Communication Technology Connectivity

Transforming Our World, Our Choices

Uma Narula

ATLANTIC

PUBLISHERS & DISTRIBUTORS (P) LTD

Published by
ATLANTIC
PUBLISHERS & DISTRIBUTORS (P) LTD
7/22, Ansari Road, Darya Ganj, New Delhi-110002
Phones : +91-11-40775252, 23273880, 23275880, 23280451
Fax : +91-11-23285873
Web : www.atlanticbooks.com
E-mail : orders@atlanticbooks.com

Branch Office
5, Nallathambi Street, Wallajah Road, Chennai-600002
Phones : +91-44-64611085, 32413319
E-mail : chennai@atlanticbooks.com

Printed in India at Nice Printing Press, A-33/3A, Site-IV,
Industrial Area, Sahibabad, Ghaziabad, U.P.

Dedicated to

My family and friends

Ameeta and Vivek
Tara and Atul

And all those who are closely associated
With invisible digital empowerment around
the globe

Acknowledgements

New technologies are becoming a way of life in work, leisure and entertainment. All of us are looking for 'what is new', innovating and satisfying technology. Many of my friends are associated with new technology domains. Whenever we meet formally or informally, we talk about them, their assimilation in our lifestyles and critically assess them as well as what else we want in that direction. Such a background associated us all with—"what is next (technology)?" Such a spirit of enquiry and attitude all around me inspired me to research the old and the new digital technology scenario globally and at India also. At times I would be curious as well mystified by the new technology concepts and products. My friends' group clarified the digital technology concepts and innovations for me. Simplifying, it is all multiple sensors and cloud. And the end product is Artificial Intelligence, or virtual reality, automation in various fields—a driverless car, robot, drone, or just a simple way how smartphone connects you to your friends and professionals. Such inspiration, knowledge and innovative spirit from my associates further stimulated me. My sincere thanks and acknowledgements are to all these associates.

Various research reports from corporates, consultants and international actors on updates about communication technology scenario highlighted the waves of communication technology connectivity globally and in India. I acknowledge their contributions with thanks. They are also acknowledged in the reference section.

The changing communication technology scenario was not only an eye-opener for me but I also thoroughly enjoyed writing it. Digital technologies are transforming our world and our choices. Further, editorial board and editors have shaped the book beautifully—my thanks.

Uma Narula

Contents

Uma Narula Books

Indian Women Across Generations

9788126904136	HB	184	2005	₹395.00

Indian Economy: Visions, Reality, Challenges

9788126906826	HB	136	2007	₹295.00

Global Empowerment: Emerging Practices

9788126909889	HB	256	2008	₹550.00

People Empowerment: Emerging Practices

9788126910281	HB	264	2009	₹550.00

Rising Expectations: India's Transformation

9788126912223	HB	568	2009	₹995.00

Dynamics of Indian Rural Economy: Growth Perspective

9788126914449	HB	480	2010	₹995.00

Business Communication Practices: Modern Trends

9788126906017	HB	388	2013	₹995.00

Communication Models

9788126906765	HB	136	2013	₹395.00
9788126906772	PB	136	2013	₹150.00

Dynamics of Mass Communication: Theory and Practice

9788126906369	HB	312	2013	₹795.00
9788126906758	PB	312	2013	₹295.00

Handbook of Communication Models, Perspectives, Strategies

9788126905133	HB	448	2014	₹1195.00
9788126906710	PB	448	2014	₹495.00

Development Shock: Dynamics of India's Current Developments

9788126920457	HB	424	2015	₹1195.00

Skeptical Voices—Economic, Political Optimism: Social Actors' Visions, Ideologues, Actions

9788126920808	HB	496	2016	₹1295.00

CHAPTER 1 Prologue

Technology challenges.
Technology is here to stay and there is no escaping its use.
It is a wonderful tool if we use it appropriately.

Disrupted technologies focusing on connectivity, convergence and digitalization have created not just ripples but 'Three Waves' over time. Digitalization and mobile telephony with their applications in the current decades are globally the most obsequious and strong with notable impacts.

Development of new media technologies and technological advancements have created communication revolutions. The technological innovations over time have supported the evolutionary process of media technologies which have generated and shaped seven communication revolutions over time. In the last seven decades the advancement and breakthrough in disrupted technologies have created seven communication revolutions which have impacted the social and working lives of people around the world.

Connectivity, convergence and digitalization have been the main focus. Connectivity is the mainstay for creating awareness, information, knowledge, and above all, an inexpensive entertainment channel. Innovative and disruptive technologies and their varied applications have been created through convergence and digitalization throughout these three 'Technology Waves'. Major communication media modalities are printing and its by-products such as newspapers, books etc.; radio, television and motion pictures and their linked subsequent products; telecommunication; telephony and its mobile applications.

More products and applications are now digitalized over time with invention of Internet, mobile phones, computers, telephones, and mobile telephony and Internet technologies. They have all become inter-dependent. The millennium era is of digitalization; and web based and mobile applications.

The 1st wave of technology focuses on communication revolutions. Three decades of communication revolution (in 19th and 20th century, from writing paper, printing press, broadcasting—radio and TV) started with analogue technology for its various media channels products such as printing, radio, television and motion pictures. The socio-cultural-eco-political impact of technologies facilitated the necessity for 'Social Technology Model', i.e. the acceptance of technology in life of people for any progression, and technologies that were shaped through communication revolutions and other technologies to come over the decades.

These media technology developments have been in global contexts and their acceptance has been in national contexts and in its societal segments according to economic parameters of affordability and market availability as well as compatible technology infrastructure. First technology wave initiated 1st, 2nd and 3rd communication revolutions.

The 2nd wave of technology focus has been on digitalization of analogue technologies developed during 1st, 2nd and 3rd communication revolutions for various media channels products and its linked subsequent products such as radio and transistors; television to video and audio players; videotapes and audio tapes; motion pictures to digitalized advance cameras, and films (black and technicolor); and sound recordings plus enhanced microphones, later developing into wireless microphones. Digitalization facilitated putting newspaper, books and other printing material on tapes, microfilm and microfiche which have been low-cost, reliable, long-term, standardized image storage media.

Innovations and technology advancements in printing, television, satellites, wireless, cellular and mobile telecommunication, computerization, laser, fiber-optics and quantum technologies have all enhanced connectivity in communication which is global in nature as well nationally inter-citizen connectivity in whichever country they live. The 2nd technology wave is also marked with evolutionary telecommunication revolution, giving high connectivity to people at low cost. Computerization, personal computers and their linked subsequent products such as fax machines, and printers revolutionized communication scenario and it marked 4th and 5th communication revolutions.

The 2nd wave of technology initiated in fourth and fifth decades of communication revolution (80s to 90s) was a transition period to digital technology, though not for all technologies and not in all countries. Both analogue and digital technologies were co-exiting. These decades focus on four salient areas (i) digital and digital shift, (ii) digital technologies of the 2nd wave, (iii) the transient period and (iv) the sustained and disruptive technologies which were a backdrop to the boom of 3rd digital wave and the digital technology progression.

This was also the transition period from analogue to digital technologies. This period was the base of many new digital technology concepts which in third digital wave accelerated into innovations and further into their innovative applications.

Over time, all these technologies have been used from varied perspectives of businesses, government, educationists, society and people themselves and posing challenges. These challenges have pushed them to explore more, create more in technology fields to achieve what they wanted.

Technologies transited to digital, and also they were not adopted globally. Many parts of the world, especially a larger population in developing countries, were and are still using analogue technology products of the first technology wave due to reach and affordability factors.

Uma Narula research based publications (2006, 1990, 2010—notes 1.1.) have highlighted that The ICTs contribute and impact changes and advances according to the time lags, because of both the advances in technology shifts and social transformation in societies, and technology diffusion is the main driver. We find that technology diffusion happens to be the main accelerator of life and work enhancement in third wave of technology in current decades. Ewa Lochman (2016) highlights the reality of accelerated ICTs contribution to global economy reshaping financial institutions. ICTs diffuse innovations in many ways and in many domains of our life and work which is progressive. She further points that for the last two decades, global landscape has been profoundly reshaped by two overwhelming processes: rapid diffusion of new technologies (ICT) and high-tech solutions that have contributed to the functioning of global economy, enhancing shifts in productivity and pervasively impacting economy, generating structural and qualitative changes; and the process of adoption and use of new technological solutions have provided foundations for the emergence of various economic networks.

India has participated and gone through communication technology revolutions and waves with its own time lags and pace. In India, its 1st and the 2nd wave of technologies did not coincide with global technologies periods of 1st and the 2nd waves. In the first wave period, India had developed and was using analogue technology for media channels products such as printing, radio, and motion pictures for its limited urban population because of low resources. But in latter half of 80s and 90s, it was catching up with global 2nd wave new technologies channels and products and transition to digital to some extent, as well as developing and manufacturing digital technology products.

In the 2nd wave India pushed ahead with newer technologies for telecommunication, computerization with digital push. The 1986-92 period, was crucial for revitalization and development of modern technology features in Indian telecommunication systems to make it efficient. It was necessary to participate in the globalization process.

Advanced cameras, films (black and technicolor) and sound recordings were enhanced. It also focused on various media channels linked ethnotronic devices such as radio and transistors, television to video and audio players; videotapes and audio tapes; motion pictures to digitalized microphones, later developing into wireless microphones. It had already successfully launched a communication satellite during this period. It was also for the first time that India focused on indigenous manufacture of fiber-optics and some of the equipment needed for satellite based communications. The manufacturing initiative had dual purpose; initially for domestic use and later to export to the neighboring developing countries.

In the 3rd wave of technology, initial period since 2000, the focus has been on enhanced digitalization, disruptive technologies in computer, and telecommunication in its various modes (6th communication revolution). The second period focused on applications and their practical utility. The computer technology has been focusing more on 'wearable' modes; and mobile telecommunication applications are focusing on novel ways to make life livable, quicker, mobile and safer, and cutting on distances (7th communication revolution). Both 6th and 7th communication revolutions are current and overlapping revolutions.

We are all currently in 2000 decades—more so from 2010 onwards—experiencing the digital technological revolution which, far from being completed, is undergoing new accelerated phases of technological acceleration. Internet—broadband and Internet of things (IoT), Artificial Intelligence and sensors, robotics; mobile technology with all pervading smartphones—all are leading to one fundamental trend of connectivity and potential social impact. These transformations, the evidences of which we already feel, and their extreme evolutionary perspectives will produce their full effect after one or two decades. We will have ample time to rationally analyze their consequences, without having deep concerns.

But now it is challenging to identify the likely or inevitable changes, the opportunities they represent or the threats they pose to our society currently. In fact, as we shall see, these trends are no more than the logical consequences of the Internetization i.e. empowerment of electronic connectivity on the national and global economy, and human connectivity.

Third wave of technology has ushered in higher level of digital technologies like Artificial Intelligence (AI), clouds, virtual realities, 3d printing, IoT, advancement in mobile technologies and social media platforms. This is an era when these technologies' focus is on digital economy and varied applications of these advanced technologies.

Computerization, automation and robotics have already shaken business and social model. Traditional economy is disappearing, followed by the digital economy, the virtual one. All this is made possible by Internet. Future is continuous acceleration.

Internet, commercially initiated in the 1st technology wave in 1993, had a very big connectivity role which created many technologies as well communication revolutions. The commercial use of the Internet started in 1993 by inventing World Wide Web (WWW) though it was innovated in 1960.

Current 2nd wave of technologies and ongoing and overlapping 6th and 7th communication revolutions are marked by speedy progress in Internet—the broadband and its products. There is wide focus on IoT, creating more widespread technologies and applications. This has created the issues of 'net neutrality'.

Internet connectivity created social media platforms over time. These have been instrumental in creating awareness, knowledge and information about technology and about wider global and national social issues among its participants. These have social ramifications in both global and national contexts.

Over the decades, amazing innovated technologies have been invented, whether it was electricity, telecommunication or television, or the 'lifts/elevators' to carry passengers or goods from ground level to higher areas. In the long run, lifts/elevators' have stimulated the idea of building skyscrapers.

All these technologies at that time were unbelievable and had their 'wow' moments. Now they are taken for granted and as a way of life. In fact, there have been efforts to make them better with more disruptive features along with other disruptive technologies.

There is an adage, 'Necessity is the mother of invention', suggesting necessity as the first component and human ingenuity as the pushing component to create disruptive technologies. But now in 2010 decades, it is the human ingenuity that is creating disruptive technologies to generate a necessity for new and better ways for lifestyle-entertainment, enterprises-workplace, and governance.

It is incremental to build on earlier achievements; the moment humans start asking—Why? and How?, new technology or gadget is likely to come up. Hence, today's science and technology has to be better than yesterday's.

Design thinking is a methodology that helps people understand and develop creative ways to solve a specific issue, generally business oriented. It is solution-based thinking. Design thinking is a process applicable to all walks of life for creating innovative ideas and solving problems.

In design thinking you identify an issue, be curious and explore and frame it, take action; sometime it works and sometime it does not work, and we reframe it. You face challenges in the process of reaching ultimate solution; and along the process you build a design team since you would be finding ultimate solutions in collaboration. When design thinking is applied to strategy and innovation, the success rate for innovation improves dramatically.

Three waves of communication technologies have proven the usefulness of design thinking in creating technology innovations over time.

Three waves of communication technologies have given us not only better but global connectivity and upgraded move towards globalization.

People, ideas and trends that are reshaping the global connectivity are travel, trade and technology. Above all, in current decades, technology through many channels and various products and formats is reshaping the global connectivity.

Further, the streamlined solutions are allowing people to participate efficiently in the global economy.

Scientists and technology community are creating, doing innovations in one country of the world, but these innovative trends spread fast to other countries of the world and connect them through these innovations. These innovations get adopted by the world and they become global innovative trends.

World awareness about the innovative trends is getting widespread, but whether people are able to adopt and make use of them is a separate issue and depends on many other country-specific factors. People, enterprises, and governments in different countries pick and choose according to need-priorities, accessibility and affordability. Many times, needs though essential, take a backseat because of other two factors.

Earlier, mobility through travels would expose people to more opportunities and access ideas and resources for education, businesses and agriculture and for better governance. Now because of Internet and other digital technologies, they have access to them without leaving their homes even. That is the power of technology innovations and Internet.

Innovative digital technologies of today are leading transformation for a better tomorrow and invigorating the human life-force. They are creating opportunities and better environment for the development of people, society and workplaces and leveraging technologies for addressing the challenges in the contemporary world.

On one hand, many local and global social issues, including protection of environment, provision of sustainable urban livelihoods, resettlement of people living in urban slums, etc. are challenging. On the other hand, there are challenges of creating productive and remunerative employment for population with innovative skill development focus. Growth of economy, business enterprises and innovative products is equally challenging. Both disruptive digital technologies and progress in sustained technologies are leveraging to tackle these issues and bring large-scale change across the world.

The last two decades have been accelerating change across economies, political and geographic boundaries, presenting daunting challenges with growing populations and limited resources in the developing world.

In the 2000 decade, more from 2010 onwards, constant streams of technology innovations are addressing these issues which will dramatically transform the future, and would boost life at home and address changing healthcare and lifestyles of changing demographics around the world. Technology disruptions are impacting businesses and industries and creating major policy impacts and implementations at city (urbanization), rural, national and international levels.

In these contexts, both disruptive, frontier and cutting edge technologies as well as sustained technologies are creating a better world for highly developed countries, and for the developing as well as countries with poor economies. This is being implemented according to their urgent and affordable needs.

Comprehensive and wide-ranging perspective of technologies will drive our future. Leaders and innovators can create vision of better future through evolving digital technologies, but leaders, governance and people can achieve the vision only by their committed efforts.

Hassabis of Google DeepMind (2016) along with his team is focusing on creating what he calls *general artificial intelligence*—something that, like a human, learns to take on just about any task. He envisions it doing things as diverse as advancing medicine by formulating and testing scientific theories, and bounding around in agile robot bodies. He has to develop smarter software to invent his way around some long-standing challenges in Artificial Intelligence.

The disruptive and sustained digital technologies are focusing currently on some of the following major areas:

- Development and deployment of advanced computing solutions based on natural sensing and interactions, interactive computing;

- Immersive virtual reality—a hypothetical future technology that exists today as virtual reality art projects;
- Robots—autonomous and intelligent, robotic ocean exploration to deep space; applications of robotics in medicine and other walks of life;
- Challenges of Artificial Intelligence (AI), Big Data and Analytics, and convergence of AI and big data;
- Cloud computing and challenges of cloud based enterprises;
- Unmanned aviation systems, electric and driverless cars, and hyperloop technologies;
- Drones for e-commerce to defence;
- Physical and virtual infrastructure for global e-commerce;
- Personalized medical devices and efficient healthcare delivery, genetically driven treatments, and advances in vaccines;
- Digital learning–educational technology;
- Breakthrough digital financial technologies, and blockchain technologies;
- Innovations in cleantech and smarter power;
- Internet of things (IoT);
- Mobile technology—mobile phones;
- Social media platforms.

Gartner, Inc. (2016) highlights that a new type of infrastructure needs to be built, which will not only reshape businesses, but also the way people live. Gartner calls it 'civilization infrastructure'. Software and IT services will be keys to the development of civilization infrastructure.

Gartner forecasts worldwide IT spending to total \$3.4 trillion in 2016. In 2017, global IT spending is projected to grow 2.9 percent and reach \$3.5 trillion. Worldwide spending on software is projected to grow 7.2 percent, and IT services 4.8 percent.

Analysts say, this growth will be driven by the software and IT services segments and lead to higher growth of civilization infrastructure.

Peter Sondergaard, Senior Vice President and global head of Research Gartner, explained to an audience of more than 8,000 CIOs and IT leaders at Gartner Symposium/ITxpo (2016), that this civilization infrastructure will be the most important thing IT accomplishes in the next decade. CIOs are the builders of this infrastructure. His further observations are:

Civilization infrastructure will forever change the way people engage socially, digitally, and physically through connected sensors and digital intelligence. CIOs will participate in the building of a new digital platform with Artificial Intelligence at the center. That platform will enable ecosystems, connecting businesses and collapsing industries. It will change society itself, and the way people live.

Civilization infrastructure will be a new digital platform that extends beyond traditional IT infrastructure, using new technologies not familiar to the typical IT department. The new digital platform allows participation in evolving business, government, and consumer ecosystems, because ecosystems are the next evolution for the digital; it is how you compete at scale.

The new digital platform consists of five domains: traditional IT systems, customer experience, IoT, Artificial Intelligence and the ecosystem foundation.

Each of these domains is interconnected and interdependent. All domains have a role, and all are required.

Insight into the five elements of the new digital platform: Traditional core IT systems: This is how CIOs run and scale operations. It's building on what's already been built. It's taking high performing traditional IT systems (such as the data centers and networks) and modernizing them to be part of the digital platform. For example, leading organizations are halfway through the transition to the cloud. It started with sales and marketing, and now half of sales-support capabilities are in the cloud. This migration will continue through the end of the decade into functions such as HR, procurement and financial management.

You now need to make cloud, mobile, social and data your core capabilities while investing in resilience, business continuity and disaster recovery insight and outside in a hybrid approach, Sondergaard said.

Customer experience: How the business will connect and engage customers in the digital world through new digital technologies. The pioneers are exploring how new experiences such as virtual and augmented reality will change the way customers engage.

Chatbots and virtual personal assistants (VPAs), mobile apps, and even web presence, will be much less relevant. The new competitive differentiator is understanding the customer's intent through advanced algorithms and Artificial Intelligence. Creating new experiences that solve problems customers didn't realize they had.

The Internet of Things (IoT) is how the organization senses and acts in the physical world. Adding devices to the domain is the easy part. Processes, workflows, and data integration are much harder. In fact, two-thirds of organizations have to rework their existing IT systems to accommodate IoT.

Real-time analytics: IoT also changes how CIOs should invest in real-time analytics because decisions must move from days to minutes to instant. Real-time analytics will outpace traditional analytics by a factor of three by 2020 to become 30 percent of the market.

Artificial Intelligence is the new type of intelligence, driven by machine learning by which the systems analyze, learn, and decide independently. CIOs start with traditional data management, data science and data intelligence. Algorithms determine the action.

As digitalization matures, enterprises are increasingly finding themselves part of a digital ecosystem—a grouping of enterprises, competitors, customers, regulators and other stakeholders that exchange information and interact electronically.

Gartner CIO Agenda Survey 2017 gathered data from 2,598 CIO respondents in 93 countries and all major industries, representing approximately $9.4 trillion in revenue/public-sector budgets and $292 billion in IT spending. For the purposes of the survey, respondents were categorized as top, average and trailing performers in digitalization.

Survey data highlights that the high performance of digital mature companies depends on their technology core, i.e. having latest digital skill technology employees, plus adoption of bimodal IT; a combination of core and evolving digital technologies reinforces the transition to digital ecosystem participation; need for organizational capabilities, and enterprise leadership, i.e. digital ecosystem-ready leadership is important and necessary.

Survey data reveals that CIOs are shifting their investment pattern in response to digital business, with average CIOs already spending 18 percent of their budget in support of digitalization, a figure set to increase to 28 percent by 2018. Top performing businesses (where digitalization is fully into their planning processes and business model) are already spending 34 percent of their IT budget on digital, and this is predicted to increase to 44 percent by 2018.

Survey responses also point to the fact that digital ecosystem membership increases with digital maturity. One of the differentiating factors of a high-performance digital business is the creation of and/or participation in a digital ecosystem. Making deliberate, wide-ranging use of an ecosystem to co-create solutions and taking advantage of distributed capabilities separates top performers from the rest of the pack. Seventy-nine percent of top performers indicate their participation in digital ecosystems compared with 49 percent and 24 percent for average and trailing performers, respectively.

A digital ecosystem amplifies the reach of a company; it blurs industry boundaries and gives rise to entirely new kinds of companies, products and services. It enables scalable connections between known partners and customers, but also provides a platform for unknown parties to connect with one another.

In order to fully participate in a digital ecosystem, businesses will need to focus on three core domains: their technology core, organizational capabilities, and their enterprise leadership. A combination of core and evolving digital technologies reinforces the transition to digital ecosystem participation.

Investment priorities: Analytics, cloud services, digital market management and security, business intelligence (BI) and analytics, and modernizing enterprise resource planning (ERP) continue to top technology investment priorities across all organization types.

IT skills gap: When there is low availability of skilled employees, especially having those skills which are needed for the latest, most advanced analytics environments, this can hamper the progress of digitalization of organizations. The skills that have previously been applied to pre-digital diagnostic analytics are not sufficient for the new real-time data scenarios presented by the IoT, personal analytics, operational technology, and information ecosystems. Newer skills are in short supply and expensive for the time being. Therefore, adoption of bimodal IT is vital to the creation of a digital ecosystem-ready organization. Survey findings indicate that 43% average performers are bimodal, and 68% of top performers are bimodal.

Customer ecosystems are business networks that are aligned to help customers get things done. Economies, society and consumers are in the natural ecosystems that impact economies and society.

Master digital ecosystem-ready leadership: Understanding business priorities and applying value disciplines to inform management and execution are foundational to the transition to a digital ecosystem. The survey showed that high-performing CIO leaders, together with their CEOs, focus on growth and digitization. Digital business/digitalization is a high strategic business priority among the top and average performers (28 and 20 percent, respectively).

To create digital ecosystem-ready leadership, business leaders must re-evaluate leadership priorities, engage stakeholders and involve them across digital initiatives. Leaders that are digital ecosystem-ready are panoramic thinkers, having unobstructed and wide view of an extensive area in all directions. They look for opportunity in every direction, cultivate diverse partnerships, and question the value propositions and business models of the past.

Accumulation of knowledge and use of digital technology is driving higher and better quality change in productivity. Previously, investment in physical infrastructure, factories and distribution was the key to higher and quality productivity. But new technologies do create their own demands, a highly dislocating process, eliminating hitherto successful business models, dissolving labor markets and altering societies. Some of these dislocations are driving reactions throughout companies, economies and individuals for example, (i) there are more Mergers and Acquisitions (M&A) to strengthen their market dominance by trying to create monopolies, (ii) economies are using technology to boost productivity, and (iii) individuals are learning latest digital IT skills as well. Companies are also imparting latest digital training to strengthen the technology skilled core employees. The third Industrial Revolution and the 3rd wave of digital technology revolution are aiming to completely replace humans, rather than just complement them, with potentially up to half of current jobs and traditional professions in danger of extinction over the next one or two decades; drivers being replaced by autonomous cars, AI and robots doing machine and human work, and Algorithm replacing financials.

Digital economies: India focus has been highlighting its stake throughout the seven revolutions and all the three waves of technology and its acceptance in national contexts and in its societal segments according to economic parameters of affordability and market availability, and compatible technology infrastructure in India, though political will and ideology to push the technology products for masses has been also one of the deciding factors. The political will and ideology factor has been stronger and significant in 90's decade. Currently, the political will and ideology is impacting the digital technology scenario by pushing harder the 'digital' applications of technology in social segments and issues benefiting the lower, uneducated, especially the rural strata of society and through 'Make in India' program and in governance. Interestingly, 'people's will' of the rural and lower segments of society is also a strong factor to make 'digital' revolutionary since they want to be part of the digital wave and not in for digital divide any more. That contributes to the success of mobile telephony and its smart applications in India.

Why India focus? Because many more developing countries have ventured into outsourcing and insourcing of technologies. A few countries like China are venturing faster into digital economy with digital technologies, and digital modes. To narrow down, India focus is chosen, since this is our research base and anchor.

Internet, thriving since 1993, facilitated connectivity and information for people. Information communication technologies (ICTs) flourished. There was dot.com boom period. All this resulted in information load for people which overwhelmed them.

From in 2010 onwards, disruptive digital technologies and their applications are booming. Every day, one encounters a disruptive digital technology in the making, a new application in the market from a big company or a startup. People are excited about these as these are going to change the lifestyle and entertainment for people, expedite efficiency in businesses and enterprises and governance and create better frame for overall connectivity.

People want to experience the efficiency, speed, ease, novelty of digital economy but they do not want to be overwhelmed by the digital technologies and their applications too rapid too many.

This is likely to overwhelm them surely. Enjoy the digital scenario and be excited and overwhelmed!

The 3rd wave technologies may be a compilation of the current technologies and their applications but read in the background of 1st and 2nd wave technologies and the ensuing communication revolutions, it does reflect how much the machine-made technologies and the human thinking, intelligence, ingenuity and innovativeness have evolved in the past seven decades along with economic and social-cultural gains; and as understood in the right contexts, the political agenda both national and international, has played a prominent role.

India, through its technology companies, holds a very high and significant position in outsourcing technologies, creating technologies in global contexts though it has been creating benefits for India also, through national constraints and barriers. The book highlights the global and India's role in communication technology revolutions through three technology waves. This would be of wide interest in India and abroad.

Information technologies, big and small, available today challenge the traditional notions and practices. One important concept is that information technology relies on a global grid for international use. Any one's nation's desire, decision or trial with IT inevitably links that nation to a larger, global system. It could have ramifications for that global system—depending whether that nation is adopting their older technologies or newer technologies for their use; or a section of that nation such as Indian technology outsourcing companies is using as well as developing innovative technologies.

The significant points are that the technologies worldwide developed over time during the communication technologies waves and through communication revolutions had evolved for the better from one wave to another along with some disruptive technologies and not for getting obsolete. Secondly, some of these evolving technologies emerge in the developing countries or countries with low resources and quite likely they may also contribute certain new perspectives to these evolving technologies because of their societal demands. The initiatives to develop and implement these have come from scientists and private entrepreneurs.

The significant trends that we have observed with regard to acceptance of these technologies are: (i) They are always initiated by the government; (ii) A few globally developed are implemented according to the resources; (iii) Though initiated by the government, private initiative and entrepreneurs bring them to the market, such as newspapers, books always published by private entrepreneurs; (iv) In the 2nd technology wave, media channels, telecommunication and computer policies and products are governed by government, but in the latter half of the 2nd wave, some of the telecommunication and computer products were being indigenously manufactured by private enterprises; there was greater demand and use of these products by private enterprises. But government codes, guidelines and basic censorship always existed. (v) In the 3rd wave, the communication technologies are produced by global and domestic private business enterprises; even media channels are run by private entities. There is larger consumer base for these, both in urban and rural areas, because of enhanced reach and affordability. Most of these are directed by global codes and guidelines. But Indian Government does step in against consumer protection for price wars, exploitation and for basic censorship.

Prologue initiates us to the technology scenarios—the backdrop and the upcoming digitalization for digital economy and its vital economic parameters. These will be discussed in detail in the subsequent chapters.

Organization of Book

Book reflects the three waves of technologies and the seven communication revolutions incorporated by these waves in the last seven decades mainly in global contexts. It does highlight India's technology scenario during these Waves and Communication revolutions and contribution of technologies in its socio-eco-cultural and political development when insourcing and economic enhancement in global contexts when outsourcing technologies.

Prologue initiates us to the technology scenarios—the backdrop and the upcoming digitalization for digital economy and its vital economic parameters.

The Innovative and disruptive technologies which have supported the evolutionary process of communication technologies over seven decades and shaped seven communication revolutions and three waves of communication technologies are discussed in *chapter* 2. There have been technology shifts and transient periods of technologies during these decades.

Connectivity, convergence and digitalization have been the main focus. Connectivity was the main stay for creating awareness, information, knowledge; and above all a digital world of work, lifestyle-entertainment where machines are delivering everything in split seconds.

Innovative and disruptive technologies and its varied applications are being created through convergence and digitalization.

Chapter 3 divulges how Innovative and Disruptive technologies and its varied applications are being created through convergence and digitalization. In first wave the focus was on developing the technology e.g. radio, television, motion pictures etc.; though in second wave the focus was on developing the enhanced features in radio, television, motion pictures and their ethnotronic devices.

The recent focus has been on varied applications of digital technologies in several domains of life, work and enterprises, and governance through major digital technologies of Cloud, Artificial Intelligence—automation, robotics, cognitive technologies, Augmented reality (AR), visual reality (VR), blockchain technologies and Digital development of Internet of things (IoT), remote sensing and mobile—Smart phone technologies.

The other focus is on innovative and enhanced applications of the sustained technologies RFID, Quantum computer, Laser, fuel cells, and nano technologies.

Chapter illustrates a few upcoming applications in Digital-Healthcare: Medical devices, wearables; e-commerce, m-commerce, biometrics, payment technology, financials, data analytics, and Mobile technology—Smartphone technology apps using the AI, cognitive technologies, remote sensors, and robotics.

Internet was commercially initiated in 1993 and contributed to dot.com boom and its varied applications. Current 3rd wave of technologies and ongoing and overlapping 6th and 7th communication revolutions are marked by speedy progress in Internet—the broadband and its products. There is wide focus on *Internet of things* (IOE) creating more widespread technologies and applications. This has created the issues of

'*Net Neutrality*'. This is discussed in *Chapter 4*. Timeline for Internet is given in appendix.

Internet connectivity created overtime *social media platforms* which are focusing on political, business, governance besides social networking.

India focus highlights India's technology role in global and domestic contexts. It is discussed in *Chapter 5*. It reflects how in national contexts and in societal segments; India has been forging ahead in technology according to economic parameters of affordability and market availability; and compatible technology infrastructure in India throughout all 7th revolutions and all the three waves of technology. Interestingly, 'People's Will' of the rural and lower segments of society is also a strong factor to make 'digital' revolutionary since they want to be part of the digital wave and not in for digital divide any more That contributes to the success of Mobile telephony and its smart applications in India.

In global contexts, since the 2nd wave of technology India has been developing and implementing some of the frontier and cutting edge technologies. They have been outsourcing these globally to businesses and enterprises. India through its technology companies holds a very high and significant position in outsourcing technologies, creating technologies in global contexts though it has been creating benefits for India also through national constraints and barriers. Book highlights the global and India's role in communication technology revolutions through three technology waves. This would be of wide interest in India and abroad.

Why India focus? Since many more developing countries have ventured into outsourcing and insourcing of technologies. A few countries like China are venturing faster into Digital economy with digital technologies, and digital modes. To narrow down, India focus is chosen; as this is our research base and anchor. Book highlights the global and India's role in communication technology revolutions through three technology waves. This would interest wide audience in India and abroad.

Post script chapter 6 gives interesting insights. It is significant as it reflects on technology scenarios in the coming decades now and in future.

The book is likely to evoke interest in digital economy through use of disruptive as well sustained digital technologies and their applications in various domains of life, enterprises and governance because of their shaping faster and easy connectivity with one and all; efficiency, speed, novelty and human efforts replacing machine learning both globally and in India.

The book would interest people in digital Communication technology industries such as (mobile telephones, smart telephone and many more both in India and abroad), those associated with digital Communication technology policy initiatives, and above all consumers and beneficiaries of these technologies both in global and Indian contexts. In general, those interested in digital technologies would find this book of immense interest.

CHAPTER 2

Waves: Communication Technology Connectivity

Technology challenges: pushing the boundaries of what is possible is what keeps us moving forward.

You need intelligence, technology and human expertise to find trusted answers.

Waves: Communication Technology Connectivity

There have been technology shifts. A particular technology say telephone, TV at one point of time might have appeared, sounded miraculous and had given the *Wow and Aha-ha* moments but now they sound very normal. So it happens with all the innovative technologies.

The millennium era is of digitalization and web based; and of mobile telecommunications and applications. Development of new media technologies and technological advancements created Communication Revolutions. The technological innovations over time have supported the evolutionary process of media technologies which have shaped *seven communication revolutions*.

Connectivity, convergence and digitalization have been the main focus. Connectivity was the main stay for creating awareness, information, knowledge and above all an inexpensive entertainment channel. Innovative and disruptive technologies and its varied applications are being created through convergence and digitalization.

Connectivity—institutional, physical, people-to-people and ICT development and co-operation through science, technology and innovation create upcoming technologies that address and provide solutions to development challenges in diverse fields.

Seven Communication Revolutions

In 14th century when paper and writing were discovered, they became the isolated technologies. But as inventions and innovations moved on from printing, broadcasting—radio and TV, satellites, telecommunication, and computer; the technologies were getting more and more integrated. The innovations of silicon computer chips, digitalization, and laser have added more integration, depth and breadth to communication technologies. People feel coming closer to the idea of a network society. *The update model is technology networking and technology convergence.*

Three decades of Communication Revolution (in 19th and 20th centuries from writing paper, printing press, broadcasting—radio and T.V.) started with analogue technology. Fourth and fifth decades of Communication Revolution (80s to 90s) were transition period to digital technology; though not all technologies and not in all countries. Both analogue and digital are co-exiting. (Information communication technology models 4.1, to 4.19, in Chapter 4 of Uma Narula, *Handbook of Communication Models*, 2006).

These models highlight the evolutionary and revolutionary 1st to 5th communication technology revolutions and their impact on people from entertainment, economic, social, political and development perspectives; and how these upcoming disruptive technologies have been making demands on market, finance resources, and information resources.

Social Technology Model becomes crucial and important to overcome resistance, barriers in accepting upcoming technologies. First tier is resistance to information flow because of source credibility and accountability. Second tier is limitations for potential for technology diffusion, third tier is policies for technological applications and social practices, fourth tier is forms of technology provided by government policies and people's preferences are appropriate as well as desirable technologies for better life, businesses and governance. Fifth tier is where technology becomes continuous process where technologies are reorganized; their applications are redirected and refocused.

Social Technology Model creates strategies for accepting technologies in individual, social, family, community and nation and international lifestyle from information, educational, socio-eco-political and cultural contexts. (Social Technology Model Uma Narula 1990: In its earlier conceptual model, the major focus was acceptance/diffusion of technologies by people. But in its progressive conceptualizations; the model and its five tiers strategies holds good for technology innovations from analogue to digital.)

Over time, all these technologies have been used from varied perspectives of government, businesses, educationalists, society and people themselves and posing challenges. These challenges have pushed them to explore more, create more in technology fields to achieve what they wanted.

Technologies transited to digital and also it was not adopted globally. Many parts of the world especially a larger population in developing countries were and are still using analogue technology products due to reach and affordability factors.

The current sixth and seventh decades of Communication Revolution is happening fast in 2000 decades; the basic and advance digital technologies are ubiquitous globally, though differentiated by high-low grade technologies according to the reach, affordability and need-demand.

These seven Communication Revolutions decades have marked the three Technology Waves. First Technology Wave started with analogue technology, digital transition is Second Technology Wave, and high and low grade new digital technologies in various arenas define the current Third Technology Wave.

These technologies have produced products, and applications for home, industry, businesses and governance. These were contributory in bringing better lifestyle and industrial revolution and many shifts from products to service economy and for political strategies for governance.

Socio-cultural-eco, Politico Impact

It is observed that 'Technology Diffusion' at grassroots level has focused on social transformation and information power to people through connectivity, accessibility and reliability and through specific information technology model creating an information and empowered society and over time through better economy, adding variety of occupations, professions, work arenas, and organizational practices.

The economic impact is highlighted by increased economic growth and productivity. People are connected more at all levels, family, community, society, nation, and international. A network global society is created facilitating cross-cultural communication. Socially and politically, the development of 'Networked' society has not only overcome space and time but has created more economic and political growth; and cooperation on global issues but at the same time the ensuing growing political disorders cannot be ignored. In practice, the diffusion and leapfrog in certain technologies is bound by resources, technological visions, policies and implementations.

These impacts are not static but change according to the demands of the 'Social Technology Model' of a country. Even the social technology model parameters have undergone change with invasion and leapfrog of new and advanced technologies.

These impacts have further innovated and shape many new technologies and technology challenges.

Technologies They Shaped

First Wave of Technology: Technology focus was *analogue* in its various modes of communication technologies. These were later termed as information communication technologies (ICT); though as evident later these have wider role to play for individuals, society, nations, and globally.

It was the innovation of print along with paper; radio, TV in its analogue forms that ushered this wave. Print assumed literacy which was extremely low among the masses but radio—its transistor mode, TV over time revolutionized masses contact with these technologies and were/are powerful means of creating awareness, information, knowledge and above all an inexpensive entertainment channel available at their door steps.

In the last seven decades, the advancement in technologies has created seven Communication Revolutions which have impacted the social and working lives of people around the world.

Different issues were brought on the forefront due to these technological changes. These focused on giving better connectivity to human beings through both machines and humans. Innovations and technology advancement in printing, television, satellites wireless, cellular and mobile telecommunication, computerization, laser, fiber optics and quantum technologies have all enhanced connectivity in communication which is global in nature as well as nationally inter-citizen connectivity wherever in the country they live.

Communication Revolutions Focus

First and Second Communication Revolution focus was on paper, writing, printing of books and newspaper. In late 19th century focus was on paper, and writing; but in early 20th century focus shifted to printing of books and newspapers through innovation of printing press technologies which were analogue at that time.

The Third Communication Revolution in 70s-90s focus was on broadcasting.

The conventional electronic mass media channels comprised of print, broadcasting—radio and television, films, telegraph and telephone. These conventional channels further expanded to supporting channels for these, such as VCR for television, audio players for radio and television, etc.

Over a period of time these basic channels have expanded in its different functional forms such as television expanded from black and white to color and from cable to satellites. Radio evolved in its frequencies modulates from its AM and FM modes and transistors. Films changed from silent to talkies, from black to technicolor. These films are even presented on different kind of screens.

Fourth Communication Revolution in 80s to 90s focused on computer, and telecommunication revolution through integrated technologies.

Fifth Communication Revolution in 90s onwards focused on innovations of digital, fiber optics and laser and advancement in silicon chips which led to digitalization giving high speed, clear images, text, sound and pictures over global network of computers. Thus, enhanced focus on computerization and its new products and convergence of diverse technologies.

Sixth Communication Revolution in 2000 focus on convergence of technologies through Internet revolution and development of mobile technologies.

Seventh Communication Revolution (2010) onwards is focusing on Internet of things (IOE) and mobile technology applications through advancement in mobile technologies.

To reiterate communications revolutions over the centuries created more and more of industrial products, consumer products and cultural and personal products and services to develop and improve the living conditions around the world. The Seven Communication Revolutions since early 14th century to date have exploded in information revolution and created new perspectives and contexts for media technologies, and their impact through changing media technologies over time and beginnings of information society.

Paradigms, Revolution, Perceptions: The new generation is looking for better pictures, better sound and more ways to spend leisure time. Tech-savvy consumers have 'an affinity' for the benefits that advance products provide. This approach is categorized in two. First, is the repositioning and repackaging of the existing technology to cater to consumer needs. The second includes technology that does not yet exist, but consumers have expressed interest in that. Scientists, technologists, and entrepreneurs are developing new technologies for these consumer needs of today and of future.

Technologies Impact: As evident from history these revolutions overtime impacted the personal, social, national and global lives. The first and second revolutions were slow and steady with wider ramifications but eroded barriers of isolation, and increased pace in communicative behavior.

Third broadcasting revolution impacted psychological well-being of individuals and educational projects and programs in a society, and creating political and economic awareness, expectations and participation among public. The overlapping Fourth Communication Revolution in 80s to 90s focused on start of computer, and telecommunication revolution integrated technologies impacted political, economic, social and development scenario through global perspectives; and that was the start of globalization. Computerization, software development and telecommunication both hardware and software by researchers around the world has been the start of ubiquitous advancement in such technologies in the years to come. Fifth Communication Revolution and subsequent revolutions in 90s onwards; innovations in digitalization and fiber optics and advent of Internet created more disruptive technologies.

The social technology—that is public assimilating these in their lifestyles created demands for advance technologies; and Sixth and Seven Communication Revolutions 2000 onwards to date are provoking, stimulating, and pushing those demands in unprecedented ways globally.

Technology model, social technology model and diffusion model together are promoting the disruptive mobile technologies and its varied applications; and these are the harbinger of Sixth and Seven Communication Revolutions. The modalities of the earlier technologies are reshaping and reinventing the current (sixth and seventh revolutions) modalities replacing with newer products and the earlier products becoming obsolete and having only historic value such as VCR, audio player, the conventional camera, etc.

Governance over the world are pushing current communication technologies and specifically mobile technologies and its varied applications for efficient Communication Network to accelerate all-round development and good governance through optimum awareness, information and knowledge and entertainment available to majority of multitude. There is fast realization that technologies should be available, accessible and cost effective for meaningful performance and improving quality of life for all sections of society including grassroots levels.

Science and Technology Researchers around the globe are working around these challenges.

The multi-tier technology diffusion and social practices call for social media platforms which have assumed a diversified and important role through sixth and seventh communication revolutions starting from chat sites to significant social, political and economic platforms for social, development and more importantly for global political changes from democratic political orders to political disorders of agitations, uprisings, and wars.

Second Wave of Technology

Digital Technology

What's the difference between analog and digital technology. Digital is entirely different. Instead of storing words, pictures, and sounds as representations on things like plastic film or magnetic tape, we first convert the information into numbers (digits) and display or store the numbers through computers—start of digital technology. Digital describes things that rely on computing technology to operate. Digital is also the language that unites chips, software, and all computing devices. The ones and zeros of digital codes allow engineer to pack more calls into a radio channel or a beam of light; to record and manipulate sounds and images; and to store all that data into a computer file, on a disk, or chip to replay later. Digital happened in early decades of 20th century.

Two driving forces for digital came about in 60s and 70s as methods were developed in turning information—a sound, a moving image, an odor into binary or digital language of computers.

Digitalization converts all information—text, sound, and pictures into binary codes that can promptly travel through a global network of computers linked by telephones, fiber optics, and satellites. Miniaturization has been the driving force in the digital revolution, yielding faster, smaller and better computers every year.

Digital is setting aside the old analog ways. It may be more efficient. It may allow all sorts of gadgets to do all sorts of tricks. For starters, the wonders of digital come at the expense of clarity and depth.

Disruptions in science and technology have innovated many products and applications. After computers, mobile technology, Internet has been the disrupting factor and now Internet of things (IOE) is making things happen.

All kinds of everyday technology also work using digital rather than analog technology. Cellphones, for example, transmit and receive calls by converting the sounds of a person's voice into numbers and then sending the numbers from one place to another in the form of radio waves. Used this way, digital technology has many advantages. It's easier to store information in digital form and it generally takes up less room. Digital information is generally more secure: cellphone conversations are encrypted before transmission—something easy to do when information is in numeric form to begin with.

In late 1970s, *digital* watch was invented. Instead of trying to figure out the time from slowly rotating hands, as you had to do with an old-style *analog* watch, you simply read the numbers off a digital display. Since then, we've got more used to the idea of digital technology. Now pretty much everything seems to be digital, from television and radio to music players, cameras, cellphones, and even books.

Many digital technologies such as automatic doors—the door opening/closing as the human feet touch the landing, or opening a heavy door with the push of a button are ubiquitous now.

This period is marked by digital and digital shift. This is the transient period for digital technology. Convergence of media forms was the main stay. Satellites and fiber optics offered the technological possibility of digitalization of information in the early decades through a universal system. It makes the same channel of communication more useful by doubling up the amount of information carried through conventional conduits.

The potential impact of *digital convergence* and satellite communications has been on the pre-digital media systems of print, film, radio, television, computer and telecommunications. Production technology has become more computers based and is now creating new convergence media forms.

It is having impact on design, control and competition of converged products and markets. The technological and economic drivers of such convergence have been impacting social, cultural, and economic; policy makers, practitioners and consumers concerns.

70-90s observed the third broadcasting revolution due to convergence and digitalization of telegraph, radio, TV terrestrial, cable and satellite and support from audio, video technologies and transistors. Further space satellites revolutionized broadcasting and telecommunication. These had psychological, political, economic, educational and creative impact.

80s to 90s witnessed computer and telecommunication revolution through converged and integrated technologies. Innovations of silicon chips and digitalization created ubiquity and speedy communication over distances. The impact was economic, political, social, development through global exposure. In 90s, there was further innovative development in digital technologies through fiber optics, laser, silicon chips innovations. There was convergence of communication satellites. More innovations in digitalization of other technologies and advance computerization resulted in high speed, clear images, text, sound, and pictures over global network of computers. This facilitated global communication and a big contributory factor in globalization.

In 2000 decades, specifically 2012 onwards many futuristic high digital technologies are being innovated through applications of Internet of things (IOE).

Technology Revisited: Behind the Boom of Third Digital Wave

Sustained vs Disruptive Technologies: Most new technologies foster improved product performance. These are called sustained technologies. Some sustaining technologies can be discontinuous or radical in character while others are of incremental nature. What is common among all sustaining technologies is that they improve the performance of established products. Most technological advances in a given industry are sustaining in character.

A disruptive technology is one that displaces an established technology and shakes up the industry. Harvard Business School professor Clayton M. Christensen coined the phrase.

Initially, a disruptive technology generally promises lower margins and not greater profits. They are first commercialized in emerging and insignificant markets. By and large, these are initially used by the least profitable customers.

Transistors were disruptive technologies in 40s; IBM's 'personal data network' (1998); IOE for 'Internet appliances' may become disruptive technologies relative to personal computer hardware and software in the near future. More important is that disruptive technologies that underperform today, relative to the market what users demand; may be fully market-competitive in that same market tomorrow.

Dilemmas of Innovations: Christensen Clayton (1997) highlighted that dilemmas are posed to the technology innovators by the conflicting demands of the DT (disruptive technologies) and ST (sustained technology). First, the pace of progress that markets demand or can absorb is different from the progress offered by technology. We cannot expect consumers to lead us to innovations; though keeping close to consumers is an important management paradigm for handling sustaining technologies; but it may provide misleading data for handling disruptive technologies.

Two, managing innovations need resource allocation. Innovation proposals which get the required funding and manpower may succeed. Others lacking resources and given lower priority have little chance of success.

Third is matching the market to the technology. Successful companies will have the practiced capability of giving sustaining technologies to the consumer in improved versions of products. But this valued capability does not help in disruptive technologies.

Fourth, organizations have capabilities to take certain new technologies to certain markets. They have disabilities in taking technologies to market in other ways.

Fifth, the information required to make large and decisive investments for disruptive technologies is not available. It needs to be created through fast, inexpensive, and flexible forays into the market and the product. Failure and interactive learning are intrinsic to the search for disruptive technologies. The mortality rate for ideas for DT is high.

Sixth, companies address different strategies for DT and ST. DT entails first-mover advantages so leadership is important.

Seventh, there are powerful barriers to entry and mobility that differ on the type of technology.

Tim Fohl's Model of Technology Development suggests that at a constant level of efforts, technologies first advanced slowly—then erupted—like water at the boiling point. After the explosive period they return to slow advance. In other words, their progress follows a clear S curve. The model proved so reliable that it could forecast product development cycles.

*Many disruptive technologies did not connect for various reasons (refer Appendix 2).

Technology: Digital Progression

Broadcasting

The broadcasting sector in the whole world is redesigning its structures, operations, programming, and technology to adapt to change. The efforts involve diverse conceptual and strategic approaches as the industry confronts new communication technologies, expanding markets, increased competition, and changing audience preferences. It is a challenge for both private and public service broadcasting to survive and thrive in this changing environment. Cable technology made Internet as accessible as TV variations occurred such as web TV, Internet TV, HD TV, digital television. Digitalization began with CD, other products DVD (digital video disk). Peripheral devices like camcorders and tape players were going digital. DVD players were launched in 1996.

Video technology was innovated for their potential in supporting working from home, teaching and learning at a distance, conferencing, and interpersonal communication. These new media forms had changed the way we think about entertainment and leisure.

Digitalization in broadcasting and the growing use of satellite communication technology has provided the opportunities to reach wider audience, and people in remote areas, in different regions, and internationally. It creates new markets, programs, and products in the regions. Digital age is further posing challenges and opportunities for broadcasting. The issue is which new digital communication technology is going to benefit broadcasting, impact programming, and manpower needs. Further, the multichannel age creates competition.

The airwaves using a digital signal could handle more information, produces a more detailed picture with clearer images, brighter colors and sharper sounds. The TV sets were getting flatter like the screens at the movie theaters.

More choices in programs were being offered. Some broadcasters will compress digital data to offer a single high definition channel; others will offer several different channels which may not be as super sharp but will be sharper than what you get now. Broadcasters could also use the channels to offer paging or other data services, or to combine conventional programming with chunks of data.

Technology companies, Microsoft, Compaq, and Intel were teaming up to develop digital computer screen that would carry TV programs.

Earliest digital TV sets were available in 1998 at expensive price but prices tumble as more people were buying digital sets and makers cut manufacturing costs.

In USA in mid-1998, the digital services were available in metropolitan areas, though not for several years in the smaller markets in USA and other markets in the world. Broadcasters must install transmitters and production equipment that would enable them to broadcast a digital signal. Other stations continued to broadcast in current analog signals. Broadcasters' commitment to transition to digital and high-definition TV was faster than turning black and white to color TV.

The digital signal reception could be received on the conventional TV sets through convertors; though the reception may not be as crisp as on the digital unit. Consumers did not have to replace their TV sets immediately, because broadcasters continued to transmit in the current analog technology for several years.

Digital TV enhances reception for satellite customers, because satellite carriers already broadcast in digital and cable industry would convert to a digital feed over the next several years. Several digital technology-oriented countries of Japan, USA, South Korea, and Singapore hoped that traditional broadcast feeds will end.

Every day there is change in finer points of this technology for better connectivity and affordable prices and that adds on more consumers. Television has impacted cultural, social, economic, political and overall globalization of values with its wider reach.

The *chip innovations* were enabling designers to put more functions on a single chip. Designers can use smaller chips; expand capability and cramming more circuitry on each chip. Such integration was innovating digital cameras, advanced video games. Chip makers use fine lenses and etching materials to miniaturize them. Wavelet-based compression chips would work five or ten times more efficiently; MPEG-2 compression, allowing for faster processing. The next generation video-encoding method—compression algorithms that take snapshot of an entire image, then look at eliminating the redundancies across a much larger amount of data. With chip innovations, credit cards were getting smarter with features such as touch-sensitive fingerprint identification.

Another innovation in audio digital technology could separate sound among five or more speakers; with this consumers could turn TV watching rooms into home theaters.

The product most associated with digital wave is Personal Computer. It first brought new productivity and educational tools in the home. Later, it became new portal to connect people to Internet.

Following Tim Fohl's Technology Model many small incremental advances followed by an explosion of change. Fads and fashions break out like that. A deeper understanding of dynamics of Innovations becomes imperative. Traditional models of innovation show a steep increase followed by diminishing returns—the familiar 'learning curve'. This model can forecast the course of technology development efforts and find out about dynamics of progress. Whereas traditional diffusion model of innovation focus is on diffusing the innovative products and practices by spread out process of initiating products through creating awareness, knowledge and practice and through early adopters to others.

Social technology model focus is in assimilating the innovative products and practices by accepting a technology and assimilating it in people's lifestyle. Thus, social technology model can vary society to society and from technology to technology. Thus, all the three technology development model highlight different ways and aspects.

Computers, Telecommunication

Important hardware technologies involved are chips technology and modem technology. Software technology develops on the use of various computer languages, software packages, and the services as Internet, Fax, e-mail, etc.

Telecommunication: Fourth revolution focused also on telecommunication that was stimulated and advanced by advance wireless and cellular technology and advancement in computerization.

Telegraph, telephone, cell and wireless technology, and computer are the four main pillars of telecommunication.

More than a century ago, technology efforts were made to bring people close together. Telegraph and telephone gave people means to communicate and help people stay in touch. As part of global activities, the advanced global communication network brings people close together; growing to shape the way people interact with each other in global telecommunication. There were many innovations and modifications in telecommunications and its products during the many communication revolutions.

People were exposed to landline telephones a century and half back after its invention. It took many decades to develop variety of features and applications both in hardware and usage. Also lots of efforts have been put since then to increase the telephone density all over the world. Landline improved in its many services including long distance within the country and internationally which provided worldwide connectivity. It also added many technical features to improve on voice quality and products—from rotary to push button phones, and delivery of services.

Initially, landline telephones were concentrated mainly in the urban areas particularly in developing countries. Rural areas had no telephone connectivity. In decades of 80s, India made efforts to develop rural telephone exchange but it was not implemented in majority of the villages. It only remained at experiment stage. In developing countries including India, the landline telephone density had been very low till 90s.

The copper wire telephone system invented by Alexander Graham Bell had gone through tremendous innovations. During the past few decades, these innovations have changed the Graham Bell system to fiber optic cables, satellites, wireless telephone technology, cellular technology and now to Internet telephony—VOIP (Voice Over Internet Protocol) technology. The decades of 90s and 2000 have been the fastest in innovations in telecommunications. It is still an ongoing process.

Decades of 80s onwards have been the revolutionary period for telephones. People are enjoying wireless and cellular telephones. As part of global activities, the advanced global telecommunication network is bringing people closer together. People's needs for reliable means for communicating over long distances increased as society grew in complexity.

Hudson (1997) writes that four major technological trends—capacity, digitalization, ubiquity, and convergence are driving the current telecommunication revolution, which parallels the emergence of a global economy. Investment in telecommunication revolution itself can contribute to economic, social, and political development. Reliable telecommunication could improve agriculture, industries, and social services.

Various research studies of World Bank and the Maitland Commission (1994) have all pointed out to the telecommunication-produced benefits across the spectrum of development activities. Hanson and Narula (1990, 2010) endorsed these benefits for developing country of India.

The wireless and cell telecommunication technology has been revolutionary and the development of its infrastructure as well the hardware and software components of telephones have been revolutionary. Further, these technologies impacted people's lifestyle and businesses in unheard ways. An expanded scenario of innovations in both these areas created ongoing fast changes; price wars and competition have been stimulating the new products and services worldwide.

Wireless and Cellular Technology: The first automatic analog cellular phone was made in the 1960s. Commercial models were introduced in Japan by NTT on December 3, 1979. They were introduced in Scandinavia in 1981, in Chicago, USA, on October 13, 1983 (by Motorola), and in Europe in the late 1980s, and in India in late 90s. A team of researchers at Bell Labs devised this cellular phone concept in 1947, but there were no computers available to do the switching. As small inexpensive computers were developed, cell phones could be produced. Motorola holds the US patents for the cell phone. Henry Taylor Sampson and George H. Miley hold a 1968 patent on a 'gamma electric cell' which is not a component of cellular phones.

The (tele) communication became wireless and in this *New World*, the invisible communication-network grid in every metropolitan area, link people all over, workers inside office buildings and warehouses; through surrounding the earth via flotillas of satellites. It is a world in which wireless devices combine the functions of telephone and computers, sending and receiving voice, text and graphics and sifting through rims of information. We are reachable any time any place.

For years, the technology and costs have conspired to ensure that most communication flow through wires and the gadget that we communicate through such as phones, faxes, computers, etc. were tethered to wires. The advance technology is making wireless technology vision come true and through cordless phones, cellular phone, worldwide wireless satellite system, and personal communication services, etc. Microchips and software technology developments have allowed miniaturization of the cellular phones, driving down prices, and driving up performances.

The cellular phone is on the scene; cordless telephone was the first application of wireless phones, VOIP phones and through skype, facetime applications and smart mobile phones with various apps.

The changing communication scenario gives a sense that telecommunication revolution is a volcano ready to erupt, though in some ways it has already erupted. The wireless vision is possible because of advances in technology of microchips and software that helps in building wireless networks.

Another breakthrough is the moving cellular technology from analog to digital. This greatly speeds up the traffic and it is also free from static interference and transmission errors. Since 2000 decades, more and more new features of geo mobility and message access are being provided on cell phones. There is stiff competition even in developing countries both for its hardware and software. This has brought down the prices of both cell services and cell phones and increasing consumer density.

Thus, cell phones are becoming an essential part of life of consumers and they are ubiquitous rather than status symbol in these countries. SMS messages on cell are useful, cost effective and are boon to the hearing disabled. The Internet on cell phone is likely to have a huge appeal. Typing e-mail (on phone screen) is a hassle even with the latest technology; voice recognition software will enable users to dictate directly to their cell phones.

Cellular technology has great telecommunication potentialities. Cellular phones are expected to grow worldwide usage to millions and increasing substantially in years in developing countries because of accessibility and affordability. More and more developing countries are introducing cellular phones with new features suiting to their consumers' indigenous needs. They could bring down to affordable prices and accessibility and thus add on millions of consumers and with stiff competition from many players in the field due to liberalized government telecom policies in these countries and less restrictions for import of technology.

Cell phones have added applications from sending SMS to e-mail. It has keyboard, camcorder, TV, videogame, MP3Player, camera, and etch-a-sketch and GPS (providing location information for emergency calls). The new software development has exploited the possibility of video, sound, messaging, and color screen technology. Even with these new applications cell phones are becoming smaller and smaller in size.

Consumers are ready to pay great deal of money for these; for people want mobility and access to messages and data. This can be evidenced by explosion of cellular phones, pagers, portable computers, e-mail users, and Internet subscribers.

Now major players for smart phones are: Apple, Android, Samsung Galaxy, Jio Reliance.

Many innovative applications on mobile phones are happening around the world. We discuss this in Chapter 2 Applications of technologies—on mobile phones.

Shift to Digital Transmission of Cellular Technology

In 1994, the digital telephone switch was manufactured by Siemens Corporation. It could handle 10,00000 calls an hour. It could even carry data, text, and voice simultaneously on a single line. These voice and data solutions helped both large corporations and small businesses improve productivity.

A British company Psion was giving brains to new mobile phones that receive e-mail, surf the Internet, and can even pay for transactions. The satellite phones—the super cell phones. The Iridium Consortium and rival joint ventures were closing on their goal of making sat-phones into multibillion-dollar mainstays of the Info-superhighway. At present phone users without any intervention by an operator. Nokia and other cell phone that this manufacturers hope feature would spur consumers to replace handsets and that would boost the cell phone industries. Nokia and other cell phone manufacturers hope that this feature would spur consumers to replace handsets and that would boost the cell phone industries.

Nokia began selling 9110 Communicator to Europe in 1998. It is a second-generation device about the size of a large mobile phone with a flip-top computer screen, capable of composing faxes, sending and reading e-mail, and accessing the Internet.

In consequence to Nokia's 9110 Communicator, Nokia is bringing into the market Communicator 9500—Wi-Fi (wireless local area) compatible handsets. The Wi-Fi chips are built-in the handsets. It will be able to bypass conventional cell phone networks, but still access the web and even make phone calls using the Wi-Fi (wireless local area) network. Key to its operation is 'hot spots' within 300 ft. of a Wi-Fi base station connected to the Internet by a fixed line. Its limitation is that people will be able to use the Wi-Fi function within a hot spot. At present phone users without any intervention by an operator. Nokia and other cell phone manufacturers hope that this feature would spur consumers to replace handsets and that would boost the cell phone industries. Nokia faces competition from Motorola and other cell phone manufacturers to get Wi-Fi compatible sets in the market by year-end. Nokia intends retailing it. It would be several years before they are commonplace. Consumers would need a specially equipped laptop or a personal organizer to use these hot spots.

Communicator 9500 set was a threat to other cell operators who were trying to sell data wireless services such as web browsing and e-mail (March 2004). Wi-Fi uses unlicensed spectrum meaning any property owner can offer wireless Internet access in the proximity of their premises. Today cell phone operators can largely access the content delivered over their networks. But media companies using Wi-Fi networks can sell video clips and music on mobile.

Alcatel, Cisco, Nokia, Motorola Qualcomm Inc. (chips for mobile phones) with 3Com Corp, Unwired Planet Inc. Calif, Nortel have been the other major players.

A new Internet-based phone technology known as VOIP is available since early 2003. VOIP is still in infancy mode and is being protected by governments to encourage it. Introduced in mid-90s, this new technology overpromised and under-delivered; creating frustrations for early adopters and huge losses for investors. Some of the earliest businesses that installed VOIP were critical of the sound quality. Enough improvement has been made now to let businesses install it now as a way of increasing efficiency and productivity and cutting costs.

Currently, phone companies have an interest in promoting other services such as caller ID, call waiting, and three-way calling. Special electronic commerce phones are proving popular. Nortel is testing it in conjunction with several Canadian banks and international smart card companies. These phones allow consumers to access their bank accounts and add money to smart cards from homes.

Currently, cell phone has become everyday consumer appliance; even a fashion accessory, and a status symbol in Asian countries; earlier the preserve of business users only. Since 2000, cell phones by many big players in the field connected India heavily. It has added many indigenous applications and features in the cell phone services.

This has made cell phones affordable and useful in India. Even a roaming real estate agent or a car mechanic or a plumber would own cell phone, since it would give them better connectivity with their customers. They find it cost effective and useful; even rural areas closer to the cellular range use cell phones. In many of these areas even landlines are not connected.

Cell phones have become so ubiquitous that landline is pushed into the background for household or for businesses.

The roaming (within the country) feature on the cell has greatly facilitated the connectivity for the businesses. The prepaid calling cards, both for domestic long distance and international calls and cheap mobile phones have made markets grow worldwide. In Israel, children have got some 200,000 units of a phone known as 'Mango'. It can only ring one specific phone number.

Airplane Phones: Eventually, air phones will be cheaper than today. In the 'virtual office' in the sky where business fliers send and receive faxes, plug in their laptops and select and watch videos. Even some of the airlines provide TV monitor in front of every seat; not only have you watched video but you can surf the Internet also on these monitors. Analog ground stations used by most airplanes installed in 80s are outdated in its capabilities. Analog calls are full of interference of air whooshing, noise, and getting disconnected when moving away from the range of one ground station to the next.

Now in-flight phone companies are converting its analog system to digital or going directly to digital system skipping the analog phase. Digital phone systems will translate sound into electronic pulses that register in ground station computers as zeros and ones.

A 'call hand off' will pass the pulses from one ground station to another. A 'Doppler effect' detect when the signal is weakening, the system than begin phoning the next ground station to transfer the call when the airplane gets close enough. The most important is before the calls get disconnected; this sophisticated technology can switch calls back and forth between ground stations when necessary. A second big advantage of the digital technology is its ability to screen out background noise. The ground station computers are programmed to recognize voices as opposed to things like static and whooshing. Similarly, ground computers are programmed to recognize word patterns. If there is a blip, they will fill in synthesized voice thus making up broken conversations whole again. This brings up two concerns about digital: synthetic voice gives a metallic quality and the technology causes the kind of voice delay that makes many users uncomfortable.

The concept of global cellular communication using intermediate-circular-orbit, and low-earth-orbit offer a hope for rural communication for rural areas in developing countries. Four mobile satellite operators—Globalstar, Odyssey, Iridium, and Immarsat ICO are developing such systems to offer a global system by 2000 (*The APT Yearbook* 1997). The current cost of such global cellular is beyond the reach of rural folks.

Personal Communication Services (PCS): This is another kind of micro-cellular digital network, which use low power and high frequency radio all over again in each micro-cell transmission area. PCS networks will be twenty times as waves. Current cellular transmissions move from cell to cell geo unit, each of which is equipped with high-powered transmitter. Micro cells will be much smaller, allowing phones to use less power and smaller batteries thus reducing the size and cost. Low power also means the ability to use the entire frequency efficient as existing cellular analog systems and provide much better services and quality.

In the 2000 decade, another feat of integration of technologies will occur. Cellular phones and pagers will exist on single microchips making them extraordinary cheap and capable, being built into a single device. This will be possible when the functions and capabilities of cellular phones, pagers, faster microprocessors, color screens and more powerful batteries are blended together.

Worldwide Wireless Satellite System: This system would beam voice, data, fax, or physical location from a small handset, anywhere in the world to anywhere (Motorola Iridium phone). Transmitters as small as bricks are developed that can be hung from utility (electrical) poles, creating wireless networks inside buildings, on campuses, and in downtown areas. Soon there will be credit card size wireless modems that will easily slip into hand-held communicators and portable computers.

Tech-savvy consumers have 'an affinity' for the benefits that advance products provide. Technology-related multinational companies come up with the offerings. This approach is categorized in two. First is the repositioning and repackaging of the existing technology to cater to individual needs. An example is prototype-messaging center IBM is working on, which lets consumers' access computer information in the kitchen. The second part includes technology that does not yet exist, but consumers have expressed interest in that, such as the transmission of high-speed data on power lines.

It is advocated that development and deployment of open source software should be encouraged, as appropriate open standard for ICT. 2004 year was a broadband era. Broadband is through analog, DSL and cable modem. Internet is being casted as multimedia platform with a flexible data expecting maximum connecting through broadband. Internet telephoning is a bright spot in the telecom world because it is more cost efficient method of transmitting voice calls. Earlier, users needed to speak into microphone attached to a computer now it is inbuilt because of WI-FI. *Broadband is getting digital.*

VOIP: VOIP makes an Internet call (skype through computers or face time through mobile phones). But today most of these calls originate from ordinary phones. Many phone companies sell Internet-based services and sell pre-paid phone cards also. Though, initially, the sound quality of the Internet-based calls did not match that of standard calls but the service is growing with new features and has improved a lot.

Telecom expert says most business people will convert to VOIP for cost saving and wide range of new features the technology will offer, such as improved conference calling, and combining voice and e-mail messages on one directory and eventually video phone. This technology could make dramatic changes the way businesses operate comparable to those by the Internet and the PC. VOIP works by transforming voice into data and then transmitting over the Internet or some other data network in the same way text, photos and e-mail are sent.

VOIP can make a wide range of existing phone features easier to use because when voice turned into data, it is essentially another application on the computer. Features can also be combined with other data applications. For instance, voice mail and e-mail can be combined in a single directory. Another plus for VOIP is their portability. VOIP phones with a particular number can be taken anywhere, connected to a broadband connection and still receives call at the same number. Moving employees from one location to another can use this efficiently. There are savings on the long-distance calls for businesses, given VOIP calls between the offices cost the same as sending e-mail. VOIP phone systems are proving useful for businesses that rely heavily on roving employees like a hotel, a warehouse, and multinationals with global operations and offices; and in some cases enabling companies to replace big centralized facilities with virtual operations. VOIP has also been facilitating better operations of 'Call Centers'. It generates significant network efficiencies, reduces capital expenditures, and produces considerable cost savings.

Businesses can expect a wide range of new features. Major telecom companies and startups are busy developing new software that will incorporate videophone, voice recognition, wireless technology and other applications in the VOIP system.

A battle is heating up in phone industry over the growing number of voice calls sent over the Internet, pitting local phone companies against long-distance providers. Issue is whether long-distance companies pay the local phone companies access fees. Since the carriers generally do not own the lines that go into homes and businesses. They are not ready to pay for transmitting Internet calls to customers.

There are ongoing debates for legislation of VOIP. The questions posed are: 1. Should local government regulate and tax any communication between two individuals? 2. Should we discourage the use of broadband networks for fast, reliable and cheap communications because a new technology does not fit into existing regulatory slot? 3. Should regulations discriminate between two data files simply because one carries instant messaging and other someone's voice? Today these issues have become practical and substantive questions that will make or break the implementation of VOIP.

Supporters of VOIP to protect this new technology advocate that it should be treated as an information service. The broadband cable, DSL or high speed line that you are using does not care whether data packaged using the Internet protocol is spread sheet, e-mail, instant message or voice traffic. There exist no sound basis for discriminating among different types of data. Would anyone argue that e-mail, power point presentations should be differently taxed than VOIP. Secondly, it will be costly and unnecessary burden on a country's communication network to regulate a global network that transcends country's boundaries. Thirdly, VOIP as a data service should be protected from taxation.

Other innovation would offer high-speed Internet access over electrical power lines. Web's new outlet is household power line. So far we have dial-up, cable, DSL and broadband outlets. The idea of using power lines has been around for years. It is based on the fact that electricity travels at a far lower frequency than the Internet signal, so the two generally do not interfere. But earlier results were disappointments because of equipment needed and technical issues.

Two years ago there was a breakthrough for the modem called Home-Plug. This has to be plugged into the wall sockets to bring the Internet into homes. Another technical issue has been how to get the Internet signal through the transformers that step the power down from the medium voltage, which runs along the street, to low voltage that goes into homes. Current communications have solved this problem with a 'bridge' that skips the transformer, allowing the signal to go through uninterrupted. The technology is ready for prime time. This outlet is being offered initially in early 2004 as an experiment to wrinkle out the product and service problems and would be available at a larger scale at the end of year. This innovative service could help spread high speed Internet in rural and inner-city areas of the country that are not wired for Internet. We observe that modes, types of channel are the same. The concept is the same but it is getting complex and more people oriented and adding further interaction complexity of non-human communication process, form, and focus. In 2000 decade, Internet telephony—VOIP was being marketed.

Can optical chips replace telecom gear? The goal is to replace bulky telecommunication gear with devices the size of a quarter that combines lasers routers, receivers, and other devices commonly used in fiber-optic networks. Simple optical chips are in the market but they are not as nearly sophisticated as chips inside a personal computer whose processor contains billions of transistors. Still the technology is advancing fast and in five years mass-produced versions can slash the cost of voice and data networks and could eventually become a new gateway to deliver high-bandwidth movies, music and games directly to homes. The possibility of miniature optical circuits has drawn interests from computer-chip manufacturers.

If telecommunications components can be manufactured from optical chips than computer-processor performance may double. Developments in optical chips may add intelligence and reduce cost. Optical chips are not a new idea. In 1969, Bell Lab engineer Stewart E. Miller envisioned, 'guiding laser beams on miniature transmission lines' using the same manufacturing methods as for integrated circuits. But due to technical challenges, his ideas were goals rather than accomplishments. Today, many of those issues are solved but real product is still challenging.

Integrating digital technology into communication networks computerized switches, laser-driven fiber optics and signaling systems replaced the old electro-mechanical gear to bring efficiency.

The third generation of mobile phones will switch on around 2003 resulting in real sprint for technological superiority. For this, European and Japanese have agreed on a technical standard called Wideband Code—Division Multiple Access (DMA) as the successor to GSM. Probably, Qualcomm USA will adopt different standard from Europe and Asia.

The vision of the future may be: Hand-held computer makers could offer machines made with Symbian's software in the hope of making them more appealing to consumers with mobile phones. Or the mobile phone industry could adopt Window CE to ensure that their devices link easily with existing desktop PCs. That depends how the battle between Microsoft and Symbian is resolved. But likelihood is Europe will be communicating with a single standard. "Watch out Bill Gates: Europeans are getting a jump on the next information revolution".

Ethnotronic Devices—Entertainment

In 90s, the world was going through fifth communication revolution of digitalization supported by computerizations resulting from the convergence of communication satellites. It exploded the information revolution and changed media technology perspective in information, entertainment and business by introducing new devices and new modes of communications—the ethnotronic devices for entertainment.

In current 2000 decades of technology advancement; VCR, VCR tapes and other products have also grown outdated with the advance of digital and other technology. That includes film cameras and floppy disks once used to store computer content, which were displaced by smaller memory devices with larger capacity and by cloud storage.

Digital Media: Entertainment Plus Technology

Telecommunication

Multi-media mix led to revolution in telecommunication from basic local telephony to regional, national and international and its quality is further facilitated by satellites. It matured from cordless to wireless and cellular telephones roaming across the national and international boundaries and with its varied features facilitating better connectivity.

Internet revolution through advancements in computers and telecommunications has created better connectivity, information and knowledge sharing globally.

The technologies have changed the way we act and interact. The growing integration between digital devices and the widespread use of Internet and wireless communications have altered the way we view personal computing, entertainment, shopping, gaming, banking and financial services, information access and much more. The threads of information technology reach us through our society and across globe.

Both desktop and laptop computers, PDAs (personal digital assistants) and smart phones are everywhere. Today, it is difficult to imagine a world without e-mail, web pages, wireless communications, telephones, and on-the-go presentations.

We had VCR since 70s and CD in early 80s, and digitalization began with CD. The other products are DVD (digital videodisk), web TV, digital television, and Dolby digital sound system. DVIX (digital video express) is a DVD player with additional encryption technology in a 'modem' that allows you to buy disk whenever you want and when you want to watch it.

The computers and the consumer electronic industries are always looking for new storage media that can hold more software programs, data, and entertainment contents. For years, CD both in its common audio format and CD-ROM variant used in personal computers has been in the market. Earlier computer CDs is read only but now newer CDs allow you both read and write (editing) functions.

DVD also come in two forms: one for consumer electronic playback and DVD-ROM for use in PCs. Unlike videotape both formats are digital. They store text, graphics, video and audio in the formats computers can read.

DVD is assembled and encoded differently and can hold material seven times more than a CD. The technology permits with two layers of data on them, totaling 8.5 gigabytes, and even greater capacity in the future. Both DVD players and DVD-ROM drives for personal computers are also designed to be backward compatible. That means they can play music CDs and CD-ROMs, so consumers need not discard their old collections. DVD offers many viewing options than videotape.

Each movie is divided onto sections or chapters and you can move around according to your choice. You can view the movie in several language options. You will be able to see scenes from various angles. DVD disks do not wear like videotapes and does not need to be rewound. But you cannot record on it. The latest DVDs have more storage space.

Digital photography is on the anvil. Digital cameras are in the market. Digital pictures are stored in the camera itself. Its printing is computerized. Interesting point is one can play around with these pictures with background colors and other details the way one wants and original pictures may look different when these are moved around. The printing gives them life like painting quality. These cameras are still expensive for everyone to own.

Digital is efficient, but not enough to satisfy those who work with the technology and many of those who use it.

Take the problems of integrating digital technology into telecommunication networks. Such networks with computerized switches, laser-driven fiber optics and signaling systems, have replaced the old electro-mechanical gear that once required larger number of maintenance and technicians to run the system. The newer digital gear is more efficient, able to handle more calls and data traffic. Digital communication is tough to tap with cell phones and other security features.

Now much of the discussion about digital technology advance is about how to make connections happen. Most of the today's advances in digital in consumer electronics are done with an eye towards more connections in the future. Digital technology will change the face of consumer electronics in near future—and the obstacles that each of the products has to overcome. Just as in the 90s the Internet has changed the ways companies behave internally, and with customers and suppliers. It has changed from relatively obscure network being used by government agencies and colleges to a global library and business tool used by millions. Digital media are still in their infancy. But the early efforts are beginning to provide hints about what will and what won't work.

Soon the digital media from the world wide web to 3-D video games, to popular digital technology responsible for popular innovation in audio, i.e. separation of sound among five or more speakers, which drive consumers to turn TV watching rooms into home theaters.

Personal computer is the product most associated with digital wave. It first brought new productivity and educational tools in the home. Recently, it has become new portal to connect people to Internet.

Soft Corder PSS (Pace Soft Silicon) solution is a camcorder application for mobile devices including PDAs and hand-held devices, which captures video and audio, playable on devices ranging from mobile phones to windows and Mac personal computers.

PSS has optimized the computational efforts, quality of video, network bandwidth, and power consumption of its embedded software product. The soft corder allows the user of the handset to optimize it, since it allows other functions to run in parallel. For instance, if the camcorder is in use, the other functions of phone, browsing does not stop.

These new media will bring us drama and diversions unlike anything we have known. They will change the way we think about entertainment and leisure.

What will make digital media work? There is disagreement among broadcasters, cable companies, and computer industries as how to use the extra transmission or the bandwidth that is being allotted for digital signals. Digital channels can be used in multitude ways. The broadcasters can use that space for one channel to give an ultra-clear picture and CD quality sound. Cable companies are worried; they have to sacrifice the variety of channels they offer in order to squeeze in the thicker digital channels. Cable companies' capacity difficulty may provide an opening for satellite program firms to win more customers.

There are still-to-come digital technologies that will exercise a force as pervasive and powerful in our lives as films and television today.

These new perspectives in mass media technologies ushered information society to a technology society. In the technology society, the applications of advance technology are used for well-being of humanity primarily. Therefore, we find the same technologies covering a wide range from information, knowledge, entertainment, network, medical applications, genetics, drug development, space applications, to war weapons and nuclear advancement. The focus is entertainment, wealth, health, prosperity with speed, efficiency and connectivity; shrinking time and space.

We have discussed and highlighted in the earlier sections of the chapter the development of ICTs through six communication revolutions through the last many decades and even some spreading over a century.

These highlights provide background for ICT initiatives in multiple domains. The current integrated ICTs are revolutionary in their development and applications. The benefits that people, a country, and the world reap from these commensurate with their efforts and initiatives (details—ICT Initiative, Appendix 4).

Future Demands of Telecommunications

Mobile technologies
Internet
Broadband—the next wave
Printer

Internet

Marshall McLuhan in 60s had vision of globalization—the global village; a conceptual vision looking for an implementer. A notion that needed vision of course but also some down to earth things such as a network big enough to bring all the existing countries, people together and connected, a commitment to be competitive and break up monopolies both local and global and to create new ideas in global development. Internet initiated that, and now being followed by other revolutionary digital technologies.

In the 1990s, this was used as a marketing term for Internet access that was faster than dialup access. Initially, Broadband started through analog, DSL (digital subscriber lines) and cable modem. In the late 1980s, the Broadband Integrated Services Digital Network (B-ISDN) used the term to refer to a broad range of bit rates, independent of physical modulation details.

The various forms of digital subscriber line (DSL) services are *broadband* in the sense that digital information is sent over multiple channels. Each channel is at higher frequency than the base band voice channel, so it can support plain old telephone service on a single pair of wires at the same time. In the context of Internet access, the term "broadband" is used loosely to mean "access that is always on and faster than the traditional dial-up access."

Broadband is the next digital wave. Internet usage would become completely mainstream by November 1999. As more and more ISPs appeared it became a buyers' market. By the mid to late 2000s more people were using broadband service in their homes than there are using dial-up service. 2004 has been broadband era.

Wi-Fi Wireless Broadband: Wireless networks can feature data rates roughly equivalent to some wired networks, such as that of asymmetric digital subscriber line (ADSL) or a cable modem. Wireless networks can also be symmetrical, meaning the same rate in both directions (downstream and upstream), which is most commonly associated with fixed wireless networks. A fixed wireless network link is a stationary terrestrial wireless connection, which can support higher data rates for the same power as mobile or satellite systems.

Cable modems can be fast. It can deliver up to 10 million bits of data per second, nearly 350 times the speed of the fastest standard modem. Telephone modems on standard telephone lines can deliver 28,800 bits of data per second to the PC. With a special kind of modem-ISDN, one can get up to 128,000 bit per second. Moreover, cable modems are always switched on. It essentially combines the analog and digital systems in one single chip. A DSL (analog digital subscriber line) is faster for Internet and can be used for video-on demand through subscriber telephone lines and for any other applications on the Internet. This modem will meet the demand for high-speed connectivity worldwide and for faster data download. The cost of modems will also come down overtime.

So far Internet has three kinds of modem connections, dial on connection through telephone modem, ISDN cable modem, and DSL and wireless Wi-Fi connection.

Broadband has gone digital and Wi-Fi through progression in 2007. WiMAX is highly popular in Europe, started in USA in residences, business, and Wi-Fi—Hotspots. On June 2, 2010 mobile broadband started in smart phones.

With the Internet growing at exponential rates and more and more software applications becoming available, such as digital photos, downloading music, movies, and online gaming with people you have never even met, the future for broadband appears very bright. (Refer Appendix 1 Timeline for Internet (detail discussion other Internet innovations discussed in Chapter 4).)

Despite such changes innovation remains at the center of computing and IT industry. Currently, five technology themes are challenging the economy. One is wireless and mobility through technology. Wireless networks including LANs have become more pervasive and they are changing the way individuals and companies access and use data. An array of new technologies and devices including PDAs and its applications are making it possible to tap into data including Internet anytime and anywhere. Two, enterprise infrastructure, enterprise resource planning (ERP) and customer relation management (CRM), procurement, logistics and supply chain management are becoming crucial to today's enterprise. Third is information security. The Internet and the increasing use of the digital data has fueled the need for a wide range of security solutions including virtual private networks (VPNs), firewalls, biometric devices, file encryption, and advanced network monitoring.

Fourth is web services. The emergence of web into everyday life has created opportunities for an array of new applications and services, ranging from weather reports and mapping to group collaboration software and file storage and backup, software-based automation tools and web service foundation platforms.

Fifth is emergence of digital lifestyles. Over the last few years, home networking, interactive TV satellite, radio MP3 players, etc. have created new ways to live and work. There is better broadband to satisfy the demand, and wireless ubiquity for connecting people, devices, and businesses.

There is progression in Ethnotronic Technologies due to Wi-Fi progression: People from a variety of disciplines have produced a substantial body of research addressing the issues related to supportive-ethnotronic and advancement of a specific technology from a wide range of analytical perspectives. For instance, decades after their introduction, video systems (supportive-ethnotronic technology of TV) are beginning to realize their potential in supporting working from home, teaching and learning at a distance, conferencing, and interpersonal communication; video on demand, and streaming videos. There is upsurge of use of video technology for diverse functions.

Future demands in telecommunications and Broadband wave "Unconstrained connectivity" in terms of coverage in the urban and the rural and remote area populations, coverage of broadband networks along corridors between cities thus covering less-densely populated areas as well and rural areas has become imperative.

Vital and daily services, such as eHealth, connected smart cities, and the 'Internet of things' (IoT) and advantageous working of digital economy would simply not be available without high capacity networks.

Transition to high capacity networks is necessary to make sure that all citizens and business can take advantage of the digital economy. For improving opportunities for businesses and citizens everywhere, we must make connectivity available not only in urban areas, but also in rural and less densely populated areas, for all SMEs, research centers and the wider economy in general. Powerful broadband, strong Wi-Fi and Hot-Spot are utmost necessity to satisfy the demand, and wireless ubiquity for connecting people, devices, and businesses.

Ubiquitous and leading-edge connectivity in all domains will remain the main precondition for the realization of a successful digital technology revolution.

The role of important players of the digital economy: innovators, providers (through funding and accessibility), and consumers specifically in signaling demand needs—both in terms of broadband coverage, ubiquitous availability of connectivity, in terms of speeds and quality of connectivity. This only would enable the Internet of things to happen.

5G mobile will bring an exponential change to what we are used to today. It will be an innovation platform beyond the traditional telecom industry. It will become the lifeblood of the digital economy and society supporting the requirements of an array of business sectors like health, energy, transport and many more. 5G mobile has the potential to be a game changer, not only in terms of spectrum access but more fundamentally in terms of ecosystems and business models. It should also serve many more user communities than today and should have a true societal dimension. 5G will be key for mobile networks in the relatively near future.

Therefore, also an ambitious spectrum policy is fundamental in creating growth and investment, spectrum coordination mechanisms to ensure its proper and efficient roll-out; and stimulating the digital market.

In this context, it is important to streamline the technical harmonization process, which is currently extremely resource- and time-consuming. It is important that providers of equipment, devices, online services and end users need to evolve at a fast pace to keep up with exploding demand. So we need the quick, coordinated assignment of 4G—and soon 5G—spectrum bands.

But first we need to look at lessons learned of whether our telecoms regulatory framework was successful, or not, in delivering what it was meant to deliver; to bring end-users with more choice, good quality communications services, and lower prices.

We need significant investment in next generation networks. The investment must be efficient so that it achieves our connectivity aspirations.

The affordability and accessibility factor is challenging for developing countries' populations specifically the underserved; once if those countries want to use Internet, IoT for digital economy.

Third Wave of Technology Focus

Our use of data on phone or computers everywhere and all the time is possible because of Internet digital technology, even more so when billions of objects will soon be connected to the Internet. *Connectivity* is the basis for everything. Without connectivity and high-performing broadband networks, '*Digital Wave Revolution*' would not happen. Access to 'High capacity Next Generation Networks' is must.

The vision of third digital technology wave can only become a reality if we have unconstrained, ubiquitous connectivity and there is *connectivity diffusion* (anywhere connectivity) to enhance the user's experience, add value to the product, update new features; as well create more awareness and consideration of the product or services.

Going "digital" is the next big thing in the human, enterprise and governance space. But what actually is this big and new 'digital shift'? How that shift is made? What are the implications?

Digital Technologies: Digital Five Forces

Current 2000 decades are witnessing the digital five forces of mobility and pervasive computing, cloud, big data, artificial intelligence and robotics and social media sweeping the modern world and changing the technology scenario globally.

The focus is on innovative technologies of artificial intelligence—cognitive technologies, machine learning and robotics; cloud computing, big data analytics—the visual and predictive analytics: predictive technology, block chain technologies. The recent focus has been increasing on varied applications in various domains through major digital technologies of cloud, artificial intelligence, automation—robotics, cognitive technologies, mobile technologies, augmented reality (AR), visual reality (VR), and digital development of Internet of things (IoT) in several domains of enterprises, life, and governance.

The second focus is on the sustained technologies of RFID, quantum computer, laser, nanotechnologies, fuel cells and their innovative and enhanced applications.

2010 has been observing the high, fast and revolutionary level of development in these technologies; and innovations in applications of these technologies. Innovative applications have also been possible by developing other innovative digital technologies to connect, interconnect, integrate and converge.

Fifty global big companies are innovating and reshaping the digital technologies of today. Many smaller companies and many startups worldwide are also contributing towards this digital revolution. The efforts are towards research in enhancing digital features for earlier sustained technologies, developing innovative digital technologies, enhancing their features, and innovative applications of these technologies in life, enterprise and governance domains.

In these decades, larger companies such as IBM Corp, Intel, Wipro, Tata Consultancy Services and Infosys Ltd. (India based—global technology outsourcing companies), Google, Facebook, Amazon and many more; are having big shift in focus towards digitalization and also developing innovative digital technologies and their applications.

These have created not only Seventh Communication Technology Revolution, a third wave focusing on digital revolution but has also nurtured a bigger leap towards more progressive and integrated global world.

Digital Business: Five Major Platforms

1. Information systems platform, which support the back office, and operations such as enterprise resource planning and core systems.

2. Customer experience platform, which contains the main customer-facing elements, such as customer and citizen portals, multichannel commerce and customer apps.
3. Data and analytics platform, which contains information management and analytical capabilities. Data management programs and analytical applications, data-driven decision making, and algorithms automate discovery and action.
4. Internet of things (IoT) platform, which connects physical assets for monitoring, optimization, control and monetization. Capabilities include connectivity, analytics and integration to core and operational technology systems.
5. Ecosystems platform, which supports the creation of, and connection to, external ecosystems, marketplaces and communities; API management, control and security are its main elements. Infosys: Vishal Sikka CEO (2016) commented that "digital transformation can best be achieved by adopting automation and artificial intelligence (AI). The world is looking at providing services in a better way. I observe three major shifts—focus on experience among consumers, emergence of AI and the ultimate cloud phenomenon. This is a new offering that comprise three enhanced service offerings in knowledge-based IT (KBIT), platforms and design thinking".

Infosys has deployed a number of systems that replicate human decision-making in areas such as financial service regulation and ticketing of IT issues, thus enabling productivity improvements by up to 40 percent and saving customers millions of dollars annually.

Infosys is currently in 2016 is developing solutions based on artificial intelligence to solve complex problems in the engineering space—in design, testing, and certification of complex engineering products.

"I am optimistic that artificial intelligence techniques will help us solve next-generation problems, and that humans will play the most important part in this process," Sikka added.

All our clients look to us for help with innovation, in bringing digital and computing technologies to their businesses' future: "We must bring massive automation to enable innovation. If a human has done it once, it should never be done by a human again. This must be our aspiration."

Sikka believes that the current global delivery model should be transformed into a virtual one, based on value delivered, and make the location of the person doing the work irrelevant (having blockchain technologies station).

Tata Consultancy Services (TCS)

(Dr. Satya Ramaswamy, Head of Digital Enterprise Unit, TCS Tata Consultancy Newsletter Sept. 2016)

Our global study on the use of digital technologies, strongly suggests that while these are the early days of digital forces technology cycle, more companies need to start planning and strategizing on how to reimagine their businesses in multiple dimensions.

TCS has been working globally with different brands adapting the capabilities of *Digital Five Forces*, i.e. Mobility and Pervasive Computing, Cloud, Big Data, Artificial Intelligence & Robotics and Social Media are sweeping the modern world. These are changing the way we evolve, operate and interact with our customers; and to the unique needs of each industry to—'Digital Reimagination' to reimagine—Business Models, Products & Services, Customer Segments, Channels, Business Processes and Workplaces'.

The Digital Five Forces are combining to fundamentally to reimagine digital. The world economy today is in the midst of a tectonic shift from the '*Internet Economy*' to what we call the '*Digital Consumer Economy*'. This represents both an opportunity and a threat depending on the readiness of the company. Every industry—from banking to insurance, from retail to even engineering products—is being dramatically transformed.

Digital Five Forces are shaping the Digital Consumer Economy, Digitization and Digital Transformation. A more comprehensive response—'*Digital Reimagination*' is needed (having blockchain technologies station).

Cloud computing: TCS' Cloud Application Services provide an end-to-end roadmap to benefit through transformation initiatives around cloud leverage by working with you to build, execute and manage your services using cloud optimized service delivery architectures; solutions are offered through spectrum of services—from consulting, architecture definition, building and migration, to governance.

Wipro (India-based a global technology outsourcing company): Premji formed new 'Wipro Digital business—commando force' commented: "After decades of low-margin work including server maintenance, India's $150 billion IT services industry is looking towards artificial intelligence, cloud solutions and other more sophisticated digital services for growth." Rajan Kohli, who will head the newly Industry Advisory Offshore Insights estimates automation and artificial intelligence work will grow to 25 to 30 percent of India's IT outsourcing market by 2020 from less than 5 percent now. The entire sector is expected to double in value to $300 billion by then, the national industry association says.

Wipro announced on 20 September 2016, global partnership with Witbe, a leading innovator in the field of test automation and services quality of experience (QoE) monitoring robots for broadband, voice and TV triple-play monitoring. This partnership is of strategic importance to Wipro, and will offer integrated test automation and video services monitoring solutions for customer deployments across set top box, mobile platforms and other handheld devices. These solutions will benefit new and existing customers of Wipro and Witbe including semiconductor players, Original Equipment Manufacturers (OEMs), Original Design Manufacturers (ODMs) and service providers in the media industry.

Wipro Boundaryless Data Center (BLDC) offering is based on an innovative IT transformational approach that enables enterprise ITaaS (IT as a Service) through a universal marketplace. BLDC is integrated with Oracle IaaS (Infrastructure as a Service) and PaaS (Platform as a Service) services, and provides a unified platform to drive hybrid IT journey for enterprises by enabling dynamic sourcing, automated provisioning, monitoring and management. In collaboration with Oracle, Wipro will build standard reference architectures, workload blueprints and continuous deployment solutions for accelerated cloud transformation (Capital Market—Live News, New Delhi, 20 Sept. 2016).

Wipro announced the launch of Treasury DNA Decisions and Analytics platform that will digitally enable global treasuries using cloud technologies. Treasury DNA is powered by BELLIN's tm5, a leading treasury management systems provider. The announcement was made 13 October 2016 (Capital Market—Live News New Delhi, 14 Oct. 2016).

Mumbai: Wipro's $500 million of cloud services company Appirio was not just to gain access to its cloud-integration business, it was also part of a bet that the IT industry would be disrupted the way cab-hailing company Uber disrupted the transport sector. Buried inside Appirio is a crowd sourcing platform for developers and data scientists called TopCoder. Clients contact the platform with their IT requirements and with a budget. The project is then broken down into different parts that need to be implemented. Then competitions are where experts in different fields do the actual work, experienced top coders act as reviewers and then the developers on the platform are paid for the code. When Appirio bought TopCoder in September 2013, it counted NASA, Harvard University, and cable giant Comcast as customers. Appirio uses the TopCoder platform to some services to its customers. In 2016, TopCoder had over one million IT professionals.

This has, in fact, already started happening. Last year, in an interview with ET, Appirio CEO Chris Barbin said that out of the nearly one million coders on the platform, over 200,000 were from India. ET also reported that IT companies said they were aware that their employees were moonlighting on the site, but had few ways of combating it. So, it is not conceivable that in the future, Wipro could tap a full-time

TCS employee on TopCoder to do project work for it. Wipro is on TopCoder to do project work for it. At the start of the year, Wipro started a Top Gear program—creating an internal crowdsourcing platform that was meant to tap its bench to work on projects. Crowdsourcing will supplement, not replace, traditional staffing capabilities and provide flexible access to in-demand talent that can help clients improve the end-to-end performance of their websites mobile applications and Internet of things devices.

IT industry experts are also intrigued with what Wipro could do with TopCoder. "It's the crowdsourcing angle that makes this acquisition so interesting. Pairing a Cloud-first company that happens to have a successful crowdsourcing platform with one of the biggest IT outsourcing companies in the world does create the potential for some compelling developments," Stanton Jones, Principal Analyst at Saugatuck Technology, said in a note.

He added this disruption would take longer than the cloud took to get a hold on the IT space, given that the company will have to figure out how to prevent the same coder working on similar projects from two rival clients, manage enterprise security and even the geographical location of the coders.

Cloud computing make sure you are in the right cloud. No two clouds are the same. IBM SoftLayer gives you the highest performing cloud infrastructure available. "One platform that takes data centers around the world that are full of the widest range of cloud computing options, and then integrates and automates everything. They should be able to watch people, understand what they are doing and make decisions about how to help them".

IBM Corp. is also in forefront for automation, cloud, Robot, AI technologies and Cognitive technologies. It has been developing many applications of these for e-health also.

In 2016, IBM Corp. and MIT are teaming up to tackle a major challenge facing computers: teaching machines to recognize images and sounds as people do and react in useful ways. This is a formidable technical challenge.

They announced a multiyear research program in Artificial Intelligence—'Brain-inspired Multimedia Machine Comprehension' for IBM-MIT Lab.

Guru Banavar, chief science officer for cognitive computing IBM (2016), "we think of people and machine working together to solve problems; but before machines can do that, and Research could also do: (i) for instance, a home video cameras might some day at a glance recognize an ailing parent had fallen down and transmit information to family members or the health caregiver and (ii) to enable machines to learn from other machines; a robot in an assembly line can learn a new task by watching another robot perform it".

Learning by watching and listening comes naturally to humans. IBM will work with MITs department of Brain and Cognitive sciences to find ways to teach this innate human capability to computers and robots.

James DiCarlo head MITs department of Brain and Cognitive sciences, commented: "there is much less progress in recognizing or predicting actions. Even the scientists still do not know how our own brains manage it. We must learn ways our brains might be doing it. To emulate human brains ability to recognize and respond to events—these are all cutting edge problems".

Artificial Intelligence (AI)

At the high end of artificial intelligence are systems like cognitive computing that are allowing driverless cars and other machines to develop the capacity to learn from their experiences in the world—by incorporating nuances, remembering outcomes, and adapting to mistakes. (A recent accident involving a Tesla "autonomous car" has raised questions about AI's current limits.)

At the less-expensive end is a knowledge-based approach that organizes data and language into highly malleable and helpful blocks of information ("AI Lite" systems). These "AI Lite" systems don't learn new tricks—unless their human minds use new code instructions to "teach" them. But they can become very smart indeed about sorting and distributing their information in extremely fast ways. Even in this new information age, not everything requires the high-end of AI. But companies and government agencies are finding plenty of places where knowledge-based tools can make a huge difference. These include improving data-mining operations, helping with training, and making structured, repeatable tasks and processes far more efficient and less costly. And they are finding the tools increasingly useful in dealing with online customers. AI Lite is far less complicated and less expensive than the high end of the spectrum.

Three foundational elements are required for deploying the incremental power of AI Lite and other revolutionary changes that AI bring at high spectrum. AI whether at the knowledge-based end of the spectrum or with more extensive and expensive applications: (i) careful analysis and preparation, which takes into account each department but keeps the focus on the full enterprise. (ii) It must have a formal (and nuanced) governance structure. (iii) Someone at the most senior level of the company must sponsor it.

Platforms for Artificial Intelligence (AI) are big data, social networks and mobility. AI facilitates four pillar strategies that count industrialization, resource management, efficiency in procurement and automation.

As part of effective resource management, has created a new categorization of employee skills—classifying them from level 1 to level 4. By mapping out the technology and skill levels of all employees, the company is able to cross-train them in different technologies as and when the need arises. Experts say that increasingly IT companies will look at automation for their internal and service delivery.

Evolution of artificial intelligence; there is another possible scenario, Vernor Vinge in his essay *The Coming Technological Singularity* commented that this would signal the end of the human era, as the new superintelligence would continue to upgrade itself and would advance technologically at an incomprehensible rate.

The technological singularity is the hypothesis that the invention of artificial superintelligence will abruptly trigger runaway technological growth, resulting in unfathomable changes to human civilization. According to this hypothesis, an upgradable intelligent agent (such as a computer running software-based artificial general intelligence) would enter a 'runaway reaction' of self-improvement cycles, with each new and more intelligent generation appearing more and more rapidly, causing an intelligence explosion and resulting in a powerful superintelligence that would, qualitatively, far surpass all human intelligence. Thus, leading naturally to the next stage of the "enhanced man" and running the risk (if we are not careful enough) of changing him into an "obsolete man".

Vernor Vinge commenting about the Technological Singularity argues that the acceleration of technological progress has been the central feature of this century. We are on the edge of change comparable to the rise of human life on Earth. The precise cause of this change is the imminent creation by technology of entities with greater-than-human intelligence. Science may achieve this breakthrough by several means (and this is another reason for having confidence that the event will occur): (i) Computers that are awake and superhumanly intelligent may be developed. (To date, there has been much controversy as to whether we can create human equivalence in a machine. But if the answer is yes, then there is little doubt that more intelligent beings can be constructed shortly thereafter.) (ii) Large computer networks (and their associated users) may wake up as superhumanly intelligent entities. (iii) Computer/human interfaces may become so intimate that users may reasonably be considered superhumanly intelligent. (iv) Biological science may provide means to improve natural human intellect. The first three possibilities depend on improvements in computer hardware. Actually, the fourth possibility also depends on improvements in computer hardware, although in an indirect way.

Augmented Reality is future-looking technologies: These are Augmented Reality (AR), Virtual Reality (VR), a Mixed Reality (MR) and Mobile Reality (MR).

These could lead us to very different paths in entertainment, gaming, communication and industry. Augmented reality which overlays virtual 3D graphics onto our view of the real world or virtual reality which immerses us in 360 degree views of new worlds with little or no sensory input from the room your body is actually in; a new vision-based context-aware approach for mobile augmented reality that allows users to query and access semantically-rich 3D cyber-information related to real-world physical objects and sees it precisely overlaid on top of imagery of the associated physical objects.

Augmented Reality (AR)

Augmented reality, or AR, is similar to VR in that it is often delivered through a sensor-packed wearable device, such as Google Glass, the Daqri Smart Helmet or Epson's Moverio brand of smart glasses.

AR takes your view of the real world and adds digital information and/or data on top of it. But, in general, AR lets you see both synthetic light as well as natural light bouncing off objects in the real world. AR makes it possible to get that sort of digital information without checking another device, leaving both of the user's hands free for other tasks.

The difference between VR and AR is significant, but sometimes hard to assess given that both technologies are not currently in lots of consumers' hands.

The ability to use AR wearables while out and about, rather than just at home, may make them useful to a broader range of consumers, like direct evolutions of existing mobile devices, smart phones and tablets.

Emerging Trends and Challenges in Augmented Reality (AR)

AR is an approach to visualizing cyber information on top of physical imagery and manipulating cyber information through interactions with real world objects. In AR systems, sensors (such as a mobile device's camera) are used to derive information about user interactions with the real world. This derived information can then be applied via smart devices (such as phones or tablets) to help visualize information related to real-world objects (such as highlighted regions of a construction site image) or infer interactions with virtual information (such as inferring the change in shape of a virtual 3-D model created by using a knife to cut it) around the user.

The widespread adoption of smartphones has driven rapid advances in the mobile computing industry and removed this key barrier to entry. Current-generation mobile devices, such as smartphones and tablets, have an array of sophisticated sensors, powerful processing and storage capabilities and persistent network connections that make them ideal platforms for building AR applications.

Virtual Reality

Virtual reality (VR) is an artificial, computer-generated simulation or recreation of a real life environment or situation. It immerses the user by making them feel like they are experiencing the 'simulated reality' firsthand, primarily by stimulating their vision and hearing.

In VR, you wear something on your head—currently, a "head-mounted display" that can look like a boxy set of goggles or a space helmet—that holds a screen in front of your eyes, which in turn is powered by a computer, gaming console or mobile phone. This experience becomes your reality, filling your vision due to specialized software and sensors; at the high end, this is often accompanied by 3-D audio that feels like a personal surround-sound system on your head, or controllers that let you reach out and interact with this artificial world in an intuitive way.

What distinguishes VR from adjacent technologies is the level of immersion it promises. When VR users look around—or, in more advanced headsets, walk around—their view of that world adjusts the same way it would if they were looking or moving in real reality.

The key buzzword here is ***presence*** (technology and content) that can trick the brain into believing it is somewhere it's not. That's one of VR's toughest challenges. Our brains are actually pretty smart at sniffing out badly delivered presence. For example, the VR of roller coaster but when your body does not feel the sensation of being on a roller coaster. Recent tech advances have cut down on the latency, the time between when you move your head and when the virtual picture adjusts; that's crucial for not making the brain feel sick.

Virtual reality is the technology that is set to see big consumer releases within the next year, in devices like Facebook's Oculus Rift, Sony's Project Morpheus and the Samsung Gear VR.

Which is the future technology AR or VR?

This is really the question of whether humans want what they experience in the future to be based in reality, or constructed, artificial and cut off from what we now refer to as reality.

We are social creatures. So you might think VR has a slight disadvantage—augmented reality demos such as HoloLens' Halo 5 demo allow a group of users to stand in a circle around 'holograms' simultaneously.

But steps are already being taken to make VR more social—Facebook is betting big on it and we are beginning to see real investment in platforms which allow virtual hangouts such as *AltSpaceVR*. And look no further than at art projects such as the telepresence installation, 'Me and My Shadow'; which connects visitors from four cities in a virtual space.

Neither of these technologies is as passive or as social in a physical location sense of the word as compared to reading, talking and half-watching TV. To play a game or experience on Oculus or HTC Vive, you have to commit yourself fully. And VR is thrilling and entertaining for gamers, to students, say, getting their heads around anatomy.

Perhaps the difference will be VR as an at-home treat, as console gaming or kicking back to a Blu-ray is today and AR for more of a social, everyday experience that doesn't take you away from smartphone alerts, walking down the street or playing with your kids. Both will be used.

Both technologies have potential limitations: Motion sickness in VR and privacy concerns in AR.

Key term for Mixed Reality is *flexibility*. It tries to combine the best aspects of both VR and AR. In theory, mixed reality lets the user see the real world (like AR) while also seeing believable, virtual objects (like VR); and then it anchors those virtual objects to a point in real space, making it possible to treat them as "real," at least from the perspective of the person who can see the MR experience.

Update 7/13/16: Continuing the Pokémon Go update from above, characters seen in that game *do not* follow the rules of mixed reality, which some describe as "real" augmented reality. Once a Pokémon is encountered in the real world, its distance from the player does not change as that player's phone moves around; in other words, the character appears to be on top of the real world when viewed through the phone, but it's easy to break the illusion that it is in that real world.

With mixed reality, the illusion is harder to break. Examples, from Microsoft's presentation at the gaming trade show E3; you might be looking at an ordinary table, but you see an interactive virtual world from the video game 'Minecraft' sitting on top of it. As you walk around, the virtual landscape holds its position, and when you lean in close, it gets closer in the way a real object would.

Real-world applications for MR are still largely happening behind closed doors. HoloLens lenses from Microsoft and other "mixed reality" tech like Magic Leap is different from augmented reality—and both are different from virtual reality.

For certain developers tracking the ecosystem, it may make sense to redefine applications that once were called augmented reality as mixed reality.

Mobile augmented reality focuses on mobile computing. A key problem in mobile computing is providing people access to cyber-information associated with their surrounding physical objects. Mobile augmented reality is one of the emerging techniques that address this problem by allowing users to see the cyber-information associated with real-world physical objects by overlaying that cyber-information on the physical objects' imagery.

Hyojoon Bae and Michael Walker et al. *Realization for high-precision mobile augmented reality systems*

In this paper presents a new vision-based context-aware approach for mobile augmented reality that allows users to query and access semantically-rich 3D cyber-information related to real-world physical objects and sees it precisely overlaid on top of imagery of the associated physical objects.

The approach does not require any RF-based location tracking modules, external hardware attachments on the mobile devices, and/or optical/fiducial markers for localizing a user's position. Rather, the user's 3D location and orientation are automatically and purely derived by comparing images from the user's mobile device to a 3D point cloud model generated from a set of pre-collected photographs.

This approach supports content authoring where collaboration on editing the content stored in the 3D cloud is possible and content added by one user can be immediately accessible by others. In general, mobile augmented reality is required to work regardless of users' location and environment, in terms of physical scale, such as size of objects, and in terms of cyber-information scale, such as total number of cyber-information entities associated with physical objects.

However, many existing approaches for mobile augmented reality have mainly tested their approaches on limited real-world use-cases and have challenges in scaling their approaches. By designing a multi-model based direct 2D-to-3D matching algorithms for localization, as well as applying a caching scheme, the proposed research consistently supports near real-time localization and information association regardless of users' location, size of physical objects, and number of cyber-physical information items. Empirical results presented in the paper show that the approach can provide millimeter-level augmented reality across several hundred or thousand objects without the need for additional non-imagery sensor inputs.

In addition, a key challenge is required to work regardless of users' location and environment, in terms of physical scale, such as size of objects, and in terms of cyber-information scale, such as total number of cyber-information entities associated with physical objects. However, many existing approaches for mobile augmented reality have mainly tested their approaches on limited real-world use-cases and have challenges in scaling their approaches. By designing a multi-model based direct 2D-to-3D matching algorithms for localization, as well as applying a caching scheme, the proposed research consistently supports near real-time localization and information association regardless of users' location, size of physical objects, and number of cyber-physical information items.

Fard, Nov. 2016, highlighted that a key problem in mobile computing is providing people access to cyber-information associated with their surrounding physical objects. This paper presents a new vision-based context-aware approach for mobile augmented reality.

November 2015, presenting a context-aware service and information is a key aspect of ubiquitous computing, but development of such applications is quite complicated. Context-aware applications should be able to obtain raw data from sensors, create high level context information, detect the user's situation, and adapt the behavior of the application to the recognized situation. These complexities caused to reduce the impact of context -awareness in mobile computing while sensors of smartphones have made huge potential for developing.

Robots

Earlier, decades back, big robots were in use—say on the manufacturing floor in industries, at construction sites to lift heavy equipment, material at higher levels.

In current decades, AI technologies have developed Robot to perform various functions more efficiently. This development is from virtual assistant to robot use in devices. There is development of bigger and smaller robots according to the functionality; the human robot pushing a vacuum cleaner to driving cars. AI, cognitive technologies and development of sensors have facilitated the higher level functionality of robots.

Intelligent robot has many different sensors, large processors and a large memory in order to show that they have intelligence.

The robots will learn from their mistakes and be able to adapt to any new situation that may arise. An intelligent robot can be programmed with its own expert system, e.g. a factory floor is blocked with fallen boxes. An intelligent robot will remember this and take a different route. These intelligent robots carry out many different tasks such as automated delivery in a factory, pipe inspection, bomb disposal, exploration of dangerous/ unknown environments. It is safer than sending a human into dangerous places, e.g. nuclear power.

The last "humanoid" robot made by Boston Dynamics another subsidiary of Google seems to signal a breaking point from a machine beginning to do all that is expected from a "real" robot.

It is not that basic jobs will be replaced by robots but even medical doctor's job. In ten years' time, doctor's job will only be a question of asking an expert automated system for diagnosis, a better system than himself, one similar to Watson IBM. In fifteen years' time, half of his patients will do the same thing, by themselves, using the Internet, while remaining comfortable on their couch.

Technological acceleration suggests to us that this objective will be achieved in 2040 and that starting with 2030, we will probably have robots which will be able to accomplish essential tasks of everyday life. For example, we can look toward the Franco-Japanese partnership to provide Airbus with versatile humanoid robots capable of working among humans in the confined space of airline cabins. If they prove capable of such prowess, they will certainly be useful in many other situations.

Recently in 2017, online delivery companies are experimenting with knee-high size robots to deliver 10 kg goods to the customer within 30 minutes. They are in the process of studying the obstacles in roads and sidewalks for robots to walk efficiently.

Chatbot may change your life: Chatbots, which are built to sound like human beings, find solutions to everything from where to order dinner to what to do for that sprained ankle. If you're tired of downloading an app for every other thing you need, you might want to consider using a chatbot. Just fire a simple text message to your food delivery service or cab-hailing company, and you are good to go. A chatbot ('bot' comes from the word 'robot') is essentially an artificial intelligence tool built into a chat platform. Simply put, instead of going through countless app or website menus, one can simply chat with a computer to get things done, be it ordering food or browsing the day's news.

A report from US-based Credence Research published pegged the chatbot market at $88.3 million in 2015. It said the market would witness "exponential growth" in 2016-23. And it's easy to see why chatbots are likely to take over. According to a 2016 report from consumer statistics firm Statista, over 2.5 billion people have at least one messaging app installed on their phones. So, when Facebook opened up its Messenger platform to developers in April 2016, to build and run chatbots, it became the talk of tech town. Many Indian app developers say they got their bots up and running within a week or two of the Facebook announcement. "Big companies like Apple or Facebook have the resources to make a platform for artificial intelligence. Smaller developers can take advantage of those platforms to build their own products, as is happening with Messenger bots right now. Two years ago, no one would have thought that it would be possible to book autos on a phone app. After apps, chatbots are the next thing." Chatbot have been around for almost 20 years now and undoubtedly this technology will be transformative. If people want to get the tracking information of their orders online, chatbots are a perfect solution for a successful communication, but the story is not same when it comes to sensitive data like bank account information or insurance companies. The need of privacy and security for such communication and transactions is high and Facebook as the primary platform for this may not work as more than half of adults do not trust Facebook with their data. Another reason for 'Messenger chatbot' failure is the desire of businesses of owning the data.

The changing scenarios will be many jobs going obsolete. In education domain; cognitive education development of Massive

Open Online Courses (MOOC) for each discipline and at each level; only the three best courses in the world survive and are followed by millions of students. Without students left in her classes, Ms. Y is not profitable anymore, so she is fired, and her university closes down.

Many and overtime all jobs are going to be obsolete. The most skill-demanding jobs as well as basic jobs are going to be obsolete fast. Engineers will be soon replaced by some new software able to do the same job better and faster. Traders, sales assistants perhaps these will survive longer, but the purchases made online without them are increasing. Smartphones will replace tourist guides and translators, etc. Cashier in supermarkets is already an obsolete job. Local commerce is already shattered by the Internet.

Workers in factories and warehouses; restaurant chefs, taxi drivers, banking queries are all being robotized. Builders are robotized or unnecessary because of workshop pre-assembly construction. Vehicles are replaced by automatic, driverless vehicles or by sensor driving.

A drastic transformation of our social model, and another twenty years to invent a new model, no longer based on human labor. A communication revolution in quite a short time but very powerful when we approach the moment when machine capacities totally exceed those of men; it could pose a real threat to humanity.

Promises are at least as great as threats. On the side of labor, it will be the end of the laborious and unrewarding jobs. On the side of humans, for better or for worse, the interconnected men, born in an Internet era, are gradually transformed into "enhanced" men, with a kind of collective intelligence and capabilities (both physical and intellectual) enhanced by computer science, robotics and biotechnology, while remaining, at the same time, the foundation of the social unit. This is somehow the advent of "homo connecticus" humans, forming a human anthill whose overall intelligence becomes collective and transcends individual intelligence.

The same goes for artificial intelligence, robotics and full interconnection of humans: it is seen as progress, when it causes mankind to evolve; it is seen as a problem when it challenges the human's role. With no work and no individuality, man can quickly become "useless", knowing that the technological revolution can also turn against the mental health of the population in the best scenario.

Cloud computing focuses on:

(i) Cloud Architect—Application and Platform Architecture: Optimal cost-sensitive design with high availability features.

(ii) Cloud Building Migration Services: Semi-automated tool-led application migrations for quicker implementation.

(iii) Cloud Mpower: Business and IT portfolio analysis leading to risk-calibrated recommendations on cloud leverage leading to cost and business agility.

(iv) Cloud Security, Governance, Risk Management and Compliance: Granular recommendations on cloud architecture and workload management in light of customers' regulatory, cost and technology constraints.

(v) Cloud Service Brokerage Aggregation, integration, and customization of cloud deployment components.

(vi) Hybrid Cloud Services: Bringing together legacy on-premise assets with public and private cloud workloads.

(vii) Cloud Govern Unified Cloud Management and Monitoring: Framework to seamlessly manage workloads running in hybrid environments, typically in complex service deployment models with a mix of on-premise and private/public assets.

(viii) Dev-Ops Services: Accelerated software development integrated with operations, using agile technologies on a cloud-based architecture, to deliver more effective development artifacts faster.

There are public clouds which allow companies to buy computing and storage power without needing to own data centers; also called infrastructure-as-a-service. There are personal clouds which individuals use on their computers.

Cloud systems are cheap and flexible, and companies are quickly shifting their technologies for that environment. According to analysts at Gartner, the global cloud-computing business will be worth $67 billion by 2020, compared with $23 billion at the end of this year. "The world's biggest maker of computer servers is making machines just for it" (2016).

Currently, Amazon and Microsoft are leading in cloud computing. Google is competing Amazon and Microsoft for control of the next generation of business technology in enormous cloud-computing data centers.

Google has used artificial intelligence to cut the power use in its data centers by 15 per cent, a huge decrease considering how efficient these data factories were already. Power use is the most costly in cloud computing. That ability to find energy efficiency may be a powerful tool to sell to others over Google Compute.

Mustafa Suleyman (2016), the head of applied artificial intelligence at the company's DeepMind subsidiary of Google, said "the techniques could be used at power plants, refineries and other big industrial systems. This certainly gives Google an edge. Other people focused on narrow problems. We've focused on the widest possible problem." For Google, a loss in cloud computing would be a rare misstep for a company.

Google, however, could change how we work, turning advanced computing into an everyday utility that we use to run factories, interact in virtual reality or read one another's emotions. Google also released for public use; ways to transcribe and analyze recorded speech for things like meaning, emotional content and whether a speaker was happy or sad. An outside company that worked on the project used it to analyze over two billion minutes of customer service calls. It works in 80 languages, Google said.

A move like that only makes sense when a company wants to offer the kind of split-second performance needed for virtual reality or instantaneous customer interactions over networks of cell phones and sensors.

At a recent conference at Amazon Web Services for software developers, an executive from iRobot, which makes the Roomba vacuuming robot, talked about using the cloud to map homes and human behavior in houses with potentially "hundreds" of connected devices. Doing something like that would require instantaneous connections.

Faster networks, lower prices and lots of artificial intelligence can put Google ahead. Amazon's lead seems to give it an edge for at least the next couple of years, as its cloud branch has perfected a method of developing hundreds of new cloud features annually. Yet Amazon appears to have some basic artificial intelligence features, called machine learning, it seems to have little in the way of speech recognition or translation. "Everyone has to play to the strengths the market already sees they have."

Public clouds allow companies to buy computing and storage power without needing to own data centers. Also called infrastructure-as-a-service, the business was created by ecommerce company Amazon. Its Amazon Web Services division is now on track to $10 billion in revenue this year. Microsoft, which was a later entrant to the space with Azure offering, has said its public cloud revenue doubled this year.

India is the sleeping giant in the public cloud space. Gartner expects public cloud services in the country to reach $1.26 billion this year and it is growing at over 30%. India would provide a considerable edge to whichever company corners a lead in the market. The battle for the public cloud is heating up in India, become more intense in FY17 and FY18. It is one of the fastest growing markets in the world. Microsoft and Amazon are in competition for dominance.

The worldwide public cloud services market is projected to grow 17.2 per cent in 2016 to total $208.6 billion, up from $178 billion in 2015, according to Gartner Inc. The highest growth will come from cloud system infrastructure services (infrastructure as a service [IaaS]), which is projected to grow 42.8 per cent in 2016. Cloud application services (software as a service [SaaS]), one of the largest segments in the global cloud services market, is expected to grow 21.7 percent in 2016 to reach $38.9 billion.

Growth of public cloud is supported by the fact that organizations are saving 14 per cent of their budgets as an outcome of public cloud adoption, according to Gartner's 2015 cloud adoption survey, said Sid Nag, research director at Gartner. However, the aspiration for using cloud services outpaces actual adoption. There's no question there is great appetite within organizations to use cloud services, but there are still challenges for organizations as they make the move to the cloud. Even with the high rate of predicted growth, a large number of organizations still have no current plans to use cloud services".

Blockchain Technologies

Blockchain is a peer-to-peer distributed ledger *technology* for a new generation of transactional applications (*Source*: IBM).

"Over the past two decades, the Internet has revolutionized many aspects of business and society-making individuals and organizations more productive. Yet the basic mechanics of how people and organizations execute transactions with one another have not been updated for the 21st century. Blockchain could bring to those processes the openness and efficiency we have come to expect in the Internet Era."—Arvind Krishna, Senior VP, IBM Research.

Blockchain is technology for new generation of transactional applications that establishes trust, accountability and transparency while streamlining business processes. With it, we can re-imagine the world's most fundamental business interactions and open the door to invent new styles of digital interactions. It has the potential to vastly reduce the cost and complexity of cross-enterprise business processes. The distributed ledger makes it easier to create cost-efficient business networks where virtually anything of value can be tracked and traded—without requiring a central point of control.

The application of this emerging technology is showing great promise across a broad range of business applications.

Key Concepts of Blockchain Technologies

A blockchain has four main concepts: (i) *a business network*, in which members exchange items of value through a ledger, which each member possesses and whose content is always in sync with the others. A business network is a decentralized peer-to-peer architecture with nodes consisting of market participants (such as banks and securities firms). Protocol peers validate and commit transactions in order to reach consensus.

(ii) *Shared ledger*, it can act as a source of truth for businesses doing transactions on a blockchain: Records all transactions across the business network. It is shared among participants. It is replicated so each participant has their own copy. It is permissioned, so participants see only appropriate transactions.

Often, companies have multiple ledgers for multiple business networks in which they participate. It can be used for recording and totaling financial transactions.

(iii) *Smart contracts* can include a digital asset; it can be tangible or intangible. A smart contract can also include a digital representation of a set of business rules. It is embedded in the blockchain, is executed in a transaction, and is verifiable, signed, and encoded in a programming language. Entries in the ledger are synchronized to all ledgers in the network.

Consensus ensures that these shared ledgers are exact copies, and lowers the risk of fraudulent transactions since tampering would have to occur across many places at the exact same time. All parties agree to the transaction and validate it via the peer network. Rules can also be established to validate transactions. This trusted and trustless participation makes commitment possible at a low cost.

IBM Blockchain uses a "pluggable" consensus system to meet the needs of different industry segments.

(iv) *Privacy and confidentiality*: Ability to protect records with a personal digital signature—the blockchain generates a private and public key to seal that record. It is encrypted, hashed, and sent to the network of validating nodes. There is Unique IDs for customer, invoice and reference numbers.

Transactions need to be authenticated, and cryptography is central to these processes.

Although the ledger is shared, sometimes participants require private transactions. Identities that cannot be linked to specific transactions.

IBM (August 2016) said that the new framework will help organizations create "secure cloud environments" for permissioned blockchain that exceed security and compliance requirements for industries that could benefit from the technology.

These include governments or healthcare providers that want to leverage blockchain-based systems given that they must adhere to standards such as the Federal Information Processing Standards (FIPS) and the Health Insurance Portability and Accountability Act (HIPAA). Further, that it made improvements to its cloud service that will now allow networks to be deployed in minutes, with upgrades made to its documentation and dashboards.

Like every technology, blockchain has limitations and is not suited for application to all scenarios. It is not well suited for high performance (millisecond) transactions involving just one participant with no business network involved, or for replicated database replacement. It is not useful as a transaction-processing replacement and is unsuitable for low-value, high-volume transactions. Scalability is a significant challenge currently, with differences between public and private blockchains.

In a public blockchain such as bitcoin, thousands of nodes store copies of the relevant content, forcing a limit on transaction volumes to preserve decentralization. In private blockchains, only nodes with a direct interest in the successful processing of the transactions are running. In addition, blockchains are not ideal for high-frequency trading because of delays introduced by the asynchronous, ad-hoc, peer-to-peer nature of the networked blockchain nodes (this can be resolved if, rather than storing complete transactional histories, the blockchain hosts just an ongoing verified representation of the transactions). There are also challenges with throughput capacity and storage limits related to permissions, as well as integration challenges when corporate legacy systems and systems of record are involved. As blockchain technologies develop, many of the initial disadvantages are being eliminated, with further refinements in the blockchain ecosystem.

IBM is out to merge blockchain with Watson cognitive computing tools to build an even more powerful technology (IBM report 2016).

In Chapter 3, Healthcare Challenges and how Blockchain can solve them is discussed.

Drones

Commercial Drones will facilitate e-commerce. Google and Facebook are already testing drones (an unmanned aerial vehicle (UAV), an unmanned aircraft system (UAS)). Facebook drone is a solar-powered and wider than a 747.

Drones could eliminate the need for shipping via post or UPS. In the not-too-distant future, Amazon could use a drone to deliver a package from a country warehouse all the way to...a nearby farm. USA Obama administration (2016) was not ready to let Google and Amazon launch automated drone delivery fleet across urban areas. The Federal Aviation Administration (US) said commercial drones are OK so long as the drone and its payload weigh less than 55 lb, stay within unaided sight of the pilot and operators pass a test every two years. In addition, each drone must have its own pilot.

The government said it is comfortable with companies using drones for inspecting crops, search and rescue, aerial photography and other infrastructure inspection. But when it comes to deliveries, the Obama administration said drones are only clear for take-off in a very limited set of circumstances. There is risk from automated package delivery.

The government said it lacks data on the safety of flying drones outside the line-of-sight of the pilot; though it said operators could apply for a waiver on a case by case basis.

Commercial drones can only fly during daylight and 30 minutes before sunrise and 30 minutes after sunset. Speeds must be kept under 100 mph and the drones can't fly above 400 ft. (122 m).

Amazon has announced (2016) that it will partner with the British Government to run tests exploring the viability of delivery of small parcels by drone—the first time such tests have been run in the UK.

The company announced that a cross-government team supported by the Civil Aviation Authority (CAA) gave permission to Amazon to explore three key areas: operations beyond line of sight, obstacle avoidance and flights where one person operates multiple autonomous drones.

The experiment will look at drones carrying deliveries weighing 2.3 kg (5 lb) or less—which makes up 90 per cent of Amazon's sales, a company spokeswoman said.

A representative for the CAA said that a priority during the tests would be making sure that drone delivery did not adversely affect other airspace users.

During the test the drones will be limited to an altitude of 400 ft (122 m)—as is standard among private drone operations—and kept away from operating near airport flightpaths.

There are still many hurdles to fly commercial drones, not to mention these being shot down.

Biometrics

Next wave of identification by biometrics: So far the biometric recognition focus has been on physical touch whether unlocking the door or using bank ATM with finger or thumb swipe or using/opening smart phone with thumb touch. In technical terms these are physical/body touch.

Now fingerprint left behind on public computers can identify your location and your browser history. Computer unique online 'fingerprints' left behind while using your device in public locations can reveal your identity, and can be used to track your movements, say scientists who are trying to find ways to protect against the fingerprinting of personal computers. People's leave behind online browser "fingerprints" at each location they visit on their Internet browser, researchers said.

Every individual has 'unique browser Print". You may not see it but companies/hackers have special way to view it.

Researchers at the University of Adelaide in Australia are working to find new methods of protecting against the fingerprinting of personal computers—and are now giving members of the community the chance to see their own computer browser print.

This is because fingerprints build up in between the websites you're visiting—your browsing history and personal information can be pooled in the gaps between those websites," he said. "Simply clearing your browsing history won't make any difference to this, because the information is already out there," he added.

Data collected through browserprint can be targeted by advertisers, for spying, etc. privacy issues are targeted.

Scientists and researchers are doing research to protect the privacy re browserprints. They are seeking the public's help to better understand which fingerprinting techniques are the most powerful, so that they can help to build defenses against them.

Iris program: The new Iris biometrics focus is on our eyes—supposed to tell us about a person what words cannot express; it has its own eye-language to tell about the person.

It is a push to develop more sophisticated identification systems for identifying person for various purposes from banking to spying and other law enforcement programs; to run parallel to existing and expanding technologies such as of finger printing, face recognition. The focus is on creating and using Iris biometrics. Iris scanning technologies are coming up fast.

Even the existing Iris technology is improving rapidly. Researchers at Carnegie Mellon USA have been working on long-range Iris recognition systems that can scan and identify eyes from up to 40 feet even captured from rear-view mirror of a car. Parallel to this trend is the eye-tracking technology.

There are more and big technological shifts to come in eye biometrics.

Payment Technology

A fast and efficient payment network also has implications for the economy. The banks now face a challenge to make their real-time technology work for customers. Electronic payment technology is fast developing for individuals; from the conventional cards—credit, debit, prepaid; ATM (automated teller machines), through Internet, use of e-wallet through its varied products, and mobile phone apps.

Banks have also devised technology to transfer large sums of moneys for customers through inter-banking system and instantaneously. Bank uses various codes such as IFSC on mobile phones to transfer to any vendor, RTGL, to transfer larger amounts.

Mobile Technology—Mobile Phones; Enhanced Telecommunications, Towers

Mobile technology is a megatrend since last 10 years. It is igniting opportunities that will shape our world; it is stimulating more prosperous and innovating and compassionate world.

We are in the midst of mobile revolution that extends far beyond our mobile phones. It is creating new global connections, empowering individuals, and driving societal change.

Digital mobile technology is creating all the transformational, logistical and social changes critical to e-commerce. Mobile technology is empowering people as consumers and part of global workforce. e-commerce world is doing commerce anywhere, anytime. Businesses are launched in an iPad tap. Supply chains are powered by just-in-time deliveries; increasingly mobile workforce offices anywhere are using three or more mobile devices.

Development of Cell Phones

It has taken 120 years from Alexander Graham Bell's invention of the conventional telephone to wire up one billion customers worldwide. Now cellular technology has created worldwide connectivity through Internet phones and cell phones.

Development of cellular technology ushered mobile (cell) phones in the market. Feature phone came first but are big hit for connectivity. Now there are smart mobile phones—iPhones of 2G, 3G, 4G, etc. with enhanced features of connectivity of not only telephones but web-surfing, e-mail access, and faxing, a speaker phone and camera for pictures and downloading and uploading of these pictures. It allows many apps for e-commerce to entertainment. e-wallet skype and facetime are likely to be used with biometric technology also.

Once the preserve of business users, cell have become everyday consumer appliance and even important mode of connectivity where people cannot have landlines such as rural and hinterlands.

Unlike Psion which produced Palmtop organizer in 1980s; the Microsoft entry into the world of palmtop computing began only in 1995. Following the huge success of 'palm pilot' the tiny organizer that uses a plastic pen instead of keyboard; Microsoft enlisted another eight manufacturers to make a competing version of a similar unit.

Symbian a joint venture of Nokia, Ericsson, and Motorola are planning to use Psion operating system EPOC as the basis for the smart phones. So far only Philips has licensed Psion software for smart phone. An Ericsson Vice President Jan Ahrenbring (1998) adds that Microsoft operating system was not actually applicable for mobile. But Microsoft maintains that its software is modular and can be customized to suit customers' needs.

In addition to Symbion, telecommunication industry has formed two other alliances to improve the usability of wireless devices. One of them is WAP forum (for wireless applications protocol) is designing special browsers to being Internet data to mobile phones. The second group Bluetooth is trying to set a universal standard for radio communication between smart devices like palm computers and mobile phones. Microsoft has not joined either group.

Finland offers some interesting insights into some of these devices side shows. At the Helsinki airport, a coke wending machine has a mobile number instead of coin slot—dial up the machine and a coke drops out with the charge appearing on your phone bill. Similar practices are spreading across Europe. In Italy, operator Omnitel lets users call a special number while standing in front of designated piazzas; the computer figures out where you are and plays back a recorded discourse on the art and history of the location in one of the five languages. Soon an advertiser like McDonald will be able to send a data message to every mobile phone at a football stadium urging their owners to eat a Big Mac at half time. Or a pedestrian walking past a car showroom might receive a message inviting him inside for special deal.

The Internet is likely to have a huge appeal; but surfing the web on the phone is impractical on the tiny screen. So designers have come up with a micro browser that let the users surf for information by pressing a number on the dialing pad instead of fumbling with a computer mouse. Typing an e-mail (on phone screen) is an hassle even with the latest technology; voice recognition software will enable users to dictate directly to their cell phones.

Data transmission on mobile phone is currently limited to 9.6 kbps. The Europeon telcom industry will receive a huge boost in 1999 with the arrival of an enhanced GSM system: General packet radio service or GPRS. This will boost transmission speed to 150 kbps—faster than high speed ISDN (Integrated Services Digital Network) computer line.

The third generation of mobile phones will switch on around 2003 resulting in real sprint for technological superiority for this, European and Japanese have agreed on a technical standard called Wideband Code Division Multiple Access as the successor to GSM. Probably, Qualcomm USA will adopt different standard from Europe and Asia.

The vision of the future may be: Hand-held computer makers could offer machines made with Symbian's software in the hope of making them more appealing to consumers with mobile phones. Or the mobile phone industry could adopt Window CE to ensure that there devices link easily with existing desktop PCs that depends how the battle between Microsoft and Symbian is resolved but likelihood is Europe will be communicating with a single standard.

"Watch out Bill Gates: Europeaons are getting a jump on the next information revolution. A British company Psion is giving brains to new mobile phones that receive e-mail, surf the internet, and can even pay for transactions" (material is based on—High Flying phones by Charles P. Wallace, *Times,* Sept. 28, 1998).

The satellite phones—The super cell phones. The Iridium Consortium and rival joint ventures are closing on their goal of making sat-phones into multibillion dollar mainstays of the Info-superhighway.

Other Digital Technologies

RFID

In 2004, RFID (radio frequency identification) is another technology making new headway. RFID involves tiny computer chips that transmit radio signals that can be read by a scanner. RFID chips are already common, such as being used by drivers to zip past toll-booths and in the ID cards that employee use to open the office doors or for using hotel room doors by the customer. But in its new use, the big retailers are using them to tag all sorts of product to make inventory tracking more efficient and help prevent theft. Because of its higher cost, RFID will be initially used in warehouses and back of its stores and not at cash registers. The fifth revolution might shift the national and global power structures in different ways.

As we will note RFID has developed in more ways for its utilization in third wave technology.

Quantum Computing

Sixth Communication Revolution of 2000 decade is the Quantum Computing. Other technologies, such as laser and quantum are facilitating information revolution. Taking a quantum leap researchers are now harnessing the bizarre laws of quantum physics to make computers out of single molecule. Will molecule-sized computers revolutionize the world? In classical computing, a computer can store one piece of data, either a 1 or a 0. In quantum computing, the qubits can be both 0 and 1 at the same time meaning that they can specify numbers simultaneously. In quantum computers, researchers can use atom nuclei to store information. If mixed up together, in quantum physics, an object's attributes can be linked or entangled with another object.

Seth Lloyds, MIT professor (2000) is experimenting with Quantum computing, a completely new way to crunch numbers and process data. If quantum computing can be perfected, it will revolutionize everything we know about computers. Sometimes, around 2020, researchers reckon, each transistor will shrunk to the size of a single atom. The magnitude of data storage at this scale is unprecedented. "If you could put a bit of information on a single atom, you could store way more than the library of congress", Lloyd said. If new rule of quantum physics can be mastered by new generation of computer scientists, the payoff would be astounding, allowing hard secret codes to be made and broken and instant searching of incredibly voluminous databases.

This extraordinary power is possible in the counter-intuitive world of quantum mechanics, the physical laws that govern microscopic things like atoms. Unlike our everyday existence, in quantum mechanics you really can be in two places at once. Even qubits can exhibit a totally bizarre property called entanglement. This purely quantum effect means that all qubits in a quantum computer are hooked together—entangled, so that a computer operation on qubits can influence other qubits. It is this strange communication among qubits that allows huge amounts of quantum data to be searched and manipulated simultaneously. (Quantum bit—qubit is a unit of quantum information—the quantum analogue of the classical bit.)

The experimental challenges are incredibly difficult. Quantum computing is still in its infancy. Issac Chuang MIT professor, Peter Shor at Bell Lab, and David Cory (MIT) are into 'quantum computer building' (for details see Notes 2.1). A general-purpose quantum computer (like desktop PC) is decades away. Nonetheless the interest is high in its applications like ultra-secure communications, cryptography and other InfoTech applications.

Unlike the CMOS-integrated circuit technology, which is the backbone of today's communication revolution, it is difficult to predict the trajectory of future developments in quantum computing. We must remember that the exponential advances in CMOS technology, during the last 60 years, are largely due to the evolution of planar technology based solely on silicon. The historical lesson that we need to learn here is that unless we zero-in on one or two possible technologies using a material whose properties are well understood, the evolution of any technology becomes unpredictable. Unfortunately, during the last two decades, researchers have been grappling with too many alternate technological approaches (nearly 16 ways) from diverse fields of science to realize quantum computers. Some of these are based on electronic, optical, and NMR experimental methods while others draw their strength based on advances in semiconductor and superconductor technologies. Our current inability to make a clear choice from among the available technologies is an indication of our immature status in building a working quantum computer. Unless we narrow down these approaches to a small band of realizable technologies, a quantum computer will only remain as an abstract idea.

To make quantum computing a reality in near future developments in nanotechnology will, therefore, form the backbone for advancing and realizing quantum computers. In addition, since quantum computing is prone to errors due to imperfections and noise, developing efficient algorithms to take care of quantum error corrections should be an inherent part of any quantum computing initiative. The challenges for the research community, therefore, include creating new models and quantum algorithms, sorting out architectural issues, and developing technological solutions if quantum computers are to become a certainty.

Broadly, the major research groups in various parts of the world are working on: (1) superconducting qubits, (2) flux-based qubits, (3) charge-based qubits, and (4) phase-based qubits.

The quantum revolution will give us new material, new energy sources, and perhaps ability to create new forms of matter.

Laser Technology

The word Laser is acronym for Light Amplification through Stimulated Emission of Radiation. Light moves in waves, and sunlight or artificial light contains a mixture of wavelengths. By contrast, laser is a beam of light that has a single frequency or wavelength. The laser is created by subjecting a substance, such as crystal or gas mixture, to energy in the form of strong light, electricity, or a chemical or a nuclear reaction. This excites the atoms of the substance, which emits light of a particular wavelength. The advantage of a laser is that all the photons or particles of light have the same wavelength, so they are the same color, unlike a flash light which gives off a whole range of wavelengths. With a tight energy-rich beam you can do useful things like cutting metal.

A light's wavelength—the distance between the tips of two successive waves determines the color that our eyes perceive. Wavelengths are measured in nanometers. The spectrum of rainbow runs roughly from 400 nm for the violet end to the 750 nm for the red. Below 400 nm are ultraviolet light, then X-rays and gamma rays. Above 750 nm is infrared, and then microwaves, then radio waves. At present the commercial devices use infrared lasers and red lasers. In 1999, the hottest research in laser was finding a way to harness the power of a blue laser, which could lead to vastly increased storage capacity of CDs and DVDs, faster laser printers, and a better way to identify cancerous cells with blue light. Most semiconductor diode lasers—those in CD players and printers are infrared, their beams invisible to the naked eye. The ones that you can see at the checkout counter and laser pointers are on the red end of the spectrum and have been around for years.

Red lasers are tiny chips of crystal, the size of a small, square pebble. They put out bright single-colored light a few thousandth of a watt in power. But lasers that shine blue have much shorter wavelength and are difficult to make.

A decade ago researchers could make crystals that would emit blue light, but that would only work few seconds and would fade. Scientists say they can improve the laser if they can find a way to turn it from red to blue. Infrared lasers capacity is 650 mb (such as in CD). Red lasers capacity is 4,700 mb (as in DVD), and blue lasers capacity will be 16,000 mb. Lasers with smaller wavelengths can read smaller pits in a disc. Comparatively, red lasers have shorter wavelengths than infrared, blue lasers with smaller wavelengths would greatly increase the amount of data stored in a disc. Light's different wavelengths correspond to different colors: red at one end of the spectrum has a wavelength nearly twice that of blue at the other end. Lasers emit light only in one frequency; all are parallel and aligned so their peaks and troughs are synchronized.

LEDs (light emitting diodes) are less powerful cousins of lasers. The green light that says computer is on is an LED.

Shuji Nakamura of Nichia—a company based in Japan in 1994 made marketable blue LEDs. He is the leader in blue laser development through gallium nitride. What silicon did for computer chips; gallium nitride is doing for blue laser. Making the blue lasers continues to be a challenge because gallium nitride is very hard, very strong, but difficult to synthesize. It takes temperature of 1000°C to grow gallium nitride crystals. Nakamura could find a way to reduce the temperature to 500 or 600°C by working in a nitrogen-hydrogen atmosphere. This way defects did not spread throughout the crystal. Nichia was expecting to start selling samples of *high power laser diode* in October 1999. Nichia's laser lasts 2000 hours. It is necessary that a laser have a lifetime of 10000 hours to put in a commercial device.

In the early 1990s, the Institute of High Pressure Physics at the Polish Academy of Sciences in Warsaw (Poland), under the leadership of Dr. Sylwester Porowski developed technology to create gallium nitride crystals with high structural quality and fewer than 100 defects per square centimeter—at least 10,000 times better than the best sapphire-supported crystal.

In 1999, Nakamura tried Polish crystals, producing lasers with twice the yield and ten times the lifetime—3,000 hours at 30 mW. For his work, Nakamura received the Millennium Technology Prize awarded in 2006, and a Nobel Prize for

Physics awarded in 2014 "for the invention of efficient blue light-emitting diodes which has enabled bright and energy-saving white light sources".

A further development of the technology has led to mass production of the device. Today, blue lasers use a sapphire surface covered with a layer of gallium nitride (this technology is used by Japanese company Nichia, which has an agreement with Sony), and blue semiconductor lasers use a gallium nitride mono-crystal surface by Polish company TopGaN.

Diode-pumped solid state lasers: Diode lasers which emit light at 445 nm are becoming popular as handheld lasers. Lasers emitting wavelengths below 445 nm appear violet (but are sometimes called blue lasers). Some of the most commercially common blue lasers are the diode lasers used in Blu-ray applications which emit 405 nm "violet" light, which is a short enough wavelength to cause fluorescence in some chemicals, in the same way as radiation further into the ultraviolet ("black light") does. Light of a shorter wavelength than 400 nm is classified as ultraviolet.

Devices that employ blue laser light have applications in many areas ranging from optoelectronic data storage at high density to medical applications.

Applications of the Laser Technology

Since the laser invention in 1960, researchers have been hard at work looking for more useful applications of the technology—mainly for the good of the humanity. Today, lasers are familiar part of everyday life, used in everything from surgical instruments to supermarket checkout scanners to compact disc players. Laser is creating information revolution. It has the ability to send billions of telephone calls along beams of light using fiber optics. Beside telecommunication, laser has created and revolutionized laser printing, laser CDs, laser surgery, and laser diamond cutters and other metal cutters for the industry.

The next generation of lasers may open new realms, as they become microscopic as well as massive. As you get to the shorter wavelength, you get a big increase in data storage. For example, the blue lasers would give Xerox the ability to print with smaller dots, and to cluster more individual lasers together giving better resolution and faster speed. The blue diodes can aid in the building of new medical devices. Already dentists are using blue light to harden the fillings or whiten teeth. The blue laser under the right wavelength can find cancerous cells.

Lasers are also used by military in designing weapons of destruction. The military would like shorter wavelength lasers to apply similar fluorescence techniques for detection of chemical and biological weapons. The light blue-green color allows underwater communication between submarines.

Despite difficulties still to overcome, scientists believe the widespread manufacturing of blue diode laser will take only a few years more. Micro-lasers are the key link in optical computers. There are X-ray lasers. A great deal more information can be packed on them. X-ray lasers can etch fine lines onto silicon microprocessors. X-ray lasers may be able to illuminate the world of bacteria and viruses in greater detail, giving us the atomic structure of these living entities because they have short wavelengths (information based on Wikipedia, Boston Globe).

Nontechnology. Nanotechnology is a technology executed on the scale of less than 100 nanometers, the goal of which is to control individual atoms and molecules, especially to create computer chips and other microscopic devices.

It is the engineering of functional systems at the molecular scale. It is projected ability to construct items from the bottom up, using techniques and tools being developed today to make complete, high performance products. It will offer better built, longer lasting, cleaner, safer, and smarter products for the home, for communications, for medicine, for transportation, for agriculture, and for industry in general. Current application of nano technologies are in textiles, renewable energy, biomedical and healthcare, environment, food and agriculture, electronics and industrial.

Nanotech will offer greatly improved efficiency in almost every facet of life. But as a general-purpose technology, it will be dual-use, meaning it will have many commercial uses and it also will have many military uses—making far more powerful weapons and tools of surveillance. Thus, it represents not only wonderful benefits for humanity, but also grave risks.

Mihail (Mike) Roco of the U.S. National Nanotechnology Initiative has described *four generations* of nanotechnology development. The current era, as Roco depicts it, is that of passive nanostructures, materials designed to perform one task. The second phase, which we are just entering, introduces active nanostructures for multitasking; for example, actuators, drug delivery devices, and sensors. The third generation is expected to begin emerging around 2010 and will feature nano systems with thousands of interacting components. A few years after that, the first integrated nano systems, functioning (according to Roco) much like a mammalian cell with hierarchical systems within systems, are expected to be developed.

A key understanding of nanotechnology is that it offers not just better products, but a vastly improved manufacturing process. A computer can make copies of data files—essentially as many copies as you want at little or no cost. It may be only a matter of time until the building of products becomes as cheap as the copying of files. That's the real meaning of nanotechnology, and why it is sometimes seen as "the next industrial revolution."

Imagine a medical device that travels through the human body to seek out and destroy small clusters of cancerous cells before they can spread; or a box no larger than a sugar cube that contains the entire contents of the Library of Congress. Or materials much lighter than steel that possess ten times as much strength (US national science foundation).

Digital Economics

Gartner Consultants Inc. (2016) defines digital economics as the creation, consumption and control of value associated with digital products, services and assets in organizations. Digital economics creates a framework for organizations to understand and account for how much of an organization's business value can be defined as potential or realized digital value. It guides CIOs and CDOs in creating new value mechanisms and complementing or extending existing ones. By doing so, they are able to monetize the value of digital innovation and link that value with the organization's business objectives. Organizations have been able to cause real market disruptions because they have applied digital economics to exploit new value creation opportunities.

In these contexts, Chris Howard and Saul Judah of Gartner made some salient points.

Howard Chris, Vice-President and analyst at Gartner (2016) highlights that digital technologies are expanding the value of traditional products and services by using data, content, algorithms, analytics, and the connections between economic agents in a digital ecosystem. The deepening and widening of digital business initiatives puts CIOs, chief data officers (CDOs) and digital leaders at the center of creating measurable new business value. These leaders are uniquely positioned to connect digital technology advances with emerging flexible business models to fuel growth. *The framework for exploiting the value of digital business is digital economics.*

Judah Saul, research director at Gartner, said "IT leaders should establish a digital economic framework that connects digital value to a renovated economic architecture. This will help them establish a strategic, commercially sustainable foundation for creating new markets and new revenue sources. Without a corresponding economic framework, these elements of digital value remain a loose collection of digital tools and techniques."

All too often IT leaders focus value creation more narrowly, with the result that most digital initiatives are aimed at operational improvements, rather than value transformation. While this tactical approach to digital value can result in very real process and financial improvements. *But the greatest potential for digital value lies in more strategic initiatives, such as creating new markets, empowering employees, changing the basis of competition and crossing industry boundaries.*

IT leaders should engage with business leaders to identify the sources of digital value, catalog existing digital assets, products and services, and assess and assign value to them. Digital products, assets and services can be understood, cataloged and valued based on several methods such as:

Using Infonomics to Exploit Information as an Asset: Information, such as customer data and digital content, is increasingly understood as an asset; these assets have real business value measured, by intrinsic value or market value. Organizations invest in increasing the quality and consistency of their customer contact data so that they can, for example, run marketing campaigns that yield better returns. *The theory of infonomics applies information valuation techniques to information assets and can be used by organizations to understand its business value as an asset.*

Exploiting the Economics of Connections: Connections between people, businesses and things have business value. Gartner predicts that by 2018, the new economics of connections will drive organizations to increase investments in connected physical assets and systems by 30 per cent. That business value exists in the connection itself (for example, charging for usage of an API) as well as the asset being exchanged through the connection. Economic value, therefore, is a function of the number, context and usage of connections in the enterprise.

Exploiting the Power of Algorithms: Algorithms and analytics offer accelerators of value and are themselves of exchangeable and monetizable value; an analytics process may use algorithms in its creation, which could also be monetizable through an algorithmic marketplace, making it available to enterprises of all types and sizes to use.

Information technologies big and small available today challenges the traditional notions and practices. One important concept is information technology relies on a global grid for international use. Anyone's nation's desire, decision or trial with IT inevitably links that nation to a larger, global system. It could have ramifications for that global system—depending whether that nation is adopting their older technologies or newer technologies for their use. Or a section of that nation—such as Indian technology outsourcing companies is using as well developing innovative technologies.

CHAPTER 3 Applications of Current Digital Technologies

Applications of Current Digital Technologies

The recent focus has been increasing on varied applications in several domains of life, work and enterprises, and governance through major digital technologies of Cloud, Artificial Intelligence—automation, robotics, cognitive technologies, Augmented reality (AR), visual reality (VR)), and Digital development of Internet of things (IoT), remote sensing and mobile—smart phone technologies.

The second focus is on innovative and enhanced applications of the sustained technologies of second wave; RFID, quantum computer, laser and fuel cells.

Artificial Intelligence applications focus on a wide range of areas—automation, robotics, cognitive technologies, augmented reality (AR), visual reality (VR) and mixed reality; including big data-mining operations—predictive and visual analytics, financial applications—algorithm, blockchain technologies; digital health—medical devices, interpreting medical images and applications, remote sensing, biometrics—speech, handwriting and iris recognition, payment technologies. Other applications include detecting credit-card fraud, studying crop-growth and enabling drones and self-driving cars to navigate; and high level of scientific discoveries like driverless cars, hyperloop technologies.

Artificial Intelligence applications are growing fast and in numerous ways, some innovative and disruptive, some on innovative applications on sustained technologies. Human ingenuity need more—look for more and sustain more and global minds are put together to achieve these.

AI is a broad term referring to ways to make computers emulate attributes of human brain. An initial cycle of excitement about this technology rose in 80s but fizzled. Recent interest in AI boomed due to breakthroughs in field known as *machine learning* especially in the specific area of '*deep learning*'. For example, instead of programming machines explicitly to recognize human face; deep learning analyzes vast troves of images of faces. Apple, for example, uses *deep learning* to analyze speech commands issued to Siri—the software used by Apple for variety of tasks on iPhones.

Deep learning is an AI technique and other techniques and applications are widening. Any solution to an AI problem can be solved as the human has a series of choices. AI is about to transform industry after industry said AndrewNg, a deep learning pioneer and a chief scientist at Baidu Inc.

IBM 'Watson Explorer' is a cognitive exploration solution that combines search and content analytics with unique cognitive computing capabilities to help users find and understand the information they need to work more efficiently and make better, more confident decisions.

Former IBM Watson executive Stephen Pratt's new venture Noodle.ai that offers enterprises artificial intelligence solutions has launched its development center in Bengaluru India. *The TPG-funded venture's enterprise solutions include applied artificial intelligence technologies using machine learning, predictive data analytics, and data sciences with human-centered design, business process engineering and big data.* The team brings deep experience in AI, big data, data science, machine learning and data analytics across industries. Intel corporation acquired in August 2016 California-based *deep learning* start-up Nervana Systems run by an Indian-origin entrepreneur, allowing the chip maker to foray into the world of Artificial Intelligence. Intel Xeon chips handles most computing tasks in data centers but Nvidia Corp had popularized chips known as graphic processing units (GPUs) which handles more quickly specialized chores associated with *deep learning*. Nervana has AI software that exploits GPUs but expects to deliver a chip next year which expects to complete deep-learning tasks more quickly. Their IP and expertise in accelerating deep learning algorithms will expand Intel's capabilities in the field of Artificial Intelligence.

"We will apply Nervana's software expertise to further optimise the Intel Math Kernel Library and its integration into industry standard frameworks. Nervana's Engine and silicon expertise will advance Intel's AI portfolio and enhance the *deep learning* performance and TCO of our Intel Xeon and Intel Xeon Phi processors. We believe that bringing together the Intel engineers who create the Intel Xeon and Intel Xeon Phi processors with the talented Nervana Systems' team; we will be able to advance the industry faster than would have otherwise been possible. We will continue to invest in leading edge technologies that complement and enhance Intel's AI portfolio," Bryant said, Intel spokesperson.

Applications of current digital technologies foray into AI through machine learning, deep learning and cognitive technologies.

Apps on various devices are using artificial intelligence and machine learning to determine; such as the context of your questions.

Google Foray in AI—How Google Plans to Solve Artificial Intelligence: Mastering AlphaGo is just the beginning for Google DeepMind, which hopes to create human-like AI. Our goal's very big," says Hassabis. He leads a team of roughly 200 computer scientists and neuroscientists at Google's Deep Mind.

It's supposed to be just an early checkpoint in an effort Hassabis describes as the Apollo program of artificial intelligence, aimed at "solving intelligence, and then using that to solve everything else." What passes for smart software today is specialized to a particular task—say, recognizing faces. Hassabis wants to create what he calls *general artificial intelligence*—something that, like a human, learns to take on just about any task. He envisions it doing things as diverse as advancing medicine by formulating and testing scientific theories, and bounding around in agile robot bodies.

Doing that will require DeepMind's software to explore beyond Go's ordered world of black and white stones. It needs to get to grips with the messy real world—or to begin with a gloomy, pixelated approximation of it. DeepMind's simulated world is called Labyrinth, and the company is using it to confront its software with increasingly complex tasks, such as navigating mazes. That should push DeepMind's researchers to learn how to build even smarter software, and push the software to learn how to tackle more difficult decisions and problems. They're doing this by using the techniques shown off in AlphaGo and earlier DeepMind software that learned to play 1980s—vintage Atari games. But to succeed, Hassabis will also have to invent his way around some long-standing challenges in artificial intelligence.

DeepMind is working with the U.K.'s National Health Service on a project aimed at training software to help medical staff to spot signs of kidney problems that are commonly missed and cause large numbers of avoidable deaths. The group is also working with business divisions of Google, where Hassabis says: his technology could surface in virtual assistants or improve recommendation systems, which are crucial to products such as YouTube (similar systems also power some of Google's advertising products).

Communication apps are important. There are several communication apps available from SMS to WhatsApp, on smartphones, and many reasons why we use them. But that in itself creates a problem. We're using so many apps to talk to so many people in a single day, and in between all that talk, we're opening up other apps to may be search the web, find interesting GIFs to share, order stuff online, and book reservations. It can get a bit messy and stressful.

There is Artificial intelligence-powered *Google Assistant*, *Google Now*, *Google's chat app Allo*.

Wouldn't it be great if one communications app could do it all? Well, that's what Google had in mind when it created its new communications app called *Allo*. Here's everything you need to know about it, including how it works and why you would use it over anything else. But it does a lot more than just allow you to send messages to other people. It's a smart messaging app in that it has the power of Google built-in *uses artificial intelligence and machine learning to determine such as the context of your questions.*

How does Google Allo work?

Similar to WhatsApp, Allo is based on your phone number, so you can use it to send text messages to anyone in your phonebook—not just other Allo users. Apart from that, Google highlighted three aspects of Allo that make it unique: *Expression, Google Assistant, and Security.*

***Expression*:** It looked like any other messaging app; chats appeared as bubbles, with one person's chat bubbles appearing on one side in a certain color, and another person's chat bubbles appearing on the opposite side, and you could scroll up and down to see the entire threaded conversation.

Like Facebook Messenger—you could send stickers, which Google said were sourced from artists around the world. You could also send emoji. But one of the hottest features is something called Whisper or shouts. This will let you slide up or down on the send button to change the size of your reply, meaning there's no need to write in caps all the time when you're angry.

Allo offers a feature called Ink that lets you get creative with photos. You can doodle on them, for instance. Allo also took the Smart Reply feature from Google's Inbox app, so now you can quickly respond while on the go. If someone asks if you want to grab dinner, Allo might serve up responses like "I'm in" or "I'm busy".

Allo uses machine-learning and natural language processing in order to suggest replies on the fly, meaning it can anticipate what you want to say next and how you might say it.

The more you use Allo, the better your suggestions become. And they will always be unique to you. However, because messaging isn't just about texts, replies also contain stickers and emoji.

You'll even see smart reply options when someone send you a photo. Allo can understand the content and context of photos because of *Google's computer vision capabilities*. If someone sends you a photo of pasta, you will see smart replies that include mentions of pasta, yummy, or whatever. The idea here is that assistive technology can help you communicate with little to no.

Google Assistant: In 2016, Google's CEO, demoed 'Google Assistant' and said he wanted people to experience "an ongoing two-way dialog" with the virtual assistant. Keep in mind this virtual assistant trend kicked off in 2011, when Apple introduced Siri.

How it lives inside Google Allo to help you keep your conversations going without interruption. For instance, let's say you are chatting with a friend who wants to eat French food for dinner. Google Assistant will then proactively suggest French restaurants nearby at the bottom of the app's messaging window.

You can tap that suggestion to bring up restaurant cards that everyone in the chat can see. If you choose a place, you'll see options to contact the restaurant, see reviews, find it on a map, etc. You can even make an OpenTable reservation in Allo. Google Assistant will prompt in at this point to confirm number of diners, what time you want to eat, and book the table.

That means you no longer have to leave your messaging app to do a Google search for restaurants, copy and paste results, switch back again to share the options, go out again to call the restaurant and book a table, and so on.

In Allo, and with Google Assistant's help, you can get everything done in one app. OpenTable is just one partner, too (more are signed up and coming).

Google Assistant also has access to Google's Knowledge Graph, so it can help you with all sorts of situations. You can call on Google Assistant at any time just by typing "@google" in Allo. You can chat directly with it and ask anything.

Google Assistant can remember things too, including your name, address, and favorite sports team. *Allo uses artificial intelligence and machine learning to determine such as the context of your questions.* For instance, when you ask "What's playing tonight?" Google Assistant can show films at your local cinema. Google Assistant is able to string your questions together to determine context and serve up the right information. It can also do basic stuff like retrieve your travel itinerary; commute time to work, package delivery information, and more.

You are chatting with a friend about a movie you both want to watch. Behind the scenes, Google Assistant is tabulating a vast number of metrics such as your location, preferences, Cineplex you like and personal thoughts to throw up the best possible option. This tabulation requires the artificial intelligence (AI) to learn about you (read collect and analyze data) as much as possible to give you accurate results. It can make life simpler by suggesting you a restaurant, a movie hall —a movie even, tell you weather, or even crack a joke. But for this highly-personalized service, it needs data access and personal information. The more you use it, the more it learns about your habits and preferences. The protocols pertaining to artificial intelligence, or the lack of it, make our data less secure and more vulnerable.

You can therefore now use Google in your chats with friends, or you can use it to get things done, and it's all made possible with just one app.

Security: All messages in Allo are encrypted. Also, it also offers an Incognito Mode, just like Chrome browser does, meaning you get access to not only end-to-end encrypted messages but features like expiring chats and private notifications. You can therefore keep message safe from prying eyes, control how long they stick around, and permanently delete them from your device. You basically have additional controls over the privacy of your chats.

Allo can be used as main messaging app for all these reasons. Allo is tied to your phone number so you can text anyone in your phonebook. You can doodle on photos, book reservations, ask Google Assistant questions, search for information, and enter an Incognito Mode, etc. and all of that can get done within this one, free app.

Allo also works with Google Duo; it is a simple video calling app for iOS and Android smartphones. It is designed to take on Apple's FaceTime and Microsoft's Skype by making the system as easy as possible.

As featuring end-to-end encryption, Duo will work on even slow, low bandwidth Internet connections. 'Knock Knock' is another innovative feature in Duo. This enables Duo to show live previews before a call has even been answered. That way user can see what the caller is up to before they pick the call. Google has ensured that the technology is super quick.

In 2016, Google showcased how the combination of Pixel smartphones, Google Assistant and other accessories can make life simpler with its artificial intelligence-powered Google Assistant. Unlike its predecessor Google Now, it can set alarms, check your mails, help you with navigation and web searches, among many other things, Google Assistant is highly personal. The artificial intelligence-powered assistant combines machine learning and image recognition.

Google has bought 'deep mind' an AI startup. The idea behind AI pursuit is to anticipate users' needs. Google already dabbles in this when you start typing in a search and it fills in several options it thinks you want. Imagine Google being able to know exactly what you're looking for based on your Android usage, emails, etc. It sounds a bit intrusive, but it may be the way Google is looking to stay ahead in the search business.

Facebook: Facebook's foray into AI came in 2015 as it set up its own internal artificial intelligence division and hired an NYU professor with experience in machine learning. The company's artificial intelligence ambition is not unlike Google's. Facebook has massive amounts of status updates, videos, images and ads on its site and could benefit from smarter ways to sift through and deliver them to its users. *The company already uses machine learning to determine what goes into a user's News feed and depending on who you ask there's a lot of room for improvement.*

Facebook CEO Mark Zuckerberg has said that one of the company's goals is "to do world-class artificial intelligence research using all of the knowledge that people have shared on Facebook." Obviously, that would eventually entail using the research to deliver more relevant status updates, and ultimately advertising.

Amazon: Its possible move to use artificial intelligence right now from Amazon.com for anticipatory shipping. Basically, the idea is that Amazon would, based on your previous ordering history, know what you want to buy before you actually go to the site and buy it—and would ship it to you ahead of time. This type of predictive measure would require a system to view and analyze a user's previous buying history, ad interest, and real-time browsing on the site. The goal would be for Amazon to keep its customers from going out and buying an item in store, by sending it to them when they need it.

While the company isn't there right now, and it would take a lot of artificial intelligence and a lot of trial and error to get there, it is clear how this could be beneficial for Amazon. The company is constantly looking for new ways to get goods into the hands of its customers even thinking of drones to deliver in order to keep them from going out to a store and purchasing them. Sending you what you want before you click buy, may be the best way.

Alphabet Googles, Facebook, Microsoft, Apple, Samsung Electronics and other startups are working towards conversation based systems to interact with computers responses.

So *far none of these systems are true Artificial Intelligence in the sense of having real understanding of the conversations. They interact with us through scripted conversations.*

Though google has advantage and is leaning on its massive database and improving natural-language processing ability to deliver answers.

Both Google and Amazon want to deploy their voice interfaces widely by working with other partners. In 2017, Amazon Alexa plan to work with Sonos speakers among other devices. Google is pursuing partnership with automakers.

Judicial Decisions: Using Artificial intelligence (AI) or machine learning technology, a team of researchers has predicted outcomes in judicial decisions at the European Court of Human Rights (EctHR) with 79 per cent accuracy. The AI method, developed by researchers from University College London (UCL), University of Sheffield and US-based University of Pennsylvania is the first to predict the outcomes of a major international court by automatically analyzing case text using a machine learning algorithm. We don't see AI replacing judges or lawyers but we think they will find it useful for rapidly identifying patterns in cases that lead to certain outcomes," said Nikolaos Aletras, who led the study at UCL's computer science department. "It could also be a valuable tool for highlighting which cases are most likely to be violations of the European Convention on Human Rights," Aletras added.

Applications of Augmented Reality (AR), Visual Reality (VR) and Mixed Reality (MR)

Applications of AR: Potential uses for AR, according to the IEEE Report (2014), include commerce, voice calls, web browsing, film/TV streaming, enterprise apps, advertising, consumer apps, games and theme park rides.

AR has shown significant promise in overcoming cyber and physical system visualization and interaction challenges in multiple domains, including medicine, construction, advertising, manufacturing, and gaming. Despite the promise of AR and its successful application in many domains, however, significant research challenges remain related to sensor noise, precise localization, distraction, information fusion, complex information visualization, and computational complexity.

Commercializing AR applications in industries ranging from retail shopping experiences to print advertising to automotive driving assistance.

Bulks of these commercial applications are built atop commercial-off-the-shelf (COTS) mobile platforms, such as iPhone and Android so they are cost effective. Key areas of research: (1) the use of AR in safety-critical systems, such as automobiles; (2) building AR applications that fuse data from unmanned vehicles and robots to enhance user perception of their environment; (3) applications of AR in mobile computing; (4) cognitive models for understanding the impact of AR on human perception and approaches for using these models to enhance therapeutic applications; (5) research solutions for constructing real-world tools that can manipulate cyber information; (6) approaches for enhancing the perceived realism of AR experiences; and (7) application of AR for facility management in the oil industry.

Researches are going on in applications of augmented reality, as well as advances in the underlying computer vision, indoor/outdoor localization, and human computer interaction techniques that make these applications possible.

Augmented Reality in the workplace special glasses display diagrams, images of instructions on the factory floor which makes easier to visualize data. It helps factory workers wearing AR google glasses to do quality checks on tractors and chemical sprayers in AGCO Corporation Minnesota; of agriculture equipment. Quality check was 20% faster in 2016. In 2017, the company intends experimenting with computer generated Hologram-like images. Holograms are 3-D images produced by the interference of light beams that reflect-off a real physical object and can be seen by the naked eye. They intend using the three-dimensional images to help guide workers through the process of welding 30-foot booms to chemical sprayers.

Use of AR which superimposed digital content including hologram-images into the user's view of the real world is in earliest stages of commercial development. Researchers at MIT suggest that improvements in AR equipment like Microsoft HOLOLens and cost reduction would drive the technology into mainstream, specifically supply chain.

MIT is working on to hasten and improve setting of a Visual Analytics Lab where corporations and researchers can experiment with computer generated Hologram-like images and interactive touch-screen walls embedded with layers of supply chain data that often is obscured. This could range from customer and product information to real-time traffic, weather and social media data.

"AR can be a game changer in data and analytics because it is so much more immersive relating to digital technology or images that actively engage one's senses and may create an altered mental state. You are experiencing much more than analyzing" (Dr. Winkenbach MIT Lab).

Brian Mullins (2016) is working on an advanced AR headset outfitted with infrared, thermal and high speed wide angel cameras to be used in cases where you have to react with very complex amounts of information.

AGCO spokesperson said, Hologram-like images and interactive touch-screen walls envisioned by MIT could display data on heat and vibration speed of each machine her workers use to cut, weld and paint components. Visualizing her supply-chain data could be helpful in easily preventing costly disruptions at her factory.

In January 2017, GE used the improved AR to gas and turbine factory in Florence Italy, and later in GE's power and aviation businesses.

Early versions are being used by large corporations and analysts and will increase sharply with newer versions. Forrester Research Inc. predicts; large companies will spend $3.6 billion in smart glasses by 2025.

Automobiles are one of the first and most interesting safety-critical application areas for AR, where visual distractions or poor AR views could lead to real-world harm. The rapid integration of new sensory systems into automobiles that allow the vehicle to automatically steer and brake has also helped create a platform that can be used to build an AR driving experience. Automotive companies, such as BMW, have begun experimenting with AR windshields that view visual information from the sensors, such as directions and road hazards, directly on top of the driver's view of the road. Developing these applications requires a deep understanding of how to overcome key challenges related to object registration, driver distraction, and driver perception. Gabbard et al. investigate these impediments to incorporating AR systems into automobiles and evaluate promising research approaches.

The recent widespread use of unmanned aerial vehicles (UAVs) in defense, emergency response, and other mission-critical application domains has led to the potential of AR applications that increase user perception of the real world by fusing that perception with information captured from auxiliary robots that work on other unmanned vehicles.

Zollmann et al. describe their work using UAVs to create 3D models of construction sites and mobile interfaces to fuse this information into an AR experience that can be used to compare and contrast the "as-planned" models (e.g. the architectural models or drawings of the building plan) versus the "as-built" reality (e.g. what is actually being constructed) of a building.

With options of virtual reality (VR) and 3D technology becoming increasingly accessible, it is only a matter of a few clicks and customers are able to see the final images of their redecorated homes, even before the process actually begins. This gives them an opportunity to decide exactly what they want.

India-based Urban Ladder, for instance, has developed an interior design tool, where furniture can be dragged and dropped to create a 3D view of the room in question. The tool has been connected to Google Cardboard, for the customer to explore the room in VR. "With the power of technology, we are able to generate real-time output, so that the customers can actually visualize how their homes would look. These images, rendered to full quality, give a visually realistic sense to the customer, on how their homes would look," says Rajiv Srivastav, COO and co-founder, Urban Ladder. Bengaluru-based HomeLane also has 'experience centers' in several cities to educate their customers, considering the nascent stage of the industry. "Customers can visit our experience centers, to get professional inputs on the process and then take a call. We educate our customers on materials, finishes, processes and choices, so that they may make informed decisions," says Rama, co-founder of HomeLane.

HomeLane brand hosts a virtual design platform, 'SpaceCraft', which aids one with relevant designs for their home, with the option to iterate design and other elements and see how it affects costs, right away. "So, you get to walk out with a design and a quotation in hand."

One of the most rapidly evolving areas of AR applications is in the mobile computing space. Smartphones are widely used and rapidly growing in popularity around the world. One of the most pervasive AR applications in the mobile computing space is AR browsers that allow users to access and view information related to the objects around them.

A deeper understanding of how AR affects the brain will enable new applications of AR technology to therapeutic medical treatments. Regenbrecht et al. present a conceptual framework for designing such therapeutic applications of AR. Dr. Jules White, Dr. Douglas C. Schmidt, Dr. Mani Golparvar-Fard suggested medical applications while discussing various applications of AR.

Update 7/13/16: At the time of this update, the buzz around "augmented reality" has accelerated thanks to the smartphone game Pokémon Go. The game is mainly designed around maps, letting players find and catch in the real world characters from Nintendo's long-running Pokémon game franchise. When they find a Pokémon, players can enter an augmented reality mode that lets them see their target on their phone screens, superimposed over the real world.

Although prior research has investigated key technical challenges of AR, the real-world application of this technology will continue to uncover new needs. Already, privacy and security are becoming major concerns as Google Glass has gained increasing traction.

Google Glass, HoloLens is impressive but has field of vision problems at this early stage. No one has built AR technology into smart glasses we'd actually wear. But none of that means that as soon as 2016 we won't see Ray Ban and Oakley glasses running a new and improved Glass OS that actually feels like it is augmenting our view of the world in a helpful, reliable, discrete way.

Like voice controlled tech, day-to-day AR has plenty of inspiration but not comfortable so far. Of the two, AR is the one that we are supposed to be using out of the house, in public, in front of other people in the future. As for VR, the experience matches up to our expectations slightly more. The hardware is not absolutely perfect. We need higher resolution displays on the Oculus Rift, more ergonomic controllers for the HTC Vive and eye tracking as standard. But these will come.

We have seen plenty of early trials of both AR glasses and VR headsets. We'll get there quicker if businesses, universities, airlines, schools and everyone in between pick up the technologies.

Both AR and VR are being publicized as the key to training medical students by replacing textbooks—Microsoft has partnered with universities in the US and released a video to show how AR can teach anatomy. Elsewhere, the Wellcome collection and Epic Games just held a competition to find VR visualizations of research data for university academics working with big data sets.

In the area of museums and education; Samsung is trialing both VR and AR in projects such as *First Life* at the Natural History Museum and *Parthenon sculptures and Bronze Age exhibitions* at the British Museum. Samsung sees these two emerging technologies not as competing options but simply different tools available depending on the subject matter and size of the group. Likewise, the BBC wants both VR and AR projects for interactive and immersive entertainment.

The big benefit of AR in industry is offering a heads up display that keeps hands free and handy information in the worker's eye line—to NASA engineers and astronauts, construction and factory workers and airline customer service staff.

Recently, Google Glass pivot with has comeback with plans to distribute the smart spectacles to companies and enterprises depending on their specific needs. As often wearables' most useful asset is their ability to be extremely specific to a person, place or situation in terms of design, size, safety and content.

Critical Assessment: Abovitz at 'Magic Leap' Company discussed the differences between VR and AR—namely that VR headsets immerse users in an artificial world and AR incorporates objects and environments from the real world. "There is a class of devices (see-through and non-see-through) called stereoscopic 3D," he said. "We at Magic Leap believe these inputs into the eye-brain system are incorrect and can cause a spectrum of temporary and/or permanent neurologic deficits." The brain is very neuroplastic and there is no doubt that near-eye stereoscopic 3D systems have the potential to cause neurologic change."

Palmer Luckey of VR Company Oculus has no such concerns. He says that if we can make VR as satisfying and compelling as real life then it will be "one of the most important technologies in the history of man".

Mark Zuckerberg of Facebook, invested $2 billion of Facebook's money on Luckey's VR Company Oculus. "We're working on VR because I think it's the next major computing and communication platform after phones," he said in July 2016. "We will have the power to share our full sensory and emotional experience with people whenever we'd like."

Then again, some people like Jony Ive of Apple think that "face is entirely the wrong place for wearable tech."

Robotics

Currently, robots are now built in smaller size and robotic technology is put to many different applications than earlier ones which were more used in factories, etc.

Recently, advance robotics challenge competition held in India in Nov. 2016, over 50 countries showcased innovative solutions using robotics technology to reduce, manage and recycle waste.

At the moment it is a human who teaches a robot how to behave or teach, but in the next 20 years it may be possible that a robot teaches a robot or a robot develops a robot. Robot assists in risky ear plant.

Wearable Applications

In January 2015, Intel announced the sub-miniature Intel Curie module for wearable applications. This has been successfully demonstrated for playing instrumental music.

Intel Curie Low-Power Compute Module is a tiny hardware product offering design flexibility. The complete low-power solution comes with compute, motion sensors, Bluetooth Low Energy (BLE), battery charging capabilities, and pattern matching capabilities for optimized analysis of sensor data. This enables quick and easy identification of actions and motions. It's a complete low-power solution designed for use in wearable devices and consumer and industrial edge products. *The Intel Curie module offers features that are ideal for "always-on" applications such as social media, sports, and fitness activities.* The module is packaged into a very small form factor and runs a new software platform created specifically for the Intel Curie module.

It is a tiny system-on-a-chip (SoC) based on the Intel Quark SE core with 80 kB SRAM. The SoC is the size of a shirt button but includes everything required to provide compute power for wearable devices. The Curie module is designed to enable even inexperienced makers of wearable tech to make smart products. Intel Quark is a line of 32-bit × 86 SoCs and µCs by Intel, designed for small size and low power (A.R. Rehman world-known Indian musician demonstrate playing a complex piece of music by using Intel Curie in 2016).

Digital Disruptors will dominate in the next few years. AI has advanced dramatically during the past year. AI is starting to outperform humans in some areas when enhanced with machine learning through the application of capabilities such as deep neural networks. AI, Algorithms, bots and smart things will dominate business interactions during the next few years. AI and bots currently allow platforms to gain a voice, while algorithms and AI will deliver the intelligence to empower a new generation of robots, cobots and drones and self-driving vehicles.

The pace of digital disruption demands a new approach to IT. CIOs must build their digital business technology platform to support the development of digital business. The IT organization needs to design the 'big picture' of all the new information and technology capabilities required to support digital business. Businesses cannot afford to stay on the sidelines of this digital and algorithmic business wave. They need to define their algorithm, AI, ecosystem and digital platform strategies.

Digital Disrupters—Algorithm

Digital disruptors such as algorithms, artificial intelligence (AI), bots and chatbots are already transforming businesses. In the last ten years, companies have gathered enough data, through multiple channels where algorithms can be deployed. Algorithms will help companies in understanding data by going beyond traditional reporting, help in predictive analytics and will also help firms in making decisions in no matter of time. Data mining, pattern extraction, smart classification, machine learning will change things across industries in the next five years. Today Financial Tech segments like trading and lending have already integrated algorithms for faster decision making.

Today, investors and borrowers across geographies are looking for solutions that make decisions in the fraction of a second. The companies that can make decisions or contribute to decision-making in a few seconds are the one who will win. With technologies like artificial intelligence and machine learning, companies will be able to understand tons of data that has been accumulated over the years in few seconds; whether its stock trading, lending, or analyzing a fraud.

Sophisticated pattern recognition is one of the key things that every Financial Tech company is looking at. Algorithms also help in experimentation.

Gartner Inc. expects that algorithmic business will create even greater levels of disruption and new industries. To support the new capabilities and business models of digital and algorithmic business, CIOs must design and deploy their digital business technology platform.

Fueled by data, analytics and AI, algorithmic business will continue to grow and disrupt businesses. Algorithms capture the knowledge that turns raw data into valuable insight, and CIOs must use them to drive speed, scale and consistency in their digital business. Applied to huge datasets, algorithms allow highly accurate, personalized offerings, which in turn can drive revenue and differentiation.

In human resources, in order to evaluate candidates' suitability for specific roles, algorithms are used to match talent very quickly to the work that needs to be done within an organization. Eventually, algorithms will replace both manual processing of CVs by recruiters and automated CV ranking based on word matching.

Algorithms are already well established in many industries. In some industries, organizations are making advanced algorithmic models available via open marketplaces, which ultimately facilitate access to algorithms that are beyond the development reach of many organizations.

Artificial intelligence (AI) through Algorithms Models is helping in financial products machine learning for trading-lending, direct market access, behavioral biometrics, biometrics, human resources and other many more personalized offerings to come.

***Algorithmic retailing through Big Data Analytics*:** In the new digital economy, retailers can best gain competitive advantage through the application of algorithms that reduce costs and grow top-line revenue, according to Gartner Inc. Data is ubiquitous in the new retail environment, and retailers will survive only if quality data is embedded into every decision, minute by minute, across the retail organization. But retailers can't humanly scale to keep pace with growth of data, so a fundamentally different approach is necessary. Algorithmic retailing can be the application of big data through advanced analytics across an increasingly complex and detailed retail structure, to deliver an efficient and flexible, yet unified, customer experience. Algorithms connect big data to results.

According to Gartner, there are four main functions where algorithms can have a big impact in retail. (i) Cost of goods sold—Algorithms can both reduce the cost basis and increase top-line revenue. (ii) General and administrative, activities such as finance, legal, HR, advertising and IT, as well as warehousing and distribution. Algorithms used here will significantly improve cost optimization. (iii) Labor cost is rising sharply, and directly impacts the quality of the customer's experience. Algorithms can support both cost optimization and customer service. (iv) Stores is a major cost of retail operations and an integral part of the retail landscape. They provide a major source of competitive differentiation for multichannel retailers, with store services much of what employees provide to customers. Algorithms can help with pricing, inventory and improving the in-store customer experience.

Retail CIOs and their teams play a pivotal role in helping business leaders understand the benefits and limitations of algorithms, and how algorithms can support their business goals.

In this context, Gartner advises retail sector CIOs to: (i) Identify and classify all data sources, and identify data gaps that must be filled. (ii) Prepare for an explosion of Internet of Things (IoT) data generated by products, customers and stores. (iii) Review examples of how other retailers are successfully using algorithms. (iv) Develop a framework for identifying current and future opportunities to improve performance through automation by algorithms. (v) Ensure that smart data discovery technology is bringing big data discovery to the business user at the time of decision. This is a critical step on the path to process automation.

Gartner predicts that merchant leaders will use algorithms by 2020.

Applications of Blockchain Technologies

Blockchain allows financial securities to be settled in minutes instead of days. It can also be used to help companies manage the flow of goods and related payments, or enable manufacturers to share production logs with OEMs and regulators to reduce product recalls.

Asset ownership and transfer between businesses is currently inefficient, slow, costly and vulnerable to manipulation. Everyone has their own ledger where discrepancies between business parties can increase settlement times. A new way is needed for Internet-age market enablement.

Blockchain technologies can be used to share a ledger across the business network. The network will be private to the parties concerned, permissioned so only authorized parties are allowed to join, and secure using cryptographic technology to ensure that participants only see what they are allowed to see.

The shared ledger will be more robust, since it is replicated and distributed. All transactions against the ledger will require consensus across the network, where source of information is clear and transparent. Transactions will be unchallengeable, unchangeable and final.

The business network participants will be the same—disintermediation, i.e. the removal of intermediaries from a supply chain, or 'cutting out the middlemen' is a natural consequence of blockchain usage. Goods and services are provided more efficiently, with the potential to lower costs on all levels.

IBM and Samsung recently presented a proof of concept for ADEPT, which uses the block chain database to build a distributed network of devices—a sort of decentralized IoT. According to a Samsung report, ADEPT (Autonomous Decentralized Peer-to-Peer Telemetry) taps into this source to provide a secure, low-cost way for devices to interact. It is using BitTorrent to share files, Ethereum for smart contracts and TeleHash for peer-to-peer messaging to power this technology.

According to the executive report, an appliance such as a dishwasher could initiate "smart contracts" to issue commands to a detergent retailer for supplies. These contracts give the device the ability to pay for the order and later receive word from retailer that the detergent was paid for and shipped. As a proof-of-concept, Samsung has already applied this technology to WW9000 washing machine. More examples, on the potential of blockchain as a technology and why it is so exciting for so many. From the London Stock Exchange, UBS, JPMorgan to Axis Bank, everyone is dabbling with blockchain. India IT-giants like Tata Consultancy, Services now and Infosys have a dedicated track for blockchain.

The Benefits of Blockchain Applications

Blockchain can help radically improve industries, banking and insurance-creation and insurance record management; and more for digital health applications. However, the opportunities for blockchain go far beyond this. This technology in future is likely to be used to create smart(er), more efficient systems for supply chains, Internet of Things networks, gaming, multi-media rights management, car rental, government proof of identity (or license).

It can make application/systems more efficient, less risky, more cost-effective, can be used for legal contracts, corporate treasury, accounts payable and receivable, trade finance, letters of credit, smart property, internal cash management and even international payments.

Blockchain for Healthcare Applications

Blockchain technology is being used in healthcare IT; there are private and public efforts to harness it. These could be used in setting up vaccine registries or transactional histories for patients. During clinical trials, the blockchain could be used to share blood test information; for, say, five different trials, only one blood test would then be needed. The blockchain could also be paired with a patient's current electronic medical record to provide a new level of data integrity and interoperability, meaning patient data could be shared across organizations and people without compromising the security of the information that's stored (Medcity News July 2016). We face a critical need for such innovation as MedRec, as personalization and data science prompt patients to engage in the details of their healthcare and restore agency over their medical data.

MedRec: a novel, decentralized record management system to handle EHRs, using blockchain technology. This system gives patients a comprehensive, immutable log and easy access to their medical information across providers and treatment sites. Leveraging unique blockchain properties, MedRec manages authentication, confidentiality, accountability and data sharing—crucial considerations when handling sensitive information.

A modular design integrates with providers' existing, local data storage solutions, facilitating interoperability and making our system convenient and adaptable. We incentivize medical stakeholders (researchers, public health authorities, etc.) to participate in the network as blockchain "miners". This provides them with access to aggregate, anonymized data as mining rewards, in return for sustaining and securing the network via Proof of Work.

MedRec thus enables the emergence of data economics, supplying big data to empower researchers while engaging patients and providers in the choice to release metadata. The purpose is to expose, in preparation for field tests, a working prototype through which we analyze and discuss our approach and the potential for blockchain in health IT and research.

Beyond the time delay, record maintenance can prove quite challenging to initiate as patients are rarely encouraged and seldom enabled to review their full record. Patients thus interact with records in a fractured manner that reflects the nature of how these records are managed. Interoperability challenges between different provider and hospital systems pose additional barriers to effective data sharing. This lack of coordinated data management and exchange means health records are fragmented, rather than cohesive. Patients and providers may face significant hurdles in initiating data retrieval and sharing due to economic incentives that encourage "health information blocking." A recent ONC report details several examples on this topic, namely health IT developers interfering with the flow of data by charging exorbitant prices for data exchange interfaces.

Most importantly, the MedRec model restores comprehensive patient agency over healthcare information—across providers and treatment sites, empowering citizens with the data they need to make informed decisions around their care. By giving patients a long-term, trusted log of their information with data sharing functionality built-in, the MedRec system directly addresses the ONC Interoperability Roadmap's first outcome: "Individuals have access to longitudinal electronic health information, can contribute to the information, and can direct it to any electronic location". As envisioned by the Precision Medicine Initiative (PMI), the MedRec patient record would reflect the many facets of health data, by accepting not just physician data, but also data from the patient's Fitbit, Apple HealthKit, 23andMe profile, and more. Patients can build a holistic record of their medical data and authorize others for viewership, such as physicians providing a second opinion or family members and care guardians. (See Appendix 7 for blockchain structure applied to EHRs and Appendix 8 potential uses of blockchain technology in healthcare.)

Blockchain technologies for health care—Healthcare Challenges and How Blockchain can Solve Them: The healthcare ecosystem is complex, with multiple stakeholders and intricate, sensitive interactions. This leads to both data security and privacy challenges and operational inefficiencies. Ownership and trusted access to medical information and administrative data is critical, yet the process must be made simpler and less costly. In healthcare, new research is seeking to apply blockchain's distributed ledger and decentralized database solutions to the critical issues of interoperability, security, record universality, and more. Intriguing uses in other industries are being extended to healthcare, such as extending blockchain's smart contracts to provider network management or connecting myriad medical devices through common, blockchain-enabled systems of information relationships. While technical consensus on a distributed ledger for healthcare has yet to emerge, with debate ongoing regarding scalability, security, and regulatory compliance, blockchain technology and encryption will drive innovation in healthcare services and administration. With blockchain, a business network allows members to exchange items of value through a distributed ledger that each member possesses and whose content is always in sync. Its cost-efficiency and accountability is driven by these key supporting concepts.

Blockchain for Healthcare Use Cases: The potential uses of blockchain technology in healthcare are multiple and varied. IBM in its report presents a wide-ranging list of prospective healthcare-related use cases that the industry has been debating (Blockchain: The Chain of Trust and its Potential to Transform Healthcare—Our Point of View).

Blockchain Challenge: Now the blockchain is getting the attention of the federal Department of Health and Human Services' Office of the National Coordinator for Health Information Technology USA. ONC announces the 15 winners of *Use of Blockchain in Health IT and Health-related Research Challenge (2016)*. "The point of the challenge was to look at the areas that people are focused on and have the greatest potential" said Steven Posnack, director of business and technology at the ONC.

Winners are proposing different ways to use the blockchain in healthcare and health IT to secure, store, and manage different healthcare data.

"The healthcare industry and market is moving in the direction of newer technologies. Whether blockchain is the winner is still to be determined," said Debbie Bucci, an ONC IT architect who researches the intersection of new technology and healthcare privacy and security. "I believe [blockchain] is going to be an underlying technology that's just going to happen," Bucci continued. "You may not know you're using blockchain, but it has the potential to be that pervasive."

Here is a look at the five most interesting potential applications of blockchain technology gathered from the 15 white paper finalists.

Blockchain and Alternative Payment Models: What type of alternative payment e-method could be used in healthcare to rein in spending and bring some control over the fee-for-service model? But this paper argues that blockchain tech could disrupt something like the typical way for processing claims in a positive way. Put claims data on a private blockchain, accessible to the organizations that exchange the data, and have it update in real-time. By allowing claims data to be processed more quickly, this could potentially cut down on incorrect reporting and make sure the final payment or bill is correct (King Yip, senior manager at Audacious Inquiry in Catonsville, Maryland).

A Blockchain Profile for Medicaid Applicants and Recipients: Use the blockchain to create a "smart health profile," and then tie that profile to an individual patient. The profile will enable financial and patient information to be securely stored and accessed, and could alleviate one of the persistent problems in Medicaid. Namely, since Medicaid is a means-tested program, how beneficiaries enroll and re-qualify for health services and keep their information up to date. By storing patient health data and personal profile securely on the blockchain, that information can be kept up to date and made easily accessible should the need to re-qualify for Medicaid benefits arise (Authors: Kathi Vian, Alessandro Voto, and Katherine Haynes Sanstad, all affiliated with the Blockchain Futures Lab at the Institute for the Future in Palo Alto, California).

MedRec: Using Blockchain for Medical Data Access and Permission Management: How to secure, store, and exchange Electronic Health Records using new technology might be the biggest topic when it comes to the blockchain? This paper offers a prototype. The MedRec is a decentralized, modular record management system that could work with healthcare providers' existing local data storage and takes advantage of some of the blockchain's advantages such as authentication for stored information and accountability on the part of people accessing that information (Ariel Ekblaw, Asaph Azaria, and Andrew Lippman affiliated with the MIT Media Lab in Cambridge, Massachusetts; and Dr. John D. Halamka, from Beth Israel Deaconess Medical Center in Boston, Massachusetts).

Blockchain and Health IT: Algorithms, Privacy, and Data: A central growing tension in the healthcare field is that between data-sharing and privacy, as this paper illustrates. Organizations in a health IT ecosystem—providers, patients, and now the government—need information on patients. Generally, that's done with a centralized IT system, the type that's vulnerable to hacking. Make it so that the blockchain is the backbone of newer distribution technologies, and an "auditable record of actions" will follow that information wherever it goes (Allison Ackerman Shrier, Anne Chang, Nadia Diakun-thibault, Luca Forni, Fernando Landa, Jerry Mayo, and Raul van Riezen, affiliated with Project Pharm Orchard of MIT's Experimental Learning "MIT Fintech: Future Commerce"; and Thomas Hardjono of MIT Connection Science).

The Use of a Blockchain to Foster the Development of Patient-Reported Outcome Measures: The Internet of things has only made personalized medicine that much more personal. Health readings taken from people's Fitbit, Jawbone wristband, and Apple Watch get stored in the cloud, but there's a risk in storing health data there. As this paper noted: "In cloud-based architecture, data is replicated and moved frequently so the risks of unauthorized data use increases." So this paper argues if blockchain tech becomes the basis for the way personal health data is recorded and stored, it would bring greater security to private data even when they are carrying around personal health devices and other mobile devices every day (Jason C. Goldwater, MA, MPA, affiliated with the National Quality Forum in Washington, D.C.).

Besides the federal department's efforts in encouraging blockchain applications, life science companies are also getting into. Merck is exploring the use of blockchain in healthcare. The private and public efforts underscore the fact that blockchain is something that we will hear about more in the future.

Digital-Healthcare: Medical Devices and Applications

Digital health is focusing attention on how to use digital-health tools to help change healthcare behavior.

We are entering an era of digital transformation in healthcare that is fueled by the convergence and unprecedented adoption of technologies that focus on mobile, cloud, big data, and the Internet of things.

Healthcare is now on the verge of a new information wave. Call it Data 3.0. At the core of this new age of healthcare analytics is data that is actionable, explainable, trusted and contextualized. "Context is everything, especially in data." To achieve that necessary context, health data has to be explainable so clinicians can understand why it's important. The information also has to be trustworthy. Building on the notion of trusted and explainable data; it must also be actionable, so clinicians can effectively put it to work once they're convinced to do so.

The value of analytics is to influence decision making, to change behavior. "When you look at analytics are you able to answer the questions what is happening, where, who's involved and why?" Understanding those can help provider organizations architect an analytics strategy.

Guttag John, head of the Data Driven Inference Group at MIT's Computer Science and Artificial Intelligence Laboratory, 2016, that machine learning is among the fastest growing parts of computer science right now in the world. As healthcare entities continually ramp up their analytics and big data efforts and gird for precision medicine and population health, machine learning as well as artificial intelligence and cognitive computing are poised to become even more valuable for healthcare.

One of the challenges unique to healthcare is the long gap between when new knowledge is obtained and when clinicians and doctors can put it to use treating patients, which is among the reasons Guttag urged major healthcare providers to more aggressively integrate today's machine learning tools into their workflows now. "People should be using today's technology to do things today; machine learning is a huge deal. And we're going to see some pretty dramatic changes over the next few years."

Organizations can use governance to take the necessary steps in transforming data into actionable, enterprise-wide insights.

Healthcare organizations are recognizing the importance of governance through formation of committees designed to work as think tanks for devising an analytics strategy rebuilding into the organizational and IT platform structure (Healthcare IT News. Big Data and Healthcare Analytics forum Boston 24-25 Oct. 2016).

"Pharma has been talking about beyond the pill for 10 years now. The pill is old. We really need to lift the digital health portion (devices and apps) rather than the pill." Developing a digital solution differs from developing a drug. There is a series of processes and capabilities that need to be put in place.

Healthcare IT infrastructure is needed to coordinate transitions of care efficiently; sharing data with selected partners, reducing gaps in visibility and improving care coordination and care transitions by care networks continuum including hospitals, post-acute care, physicians, outpatient clinics, social service agencies, pharmacists and other community-based organizations. Neil Smiley, Loopback Analytics 2015 commented, we will see the traditional relationship-based referral process steadily displaced by data-driven informed referrals that match the right patient with the right care setting at the right time.

***Influence of Technology Players Expanding into Healthcare*:** Google, Apple, and Amazon in the U.S., China's technology giants such as Alibaba, Tencent (which launched the popular messaging service WeChat) have moved into healthcare.

The current innovation scenario for digital healthcare applications and devices is tremendous and more and more are forthcoming every day. To familiarize the readers with the importance and potentials of IT for healthcare; we will be presenting only a few selected digital healthcare solutions; patient-care at hospital, by doctors and by caregivers at home and through telemedicine services.

AI and augmented reality applications in healthcare; gesture control technology through armband and smart watches and mobile phone apps, mobile PERS (personal emergency response systems) devices use a variety of location technologies to locate users, including GPS, Wi-Fi, cellular triangulation, and U-TDOA (uplink time difference of arrival); use of wearable sensors to improve understanding of disease progression. Other wearables developers such as Jawbone, Fitbit, Basis watch, Apple.

Using music therapy to help people with a wide range of conditions, including movement disorders.

Amazon Echo's Alexa, the cloud-based personal assistant, can have powerful healthcare applications. Earlier was released in 2014. Now with improved technology in 2016, Amazon Echo is voice controlled, Internet-connected speaker powered by AI software. Amazon tracks every interaction with Alexa Echo which also powers Echo Dot and AmazonTap.

"That technology exists now and it's a matter of time before Amazon decides to create a version of the device that either interfaces with another sensor device that is a motion sensor or has a motion sensor built in," said Nathan Treloar, president and chief operating officer at Orbita, a software company that builds digital services for home health.

Treloar says that there could be several use cases for how Amazon's technology can be leveraged. The biggest potential for this is as digital care agent for people, young or old, with complex care regimes.

Orbita is working with a New England area care provider/payer to create a program that intends to leverage the voice interface of the Amazon's Echo into something that home health care agents could use to streamline their work when caring for people with those difficult conditions, said Treloar. The product was formally launched in Oct. 2016.

"Care agents are so consumed when they are visiting the patient with caring for (the patients') needs, they want to be able to record their activity—when they arrive and when they leave—and one of the things that Echo can do...is that the care providers can record medications on behalf of the patients," Treloar said.

Orbita is looking at two things: to facilitate the home visit of a care agent and to manage the transportation needs of a patient who needs to go to the clinic or even to the grocery store. The patient would simply say, "I need a ride to my clinic" and Amazon Echo would manage the conversation and get third party transportation services, even Uber, at the patient's door step, he said.

Other than the regional care provider/payer, Orbita is also working with "early adopters" to see how the device can be best used for patients. "What we are contemplating with a few early adopters is trying to use the Amazon Echo as a form factor for essentially a care agent (so that they) can do 20, 30 to 50 percent of the common home care Q&A, content delivery and support and coordination and in many ways serve as a digital triage for other more serious needs that require clinical intervention or other kinds of human intervention," he explained.

Limitations of echo technology is that echo is confounded by loud noise. Why use echo when smartphone apps can perform some of these chores also?

It's a matter of convenience for the care agents, but for some patients it can also be a much better alternative. For instance, those who find the smartphone screens to be too small to see or they have physical impediments that prevent the use of those devices.

"What we love about voice is that it's the ultimate universal remote control...," Treloar declared.

In Oct. 2016, Google rolled out 'Google Home'—Echo-like device) powered by Google Assistant. Ultimately, Google is working on to build (through the device) an emotional connection with the user.

TreatMd two-year-old, Miami-based startup, wants to be a global company by serving as a platform for any doctor anywhere to offer telemedicine services.

The site launched beta in July 2016; in 22 countries so far and that its platform hosts communications in at least 30 languages. "We market to dozens of countries every day," co-founder Bryan Lenett said.

"We started TreatMD with a mindset of mixing Zillow and telemedicine," Zillow is best known as a database for real estate valuations, but it also hosts a marketplace for connecting property buyers and sellers with related services, including agents, mortgage lenders and remodelers.

Similarly, TreatMD connects patients with physicians, but, unlike many other "on-demand" telemedicine companies, lets physicians set the terms. "You charge what you feel your rate is. "It's an open platform for everybody."

And he means everybody, as in, worldwide. "Why can't a patient in Florida suffering from an illness or disease like cancer search for and communicate with a doctor in Germany, or any country for new treatments or even second opinions?" At this point, U.S. patients can't easily get remote diagnoses and treatment from a doctor in another state due to laws prohibit.

Smartphone and Medical Technology

Everybody is very excited about the potential of the adoption of mobile phone technology into the medical workplace. Smartphones are incredibly powerful devices. Stethoscope may soon be history as millions of doctors across the world are signing up for a free iPhone app that can monitor heartbeat. Peter Bentley of the University College London has invented the iStethoscope application, which monitors heartbeat through sensors in the phone. Apple has set down some rules for digital health companies aspiring to use the technology iOS network.

Apple iphone-screening medical apps: IMedicalApps highlighted some of the changes including:

Drug dosage calculating apps have to come from the drug manufacturer, a hospital, university, health insurance company, or other approved entity. This means individual developers cannot make a medical app with drug dosages by themselves (Apple has actually been enforcing this for the past year already).

No more marijuana-related apps.

Apps that encourage people to place their iPhones under a mattress or pillow while charging (such as those that monitor sleep) will no longer be allowed.

If your app has potential to cause any physical harm, Apple could reject it. If your app provides inaccurate data or

information that could be used to diagnose or treat patients, your app will get increased scrutiny.

As iMedicalApps points out, the changes by Apple could have a more tangible impact than those made by the FDA, USA and it raises the stakes for developers.

There is no way the FDA can regulate the hundreds of thousands of health and medical apps and the updates made to them. The screening process is what has to change—and it seems like Apple is finally stepping up pace to do this (Sept. 2016).

Bluetooth, Samsung and Apple are into the wearables market as well as Google's contact lens for non-invasive glucose monitoring.

The transfer of data between devices and smartphones may become energy efficient in the near future.

Applications of AI for health:

Risk Matrix Platform: Lumiata launched its Risk Matrix platform to improve care coordination and risk management. The product is aimed at health plans and the health systems they work with to assess the future health of individuals with or at risk for chronic diseases. The product enlists artificial intelligence to help physicians make better use of the data and meet some of the goals of value-based care.

The health IT business stated in a news release that the product is designed to offer predictions for 20 chronic conditions, such as diabetes, chronic kidney disease and congestive heart failure. The idea is to help insurers allocate resources more effectively. For providers it could mean more efficient patient triage and discharge, and better prescriptive information around symptoms, medications, risk factors and diagnoses. But for payers, it can produce insights on the medical and financial risks associated with their members.

Lumiata's chief commercial officer said the company's approach offers a logical solution for physicians who are being flooded with data but have less and less time to digest it.

Eyeforpharma.com: 3D bioprinting: The high costs of clinical trials could eventually make 3-D bioprinting a go-to technology for pharma and biotech, providing better data to spot toxicity early and helping the pharma industry avoid costly mistakes.

RTLS automated created data. If the information is delivered in real-time by leveraging technologies such as real-time location systems (RTLS), caregivers can respond immediately to a patient who has been waiting too long and managers can better anticipate and eliminate bottlenecks in the overall patient flow. Hospitals have a pretty good idea of what contributes to a positive patient experience such as short wait times, meaningful interaction with caregivers, and effective communication with patients and family.

As an example, take a look at hand hygiene procedures in a typical hospital. Using real-time monitoring and dashboards, visual analytics, hospitals can show staff members how they are doing individually, and show managers how the unit or hospital is doing overall—all through visual analytics. This allows for immediate action or longer term interventions such as further education or mentoring.

Dashboards take real-time information about patients, staff and assets, and provide faster insight into how to improve the patient experience—whether by resolving issues that impact wait time or seeing what's causing reduced staff contact time.

Doctors and nurses can even access dashboards on-the-go on a tablet or wall-mounted display to gain real-time visibility into what's happening in the OR, waiting rooms or post op rooms to make sure everything is running smoothly.

Today, dashboards loaded with *predictive analytics*, predicting trends in the coming hours, weeks and months to make more informed decisions, such as using previous data on infusion pump deployments to identify how the devices should be distributed and when more will need to be ordered or rented.

RTLS data combined with clinical performance data provides caregivers with a more complete picture of the patient journey. Ensuring that the RTLS system is integrated to the clinical system and that a common "key" exists is essential to being able to blend and analyze this type of data.

Healthcare institutions either look into third-party vendors to handle and manage data analysis, or find a data expert to bring in-house team. Often these in-house teams will partner with vendor teams who are experts in their solutions as a starting point, then take over day-to-day operation of the BI systems once launched.

Business intelligence (BI) and data visualization tools like Tableau, Qlik, Microsoft and SAP are paving the way for self-service analytics so that non-technical individuals can analyze and make sense of data.

The Vera avatar guides joint replacement patients through a virtual rehab program.

There are two specific-related questions in healthcare that every player in the industry is looking to answer effectively: (i) how to lower costs, sometimes forced upon by bundled care payments, and (ii) how to move healthcare outside the doctor's office.

Reflexion health: San Diego-based digital health company is targeting joint replacement patients. The startup has developed the *Vera avatar on the Microsoft Kinect platform* that helps patients get their daily exercise for physical rehab done at home in front of a TV after their hip or knee replacement. This reduces the need to go to a physical therapist to get the exercises done post-surgery, or keep them moving in between sessions; though the patient's physical therapist is incharge at all times and can choose to bring them in at their discretion. The system also provides a technology solution for hospitals eager to lower their costs to treat joint replacement patients.

Here's how it works. An orthopedic surgeon will prescribe the technology that gets set up inside patients' home, ideally prior to surgery, which helps them get familiar with the technology. After the surgery, the patient can do the exercises while being coached by 'Vera avatar' that can even correct them when they make mistakes in the rehab routine. There is a telemedicine portal that connects patients to physicians and physical therapists.

The technology also facilitates the remote collection of data that CMS requires. Those are the Hip disability and Osteoarthritis Outcome Score (HOOS) and Knee injury and Osteoarthritis Outcome Score (KOOS), range of motion data, as well as patient reported outcomes data.

Analysis of this data is lacking in physical therapy and rehab facilities, which historically have relied on tradition and insight guide activity. This provides the opportunity to put all data in a quantitative framework so that you can know exactly what was recommended, how much of it was done, when it was done and then you link that to patient-reported outcomes and objective assessments, so that allows to persistently refine the field.

The system also provides a technology solution for hospitals eager to lower their costs to treat joint replacement patients, many of whom are now part of the bundled payment environment. In March 2016, at the annual meeting of the American Academy of Orthopedic Surgeons in Orlando, Florida, panelist after panelist talked about how post-operative care accounts for nearly 40% of joint replacement costs. That's when patients are typically released from the hospital and sent to a skilled nursing facility to recoup before they can be transitioned to the home.

And that is the movement that Reflexion's FDA-cleared Vera system can speed up.

The technology has sparked interest from hospitals contending for bundled care plan for 'Comprehensive Care for Joint Replacement'.

The Vera system is currently in use in a skilled nursing facility (SNF)—typically the place that racks up a lot of expenses in post-acute care for joint replacements. As a result, hospitals are either cutting how often patients are sent to SNFs, or if SNFs are part of an integrated health system. They look for

ways to reduce expenses there. Vera is used in a SNF that belongs to a latter category.

Even outside the bundled care environment, there is a role for reflexion's virtual rehab program. It's better for patients to get out of hospitals sooner and transition to home because of the danger of hospital-acquired infections.

There are other companies in the virtual rehab arena—the FDA-cleared Jintronix, RespondWell, Virtualrehab, which have Class I medical device designation. The market is under penetrated and can support multiple players.

Augmented reality applications in healthcare: Thalmic Labs develop Myo gesture control device. 'Thalmic Labs' tech is particularly interesting because it offers a range of applications for assisting physicians.

The *gesture control technology* of Thalmic Labs' Myo armband interprets electrical activity of the user's muscles to operate technologies through gesture and motion control.

The applications for Myo vary from gaming and lifestyle uses to helping people with limited mobility, to prosthetics and sign language. The company's gesture control tool is also finding its way into surgery to reduce the need for doctors to touch equipment to read medical images.

Thalmic Labs CEO and co-founder Stephen Lake said acknowledged that developers are actively working on healthcare applications for its technology. "We're constantly blown away by at the applications that Myo developers and researchers have brought to life through this technology. At Thalmic, the first time we saw Johnny Matheny control his modular prosthetic limb using the Myo armband, we had never been more amazed by what our technology has enabled. Our developer community and researchers have done amazing things with Myo in the healthcare field, and we will continue to support them as we work to bring other products to market." At least one person has been fitted with a prosthetic arm using the gesture control technology through collaboration with Johns Hopkins University's Applied Physics Laboratory.

Another business combining gesture control with healthcare applications is Reemo. The company works with '*Samsung's Smart Things technology*' along with the tech giant's smartwatches to help seniors use locks and lights in their home with a flick of their wrist. The goal is not only to help seniors stay in their own homes longer but independently and safely. Through the use of smartwatches, caregivers and healthcare providers can track seniors' biometric data, activity levels and GPS locations.

Other companies Augmedix, Streye, Atheer, and Vital Enterprises are accepting augmented reality that have made healthcare priorities used smartglasses, predominantly to aid physicians and surgeons.

A Goldman Sachs report published earlier this year (2016) noted the potential for augmented reality tech to disrupt patient monitoring in healthcare. The report predicted that this market will grow to $5.1 billion by 2025.

Mobile personal emergency response systems (mPERS) are fully self-contained devices with a speaker and microphone built in, and they communicate over cellular networks, but with mPERS. Users are free to stay home or go down the street, to the grocery store and even travel across the country and still have the ability to get help Mobile PERS provide 24/7 two-way voice communication with certified care specialists at the press of a button. Care specialists can view user-provided information such as medication, allergies or lockbox details, and specialists can send emergency personnel or loved ones to the user, depending on what is needed. Mobile PERS devices use a variety of location technologies to locate users, including GPS, Wi-Fi, cellular triangulation, and U-TDOA (uplink time difference of arrival).

Some mobile PERS are shower-safe and have long-lasting rechargeable batteries, making them low-maintenance and easy for users to take with them wherever they go.

This is keeping caregivers connected. There are some mobile PERS that enable caregivers to locate the user via GPS online or with a mobile app and care specialists can contact caregivers during and after emergencies to update them about the user. Some mobile PERS devices also enable caregivers to receive alerts when the device battery is low or powers off, helping them to ensure their loved ones' mobile PERS are charged and available when needed.

Caregivers both near and far work extraordinarily hard to keep their loved ones safe and comfortable. Mobile PERS add an additional layer of security and peace of mind, helping caregivers have confidence that even when they are not there, their loved ones can easily get help in an emergency.

Freeus LLC is a wholesale provider of innovative two-way voice mobile personal emergency response systems.

Wearables are enlisted to study neurodegenerative diseases such as Hutington and Parkinson. Pharma industry's growing interest in using digital health to develop a more complete understanding of patient populations to advance drug development. Neurodegenerative diseases represent a particularly interesting area for wearables to come into play as clinicians and researchers seek to better understand disease progression.

The point is to get a fuller picture of patients between doctor appointments. The machine learning component is designed to make sense of the enormous amount of data the study will gather.

As part of the sub-study within an ongoing Phase 2 Open-Pride HD Study, patients will use a smartphone and wear a smartwatch equipped with sensing technology to continuously measure their general functioning and movement, a news release said. That data will be streamed to a platform developed by Intel to analyze data from the smartwatches and score patients according to motor symptom severity. The study started in later 2016 in centers in the U.S. and Canada.

The Michael J. Fox Foundation is currently recruiting for a pilot study of Parkinson's disease patients to evaluate the feasibility and compliance for patients to use wearable sensors to improve understanding of disease progression. It involves deploying a Pebble smartwatch and fall detector to participants. The study will also assess activity level, medication intake and mood. The study at Radboud University in the Netherlands includes Philips Research and Intel Corp. as collaborators.

The Sync Project, an initiative from PureTech, is interested in using music therapy to help people with a wide range of conditions, including movement disorders. Led by Marko Ahtisaari, the former head of product development at Nokia, The Sync Project has developed a series of studies to validate music therapy data in different patient populations.

It also plans to release an app later this year as part of a crowdsourced study to *assess the biometric effect of music on things like heart rate, sleep patterns and gait by looking at beat, depth of rhythm, key, the kind of instruments used in the tunes.*

It has partnered with Wearables developers such as Jawbone, Fitbit, Basis watch, Apple.

Boltt Sports Technologies, NOIDA, India in 2015 has developed an AI-based shoe that tracks your fitness, as you walk. In order to develop smart shoes, Boltt tied-up with US-based sports tech firm Garmin to build sensors with motion sensing and human reflex reading capabilities. The smart shoe comes with an embedded sensor that records the bio-chemical activities of the user.

The company also offers a range of fitness wearables which include smart shoes, fitness band, a stride sensor and wireless headsets. All these devices come in combination with an AI-based health coach.

The common problem with most of the fitness wearables is that people don't know how to utilize data tracked by such devices. Many lose the motivation to use such devices in a short span of time. The Boltt will track the data with Artificial Intelligence and use it for achieving personalized goals.

How Boltt wearables works? Under a robust on-boarding process, the user enters lifestyle details and medical history. An app works in tandem with the wearable. It tracks your activity, fitness, sleep, and nutrition data 24×7. An AI-based chatbot called 'B' analyze this data and give real-time feedback to the user/s.

'B' guides users in two ways, (i) when user is doing any physical activity; and (ii) about wellness. 'B' can differentiate between various kinds of motions such as walking, running and brisk walking. It also analyses the quality of food intake.

Combining the data will give personalized results to the user and mentor real-time training. At the ground level, the voice-coach guides the users, telling them where they are going wrong and how they can do better.

The company has team of fitness experts and nutritionists from around the globe, who have designed various coaching and diet programs that help users to improve their lifestyle and health. These programs are constantly updated.

The "company aim is to provide holistic personalized coaching platform. We want to make more humane the AI-experience for the users than just being a robotic voice," Initially, the AI-platform will be only available for Boltt's wearables, however, the company also plans make its platform available for other wearable devices too. Boltt's AI-based chatbot will be available on iOS and Android platform (moneycontrol news 1 Nov. 2016).

Mumbai, India based, Wearables startup Goqii also on-boards coaches, yoga trainers on its platform to let people achieve their fitness goals via a smart wrist-band (moneycontrol news 1 Nov. 2016).

Wearable Technologies

Smartwatch Strap-health Implication

A new wearable smartwatch strap developed by a Korean company allows you to answer phone calls just by placing your finger in your ear no need for earphone. Sgnl is a smart strap that can be attached to existing smartwatches, and enables the user to answer phone calls through their fingertip.

"With Sgnl, you can keep your cell phone in your pocket and simply raise your hand to answer a phone call without carrying any extra headset or earphone," according to the Innomdle Lab, a company based in Seoul that developed the device. "When you place your finger to your ear, your finger not only transmits the sound but it also blocks out background noise. The device receives voice signal from the phone through Bluetooth. When a voice signal is received, it generates vibration through its Body Conduction Unit (BCU) which transmits the vibration through the hand to the fingertip. As transmission is made through vibrations, there is no risk or harm to the human body. When the fingertip is placed to the ear, the vibration echoes to create amplified sound in the ear" the company said.

Eccrine systems—a tech healthcare wearable technology "sweatronics" is used as a noninvasive wearable to measure the chemical makeup of the user's sweat.

The disposable electronic patch is designed to measure electrolytes and stress levels. It is developing several different wearable devices based on the sweatronics. "Sweat holds great promise as the best non-invasive source for acquiring the type of molecular data and physiological insights that the medical community has historically collected and analyzed from blood". "Advances in microfluidics, nanotechnology, miniaturized electronics and power management are now making it possible to engineer wearable sweat sensing systems to monitor a wide array of sweat molecules in real-time." CEO and co-founder Robert Beech said in the news release 6 Oct. 2016.

Furthermore, the device has applications in medicine from medication adherence to keeping track of electrolyte levels for cystic fibrosis and other disease states. There is also relevance for ovulation monitoring.

Beech contrasted the company's rigorous, scientific approach with the proliferation of non-invasive wearable companies seeking to measure heart rate and other vitals data. The problem with the current state of noninvasive wearables is that they lack the accuracy and specificity required to derive actionable insights from them.

A new report from Rock Health looking at the future of the biosensor wearables market shows a market in transition. The next generation of wearables is more targeted towards patient populations, particularly sufferings from chronic conditions.

In a Google hangout about the report, Malay Gandhi, a co-author of the report, talked about some of the qualities that are making these wearables more appealing to consumers and the b2b market and features that will give them staying power. Gandhi pointed to Spire, a tool that tracks respiration. It can be used for COPD or asthma and other respiratory illnesses. It can be worn in several different places and supports wireless charging.

Gandhi's example of *Lumoback—a posture improvement tool*—gives feedback on posture and instructs users on what they need to do to improve it. That's something that a heart rate tracker cannot do as effectively.

The wearables should be functional, reliable and convenient. FDA clearance is critical to building b2b customers across physician practices and hospitals that many biosensor wearable companies are following. A good example of a biosensor wearable company that's meeting this demand is the maker of the swallowable pill tracker Helius by Proteus.

Athletic trackers aimed at the mass market have lost ground.

Smartphones have catalyzed the market for biosensor wearables with an emphasis on utilizing scalable yet proven technologies. Wearables can offload the display through software apps, computing and Internet connectivity to a smartphone.

Smartphone application health technology by ResApp

Associate Professor Dr. Udantha Abeyratne at University of Queensland, Australia said the mobile application for diagnosing respiratory conditions such as pneumonia and asthma through app on smartphones. It was based on an automated algorithm that could use sound alone to diagnose respiratory conditions such as pneumonia and asthma, without the need for additional hardware.

"The technology is based on the premise that cough and breathing sounds carry vital information on the state of the respiratory tract," Dr Abeyratne said.

Recently commercialised by spin-off company ResApp, the new diagnostic tool will allow doctors to diagnose and monitor respiratory diseases via a smartphone application.

ResApp has already secured more than $4 million to develop the technology and launch it into the marketplace.

With the capability to function over multiple platforms such as smartphones, web, wearable and medical devices, potential markets for this technology range from smartphone users to telehealth providers and organisations such as the World Health Organisation.

ResApp CEO Tony Keating, said the application was expected to be available in 2016.

"ResApp is excited to be working closely with Associate Professor Abeyratne's team at the University of Queensland to commercialise technology that brings the power of a true medical diagnostic tool to everybody who owns a smartphone," Mr Keating said.

Dr. Abeyratne said he would like to see the technology clinically verified and FDA approved, "My aim is for it to be implemented on mobile phones and other ubiquitous computing devices, empowering and enhancing patient participation in managing respiratory diseases such as pneumonia, asthma and whooping cough," Dr. Abeyratne said.

Neurotrack is developing a computer diagnostic tool to detect Alzheimer's disease. It is designed to determine whether a senior who shows no signs of the disease will develop Alzheimer's within the next three to four years.

Oxitione is producing a device to measure pulse oxymetry not from the fingertip but from the wrist using a smartphone to capture the data. It could detect early signs of below average oxygen levels in the blood—a condition called hypoxemia. That can be an important gauge for people with COPD and congestive heart failure—the two lead indications for the device. It also uses the cloud to transmit data from the smartphone to physicians.

Ondello wants to make it easier for doctors and patients to communicate online through text-based chat, video and voice.

Yingo Yango has a mobile and online patient engagement tool. Its online platform helps individuals work directly with their network of professionals to organize health, prevention and wellness content and resources into "Health Circles" for specific medical conditions, interests or wellness topics, for that individual's needs, according to its website.

Adhere Tech developed a smart pill bottle with technology to "know" whether each dose of the medication has been taken. It uses text messages and rings users to remind them to take their medicine. It also uses sensors to track how often and when a patient takes their medication. It transmits HIPAA-compliant data from the pill bottle to the cloud. It can also collect feedback on why the patient is not taking their meds and inform doctors. Earlier in 2016, the Cornell HIV Clinical Trials Unit said it would test the pill bottle to assess adherence to an HIV drug regimen over a 12-week period and compare it.

Vertex Pharmaceuticals is interested in companies using data to change how we understand the progression of degenerative conditions such as Huntington's disease and speed up the drug delivery cycle.

Franciscan Children's Hospital is looking for technology that can support remote monitoring so they can reduce the intrusiveness of noisy machines.

Telemedicine and remote monitoring technologies:

We're looking for companies and solutions that we believe understand the realities of clinical care and the workflow within healthcare, and create an opportunity to do things more effectively and more efficiently. Such as companies for instance that provides automated cognitive behavioral therapy for patients with insomnia and related anxiety and depression and other behavioral health issues.

Digital health technologies such as remote monitoring and telemedicine are focusing more for caregiving than self-care, remote monitoring for chronic conditions, post-surgical recovery and to support caregiving, and behavioral health.

Telemedicine and remote monitoring company would do well to consider the needs of family and professional caregivers in the product development phase. There is focus on rural telemedicine, telemedicine is added to cloud platform.

"Many caregivers are interested in using technology—but adoption thus far is low. Some focus groups have shown that caregivers seek integrated, multifaceted platforms that help them coordinate tasks and selectively disseminate information. Most caregivers also want tools to ensure that medications are managed accurately and with ease," the report said.

Aetna digital-based preventative health and wellness strategies:

"We are incredibly excited to use iPhone, iPad and Apple Watch to create simple, intuitive, and personalized technology solutions that will transform the health and wellness experience for our members," Aetna Chairman and CEO Mark Bertolini said in a statement. "This is only the beginning—we look forward to using these tools to improve health outcomes and help more people achieve more healthy days." Aetna's iOS-exclusive health apps will aim to simplify the healthcare process through a number of features, including medication reminders; integration with Apple Wallet to allow consumers to check their deductible and pay a bill; personalized health plan onboarding; messaging and decision support; and guidance for consumers through health events like a new diagnosis.

Aetna's biggest digital health footprint is its iTriage app, which the company acquired in 2011. iTriage has evolved from just a symptom navigator, physician and hospital finder app to include price transparency tools, health education and literacy tools, prescription management tools, and—soon—maybe even video visits with physicians.

And other Aetna apps do even more: Aetna Mobile has many of iTriage's features, plus it allows Aetna members to access information about their insurance, and Aetna's *Resources for Living* app helps users to manage stress and anxiety, moderate work-life balance, and track their moods.

In 2012, the health insurance company equipped New York City area dentists with iPads to help them educate their patients about tobacco use in an effort to curb smoking.

Eye-Netra, Eye-testing medical device: Near-Eye Tool for Refractive Assessment, or NETRA

In 2015, after five years of development; project started in 2000; and about 40,000 tests worldwide, the smartphone-powered eye-test devices developed by MIT spinout EyeNetra is coming to hospitals, optometric clinics, optical stores, and even homes nationwide. But on the heels of its commercial release, EyeNetra says it's been pursuing opportunities to collaborate with virtual-reality companies seeking to use the technology to develop "vision-corrected" virtual-reality displays.

"As much as we want to solve the prescription glasses market, we could also [help] bring virtual reality to the masses," says EyeNetra co-founder Ramesh Raskar, an associate professor of media arts and sciences at the MIT Media Lab who co-invented the device.

The device, called Netra, is a plastic, binocular-like headset. Users attach a smartphone, with the startup's app, to the front and peer through the headset at the phone's display. Patterns, such as separate red and green lines or circles, appear on the screen. The user turns a dial to align the patterns and pushes a button to lock them in place. After eight interactions, the app calculates the difference between what the user sees as "aligned" and the actual alignment of the patterns. This signals any refractive errors, such as nearsightedness, farsightedness, and astigmatism. The app then displays the refractive powers, axis of astigmatism, and pupillary distance required for eyeglasses prescriptions.

According to the World Health Organization, uncorrected refractive errors are the world's second-highest cause of blindness. EyeNetra originally invented the device for the developing world—specifically, for poor and remote regions of Africa and Asia, where many people can't find health care easily.

But the United States has offered the best market, in terms of adoption, Raskar says. "The consumerization of health is happening much faster here in the U.S. than in the developing world," he says. "*If you're to play that role of smartphone-based personalized health solutions, then we have an amazing lead over anyone else 'Personalized correction'*."

Over the past six months, EyeNetra has been in discussion with virtual-reality companies in USA to integrate the technology into virtual-reality displays, Raskar says. The idea, he says, is to use the startup's technology to develop custom screens to fit a user's eyeglass prescription.

Prescription screens could make virtual-reality devices more form-fitting for a more immersive and comfortable experience, Raskar says: Right now, devices are built with extra space on the viewing end for people wearing glasses.

But it could also help solve a larger issue: aligning the eye lens, prescription lens, and the virtual-reality screen. "All three have to be aligned in the right way for you to enjoy the experience," Raskar says. If the glasses shift, for instance, optical aberrations disrupt the viewing, potentially causing headache, fatigue, and nausea.

EyeNetra's technology measures how a user's optical refractive errors will affect how they see patterns on a digital display—in an environment very similar to a virtual-reality headset, Raskar says.

Therefore, companies could use these precise measurements to display images that are pre-corrected to a user's specific refraction errors. "It's personalized correction," Raskar says. "Your [vision] correction is built into the headset."

Such an approach could be game-changing, Raskar says, as billions of dollars have recently been invested into virtual-reality technology. "In addition to the major business [EyeNetra] is doing for prescriptions, it can also disrupt virtual reality, which is potentially an even bigger market," Raskar says.

About 340 product iterations led to an improved device and better user interface. For instance, around three years ago, the team realized that people didn't perform well interacting with the phone. So, for the current design, they moved all buttons and knobs to the actual device. That change, and other small tweaks, made the device easier and more widely used, Raskar says.

"We were naive in thinking that if you solve the optics problem, it will be good. But in reality there are three parameters: the machine and its optical design, the eye and its involuntary activities, and the human perception," he says. "Getting all those right in the same design is nontrivial."

Moving forward, Raskar says EyeNetra aims to capitalize on the "consumerization of health" phenomenon in the United States, where consumers are gaining access to innovative medical tools for personal use. "The biggest impact we could have is playing a key role in bringing health solution technologies to people at their homes or schools," he says.

(MIT News Oct. 2015) Read with India focus Chapter 6. Details in Appendix 7.

Pharma stakeholders share views, and examine ways to put patients at the center of evolving pharma business models, without damaging profits. Putting patients first needs to be attractive on both the humanistic and fiscal levels in order for patient centricity this won't happen overnight (Eyeforma.com).

New strategies need to be implemented to reshape business structures and positively influence internal thinking. The message that patients are pharma's number one business priority needs to filter down from C-level to the root system of every pharma-related business.

As technology plays a greater and greater role in the medical realm, we have to maintain a much higher level of vigilance about the propensity for need and invention to get confused.

3D bioprinting: The high costs of clinical trials could eventually make 3D bioprinting a go-to technology for pharma and biotech, providing better data to spot toxicity early and helping the pharma industry avoid costly mistakes.

Mass Challenge, a Boston-based accelerator, has launched a digital health accelerator, Pulse@MassChallenge and is seeking applications. The new program at Mass Challenge is part of a push to make Boston a digital health hub. But in an unconventional approach to articulating the kinds of technologies it seeks, PULSE had its partners do that for them.

The digital health technologies currently garnering the most investments do not emphasize the elimination of health disparities for vulnerable populations. In fact, some may be at risk of exacerbating disparities. How to leverage digital health to eliminate health disparities may be the next essential focus. The socio-economic and medical risk factors limit the ability of vulnerable populations to purchase digital health technology directly. Additionally, their technological illiteracy due to language or age barriers introduces more challenges to freemium or ad-based models.

An overview of some currently available devices and products that are intended to meet home safety needs of the elderly is presented. General adaptive technologies include lever door handles, amplifiers on doorbells and telephones, grab rails and handrails in appropriate locations, ramps, stair lifts, external lighting with passive infra-red, lowered light switches, raised electrical outlets, level thresholds, wider doors and corridors, and electric window and door openers.

Passive environmental sensors are devices that monitor the safety features of the home as well as individuals in the home. These include devices to monitor gas leaks, carbon dioxide, and other potential hazards. Flood detectors, smoke detectors, and temperature extremes sensors notify the senior or caregiver of the need for corrective action. Motion and pressure sensors can alert caregivers of events such as falls, turn on bedside lights when the senior gets out of bed, activate an alarm if the person does not return to bed in a set time, or detect a person leaving the home. These devices not only help the senior, but can also be combined with alerting systems that send messages to caregivers. Some applications allow caregivers to remotely monitor home appliance use or turn appliances off and on, turn lights off and on, and open and close blinds from a distance.

Assistive technologies aid the elderly in meeting their daily needs and particularly help individuals who are physically disabled but cognitively intact. Technologies include voice-activated cell phones and wireless transmitters to issue voice commands to activate various functions within the home. Other functions include alerts that inform the senior when the mail is delivered, show who is at the door, open and close windows, and, if doors or windows are left open, close windows and doors with voice commands. Technologies are available to alert caregivers if the senior wanders or leaves the home and assist in tracking the elderly.

Advanced microwave technology can now recognize the type of food product selected for cooking, and based on the selection, show an instructional video indicating the steps for preparation. The "smart wave" can program itself for the appropriate cooking time, notify the person via audio and video that the food is cooked, and caution the user about safe food handling.

Digital technology is creating "turning point in the history of the pharmaceutical industry." Few essentials for e-health care.

In news released Oct. 2016, Siemens Healthineers and IBM said they would jointly develop technology and services to help healthcare providers operate in value-based environments. This will include analytics, reporting and patient engagement, the two companies said, though they don't have any specific offerings to announce just yet.

The alliance marks Siemens' first foray into population health management.

"We will bring the power of Siemens Healthineers' extensive relationships with providers and our deep domain expertise in clinical workflows, services and digital health technologies to bear to help bring population health management offerings to healthcare providers. The new alliance fits perfectly into the services business of Siemens Healthineers."

How IBM Watson is Helping Healthcare

IBM Watson has gone from game shows to searching for cures to cancer in five years. Watson is able to read medical images. Cancer researchers are using Watson because the supercomputer can process so much information so fast. "No one has time to read 8,000 new papers a day," Dr. Norman Sharpless, director of the University of North Carolina's Linenberger Comprehensive Cancer Center said, referencing the amount of new medical literature that gets churned out.

He echoed the words of medical informatics pioneer Dr. Larry Weed, who said in the 1960s that the human mind can't possibly keep up with the pace of change in medicine and recall all information pertinent to a specific patient when it's most needed.

After being trained to read medical literature, Watson scanned 25 billion papers in about a week, according to Kelly.

Sharpless discussed a trial he ran at UNC to test out the potential of Watson. The IBM system found the same thing as humans in 99 percent of medical cases the UNC team fed it. Plus, in 30 percent of patient Watson found something new that physicians had missed.

Is Watson like a physician assistant, a very comprehensive tool?

(CBS newsmagazine *60 Minutes* show to artificial intelligence. About 12 minutes of that discussed healthcare.)

Scientists at Disney Research USA have developed a way to wirelessly charge several electronic devices in a room, eliminating the need for electrical cords or charging cradles. The method makes it possible to power several cellphones, fans and lights simultaneously. "This new innovative method will make it possible for electrical power to become as ubiquitous as Wi-Fi." This in turn could enable new applications for robots and other small mobile devices by eliminating the need to replace batteries and wires for charging, wireless power transmission is a long-standing technological dream. The method called quasistatic cavity resonance (QSCR) involves inducing electrical currents in metallized walls, floor and ceiling of a room, which in turn generate magnetic fields that permeate the room's interior. This enables power to be transmitted efficiently to receiving coils that operate at the same resonant frequency as the magnetic fields. The induced currents in the structure are channeled through discrete capacitors, which isolate potentially harmful electrical fields. "Our simulations show we can transmit 1.9 kilowatts of power. Today, most wireless power transmission occurs over very short distances, typically involving charging stands or pads.

Basics of e-Health

Managing data analytics for health: Recent proliferation of connected devices, sensors, and other equipment has made it almost too easy for healthcare organizations to acquire data. The potential benefits are evident: mining this data to make more informed decisions about their internal operations and patient care.

The problem however is that just having access to data does not in itself produces results. Healthcare institutions need to focus on the fundamentals of data analysis to uncover the relevant nuggets of insights which help drive decision-making. Bad data muddles up analytics, and bad presentation of data can put the focus on the wrong things or miss the mark altogether—it's essential that the data be trusted and actionable. So how can healthcare facilities identify more meaningful insights that ultimately improve patient care? Here are some things to keep in mind.

Make data available in real time: Emergence of real-time data sources is having a dramatic impact across all industries. Data analysis no longer has to be a retrospective waiting game. It's now enabling organizations to ask, "What's going on right now, and what can we do about it?"

Take for example the challenge of improving patient satisfaction scores. Hospitals have a pretty good idea of what contributes to a positive patient experience: short wait times, meaningful interaction with caregivers, and effective communication with patients and family.

If the information is delivered in real-time by leveraging technologies such as real-time location systems (RTLS), caregivers can respond immediately to a patient who has been waiting too long and managers can better anticipate and eliminate bottlenecks in the overall patient flow. Data created by an automated RTLS can be much more accurate and timely than that entered manually.

Data Analytics—Visual Analytics, Predictive Analytics—Present Data in a Simple, Meaningful Way: Visual dashboards are essential to make the data actionable. They enable staff to more easily monitor and understand a patient's care process in a manner that is intuitive and doesn't require data analysis expertise, while quickly identifying pain points of procedural inefficiencies to get ahead of a problem before it occurs.

Using real-time monitoring and dashboards, however, hospitals can show staff members how they are doing individually, and show managers how the unit or hospital is doing overall—all through *visual analytics*. This allows for immediate action or longer term interventions such as further education or mentoring.

Dashboards take real-time information about patients, staff and assets, and provide faster insight into how to improve the patient experience—whether by resolving issues that impact wait time or seeing what's causing reduced staff contact time. Doctors and nurses can even access dashboards on-the-go on a tablet or wall-mounted display to gain real-time visibility into what's happening in the OR, waiting rooms or post op rooms to make sure everything is running smoothly.

Today, dashboards loaded with *predictive analytics* are becoming a reality as historical data uncovers trends. Looking at the facility's records, organizations can better predict trends in the coming hours, weeks and months to make more informed decisions, such as using previous data on infusion pump deployments to identify how the devices should be distributed and when more will need to be ordered or rented.

There's a movement to bring *self-service analytics* to the masses. Business intelligence (BI) and data visualization tools like Tableau, Qlik, Microsoft and SAP are paving the way for non-technical individuals to analyze and make sense of data.

Organizations need to be able to differentiate between "good" and "bad" data if they hope to avoid confusing or non-correlated results. An experienced analytics team knows that data integrity is the key to success.

Healthcare institutions either look into third-party vendors to handle and manage data analysis, or find a data expert to bring in-house team. Often these in-house teams will partner with vendor teams who are experts in their solutions as a starting point, then take over day-to-day operation of the BI systems once launched.

Spot and Breakdown Data Silos: When implementing new technologies, it's also important to consider data silos; particularly how to avoid creating new silos and how to eliminate old ones. Data silos are repositories of data that are isolated from other parts of the organization. Healthcare groups should use all of the data that is available to them to drive more informed decisions and ultimately help improve patient care.

For instance, being able to combine RTLS data with clinical performance data provides caregivers with a more complete picture of the patient journey. Ensuring that the RTLS system is integrated to the clinical system and that a common "key" exists is essential to being able to blend and analyze this type of data. A healthcare data strategy must evolve. Payers, providers and other organizations must leverage greater volumes of data, in a variety of formats, to improve care coordination and deliver better health outcomes and to respond to emerging healthcare challenges.

Current Applications of Nanotechnology

Nano-materials such as nanocrystals, nano particles, nanoclays and nanocomposites, nanocatalysts, nanofilters. Nano technology effect is being used in clothing industry, metals, sports industry, photovoltaic devices, food sector, and cosmetics sector. It is being used to produce nano-particulate-based synthetic bone.

Currently embedded nanoparticles are used to create stain-repellent khakis 'Stain Defender'. Researchers at Pacific Northwest National Laboratory have developed a coating process to make sponge-like silica latch onto toxic metals in water. Self-Assembled Monolayers on Mesoporous Supports easily captures such metals as lead and mercury, which are then recovered for reuse or contained in-place forever.

A plastic nanocomposite is being used for "step assists" in the GM Safari and Astro Vans. It is scratch-resistant, light-weight, and rust-proof, and generates improvements in strength and reductions in weight, which lead to fuel savings and increased longevity. And in 2001, Toyota started using nanocomposites in a bumper that makes it 60 percent lighter and twice as resistant to denting and scratching. It is likely be used on other GM and Toyota models soon, and in other areas of their vehicles, as well as by other auto manufactures, for lowering weight, increasing mileage, and creating longer-lasting autos; as weight, weather-proofing, durability, and strength are important factors. NASA, the ESA, and other space-faring organizations are seriously considering its applications which will eventually result in lower lift costs, and in more material.

Metal nanocrystals might be incorporated into car bumpers, making the parts stronger, or into aluminum, making it more wear resistant. Metal nanocrystals might be used to produce bearings that last longer than their conventional counterparts, new types of sensors and components for computers and electronic hardware. Nano-materials are used for golf clubs and tennis rackets for strong and light products.

Nanocrystals of various metals have been shown to be 100 percent, 200 percent and even as much as 300 percent harder than the same materials in bulk form. Because wear resistance often is dictated by the hardness of a metal, parts made from nanocrystals might last significantly longer than conventional parts.

Using aluminum nanoparticles, Argonide Corporate has created rocket propellants that burn at double the rate. They also produce copper nanoparticles that are incorporated into automotive lubricant to reduce engine wear.

"Nanocrystals are an ideal light harvester in photovoltaic devices. (They) absorb sunlight more strongly than dye molecules or bulk semiconductor material; therefore high optical densities can be achieved while maintaining the requirement of thin films as perfectly crystalline."

All of them contain polymer particles ranging from ten to several hundred nanometers in size. Polymer dispersions are found in exterior paints, coatings and adhesives, or are used in the finishing of paper, textiles and leather.

Nanotechnology also has applications in the food sector. Many vitamins and their precursors, such as carotenoids, are insoluble in water. However, when skillfully produced and formulated as nanoparticles, these substances can easily be mixed with cold water, and their bioavailability in the human body also increases. Many lemonades and fruit juices contain these specially formulated additives, which often also provide an attractive color.

In the cosmetics sector, BASF cosmetic company has for several years been among the leading suppliers of UV absorbers based on nano-particulate zinc oxide. Incorporated in sun creams, the small particles filter the high-energy radiation out of sunlight. Because of their tiny size, they remain invisible to the naked eye and so the cream is transparent on the skin.

Sunscreens are utilizing nanoparticles that are extremely effective at absorbing light, especially in the ultra-violet (UV) range. Due to the particle size, they spread more easily, cover better, and save money since you use less. And they are transparent, unlike traditional screens which are white. AngstroMedica has produced a nano-particulate-based synthetic bone. "Human bone is made of a calcium and phosphate composite called Hydroxyapatite. By manipulation calcium and phosphate at the molecular level, we have created a patented material that is identical in structure and composition to natural bone. This novel synthetic bone can be used in areas where natural bone is damaged or removed, such as in the treatment of fractures and soft tissue injuries."

***Nano technology use in non-structured material*:** Nanodyne Corporate makes a tungsten-carbide-cobalt composite powder (grain size less than 15 nm) that is used to make a sintered alloy as hard as diamond, which is in turn used to make cutting tools, drill bits, armor plate, and jet engine parts.

Kodak Corporate is producing OLED color screens (made of nanostructured polymer films) for use in car stereos and cellphones. OLEDs (organic light emitting diodes) may enable thinner, lighter, more flexible, less power consuming displays, and other consumer products such as cameras, PDAs, laptops, televisions, and other as yet undreamt of applications.

Nanoclays and nanocomposites are used in packaging, like beer bottles, as a barrier, allowing for thinner material, with a subsequently lighter weight, and greater shelf-life. Wilson Double Core tennis balls have a nanocomposite coating that keeps it bouncing twice as long as an old-style ball and giving the ball substantially longer shelf life. Carbon nanotubes manufactured by Nonoledge Corporate is used in a tennis racket; which make the yoke of the racket bend less during ball impact, improving the player's performance.

Nanocatalysts Examples

1. China's largest coal company (Shenhua Group) has licensed technology from Hydrocarbon Technologies that will enable it to liquefy coal and turn it into gas. The process uses a gel-based nanoscale catalyst, which improves the efficiency and reduces the cost. "If the technology lives up to its promise and can economically transform coal into diesel fuel and gasoline, coal-rich countries such as the U.S., China and Germany could depend far less on imported oil. At the same time, acid-rain pollution would be reduced because the liquefaction strips coal of harmful sulfur."

2. One of the characteristic properties of all nanoparticles has been used from the outset in the manufacture of automotive catalytic converters: The surface area of the particles increases dramatically as the particle size decreases and the weight remains the same. A variety of chemical reactions take place on the surface of the catalyst, and the larger the surface area, the more active the catalyst. Nanoscale catalysts thus open the way for numerous process innovations to make many chemical processes more efficient and resource-saving—in other words more competitive.

Nanofilters Examples

Argonide nanomaterials, an Orlando-based manufacturer of nanoparticles and nano filtration products, makes a filter that is capable of filtering the smallest of particles. The performance is due to its nano size alumina fiber, which attracts and retains sub-micron and nano size particles. This disposable filter retains 99.9999+ percent of viruses at water flow rates several hundred times greater than virus-rated ultra-porous membranes. It is useful for sterilization of biological, pharmaceutical and medical serums, protein separation, and collector/concentrator for biological warfare, detectors, and several other applications. In the future, for one application, sterilizing drinking water, this product may have an impact on so-called Third World peoples, who only have access to dubious sources of water. For more current applications, refer 'Reality is the concept that governs the new nano-business world'.

Scientists have developed a new eye transplant that may help restore vision to millions worldwide.

These are just a few of the many ways in which nanotechnology is working itself into our everyday lives. At present, there are no nano bots, no molecular-scale machines, and no assemblers—these are still in the basic research stages, and may not be seen for decades (although many would argue that a concerted effort would bring them to fruition in just a few years).

What we are seeing is the beginning of a revolution, caused by our ability to work on the same scale as nature. Nanotechnology will affect every aspect of our lives, from the medicines we use, to the power of our computers, the energy supplies we require, the food we eat, the cars we drive, the buildings we live in, and the clothes we wear. And it will happen sooner than most people think. You won't be able to count the number of businesses affected by nanotechnology. Nanotechnology involves manipulating properties and structures at the nanoscale, often involving dimensions that are just tiny fractions of the width of a human hair. Nanotechnology is already being used in products in its passive form, such as cosmetics and sunscreens, and it is expected that in the coming decades, new phases of products, such as better batteries and improved electronics equipment, will be developed and have far-reaching implications.

Nanotechnology and Medicine

One area of nanotechnology application that holds the promise of providing great benefits for society is in the future realm of medicine. The use of nanotechnology in the field of medicine could revolutionize the way we detect and treat damage to the human body and disease in the future, and many techniques only imagined a few years ago are making remarkable progress towards becoming realities.

Nanotechnology is already being used as the basis for new, more effective drug delivery systems and is in early stage development as scaffolding in nerve regeneration research. Moreover, the National Cancer Institute has created the Alliance for Nanotechnology in Cancer in the hope that investments in this branch of nanomedicine could lead to breakthroughs in terms of detecting, diagnosing, and treating various forms of cancer.

Nanotechnology medical developments over the coming years will have a wide variety of uses and could potentially save a great number of lives. Nanotechnology is already moving from being used in passive structures to active structures, through more targeted drug therapies or "smart drugs." These new drug therapies have already been shown to cause fewer side effects and be more effective than traditional therapies. In the future, nanotechnology will also aid in the formation of molecular systems that may be strikingly similar to living systems. These molecular structures could be the basis for the regeneration or replacement of body parts that are currently lost to infection, accident, or disease. These predictions for the future have great significance not only in encouraging nanotechnology research and development but also in determining a means of oversight. The number of products approaching the FDA approval and review process is likely to grow as time moves forward and as new nanotechnology medical applications are developed.

Nanotechnology in medicine involves applications of nanoparticles currently under development, as well as longer ranges research that involves the use of manufactured nano-robots to make repairs at the cellular level (sometimes referred to as nanomedicine).

Nanotechnology in Drug Delivery: One application of nanotechnology in medicine currently being developed involves employing nanoparticles to deliver drugs, heat, light or other substances to specific types of cells (such as cancer cells). Particles are engineered so that they are attracted to diseased cells, which allow direct treatment of those cells. This technique reduces damage to healthy cells in the body and allows for earlier detection of disease.

Nanotechnology in Therapy Techniques: Researchers have developed "nanosponges" that absorb toxins and remove them from the bloodstream. The nanosponges are polymer nanoparticles coated with a red blood cell membrane. The red blood cell membrane allows the nanosponges to travel freely in the bloodstream and attract the toxins.

Researchers have demonstrated a method to generate sound waves that are powerful, but also tightly focused, that may eventually be used for noninvasive surgery. They use a lens coated with carbon nanotubes to convert light from a laser to focused sound waves. The intent is to develop a method that could blast tumors or other diseased areas without damaging healthy tissue. Researchers are investigating the use of bismuth nanoparticles to concentrate radiation used in radiation therapy to treat cancer tumors. Initial results indicate that the bismuth nanoparticles would increase the radiation dose to the tumor by 90 percent.

Nanoparticles composed of polyethylene glycol-hydrophilic carbon clusters (PEG-HCC) have been shown to absorb free radicals at a much higher rate than the proteins out body uses for this function. This ability to absorb free radicals may reduce the harm that is caused by the release of free radicals after a brain injury.

Targeted heat therapy is being developed to destroy breast cancer tumors. In this method antibodies that are strongly attracted to proteins produced in one type of breast cancer cell are attached to nanotubes, causing the nanotubes to accumulate at the tumor. Infrared light from a laser is absorbed by the nanotubes and produces heat that incinerates the tumor.

Read more about nanomedicine therapy techniques.

Nanotechnology in Diagnostic Techniques

Researchers at Worcester Polytechnic Institute are using antibodies attached to carbon nanotubes in chips to *detect cancer cells in the blood stream*. The researchers believe this method could be used in simple lab tests that could provide early detection of cancer cells in the bloodstream.

Researchers at MIT have developed a sensor using carbon nanotubes embedded in a gel; that can be injected under the skin to monitor the level of nitric oxide in the bloodstream. The level of nitric oxide is important because it indicates inflammation, allowing *easy monitoring of inflammatory diseases*. In tests with laboratory mice the sensor remained functional for over a year.

Researchers at the University of Michigan are developing a sensor that can detect a very low level of cancer cells, as low as three to five cancer cells in a one milliliter in a blood sample. They grow sheets of *graphene oxide*, on which they attach molecules containing an antibody that attaches to the cancer cells. They then tag the cancer cells with fluorescent molecules to make the cancer cells stand out in a microscope.

Researchers have demonstrated a way to use nanoparticles for *early diagnosis of infectious disease*. The nanoparticles attach to molecules in the blood stream indicating the start of an infection. When the sample is scanned for Raman scattering the nanoparticles enhance the Raman signal, allowing detection of the molecules indicating an infectious disease at a very early stage.

A test for early detection of kidney damage is being developed. The method uses *gold nanorods* functionalized to attach to the type of protein generated by damaged kidneys; when protein accumulates on the nanorod the color of the nanorod shifts. The test is designed to be done quickly and inexpensively for early detection of a problem.

Nanotechnology in Anti-Microbial Techniques: Researchers at the University of Houston are developing a technique to kill bacteria using *gold nanoparticles and infrared light*. This method may lead to improved cleaning of instruments in hospital settings.

Researchers at the University of Colorado Boulder are investigating the use of *quantum dots* to treat antibiotic resistant infection. *Polymer coated iron oxide nanoparticles to treat chronic bacterial infections.*

Researchers at the University of New South Wales are investigating the use of one of the earliest nanomedicine applications; the use of *nanocrystalline silver* which is as an antimicrobial agent for the treatment of wounds, as discussed on the Nucryst Pharmaceuticals Corporation website.

A nanoparticle cream has been shown to fight staph infections. *The nanoparticles contain nitric oxide gas*, which is known to kill bacteria. Studies on mice have shown that using the nanoparticle cream to release nitric oxide gas at the site of staph abscesses significantly reduced the infection.

Burn dressing is coated with *nanocapsules containing antibiotics*. If an infection starts the harmful bacteria in the wound causes the nanocapsules to break open, releasing the antibiotics. This allows much quicker treatment of an infection and reduces the number of times a dressing has to be changed.

An idea in the early study stages is the *elimination of bacterial infections* in a patient within minutes, instead of delivering treatment with antibiotics over a period of weeks. Design analysis for the antimicrobial nanorobot are used in such treatments refer "Microbivores: Artificial Mechanical Phagocytes using Digest and Discharge Protocol".

Nanotechnology in Cell Repair

Nanorobot could actually be programmed to repair specific diseased cells, functioning in a similar way to antibodies in our natural healing processes.

Applications on mobile phones

Focus is on developing more and more of smartphone applications rather than applications for desktop or lap top and other mobile devices such as mobile phones.

Mobile-cellular Technology

Mobile technology is being used through various devices for e-commerce, m-commerce and Digital Marketing (details in Chapter 4). Mobile phones lead the way.

A corporation may track 40,000 trucks via satellite constantly monitoring their locations and even engine conditions or a wireless system for vending machines to talk to a computer at headquarters ordering more goods or reporting vandalism. In fact, the big corporates (Motorola for one) worldwide planned to sell the idea to the masses that anything that has a switch including car engines can be turned on and off by wireless network. At the same time wireless world may create hostile environment for those who have invested billions in outmoded technology and now must invest billions to convert to digital transmissions or take over the PCs networks.

Similarly, retailers, distributors, store services will be outmoded when 'virtual stores' can be shopped on a wireless device through e-commerce. What need is there for a film distribution company when it can rent a space on a satellite network to beam a new movie to 3000 theaters? Or video streaming services. Eventually, the devices and networks will be ubiquitous and the ultimate effect will increase the pace of the society, liberating people from physical constraints of time and space. Wireless assistants and alter egos will do much of the communication that we do now while we are doing something else somewhere.

Finland offers some interesting insights into some of these devices sideshows. At the Helsinki airport, a coke-wending machine has a mobile number instead of coin slot—dial up the machine and a coke drops out with the charge appearing on your phone bill. Similar practices are spreading across Europe.

In Italy, operator Omnitel let users call a special number while standing in front of designated piazzas; the computer figures out where you are and plays back a recorded discourse on the art and history of the location in one of the five languages. Soon an advertiser like McDonald will be able to send a data message to every mobile phone at football stadium urging their owners to eat a Big Mac at half time. Or a pedestrian walking past a car showroom might receive a message inviting him inside for a special deal. Though people feel some of these features will intrude on their privacy.

Applications on Mobile Phones

Mobile phones beside telephone connectivity; email, texts, web searches and social networking, banking, e-wallets, ordering consumer good to food and transport on mobile phones still lead the way. Due to the pervasiveness of web content and interactions, users have high expectations for their mobile experience. They demand an excellent user interface with a design adapted for mobile devices. Focus is on developing more and more of smartphone applications rather than applications for desktop or lap top and other mobile devices.

Smart mobile phones with 2G, 3G, 4G connectivity facilitate many of these functions through various apps programed in these phones. Many medical applications are put through Smartphones (discussed in earlier section). Scientists have developed a new smartphone app that tracks eye movement to determine, in less than a minute, if a child is showing signs of autism spectrum disorder. The autism tracking software, which can be installed in cell phones, tablets or computers, provides detection of the neurodegenerative disorder in children as young as two years old and can dramatically improve the benefits of treatment. If other neurological conditions are included, like AD attention deficit disorder.

Smartphones can be used to make high-resolution movies of living cells, without the need for expensive equipment, a new study has found. Live imaging is a very powerful tool for the study of cells, to learn about how cells respond to different treatments such as drugs or toxins.

The study by researchers at Uppsala University in Sweden makes it possible for laboratories around the world to do the same thing. In the study, old standard inverted microscopes that are very abundant at universities and hospitals were upgraded to high quality live imaging stations using a few 3D-printed parts, off-the-shelf electronics, and a smartphone. It was shown that the resultant upgraded systems provided excellent cell culture conditions and enabled high-resolution images of living cells (Johan Kreuger, senior lecturer at the Department of Medical Cell Biology at Uppsala University—Dec. 2016).

Your smartphone may soon be able to give honest answers to your queries, thanks to a new machine learning algorithm is designed to learn directly from human instructions, rather than an existing set of examples. The algorithm designed by researchers from University of Toronto in Canada.

Humans "teach" neural networks—computer networks that learn dynamically—by providing a set of labelled data and asking the neural network to make decisions based on the samples it is seen. This algorithm is different: it learns directly from human trainers. With this model, called heuristic training, humans provide direct instructions that are used to pre-classify training samples rather than a set of fixed examples. Trainers program the algorithm with guidelines such as "sky is likely to be varying shades of blue," and "pixels near the top of the image are more likely to be sky than pixels at the bottom."

This heuristic training approach holds considerable promise for addressing one of the biggest challenges for neural networks: making correct classifications of previously unknown or unlabeled data. This is crucial for applying machine learning to new situations, such as correctly identifying cancerous tissues for medical diagnostics, or classifying all the objects surrounding and approaching a self-driving car. (The study was published in the journal *IEEE Transactions on Neural Networks and Learning Systems*.)

Revolution in automated retail: Even recently automated retail is being developed through smartphones. Amazon Go initiated by Amazon Company using different automation concepts. Amazon eliminates checkouts and cash registers altogether. Customers scan their mobile smart phones as they walk into the store. The store is designed to determine automatically what items customers take from the shelves and into the shopping basket and charge their accounts when they leave.

Further for automated retail, a machine, a convenience store checkout machine by Panasonic (2016); can scan and bag items on their own; a special shopping basket fitted with electronic tag is designed to detect the merchandise in the basket and calculated the bill. When customer puts the basket on the slot; the bottom slides down and merchandise drops into a plastic bag. Customer can pay by cash or credit card and through smartphone apps.

In addition India is using mobile apps to suit its culture and societal needs. For example, in times of demonetisation in Nov. 2016 and earlier for modes of money transfer in rural areas.

Payment technologies applications are developing for individuals from the conventional cards such as credit, debit and prepaid; ATM (automated teller machines), through Internet, use of e-wallets through its varied products, and mobile phone apps.

Platforms for Building Mobile Apps

IBM MobileFirst is a platform for building mobile apps for the enterprise. New enterprise mobility platform IBM MobileFirst for iOS Garage in Bangalore India was opened in August 2016 and plans to open satellite centers in many other countries including Brazil, China and Romania and China.

The Garage is dedicated to enable clients to complete digital mobility projects as quickly as possible and into the world's largest concentration of Swift developers, IBM design and iOS device expertise and consulting services. It will serve as a global development hub for iOS apps and work with existing design locations in Atlanta, Chicago, Cupertino and Toronto.

IBM also announced Mobile at Scale for iOS, a new offering specifically for clients looking to invest in digital transformation projects that include more than three iOS apps over a multi-year period. The partnership with Apple is focused on enterprises and professionals, and at the same time the company delivers solutions for its clients across the board. So, when you get into a specific industry, we have a suite of apps that serves the industry. IBM partnered with Apple in July 2014 to transform enterprise mobility through a new class of 'made for business' apps, bringing IBM's big data and analytics capabilities to Apple devices in the enterprise. Till date, IBM has developed over 100 apps across 15 industries and delivered nearly 2,000 client engagements. The Garage will extend the design, development and delivery skills gained from IBM's partnership with Apple to serve a broader set of global clients.

Mobile Technologies—Smartphones

There are many smartphones in the market with update digital features such as Google, Samsung, Apple, Android, Lyf-Jio, Vivo.

"Advances in various technologies will drive users to interact with their smartphones in more intuitive ways", said Gartner, Inc. Gartner predicts that, by 2019, 20 percent of all user interactions with the smartphone will take place via virtual personal assistants (VPAs). The role of interactions will intensify through the growing popularity of VPAs among smartphone users and conversations made with smart machines, said Annette Zimmermann, research director at Gartner.

Apple's Siri and Google Now are currently the most widely used VPAs on smartphones. Fifty-four percent of U.K. and U.S. respondents used Siri in the last three months. Google Now is used by 41 percent of U.K. respondents and 48 percent of U.S. respondents. VPAs usage is bound to accelerate as they add many new features, including integration for business services, further language support and appear across more devices, said Jessica Ekholm, research director at Gartner.

Gartner expects that, by 2019, VPAs would have changed the way users interact with devices and become universally accepted as part of everyday life. Today, VPAs are fulfilling simple tasks such as setting the alarm or retrieving information from the web, but in the near future these systems will be able to deliver more complex tasks such as completing a transaction based on past, present and predicted context.

This trend is also intensified by the acceleration of conversational commerce, but voice is not the only UI for VPA use. In fact, Facebook Messenger is allowing users to interact with businesses to make purchases, chat with customer services and order Uber cars within the app. Moreover, Tencent's WeChat generates over $1.1 billion in revenue by offering its 440 million users an all-in-one approach, letting them pay their bills, hail cabs and order products with a text.

China represents the most mature market by far, where the increased dominance of messaging platforms is causing the traditional app market to stall. This trend is continuing to grow, not only among consumers but also among businesses or in the pro-consumer context. For example, Microsoft's integration of Cortana into Skype will allow users to chat with their VPA. Cortana will then facilitate the interaction with a third-party bot to get things done, such as a hotel or flight booking.

Biometrics: We expect AI, machine learning and VPAs to be one of the major strategic battlegrounds from 2017 onwards, and make many mobile apps fade and become sub-servants of VPAs. Voice and Gesture become increasingly important Interfaces. With a predicted installed base of about seven billion personal devices, 1.3 billion wearables and 5.7 billion other consumer Internet of Things (IoT) endpoints by 2020, the majority of devices will be designed to function with minimal or zero touch.

By 2020, Gartner predicts that zero-touch UIs will be available on two billion devices and IoT endpoints. Interactions will move away from touchscreens and will increasingly make use of voice, ambient technology, biometrics, movement and gestures. In this situation, apps using contextual information will become a crucial factor in user acceptance, as a voice-driven system's usability increases dramatically according to how much it knows about the user's surrounding environment. This is where device vendors' assets or partnerships in VPAs, natural language processing (NLP) and deep machine learning experts will matter.

Biometric Applications

In 2015, Lumia Nokia and Fujitsu phones fitted with infrared cameras that use Iris scans to unlock, no swipes or passcode required. Recently, UN World Food Program installed iris scanners within its camps as a biometric payment method for Syrian refugees who fled home without any cash or credit cards. Iris biometrics is also used for NEXUS card to expedite border crossings between USA and Canada.

Eye-tracking firm Tobil has developed custom designed glasses to track eye-movements and generate insights on viewing behavior—creating valuable data for marketers, engineers and designers; as well an eye-tracking systems for home computers that uses eye movements to control a wide range of functions.

Companies like Eye-influence are building eye-tracking technology into head mounted displays for VR and AR (augmented reality) platforms. It is also being deployed in medical field to detect diseases and disorders, from the onset of Alzheimer to concussion and autism.

Iris is used widely as Id in passports and other identification documents, bank ATMs many IOT endpoints at par with finger prints or thumb impressions.

Drone's e-commerce is increasing and it is being felt that on-line shopping delivery mode deliveries through drones could be faster than through motor cycles or trucks. Currently, drones are being used to deliver groceries, drugs and other packets with certain reservations because of their getting into airspace. Drones can be used to deliver drugs in less time than through other modes. Amazon is experimenting delivery through drones. Recently, Facebook is using laser drones. In India in 2017, a drone is designed by a 14 years old that help detect and defuse land mines on war fields. India Government is facilitating its production.

Summary

The essence and objective of communication technology innovation and development is its applications in varied domains from entertainment, business, medical, finance and home utility and safety. In earlier first two communication technology waves, the focus has been on bigger technology, such as computers, TV and its ethnotronic technologies and their applications narrow down to in one or two domains. But in third wave, not only more technologies are innovated but focus of applications for new and old technologies has widened. The recent focus has been increasing on varied applications in several domains of life, work and enterprises, and governance through major digital technologies of cloud, Artificial Intelligence—automation, robotics, cognitive technologies, augmented reality (reality (AR), visual (VR), and digital development of internet of things (IoT), remote sensing and mobile—smartphone technologies.

The other focus is on innovative and enhanced applications of the sustained technologies of second wave; nanotechnologies, RFID, quantum computer, laser and fuel cells.

CHAPTER 4 Internet

Internet

Internet commercially initiated in Second Technology Wave in 1993 had a very big connectivity role which created many technologies as well as communication revolutions. The commercial use of the Internet started in 1993 by inventing World Wide Web (WWW), though it has been innovated in 1960.

Internet access impacted technological, economic and market forces; learning and social behavior. Internet has been great influencer for learning-academic and business and offering content, news and email; search channels facilitating information and knowledge as well digital advertising. Social behavior become more focused and wider as Internet network become more efficient and help creating social platforms. Cyber security and surveillance have been the major concerns. More and more as Internet become more advanced as hackers also advance their ways.

Internet technology has created both local and global connectivity overtime. Internet access is directed by technological, economic and market forces. It has impacted learning in terms of information, knowledge, connectivity in academics, businesses, community, and applications in terms of content, news, email. The impact on social behavior is focused and efficient through wider networks. Computer literacy, Internet access and affordability are major necessary conditions for wider usage and applications of Internet.

With Internet exploding, consumers were looking for faster speed, accessible, reliable, and secure Internet connections. In 1999, DSL (digital subscriber services) was used for speedier Internet. DSL uses special equipment and modem to boost the capacity of the traditional copper telephone lines. Earlier cable modem was being used since that is less expensive. Fixed wireless is another alternative to provide high Internet services. It uses antenna and airwaves to transmit data.

Less than a decade and the technology has changed from being a novelty to integral part of everyday life. Its reach and applications are ubiquitous. It has become central to businesses, enabling real-time communications with customers, suppliers and partners. To some extent, the Internet is a tool that allows people to do things cheaper and faster. It is transformational. It allows you to do things you could never do before. The tremendous increase to information (and disinformation) generated by Internet has also resulted in knowledge revolution and creation of virtual communities and disembodied publics. The late 90s burst obscured the rapid progression of the Internet. But the current build-out marked by a proliferation of mobile Internet devices, the spread of Internet protocol telephony, and the emergence of spin off technologies will refocus attention on the Internet.

Internet Channels

Yahoo started in 1994 and was once the leading search engine for the Internet but it has been overtaken by Google, which launched in 1998. According to data compiled by Netmarketshare, Yahoo handles just 7.7 percent of global online searches compared with 70 percent for Google and 11 percent for Microsoft's Bing. For online advertising, Yahoo is only expected to take 1.5 percent of the worldwide digital advertising market in 2016 down from 2.1 percent in 2015, according to eMarket.

Broadband

People want to be connected. Internet helps connect people. Challenge is in parts of the world (such as rural areas and hinterlands in India) where Internet service is thwarted by lack of fiber, towers and other infrastructure. Creative solutions such as drones and balloons are being tried to stream Wi-Fi signals.

Elon Musk, Tesla and SpaceX founder, has asked USA federal government permission to use a fleet of 4000 tiny satellites to beam Internet service from outer space. Using gigantic balloons, Google's 'Project Loon' aims to stream Wi-Fi from the stratosphere. The stratosphere is the second major layer of the Earth's atmosphere as you go upward. The troposphere, is the lowest layer to remote parts of the world.

Broadband the Next Wave

The Internet "connectivity anywhere (IOE) is component of a big evolution or revolution. It has already procreated several of these, but the global change has only begun. Global connectivity is revolutionary.

Nagle Green Emily's (2016) book *Anywhere*, argues effectively that the future of the world and business is ubiquitous connectivity, the total interconnection of people, ideas, and products through a global digital network. Every person will have access to virtually anything in the world from virtually anywhere he or she happens to be at the moment. Key vehicles already include wireless for communication, and RFID for product location.

On the hardware side, we need better technology to provide a common digital network around the world, better broadband to satisfy the demand, and wireless ubiquity for connecting people, devices, and businesses. The needs for new software and services are just as pervasive.

The '*Anywhere Revolution*' focus could be:

1. Be eternally curious for something different, have powerful ideas, a keen sense of what people want as well as current solution strengths and weaknesses.
2. Be a ubiquitous connector. Some people are naturally "connectors," using their links with others to create or promote opportunities between them. The Internet

dramatically reduces the cost of being a connector. In fact, now we can all be connectors, and should be.

3. Be an analytic thinker. Skills in searching for information and then synthesizing that information, looking for patterns, and interpreting it, can be more valuable than the actual information amassed through your experience.

Information and Communication Technologies (ICT)

The information technology scenario has changed since decades through development and innovations in the IT. The face and shape of information societies too have undergone tremendous change world-wide.

ICT in organizations include office atomization, production atomization, telecommunication, and electronic networks connecting organizations. Beside information processing technologies, a rapid growth can be found in computer-assisted communication technologies, and computer-supported cooperative work. Organizations change as a result of socio-economic and technological developments. ICT is adapted and designed to solve problems caused by these changes. The impact of ICT becomes apparent in changes in work patterns, qualifications, and decision-making procedures.

ICTs Supporters for Inclusive Growth

ICTs have significant potential for supporting inclusive growth. For example, farmers in developing countries have benefited from new ICT services such as real-time information about commodity prices and weather, and from the ease of money transfers. The effectiveness of governments has increased as a result of their ability to provide citizen-centric online services and to involve citizens in governance. ICTs have become key enablers of business and employment creation, and of productivity growth.

Report *The Global Information Technology Report 2015—ICTs for Inclusive Growth* highlights Digital divide —Internet. The impact of ICTs, reveal that, so far, it is mostly the rich countries have been benefiting from the ICT revolution. Paradoxically, ICTs have opened up new digital divides. Although Internet access is expanding, 61 percent of the world's population is not connected yet. The distribution of high-speed broadband and the use of mobile applications and advanced data services vary widely across and within economies. And although schools and firms increasingly have access to the Internet, the skills required to leverage ICTs remain woefully inadequate in many organizations. The question of whether opportunities offered by ICTs are inclusive by nature or whether they are likely to increase the distance between the haves and the have-nots is a pertinent one.

Some segments of the population may be exposed differently than others to labor market shifts induced by technological innovation, which can aggravate inequalities across groups with different levels of skills. Progress made in improving national competitiveness may create or deepen domestic inequalities. In the absence of corrective mechanisms (e.g. specific policies to connect all citizens and give them access to relevant skills), ICTs could contribute to a non-inclusive type of growth, thus exacerbating the problem rather than moderating it.

Under the theme "ICTs for inclusive growth," 2015 year's report showcases compelling solutions and makes policy recommendations for avoiding the pitfalls. The report highlights about bridging the divides, and allowing everyone to benefit from, and participate in, the ICT revolution; highlights about: (i) *The networked readiness framework* suggests that productivity is a critical determinant of economic growth. In fact, those differences in productivity growth account for cross-country growth variations even more than capital or labor accumulation. As the World Economic Forum's research on competitiveness has shown, the determinants of productivity are many and complex; and empirical evidence shows that, among these determinants, *ICT use is a key driver of innovation, especially in advanced economies where other sources of productivity gains have dried up or produce lower returns.*

As a general-purpose technology, ICTs have an impact that extends well beyond productivity gains. ICTs act as a direction to social development and transformation by improving access to basic services, enhancing connectivity, and creating employment opportunities. In these ways, ICTs affect how people live, communicate, interact, and engage among themselves and with their governments. For these reasons, measuring the extent to which ICTs are used and understanding the determinants of ICT adoption have been the object of much research since the early 2000s.

In 2001, the World Economic Forum launched the Global Information Technology Report series and the Networked Readiness Index (NRI). This represented one of the first attempts to make conceptual sense of the complex ICT reality, identifying the common factors that enable countries to use technology effectively. *The networked readiness Index framework (NRI) reinforce that it is intended to provide guidance to policymakers on the factors that they need to take into account to fully leverage ICTs in their growth strategies.*

In recent years, the debate has moved from the issue of ensuring access to the question of how to make the best use of ICTs in order to improve business innovation, governance, citizens' political participation, and social cohesion. In light of this shift in emphasis, and after two years of research and consultations with experts, the impact subindex was added to the NRI framework in 2012.

Yet measuring the actual impact of ICTs remains a very arduous task, as data remain scarce. In addition, the complex relationships between ICTs and socio-economic performance are not fully understood and their causality not fully established.

However, opportunities are offered by ICTs and they are transforming economies and societies around the world. The networked readiness framework rests on six principles: (i) A high-quality regulatory and business environment is critical in order to fully leverage ICTs and generate impact. (ii) ICT readiness as measured by ICT affordability, skills, and infrastructure is a precondition to generating impact. (iii) Fully leveraging ICTs requires a society-wide effort. All stakeholders, the government, the businesses, and the population at large have a role to play. (iv) ICT use should not be an end in itself. The impact that ICTs actually have on the economy and society is what ultimately matters. (v) Environment, readiness, and use are set of drivers that interact, co-evolve, and reinforce each other to create greater impact.

In turn, greater impact creates more incentives for countries to further improve their framework conditions, their readiness for ICTs, and their use of ICTs, thus creating a good cycle. Conversely, weaknesses in any particular dimension are likely to hinder progress in others. (vi) Finally, the networked readiness framework should provide clear policy guidance.

ICTs act as a vector of social development and transformation by improving access to basic services, enhancing connectivity, and creating employment opportunities. Since 2001, The Global Information Technology Report series published by the World Economic Forum in partnership with Cornell University and INSEAD has measured the drivers of the ICT revolution using the Networked Readiness Index. For each of the 143 economies covered, it allows areas of priority to be identified to more fully leverage ICTs for development.

Four important messages emerge from the 2015 edition. First, as mentioned above, the ICT revolution holds the potential of transforming economies and societies and of addressing some of the most pressing global challenges of our time. Second, this ICT revolution is well under way in some parts of the world. In these places, it is even accelerating as a result of the ubiquity of broadband Internet, the democratization of technologies, and the accelerating pace of innovation. Third, the ICT revolution has not so far reached large parts of the planet. Many of those who stand to gain the most from it are not yet connected. In order to better leverage ICTs for development, a higher level of preparedness and better infrastructure and access are needed. In this context, government leadership and vision are critical. Finally, we observe that digital divides exist within countries. Even in the most advanced economies, only certain segments of the population are benefitting from ICTs. Many are left behind because of their age, limited digital literacy, lack of access, or remoteness. It would be wrong to assume that these divides will be bridged by merely increasing ICT use.

The report concludes with a call for action. Policymakers must work with other stakeholders to swiftly adopt holistic long-term strategies for ICT development, implement sound legislation, and make smart investments. Under the theme "ICTs for Inclusive Growth," The Global Information Technology Report 2015 offers many solutions and examples of enabling policies and investments to help countries to better leverage ICTs for shared prosperity As the ICT revolution unfolds, it will indeed bring benefits, but it will also bring risks and challenges. Some of these are seen in the increasing incidents related to breaches of cybersecurity or cyberwarfare, and in questions related to privacy and the neutrality of the Internet.

The World Economic Forum is addressing these issues through its Future of the Internet Global Challenge. This endeavor aims to ensure that the Internet remains a core engine of human progress and to safeguard its globally integrated, highly distributed, and multi-stakeholder nature. It further contributes to making the ICT revolution truly global, growth supportive. It includes the Cyber Resilience initiative, which aims to raise awareness of cyber risk and to build commitment regarding the need for more rigorous approaches to cyber risk mitigation.

Other major concerns about Internet are cyber security, surveillance and censorship.

Internet Surveillance and Censorship: Holding Internet platforms liable for third-party content would lead to self-censorship and reduce the free flow of information, Google Inc. said in reaction to India's new rules. "We believe that a free and open Internet is essential for the growth of (the) digital economy and safeguarding freedom of expression,"

> "If internet platforms are held liable for third-party content, it would lead to self-censorship and reduce the free flow of information. The regulatory framework should ideally help protect Internet platforms and people's abilities to access information."

Regulations introduced in Dec. 2016 by India require search engines and websites to get rid of objectionable content including information that is "grossly harmful, harassing... defamatory...hateful...and disparaging."

The rules also state the websites will not "knowingly host or publish" objectionable matter and should remove such material within 36 hours of becoming aware that it existed.

Seeking to allay concerns the new rules enabled the Indian Government to regulate content in a highly subjective manner, India's Department of Information Technology, in a separate statement, said the government had no intention of acquiring regulatory jurisdiction over content under these rules.

Referring to concerns the wording used in rules for objectionable content were broad and could be interpreted subjectively, the Department said the terms were in accordance with those used by most Internet platforms as part of their existing policies.

Cyber Security as earlier stated information security is a major concern in Internet usage. The Internet and the increasing use of the digital data has fueled the need for a wide range of security solutions including virtual private networks (VPNs), firewalls, biometric devices, file encryption, and advanced network monitoring.

Current third wave of technologies and ongoing and overlapping 6th and 7th communication revolutions are marked by speedy progress in Internet—the broadband and its products. There is wide focus on Internet of things (IoT) creating more widespread technologies and applications. This has created the issues of 'Net Neutrality'.

Internet is fast expanding. It is no longer a fad but it is becoming essentials of business as more and more businesses are utilizing Internet technology as essential office fixture for information gathering, collaboration, publicity, customer service, and on-line shopping, etc.

Now there is a revolutionary way to send documents and files quickly and securely over the Internet through UPS document exchange. At exchange you can access software that lets you address any digital file, choose the level of security you need, and send from your desktop. You get tracking and delivery confirmation; your recipient gets a universally readable file. Neither of you have to wait for delivery, stand by fax machine, or struggle with e-mail attachments (refer Appendix 1a).

To make the WEB ready for business we had to overcome many technological hurdles. Through certain software (necessary) you can use the web to work together, to get to the people or information they need. But it also lets you control who sees what and who can make changes to what they see. These are customized, interactive solutions for corporate intranets and the web. Our vision is web-tone, an Internet that is accessible, reliable, and secure. We are providing the bandwidth; you need to deliver new access speed and services.

The culture of Internet has touched the imagination of people everywhere. Suddenly, the Internet in everyday parlance, featured in talk shows, in special business 'technology' section of newspapers, etc. If the Internet is a new world of social behavior; it is also a new world for those who study social behavior. Researchers are thinking about the social processes of electronic communication and its effects on the society. For some, the emergence of new communication technologies represents a new perspective on social and behavioral processes of longstanding interest in their disciplines. Others want to draw on social science theories to understand technology. A third group holds a more activist program seeking guidance through research to improve social interventions using technology in domains such as education, mental health, work productivity, etc. The researchers highlight the human side of electronic communication and Internet. This also illustrates how scientists are thinking about the social processes and effects of electronic communication designs, applications, and policies. Many social media channels have developed through Internet facilitation and affect the social and human behavior processes in many ways through such connectivity.

Social Media Platforms: Internet facilitates social media channels which not only connect people socially and professionally but overtime have become multifunctional. The innovative technologies platforms of social media have profound influence on society; these have amazing network effects.

A few social media platforms are sites, Facebook, Twitter, LinkedIn, MySpace, Instagram, YouTube (through Google), etc. These are used for social, cultural, education, economic, professional, jobs and careers, political, development and governance. These have changed paradigms of media in the digital age; creating issues and changing perspectives. Overtime there is rise in social media channels, usage and different perspectives and influences. A new world information and media order is in the process of establishing on its own without any help of developed countries regimes, it is happening as natural process caused by technology and people's freedom they have got to unite with each other barring any border in the world.

Social media platforms like Twitter and Facebook have enabled everyone to voice their opinions and share their views on various topics, ranging from socio-political issues to market and investment ideas. The unregulated and untamable nature of the Internet has given the masses a ground to exercise their right to freedom of speech and expression without worrying about censorship. Since besides social networking, social media platforms have become multifunctional and delivering more organized information; many new specialized job-roles have come up such as Social Media Consultants helping the companies for marketing strategies through social media. In fact, it has become so specialized that a whole lot of jobs associated with have come up such as: social media digital content writer: In technology age, corporates are committed to leverage content on the web to start conversations and build communities. The power of content is to initiate an exchange of views and ideas among target audiences across verticals. This power is rooted in the medium itself because unlike traditional media where you read or listen, in the digital world you engage. This is promoted by technology journalists and backed by a strong team of writers, designers and technologists who understand content, media platforms and technologies. They have ability to combine online, social and mobile platforms to build communities for new media products. This is achieved through a vigorous process for content creation, organization and management. Creating strategy and work with social media team to improve the image of client on the web.

Social media analytic manages the social engagement across verticals, building conversations around content and engaging communities, ensuring constant engagement through response management, creating and sharing key metrics for SMM activities, monitoring social media activities and creating online communities and analysis. Social media analytics tools are social media marketing: The economics of social media, business tool, marketing and advertising. Based on research, derive insights on what motivates your brands' audiences and accordingly device an effective strategic plan to communicate and engage with them regularly. Brainstorm creative ideas to plan and design creative content and campaigns. Plan and execute platform wise campaigns based on the core brand strategy to attract and engage with the audiences on the digital medium. Monitor, listen and respond to users in the "Social" space. Execute effective integrated campaigns using social media, conventional mass media, on-ground activation's, apps, virtual reality, video content, etc. Monitor trends in digital, social media tools, applications, channels, design and strategy. Interact with clients to present the digital strategy, execution plans and also to review the effectiveness of the executed campaigns.

Social media has revolutionized marketing by forcing the analog and various digital media by outsourcing the process to end users by forcing companies to focus on consumer needs. Consumers are empowered today by social media; we need to take new perspective to marketing. Consumer empowerment improve products, companies may face scrutiny over even insignificant decisions such as when Gap; changed its logo. The good news is when companies have good products; they can harness social media to pedal it in the market to their advantage. The grassroots marketing revolution: the increasing popularity of social media has created accountability in brands.

Many companies use twitter as a form of customer service to solve customers, problems raised by them through Twitter.

Businesses get direct connections with consumers at no cost through Facebook and Twitter. As part of their business model, both these companies have created solutions to help markets connect with broader audience which is lucrative to marketers. Corporates use social networks, blogs, microblogs and forums to win new business. According to a survey even increasing number of Indian companies are using social media as an effective business tool. 83 percent corporates agreeing that without social media activity, marketing strategies cannot be successful.

For brands and consumers, mobile is increasingly becoming the primary screen of choice; have a mobile app and a mobile-friendly website. As more digital natives enter the market and smartphones become ubiquitous, this is not surprising. 80 percent of the brands surveyed advertise on web, social and mobile. Digital ad spending is expected to grow faster than other marketing channels. Brands are taking a more holistic approach. Brands and customers feel that regular engagement and customer servicing on social media are the best ways to promote engagement and conversion. However, customers it seems value referrals more than brands' that focus on exclusive promotions for fans.

Social Media for Business

TCS's Global Trend Report explores how 11 global consumer industries and large firms in the world's four largest economic regions are using social media. This is the fourth report TCS has published since 2011.

Companies across the globe, including India, will spend an average \$19 million (₹ 119 crore) on social media this year, according to global study by IT services TCS 2016. According to the Mumbai-headquartered company's Global Trend Report on social media, this average spending will rise to \$24 million (about ₹ 150 crore) by 2015. "Companies will spend an average of nearly \$19 million per company this year on social media and will increase that to \$24 million by 2015," said the report titled "Mastering Digital Feedback: How the best consumer companies use social media". Most consumer companies have become serious about social media in just the last three years, it added. Only 10 percent of enterprises are realizing significant improvements to their business as a result of social media investments. Despite the hype and increased investments, it seems that enterprises are still struggling to make the most of social media, the TCS report said. "Despite ready availability of digitized consumer to consumer interactions in social media, its use by companies is today largely limited to being a mechanism for B2C marketing," TCS Vice-President and Global Head (Digital Enterprise) Satya Ramaswamy said. It is time the companies took a multi-layered approach to social media and learnt to harness its power across enterprise in critical revenue drivers like new product design by incorporating feedback from social media in these important business functions, he added. Media and entertainment industry has the highest percentage of firms using social media, while insurance is relatively new to it, the report said. Social media are business aspects of the entertainment and media industry.

Market research firm 'Research Now' surveyed 655 respondents from mostly $1 billion plus consumer companies in June and July 2016, the average revenue of which was $15.6 billion (median of $4.9 billion), it added. "56 per cent of respondents have measured the return on social media investments and most of them say it has been positive," the report said. Marketing and customer service are the functions that most regularly view consumers' comments on social media, it added. "The three biggest success factors for using social media effectively are protecting consumer data, having a corporate culture that values consumer opinions and responding rapidly to consumers who have issues about a company or its products," the report said. It further said that since 2010, 64 percent of the firms covered have assigned at least one full-time equivalent (FTE) to use public social networks like Facebook, Twitter and LinkedIn.

Crowd Funding through Social Media: Crowd-funding typically involves young entrepreneurs and small groups of people raising funds for their ventures through various online platforms involving individuals and organisations.

Social Media for e-Governance

Social media channel twitter is being used for governance in India as well as other countries including prime ministers, presidents, ministers and diplomats.

"In India, telecom and postal service users can now file complaints with the government directly on telecom operator and DOP immediately for quick resolution and better service. The platform will also address grievances raised against private players. Twitter Sewa platform is being used as social media platform. Complaints received against any telecom operator and Department of Post (DOP) or Twitter handle will be communicated to the concerned by Railway, External Affairs and Commerce Ministry. The social media giant is in discussion with the Home Ministry, Health Ministry, MyGov, etc. for bringing them on to this platform."

Social Media and Politics: Social media has become diplomacy's second self, "a significant other", according to a recent report by Burson-Marsteller, a global PR company. Social media, Twitter in particular, has become a diplomatic weathervane as well as a research kit to analyse global trends. According to the report, today social media has become the first and foremost thought of world leaders, governments, diplomats, and civil society groups. Savvy diplomats feel that social media provides them with a platform for unrestricted communication with targeted groups.

Can cyber diplomacy replace the role of traditional diplomats? What do diplomats do? They do public diplomacy, of which cyber diplomacy is a newer version, to create goodwill and shape the international political and social environment. They do network building for information gathering and create country specific knowledge to advance trade and economic interests. Most of all they try to solve the political problematic issues. "A wicked problem is difficult to solve or unsolvable because of its complexities, because of its co-dependence on other problems, because of unknown factors impacting it, so that when you try to solve it, other problems emerge and the problem becomes more complicated. Some wicked problems such as nuclear deals, Middle East wars, bokoHaram problems are unsolvable, but what is unsolvable today might find a solution in the future.

People tell me on the one hand "it's great you played such a big role in the Arab spring, but it is also kind of scary because you enable all this sharing and collect information on people," said Zuckerberg, Facebook "But it's hard to have one without the other.... You can't isolate some things you like about the Internet and control other things that you don't" Schmidt sounded a similar note earlier when he told the assembly: "Technology will move faster than governments, so don't legislate before you understand the consequences."

To counter terrorism: Twitter and Facebook helping counter terrorism. According to a Quartz report, Facebook has posted a job description on its site for one counter-terrorism researcher. "The candidate will be responsible for helping drive our efforts around identifying the latest tools, tactics, and infrastructure used by terrorist actors as they affect Facebook and its ecosystems to better defend against and disrupt these threats," the posting read. In addition to the account suspensions, Twitter's global Public Policy team has expanded its partnerships with organizations working to counter violent extremism (CVE) online. According to a latest study by the US-based Brookings Institution, IS supporters may be operating over 46,000 active Twitter accounts.

Social Media in Schools/Classrooms Education: Public schools are trying if they should use Facebook or Twitter about school issues. There should be rules/policies how teachers, employees, schools should communicate through social media. They need to educate faculty, staff and the public on the ramification of social networking and Internet sites for any school communications.

The challenge is to balance the benefits of social media to personalize learning such as class Facebook page, while limiting the potentials for personal relationships. They have to make sure students are safe. Technology is expanding but they have to make sure we are using it appropriately and responsibly.

No matter what medium of communication teacher selects, he/she should adhere to teacher-student boundaries, a role model to student.

Tami Blumenfield's case study, "Student-Directed Blended Learning with Facebook Groups and Streaming Media: Media in Asia at Furman University," asks what happens when students in an general education course are allowed the freedom to explore a broad topic (media in Asia) in a self-directed fashion, and are then asked to share their insights and analyses through face-to-face activities and Facebook-based group discussions.

Excerpt from the Study: "By using technologies that students are comfortable with like Facebook, faculty can create a powerful learning environment through the merging of the creative, collaborative, social, and interactive capabilities of this powerful platform. Also, using Facebook in a course offered unique engagement and a different way of knowing." Sixteen students reported that Facebook and the independent emphasis of the course had a very positive or somewhat positive effect on their learning at the course mid-point, and students reported this at the end of the course.

Use in Journalism/Media Education: Emphasize social responsibility when addressing the social media. It is a key component as the social media are a new frontier.

Social Media Healthcare

We recently published this guideline on social media at Beth Israel Deaconess Medical Center (BIDMC) based on the input from a multidisciplinary working group. It might be useful to share with the community, since many healthcare organizations are at the early stage developing social media policies. To maintain our integrity, BIDMC follows the same social media guidelines as the universal online community. This means we do not delete negative posts. The only thing worse than ignoring a negative comment is deleting it. It only serves to anger the patient/consumer more and give them reason to react by telling all of their "friends" on social media about their experience. The exception is when a negative post uses hateful, obscene or discriminatory language. We do not ask for feedback or reviews from patients. BIDMC monitors all sites 24/7 using a social media dashboard.

To maintain our integrity, BIDMC follows the same social media guidelines as the universal online community. This means we do not delete negative posts; the only thing worse than ignoring a negative comment is deleting it. It only serves to anger the patient/consumer more and give them reason to react by telling all of their "friends" on social media about their experience. The exception is when a negative post uses hateful, obscene or discriminatory language.

We do not ask for feedback or reviews from patients. Sites like Yelp have rules. One among them: "Business owners should not ask customers to write reviews. Review sites work because consumers voluntarily write reviews." This is why Yelp, Healthgrades, etc. are able to provide consumers with as much trustworthy information as possible. Research has shown that when the consumer realizes that reviews and feedback have been solicited or influenced, they stop using it.

Sites like Yelp have rules. One among them: "Business owners should not ask customers to write reviews. Review sites work because consumers voluntarily write reviews." This is why Yelp, Healthgrades, etc. are able to provide consumers with as much trustworthy information as possible. Research has shown that when the consumer realizes that reviews and feedback have been solicited or influenced, they stop using it.

Why do consumers interact with an organization's social site?

In general, there is a perception gap between the reasons consumers interact with companies on social sites and why the companies think they do (*Source*: IBM Report: From Social Media to Social CRM).

After discounts and purchases (not applicable to BIDMC), consumers-ranked reviews and product rankings, general information and exclusive information as the top reasons they follow a company.

Companies ranked learning about new products, general information, sharing opinions, and reviews and product rankings as the top reasons they think consumers follow them on social sites.

Reviews and rankings are important to consumers, so we track and respond to all reviews/messages we receive. The reviews are also a great way to capture feedback about patient experience on an ongoing basis.

We receive reviews on all our social media sites. Some are informal, like a tweet. Some are formal reviews, like on Facebook, Yelp, Google+, etc.

How do we Respond to Reviews?

We respond to all messages—both praise and criticism. When we receive a complaint, we respond ASAP. We don't make excuses. ("We were short staffed" or "It was an unusually busy day.") We apologize for the experience. We have had a few instances when a physician has felt strongly about apologizing. Some physicians are of the opinion that apologizing is an admission of error, which could lead to lawsuits. We believe that enhancing communication reduces malpractice assertions, not increases that.

The marketing team along with patient relations has established a process to manage complaints/negative reviews. Our standard response in most cases is: "We are sorry that your experience didn't live up to the high standards we set for ourselves. We will forward your message to our Patient Relations team. If you'd like to contact them directly, please call...".

What does a physician need to be aware of BIDMC's social media policy?

There is risk associated with the use of social media because any content posted can reflect unfavorably on the physician as well as on BIDMC. A post conveys information about the user's personality, values, priorities, etc. To avoid errors and prevent risks, BIDMC has created a set of guidelines to help our physicians navigate the world of social media. The full policy is available on the portal. Here are some highlights:

Physicians cannot accept friend requests from patients.

If a physician engages in a discussion about the hospital on a social site, she/he should disclose that they work at BIDMC. On personal feeds, if discussing BIDMC, clarify that the posts do not express the views of the hospital.

Physicians cannot offer healthcare advice on social sites.

Physicians must respect and follow HIPAA requirements. She/he can never disclose information about a BIDMC patient.

She/he cannot endorse products on social media.

Physicians must never disclose proprietary information about BIDMC. BIDMC does not allow individual departments to open social media accounts. On rare occasions, Twitter or LinkedIn accounts are allowed. The request to open a social media account must be approved by the Social Media Policy Committee.

India: Internet Scenario Third Technology Wave

India also experienced the exposure to Internet and its associated features in its initial stages globally. Internet was more urban based, used by technology savvy people and who could afford it. But overtime through 3rd and 4th communication revolutions it was getting widespread with increase in computerization and telecommunication progress. In third wave of technology, there was less digital divide and more progress with worldwide trend.

With increased 4G and 3G penetration, the Internet user base in India is rapidly expanding and has reached a penetration of over 27% versus 50.3% penetration in China and expected to double to 600 million users by 2020 from 343 million users currently, according to an ASSOCHAM-Deloitte joint study.

India Internet user is expected to almost double to 600 million users by 2020 from approximately 343 million users currently. Going forward, rural adoption of data-enabled devices is expected to increase with the Bharat Net initiative under Digital India, reveals ASSOCHAM-Deloitte joint study.

Currently, over 55,000 villages remain deprived of mobile connectivity. This is largely due to the fact that providing mobile connectivity in such locations is not commercially viable for service providers, adds the study.

Challenges in policy, such as taxation, right of way, restrictive regulations, etc. are major roadblocks in realizing the vision of Digital India. Some of the common policy hurdles include the following lack of clarity in FDI policies; for instance, have impacted the growth of e-commerce.

Implementation of the Digital India program has been hampered by contracting challenges such as the projects assigned to PSUs are delayed given challenges related to skills, experience and technical capabilities.

Several RFPs issued by the government are not picked up by competent private sector organizations since they are not commercially feasible. Reports suggest that, as recently as 2014, nearly 70% of Indian consumers indicated that lack of awareness was the main reason for not using Internet services.

With the proliferation of cloud-based services like DigiLocker, data security has emerged as a major challenge. The recent data breach in August 2016, in which debit card data for more than 3.2 million subscribers was stolen, highlights the importance of implementing foolproof security systems.

A uniform RoW policy across all states with a reasonable cost structure is required along with a single window mechanism for granting RoW permissions.

PPP models need to be explored for sustainable development of digital infrastructure, as has been the case for civic infrastructure projects like roads and metro project.

Effective collaboration with the private sector is critical to the development of the digital infrastructure. Innovative engagement models that ensure commercial viability needs to developed jointly through consultation with industry bodies. This will encourage private sector participation and ensure a better response to infrastructure RFPs. In addition, startups need to be incentivized for the development of the last mile infrastructure and localized services and applications.

In rural and remote areas, private sector players should be incentivized to provide last mile connectivity. USOF can be effectively used to incentivize and create a viable business model. The deployment of funds so far has been erratic and not been used to effectively to fund the cost of infrastructure creation in rural areas.

Satellite communication solutions could be used to speed up broadband access in rural and remote areas. For instance, banks can use VSAT technology to connect remote ATMs, remote branches that need instant access to customer data. It could be used as a last mile connectivity solution in rural areas which lack telecom networks, highlighted the study.

For the success of the Digital India program, capacity building is crucial. In addition to infrastructure development, digital literacy, skill building and higher adoption of digital solutions is key to program success, said the study.

Despite rising smartphone penetration and Internet user base, digital literacy in India has been low. In order for the benefits of the Digital India program to reach all sections of the population, improving digital literacy is imperative. A strong skill base is required to support the initiatives and services that are envisaged under the Digital India umbrella.

India is the second largest mobile phone market globally with over one billion mobile subscriptions. Of this, smartphone users account for approximately 240 million subscriptions which is expected to grow to 520 million by 2020.

Spectrum availability in Indian metros is about a tenth of the same in cities in developed countries. This has put a major roadblock in providing high speed data services. Public Wi-Fi penetration remains low. Globally, there is one Wi-Fi hotspot for every 150 citizens. For India to reach that level of penetration, over eight million hotspots are required of which only about 31,000 hotspots are currently available, reveals the study. Currently, over 55,000 villages remain deprived of mobile connectivity. This is largely due to the fact that providing mobile connectivity in such locations is not commercially viable for service providers.

Reports suggest that, as recently as 2014, nearly 70% of Indian consumers in urban areas indicated that lack of awareness was the main reason for not using Internet services. Non-availability of digital services in local languages is also a major concern, adds the joint study.

According to a research study jointly conducted by the Internet and Mobile Association of India (IAMAI) and the Indian Market Research Bureau (IMRB) 2016, the number of Internet users in rural India will swell to 5.4 million in 2010, translating into a 30 per cent growth, primarily driven by farmers going online to check their e-mail. Active Internet users are those which have gone online in the last 30 days. The study also reveals that after communications, 67 per cent of rural users' access music and video over the Internet.

About 48 per cent of the people claim to have used the Internet for educational research and 42 per cent claim they used it for general information search. The report further highlights that about 13 per cent of the people use the Internet for knowing more about latest farming techniques and 8 per cent of the people use the Internet to find out more about fertilizers and pesticides.

"This is an important point to note considering the importance of farming in rural India. If there are Internet-related initiatives with farming as a focus, these could certainly trigger Internet literacy to rise faster," the report added.

Therefore as we discuss later the importance of rural Internet connectivity is being tackled on war footing by government, Microsoft, Google and Facebook.

Since 2015, Facebook is using the old cable operator model to get *Express Wi-Fi* working. Facebook works with the local entrepreneur with technology, business solutions and marketing to bring Wi-Fi to areas where connectivity is scarce. This model is implemented in over a 100 villages across India, and users have to come to a community area to access the Internet. Facebook has created the commercially available Wi-Fi access point technology with their software. A local entrepreneur can help users electronically buy Internet usage for as low as

₹ 10. It is "working with carriers, internet service providers and local entrepreneurs to help expand connectivity to underserved locations around the world".

Facebook did not indicate if the Wi-Fi would provide limited access to a few websites, like its Free Basics, or full access. Facebook's target with this is entry-level phones and there are no restrictions on what websites can be accessed on this Wi-Fi network. Facebook is only creating the Wi-Fi access point for users; it still uses local Internet service providers for the data. Essentially, Facebook's technology helps with the last mile connectivity where it is not available. Facebook is just the technology enabler when it comes to Express Wi-Fi. It should be noted that Express Wi-Fi is part of Facebook's larger Internet.org mission, which aims to bring Internet connectivity across the world, especially in areas where it has not been possible. Free Basics was also part of this Internet.org mission. Facebook has also been testing Express Wi-Fi in other parts of the world.

Facebook is experimenting with products like laser drones to enhance Internet connectivity for users across the world. The spokesperson said Express Wi-Fi customers could purchase fast, reliable and affordable data packs via digital vouchers to access the Internet on the Express Wi-Fi network. "We focus on building a sustainable economic model for all stakeholders involved, so that local retailer entrepreneurs, ISPs, operators and Facebook can continue to invest in and operate lasting connectivity. We believe a sustainable economic model is the one which can scale to bring all of India online". It had pulled the plug on its controversy-ridden Free Basics program in India in February 2016 after telecom regulator TRAI-barred operators from charging discriminatory rates for Internet access based on content. Facebook continues to run this program, launched in 2014, across many countries. The service was launched in India in partnership with Reliance Communications as Internet.org.

Broadband: Qualcomm is also pitching its low earth orbit satellite system that the chip maker is building with partners like Virgin Group under the OneWeb to offer broadband services. "The whole idea behind it is to provide mobile broadband to places in the world where it is very hard to get broadband coverage, which aligns very much with his (PM Narendra Modi's) ideas behind connecting people and communities. And even the smart cities aspect," Jacobs of Qualcomm met Modi to discuss issues pertaining to the telecom industry and enhancing partnership for government initiatives like Digital India and Make in India (2016).

Today consumer is the deciding factor. So let him decide. Competition is must for any industry to grow. It should be healthy competition. The government and regulators need to keep an eye on what is happening and may have to jump into if they find anything unhealthy. This price cut is the indicator that the telecoms still have the scope of price reduction and they were charging more than required from the consumer.

In 2016, "Airtel is investing across all businesses to provide broadband for all; upgrade existing broadband to make it future proof. Existing Airtel broadband customers can upgrade to V-Fiber by replacing their old modems with new modems. V-Fiber is based on vectorisation, a broadband technology which will enable superfast data speeds, HD video streaming and uploads in a multi-device environment. This latest technological step is part of Airtel's transformation initiative called Project Leap.

'Rural Information Network' Digital Divide

Digital-divide necessitates a response that encompasses fibers, computers, and the switches but also the development of the soft infrastructure required for building knowledge economies including education, cyber law, and modern regulatory institutions. Developing countries have to face the new challenges and opportunities offered by information revolution particularly Internet.

Other necessary and significant social applications of ICTs are 'Rural Information Network'. These need to be created using Internet technology for employment, education and empowerment of the villages in India particularly and other developing countries in general. It is fundamental to service industries as well as to rural development.

Efforts should be about making sure that technology becomes the great equalizer of our society. Technology can be a great enabler and you can do things more efficiently and transparently.

Maharashtra Government will be investing over ₹ 5,000 crore for taking high-speed Internet connectivity to each of the 29,000 villages in the state by 2018. "By 2018, we want to take fiber to each and every village. Once connectivity is established, we can use it for lot of applications ranging from education to healthcare to government services," Special Purpose Vehicle (SPV) will be formed with private companies as partners, who shall ensure that the project gets completed in time. "We are creating not just smart cities, but also smart villages."

There are "challenge areas", typically rural areas in developing countries, where private investments will not provide infrastructure for Next Generation Access networks. The governments have to support and provide these otherwise. Consequentially, some citizens are deprived of what digital markets can offer because of not having access to networks and affordability factor, but it will also affect the wider economy of the country.

Hence, the question arises whether operators should be given specific regulatory incentives to support their NGA deployment (for examples, co-investment models, or regulatory support for demand aggregation, etc.).

We should be extremely attentive to all possible options to exploit synergies, among all the possible stakeholders, both public and private. Recent Directive on Cost-Reduction measures for broadband deployment is a clear example.

Ongoing intense efforts in 2015-16 are being made by Microsoft, Google, Facebook and Oneweb through their projects, White Spaces & Loon, Facebook Express Wi-Fi, and Oneweb through satellites to provide Internet connectivity in rural areas. Jet Airways launched in Dec. 2016 its inflight wireless streaming technology, later being developed inflight Wi-Fi.

Google Project Loon is a research and development project being developed by X (formerly Google X) with the mission of providing Internet access to rural and remote areas. The project uses high-altitude balloons placed in the stratosphere at an altitude of about 18 km (11 mi) to create an aerial wireless network with up to 4G-LTE speeds. It was named Project Loon, since even Google itself found the idea of providing Internet access to the remaining five billion populations unprecedented and "crazy".

The balloons are maneuvered by adjusting their altitude in the stratosphere to float to a wind layer after identifying the wind layer with the desired speed and direction using wind data from the National Oceanic and Atmospheric Administration (NOAA). Users of the service connect to the balloon network using a special Internet antenna attached to their building. The signal travels through the balloon network from balloon to balloon, then to a ground-based station connected to an Internet service provider (ISP), then onto the global Internet. The system aims to bring Internet access to remote and rural areas poorly served by existing provisions, and to improve communication during natural disasters to affected regions. Key people involved in the project include Rich DeVaul, chief technical architect, who is also an expert on wearable technology; Mike Cassidy, a project leader; and Cyrus Behroozi, a networking and telecommunication lead. The balloons use patch antennas—which are directional antennas—to transmit signals to ground stations or LTE users. Some smartphones with Google SIM cards can use Google Internet services. The whole infrastructure is based on LTE; the eNodeB component (the equivalent of the "base station" that talks directly to handsets) is carried in the balloon.

Facebook is in talks with Internet service providers (ISPs) to expand its Express Wi-Fi program into a commercial launch in India, having completed a pilot roll out of 125 rural public Wi-Fi hotspots in a tie-up with state-run Bharat Sanchar Nigam Ltd. Express Wi-Fi is a Mark Zuckerberg-headed Internet giant's initiative aimed at taking affordable broadband to the rural areas of the country in partnerships with Internet service companies and small entrepreneurs. "We are testing Express Wi-Fi program in India currently that allows customers to purchase fast, reliable and affordable data packages from their local ISP to access the Internet via local hotspots," a Facebook India spokesperson said. Facebook, however, did not reveal the names of service providers that it is in discussions with, and has left it to its partners to come up with a scalable business model. The social media company on its part has developed customized software for rural markets which will help ISPs and/or entrepreneurs to run a business within their localities, helping bridge coverage gaps in the India's rural cellular data networks. "Facebook is investing in the development of the connectivity ecosystem by providing techno-commercial assistance to local ISP partners and entrepreneurs".

Facebook's previous initiative to connect the unconnected through Free Basics had to be pulled out from India after the telecom regulator banned discriminatory pricing of data services, which included zero-rated services.

Oneweb by Softbank Japan is making 720 satellites and putting in the orbit for Internet; to connect Internet to rural and unconnected areas in the world. It will be also providing to India soon announced in Dec. 2016. In this business endeavor; Softbank is partnering with Airbus, Qualcomm, Virgin group and Intelsat.

Jet Airways launch of its inflight wireless streaming technology through which passengers can stream content directly on their own devices such as mobile phones, tablets and laptops. Jetscreen will be available on domestic flights. It includes 220 hours of video and audio content such as Hollywood and Indian movies, TV shorts, music from multiple genres, interactive games, as well as children's programs. The introduction of streaming is the first step in Jet Airways' plan to eventually transform its inflight entertainment experience into a full-fledged, broadband-enabled Wi-Fi connectivity which will allow passengers to surf the Internet, send emails, browse social media, get connecting flight information, real time travel services and destination deals, it said in a release (Sept. 2016).

Constraints in India: Google's Loon project uses big balloons floating at an altitude of 20 kilometers for transmission of Internet services. The technology, used for 4G services in India, has the potential to replace mobile towers as it can directly transmit signals on 4G mobile phones. Each balloon can cover a diameter of 40 km on the ground. Further, there are security issues too that the home and civil aviation ministries have pointed out. Both the projects require spectrum assigned. Mobile operators are opposed to any assignment as they are granted the same via auctions. Government is also trying to do the same through its NOFN project.

However, in practice, there are no white spaces in India. According to a recent IIT Bombay study, more than 80% of the TV UHF band IV (470-585 MHz) is totally free and lying unused. This means what is referred to as white spaces are only free and unused spectrum and does not fall under the definition of white spaces. The answer to the next logical question—to why this unused spectrum is not being used for mobile telephony technology—is that currently the International Telecommunications Union has not recognized this band as a cellular technology band so equipment and handsets compatible with it are not being manufactured.

Industrial Internet

TCS announced that it has developed an innovative digital solution to connect Intelligent LEDs, to GE's Predix operating system for the industrial Internet through Intel Atom-based gateways, providing critical analytics to save significant time and costs in the manufacturing process.

Reliance Industries (RIL) announced the signing of a global partnership agreement in the Industrial IOT space whereby RIL and GE will work together to build out joint applications on GE's Predix platform. The partnership marks the coming together of two of the world's largest industrial conglomerates to provide Industrial IOT solutions to customers in oil and gas, fertilizer, power, healthcare, telecom and other industries. The announcement was made (17 November 2016).

GE will provide its Predix cloud offering, Industrial Internet applications and data science expertise. RIL will develop solutions on Predix as an Independent Software Vendor (ISV), bringing to bear its over 30 years of data, process and operational expertise. RIL will also offer nationwide connectivity infrastructure to customers through a 4G network powered by Jio. GE would offer the security, availability and monitoring aspects of the platform to RIL and its customers. The potential for other revenue streams includes telecom, healthcare and agriculture (Capital Market—Live News 18 Nov. 2016).

"When I talk about the Industrial Internet, it's about capturing data of the machines, turning it back into valuable insight for our customers and that's going to be worth trillions of dollars in the economy and I think it's going to transform GE," the company's CEO Jeff Immelt said at a 2015 conference of Business Insider. "We've got a digital thread that's running throughout the company...it is probably the most exciting thing I've worked on in 30 years."

GE is focusing on industrial IoT and the creation of GD Digital—which aims to be among the five largest technology businesses by 2020. GE has tied up with Microsoft, Intel, and Huawei to hasten the rollout of its IoT initiatives.

Net Neutrality is the principle that Internet service providers and governments regulating the Internet should treat all data on the Internet the same, not discriminating or charging differentially by user, content, website, platform, application, type of attached equipment, or mode of communication.

Net neutrality (i) means Internet that allows everyone to communicate freely. It means a service provider should allow access to all content and applications regardless of the source and no websites or pages should be blocked, as long as they aren't illegal. It's like a fixed-telephone line, which is equal to all, and no one gets to decide who you call or what you speak. (ii) Another aspect of net neutrality is level playing field on the Internet. This means all websites can co-exist without hampering others. All websites are accessible at the same speed and no particular website of application is favored. For instance—like electricity is common for all. (iii) Net neutrality also means all websites and content creators are treated equal, and you don't have to pay extra for faster Internet speed to a particular site/service.

If there is no net neutrality, ISPs can then create slow as well as fast Internet lanes, which will mean all websites cannot be accessed at the same speed and one can do so only on paying an additional sum. For instance, currently, you have a standard data package and access all the content at the same speed, irrespective of whether it is an international website or domestic. Similarly, ISPs can also charge extra for the free calls you make using services like WhatsApp, Skype and others, and eventually the load of additional payable sum by the OTT (over the top) players will be pushed onto consumers. On the other hand, with the increasing popularity of instant messaging apps like WhatsApp, Viber and others, telecoms are losing revenue. In India, they had wanted a fee imposed on popular OTT services as well VOIP calls. TRAI rejected telecoms' proposal to do so.

Airtel to increase its revenue, started 'Airtel Zero marketing platforms' that allows users to access apps of participating app developers (in this case Flipkart) at zero data charges; a similar platform was announced by Facebook-Reliance partnership in the form of Internet.org. Both violated 'net neutrality'. In India, the concept of net neutrality doesn't exist legally. However, ISPs try moderately not to violate any laws.

Net Neutrality is extremely important for small business owners, startups and entrepreneurs in India, who can simply launch their businesses online, advertise the products and sell them openly, without any discrimination. It is essential for innovation and creating job opportunities.

Net neutrality is very important for freedom of speech, so that one can voice their opinion without the fear of being blocked or banned.

Still government in many countries such as China and others practice Internet censorship. In India New 'IT Rules 2011' supplements the IT Act 2000 for Internet censorship.

These rules made it mandatory for Internet intermediaries to remove objectionable content within 36 hours of receiving complaint. But the terms included were vague and open to interpretations. In 2011, government also asked major sites like Google, Facebook and Yahoo to 'pre-screen' content and remove any objectionable, defamatory content from going live. Government requests for banning content have also been on rise over the past couple of years.

The Telecom Commission has approved phase II of *Bharat Net* which will digitally connect 1,50,000 Gram Panchayats (GPS) by September 2018. By March end, we will complete phase I, which entails connecting 1,00,000 GPS; 70,000 GPS in the second phase will have underground fiber, 48,000 will have overhead fiber (hilly areas); 2,000 GPSes will be connected through satellite (in forests) and 30,000 will be wireless. This is a more flexible and area-based strategy to ensure timely implementation. Secondly, implementation will be both through private and public sector. Also, certain reforms are needed in the assignment and allocation of backhaul spectrum and the use of spectrum in higher frequency bands, basically 3 GHz. It will also consider if it can make better utilization of lower band spectrum for rural broadband; say, in spectrum bands lower than 700 MHz. Also, it is further needed to improve infrastructure in the Northeast and far-flung areas where mobile connectivity is problematic. Telecom Commission will also look to auction all the spectrum left unsold in the last sale, including in the 700 MHz band, and will send a reference back to TRAI (Telecom Regulatory Authority of India) for pricing. State Governments, central public sector undertakings, private sector firms like L&T, Sterlite, and private telecom operators will lay the fiber together on a build-and-share model. We will work out the details to see whether the partnering telco, which is the building partner, should get some advantage over other teleco. Private telecom operators will build say 20,000 kms a year. Through this partnership, they will be able to build six lakh kms, use it as well as make money by leasing out.

Now, on an average, each operator holds about 25 MHz of spectrum (per circle), 40 per cent more than before and, with consolidation in future, the holdings should increase to international levels. Formulating and promulgating Rights of Way (RoW) is another big reform. So, now it will be a priority for states to align their policy to the RoW rules for setting up of infrastructure, which is more towers and more fiber. Finally, the virtual network operator (VNO) permits would be given out. For consumers, a system of Aadhaar-based KYC is being allowed. Telecom Commission abolished the wireless operating license also.

The significance of abolition of the wireless operating license is when a BTS (base station) is set up, each company has to revalidate its licenses that require a lot of paperwork and time before a BTS can start radiating. Telcoes are setting up 2,50,000 BTSes this year. Now when the license is abolished, if the infrastructure is in place, a BTS can start functioning (2015-16).

India Network readiness: India slipped two positions to 91 among 139 countries on the World Economic Forum's "networked readiness index", a parameter that measures how economies use opportunities offered by information technology and communications for increased competitiveness and well-being. According to the WEF's 'Global information technology report 2016,' affordability has long been one of the strengths of the Indian ICT ecosystem, with the country ranking 8th this year. "A deep divide persists between well-connected metropolitan hubs and remote rural areas, where even the most basic infrastructure is insufficient." The report mentioned India's ambitious Digital India program which aims to provide citizen services online, and added, "India's performance in terms of providing online services and allowing e-participation has so far been in line with that of peer countries, but far from the global best (57th and 40th, respectively)," it said. Lack of infrastructure and low levels of skills among the population remains the key bottlenecks to widespread ICT adoption, especially in terms of individual usage". Report further said that a third of the Indian population is still illiterate and about the same number is not enrolled in secondary education. Only 15 out of 100 households have access to the Internet and mobile broadband remains a privilege of the few, with only 5.5 subscriptions for every 100 people.

The need for new types of leadership, governance and behaviors necessitated by a growing and changing digital economy was also highlighted. A critical ingredient for the success and sustainability of the emerging system will be governance frameworks, which allow societies to anticipate and shape the impact of emerging technologies and react quickly to changing circumstances.

Terming technology as a tool to progress, the Minister (IT) said "from 20 to 30 years from now things would completely change lives with digital disruption impacting lives in a big way. Example, we have a target to cut travel bills by 50 per cent. Video conferencing is more efficient. He said Internet of things (IoT) promises digital realm and a focused approach was needed towards encouraging the IoT. As a nation one should look at more focused Internet usage to able to leverage IoT to impact the various programs of the government of India" (*ET* July 2016).

Mobile Internet access via smartphones can lead to a 50 per cent increase in a small farmer's revenue in India, especially if the correct inputs (read: agricultural information) are used. "Towards a more equal world: the mobile Internet revolution. One per cent increase in yields can lead to a 0.6 per cent-1.3 per cent reduction in poverty in India, having a greater impact than prices alone," said the Vodafone report on the potential of mobile Internet access in developing countries market asymmetries. Small farmers, it says, typically, have limited access to Internet resources, services, information, markets and social networks. Differential access to information has the potential to create an even bigger divide than exists now between rich and poor farmers, in effect, creating a new division between farming communities based on their access to information. The report, however, said access to spectrum in sufficient quantities at market-determined prices is critical for continued investment in mobile broadband networks. It also advocated development of locally-produced information and apps for increasing the usefulness of mobile Internet access; although this can prove a challenge due to the "high cost of creating hyperlocal apps, including those offering detailed agricultural information" (Vodafone report 2016 by independent experts).

Internet of Things (IoT)

The vision of the so-called Internet of things—giving all sorts of physical things a digital makeover has been years ahead of reality. But that gap is closing fast. Today, the range of things being computerized and connected to networks is stunning, from watches, appliances and clothing to cars, jet engines and factory equipment. Even roadways and farm fields are being upgraded with digital sensors. In the last two years, the number of Internet of things devices in the world has surged to nearly 6.4 billion, according to Gartner, a research firm. By 2020, the firm forecasts, the Internet of things population will reach 20.8 billion.

The optimistic outlook is that the IoT will be an enabling technology that will help make the people and physical systems of the world, i.e. health care, food production, transportation, energy consumption—smarter and more efficient.

Internet of things (IoT) is the term used to describe the addition of sensors and chips to machinery which allows them to be monitored and controlled over the Internet.

Kavin Ashton (2010) the man who coined the phrase "Internet of things" highlights that one of the factors in spurt of Internet of things (IoT) is needs of increasing population and its increasing capabilities. It is rapid combination of both. One of the biggest challenges is managing all the information associated with supplying those needs, and that has created demand for IoT, which basically means computer networks that gather information about the world via sensors. Information technology always follows supply chain changes.

A new generation of scientists and engineers is rising up and gaining power in the workforce, and they are the ones that fully grasp the importance and inevitability of the IoT. To them, the idea that every information system should gather its own data using networked sensors is completely intuitive.

People working in areas such as office administration, support staff and those in maintenance will see their roles being taken over by technology. The new jobs created will be IoT product managers, robot coordinators, industrial programmers and network engineers.

They will give us self-driving cars, self-operating homes and thousands of other imaginative, innovative applications. Many of these breakthroughs in IoT will come from technology startups.

These startups are hoping to cash on the massive market opportunities in IoT. There is rapidly emerging opportunity in the IoT, or devices and objects that send and receive data over the Internet. Rather than build large systems; startups are developing smaller series of IoT-based devices to "smarten" homes.

Evolution and growth of IoT is amazing in the last 15 years. Such products as the proliferation of wireless Internet and mobile broadband cellular networks, the ubiquitous use of GPS, the massive advances in digital imaging and image recognition, and the low cost and high performance of radio frequency identification (RFID) systems, and many more to come all far beyond imagination.

New technologies like the IoT and cognitive computing are enabling such an incredible period of rapid technological change. Enhance our relationship with the physical world making appliances, machines, devices, homes, cars and buildings better, safer, more intuitive and interactive.

We live in an age of immense technological and social change, much of which has been brought about by the emergence of such advanced technologies as cognitive computing, IoT and robotics. In fact, the current pace of change and the potential for further transformation is so great, that many see this as the fourth industrial revolution.

These technologies, powered by cloud computing, are changing the way we live, work, produce and consume—disrupting many of our existing models for business and innovation. Billions of sensors are improving our relationships with the physical world. We are giving objects eyes and ears so they can sense and interact with us better. As a result our relationships with buildings, cities, cars, devices and appliances are being transformed. The challenge is that over next few years, the IoT will become the biggest source of data in the world. That's where cognitive computing comes in. Machine learning and other techniques help us understand this data and turn it into insight which can help automate certain tasks, enable manufacturers to design better products, innovate new services and enable humans to make better decisions. IoT will impact our homes.

A recent McKinsey study estimated that the value of people's time spent doing domestic chores is around $11 trillion today and is expected to climb to over $23 trillion by 2025. That is staggering. IoT-enabled smart home "orchestrators" have the potential to streamline how we manage the home and all the tasks and chores within it. With natural language interfaces, access to all historical home usage data and machine learning features, these orchestrators can truly change how we manage our homes and related home activities.

Within 10 years, IoT will transform the way we manage our lives. There are plenty of data points to back this enthusiasm. In 2008, there were more objects connected to the Internet than people, and technology researcher Gartner forecasts that by 2020 there will be nearly 21 billion connected devices. If the ATM was perhaps the first popular connected device in the early 1970s, hundreds of companies have since shown an interest in getting wired up (2016). In the US technology market in 2016 there is mixed response to IoT. Several startups in the field raised significant amount of funding, including IoT software and services company. There is massive potential at global level. This growth opens up new business opportunities, as half will be attributed to new startups and 80 per cent will be in services, not products. Manufacturing, healthcare and insurance are expected to lead the IoT race. There is a lot of demand from service providers for niche IoT players with intellectual property and platforms. This will help increase the industry's market share. But the addressed market of $2.8 billion, currently, is just a fraction of the overall IoT services market of $66 billion, as companies are not as yet outsourcing their spend.

The major concerns about IoT are Security. The threat landscape has evolved to various IoT devices, tablets and smartphones. With more information being shared than ever before, it's going to be a fight for the security industry to stay ahead of them; we need to invest in zero day attacks, sophisticated tools and capabilities, machine learning, cloud-based tools and solutions to keep us at par with them but it's going to be a challenge. We are investing in a lot of technology tools and capabilities to go after the evolved threat landscape which is full of IoT devices, tons of smartphones, smart personal devices and tablets. For things like IoT, solutions are going to be different, sometimes it is going to be an antivirus, and sometimes it's going to be attacking ransomware or privacy information. We have introduced a product called True Key. It is a biometric password security tool. The app is like a tool to manage your smartphone's security to prompt you about the threats. We are investing in car IT systems. That's a little bit more on the B2B side of the business where we kind of solving the problem. I think from a consumer focus, we are solving it more from the perspective of devices that are going into the vehicle. A lot of times, a vehicle will provide Bluetooth or network connectivity and the third party devices is the intelligence. We are working with car manufacturers to build firewalls and educate the industry on how to build a secure car.

Consumers accustomed to adding security tools to their computers and phones should expect to adopt similar precautions with Internet-connected home appliances.

"If we want to put networked technologies into more and more things, we also have to find a way to make them safer," said Michael Walker, a program manager and computer security expert at the Pentagon's advanced research arm. "It's a challenge for civilization." To help address that challenge, Mr. Walker and the Defense Advanced Research Projects Agency, or DARPA, created a contest with millions of dollars in prize money, called the *Cyber Grand Challenge*. To win, contestants would have to create automated digital defense systems that could identify and fix software vulnerabilities on their own—essentially smart software robots as sentinels for digital security.

Intel product, McAfee Live safe is a cross device product that will manage all of the digital devices you interact with on a daily basis. It's like security as a service wherein you can add your new devices as and when you buy it.

IoT uses cloud-based technology and tools. Intel is doing a lot more now on the cloud front than before which will help work across platforms in a much more seamless way. Client-based technologies are great but as you start getting into other devices, you have to leverage other kinds of technologies to provide some basic security and capabilities around. It is an emerging area and Intel will continue to evolve its technology to support it. Intel is doing a lot for IoT at the chip level and trying to build some of the capabilities in the reference design earlier on in the process.

Intel started working with LG in June of 2014 wherein it embedded its MMS product into all of their G3 smartphones. In 2015, it started with Samsung on the Galaxy 6 which has its AV engine in it. Every galaxy S6, S7, Note 5, Note 7 will come embedded with the McAfee VSM AV engine powering the device. Now it is working together collaborating together on other devices.

Intel Education Digital Wellness Program in India which has been running for over two years now. We have educated over two and a half lakh kids across different states like Karnataka, Haryana, Assam and Tamil Nadu. Intel is going to keep expanding the program. This program is for public and private schools. This program will give training to faculty and students about the importance of digital wellness and ways to be secure online. Moreover, Intel has Cyberm program. The Cybermum blogs about the risks and educates not only kids but also parents about how to stay safe online. Apart from that, Intel has 'Security advice center' which has tons of information on security which is constantly updated and made available for the public for free. There are big startups active in these areas; and globally new arenas are coming up.

Researchers for Level 3 Communications, a telecommunications company, said they had detected several strains of malware that launched attacks on websites from compromised Internet of things devices. Entrepreneurs think startups have a better chance of succeeding in what is still an emerging opportunity. "IoT is a new arena where the nimbleness of a startup allows it to listen to market needs and address them quickly. Startups can bring sharp expertise and stay ahead of heftier competition. IoT is domain specific; it requires significant tech innovation and startups are suited for it. IoT requires seven or eight disciplines, including embedded computing, middleware, big data, cloud, domain knowledge and business consulting, to line up," says Vinay Nathan, CEO and co-founder of Altizon Systems, a developer of IoT platforms and solutions based in Pune. "Over the last couple of years, we have seen them mature and reach workable scale and cost." Rather than build India specific businesses, he thinks startups need to focus on being global in nature. "We need IoT companies that have clients across the world, but with solutions designed and developed in India," he reckons. Companies such as CarIQ may have already started down this road. "Right from addressing the unique needs of Indian market to needs of developed world, we have it all," he says. IoT companies are also benefiting from some other changes in technology and manufacturing. The presence of reputed international electronic manufacturing services and component makers drives international component companies to set up shop in India. "This was largely nonexistent a few years back, the availability of cost-effective solutions and component manufacturing support is driving faster development and adoption of these technologies." In 2016, we are seeing lots of IT companies, manufacturers, medical companies, insurers implementing projects; IoT is emerging from the hype cycle. "This is because of the need for automated intelligent solutions which use analytics for intelligent and predictive behavior". Other entrepreneurs think that India could witness the beginning of a technology wave rather than play catch up, like earlier. Given that IoT is a collection of technologies, businesses can be built in diverse fields such as devices, support, services, consulting and infrastructure.

Few instances: Smartron is building itself as a provider of both IoT platforms and devices for consumers. "We are not building another app...we are building an end-to-end IoT ecosystem," he says. Smartron is weeks away from closing a $25 million round of funding to fuel its plans. Towards the end of the year, we will launch Ultrabook, more smart phones, a gaming platform and Wi-Fi routers." *Home automated solutions*—which allows users to remotely manage temperature, humidity, and lighting and even mimics assorted IR devices (infrared devices that are remote controls for consumer electronics) on one device.

More connected homes are safer homes—especially for the young and elderly. We are in the midst of one of the largest demographic and technological shifts in the history of humanity. Our elderly population is expected to become the largest single age segment in the world by 2050. Our ability to create better outcomes for them while letting them live independently at home is better for patients, caregivers, family, loved ones and health providers as well. Nokia is exploring opportunities to integrate Watson IoT with Nokia's wearables and smart devices for home care. Their goal is a system that helps to detect and alert caregivers to potential problems such as: deviation from daily routines, abnormal vital signs and sudden changes in the home environment. Voice-activated interfaces in the home will be able to take simple commands (such as "call an ambulance") and offer reminders to take medicines or turn off appliances.

IBM's 'personal data network' aims to integrate the different systems within a home including computers, lighting, temperature, and security. For instance, your child comes back from school, turns off the alarm system, which will automatically signal the PC to send you an e-mail at work that your child is home. Or the system will read who is in the room and will take appropriate action; such as adjusting the temperature, playing the CD player and PC. Price-point is too high for these products at this moment for mass appeal. It is the early adopters who are willing to spend more will put this product in place. March 2016 IBM would invest $3 billion over three years in IoT business. It began with the shift of data from The Weather Service's 1,00,000-odd sensors, aircraft and drones to IBM's cloud. Recently, it created the global headquarters of its Watson IoT unit in Munich, creating a team of 1,000 to drive this business.

Bragi has innovated new generation smart earphones *The Dash* which are some of the world's most powerful micro-wearable computers with 27 unique sensors that can measure a user's vital signs while augmenting their communications and interactivity. With Kickstarter funding, Bragi has already successfully launched The Dash onto the consumer market for sport and recreation. Now with cognitive intelligence and natural language processing, this new hearable technologies will transform the way we interact with our devices, the way we communicate with each other and the way we work together. Bragi plans to apply its hearable technologies to transform the way people interact, communicate and collaborate in the workplace. The vision is for users to use the headset to receive instructions, interact with co-workers and enable management teams to keep track of the location, operating environment, well-being and safety of workers especially in industrial locations.

Samsung: In June 2016, announced a $1.2 billion investment in the US to back research and innovation in IoT. It wants to build a series of products focused on IoT, including drones, robots, autonomous vehicles, and in healthcare. It has also launched Artik, a cloud platform.

Honeywell: In April 2016, the company that makes products and solutions for a diverse range of industries made a firm step in interconnecting them by unveiling its Digital Transformation Business. This will stitch together its disparate products and solutions, including DynAMo, alarms and operations management, Industrial Cyber Security Risk Manager, which manages cyber risk for industrial companies, Assurance 360, a service pact for the firm's systems and Honeywell Pulse, an app that allows plant managers to remotely monitor their premises.

Challenges for IoT ventures are to figure out a viable business model for their products and services, which are distinct from traditional consumer model. The biggest worry is that of privacy and data security, with the amount of confidential data being transmitted between previously inanimate devices and products. "IoT is as secure as the weakest link in the chain, be it connectivity protocols like Bluetooth, hardware microcontrollers, sensors or cloud-based databases. As IoT moves from a peripheral concept to the mainstream, the field of security need get more attention."

IoT Agenda

There is pervasiveness and accessibility in IoT. This changes considerably as the device has a much focused function. In the case of the Nest Hub, it was a simple gateway controller. This means that it helps with home automation tasks. In order to function, there are costs paid for by Google (Nest) associated with securing and upgrading the gateway, hosting the web services, and maintaining the application and infrastructure. When this becomes less strategic, companies will force an update to a newer platform and deplore old services or devices. For example, if you have an iPhone 4, you cannot run the newest operating systems from Apple; you are forever stuck on iOS 7.1.2 with its security issues. iPhone 4 came out in 2010, less than six years ago. Similarly, if you have a PC with less than 1 GB of memory, you cannot run Windows 10. These are both good reminders that often times older devices or hardware are not supported forever. The same is likely to be true for IoT, especially consumer-facing devices with shorter lifespans.

End of lifespan occurs based on the strategy of the company, the cost and complexity of supporting the technology, and the need to eliminate technical debt in order to innovate.

It is being considered that for Internet of things (IoT) to work out and be meaningful, blockchain maybe the technology to adopt. IoT is hot at the moment and to envisage using Blockchain maybe the booster shot it needs to take it to the next level.

From IoT angle, the retail robot is just the visible part of a broader technology advance. With connected robots able to capture real-time inventory throughout the store and serve as a coordinated front line to field customer inquiries, a company like Lowe's can dramatically revamp its supply chain.

Jonsson (2016) highlighted developing a digital transformation strategy has become an important priority for many companies, particularly as demands for new digitized offerings are increasing from their customer base. Internet of things (IoT) presents new opportunities for mobile operators to enable that digital transformation by leveraging their core assets and moving up the value chain, through providing intelligent platforms, facilitating ecosystems, and even becoming a transformation partner to other industries. Mobile data traffic consumption is increasing.

In order to take advantage of the emerging opportunities, mobile networks will need to cope with all kinds of unique devices with different communication requirements. At one end will be simple wireless devices such as battery-powered sensors and actuators that will transmit very little data while operating unattended for several years. At the other end will be high-bandwidth, mission-critical services, and devices such as autonomous cars that require constant, reliable, and super-secure connections. Cellular networks, with their ubiquitous coverage, versatility, and rich ecosystems are well positioned to capitalize on these advantages (Peter Jonsson director Ericson Dec. 2016).

A variety of IoT solutions are already in use within different industries. Energy and utility companies are replacing old meters with remotely readable smart meters sending data from the connection points, enabling them to meet their customer needs on an individualized level. An energy company could provide consumer benefits such as more accurate and timely billing, shorter outages, and improved possibilities to reduce their power consumption. At the same time, improved network and load management leads to better capacity utilization and reduced maintenance costs for the energy company.

Agriculture is another area where IoT applications support more efficient use of resources and raise the quality of production. Wireless sensors gather real-time environmental data such as temperature, wind, humidity and carbon dioxide density enabling, e.g. calculation of crops need for water, pest management or fertilizer. Smart farms are already operational in countries like US, Japan, and Sweden. Along with improved quality of products, increased operational efficiency through remote and real-time access to information, reduction of working hours and energy consumption are achieved. There are even greenhouses specialized in cultivating tomatoes in Iceland that are connected to the Internet, enabling the owners to monitor and adjust the components of the automated cultivating system wherever they are in the world traveling.

Operators have excelled in connecting phones, tablets, and other devices, but connecting and managing growing numbers of cars, meters, machinery sensors and consumer electronics will put increased demand on them to understand how it affects pricing models, bundles, revenue mix and profitability. Today, the vast majority of operator IoT revenues come from connectivity, but in the next five years, the revenues will also come from service enablement platforms, apps, and services. Operators capable of creating and managing an eco-system of service partners, refine data from their IoT platforms and turn bulk data into smart data will be able to generate incremental revenues based on the value of the data rather than just the volume.

IoT Data Analytics will allow operators to manage their networks better as they connect increasingly more IoT devices (Peter Jonsson project manager for Ericsson Mobility Report an industry Dec. 2016).

Electronic Commerce (e-commerce), Mobile Commerce

Internet facilitated on-line business (E-commerce: Electronic commerce) in late 90s. In 1998, electronic commerce (e-commerce) that is online transaction. People and businesses are buying and selling goods and services on line. Shipping and home delivery facilitate it further. People order groceries to meals online; and at the higher end various devices, medicines, apparels, shoes, other accessories and even cars are being ordered and delivered. Small businesses get more opportunities online and more visibility also if they have a product specialization and it reduces the overhead charges for setting shop establishment; adding to profit margins. Business commerce is also flourishing due to Intranet and Extranet.

Travel and hotel sites have become popular Internet destinations. Travel companies sell airline tickets online, reserve the travel itinerary schedules including stops and other details of the travel and even deliver through email to you. Hotel reservations are made online with local information, maps of destinations and other interest areas around.

Internet banking facilitates bank operations of their accounts and other banking products on-line and paying their utility, telephone bills, etc. or buying anything online through Internet banking and even recharge of their phones.

Buying and trading stocks and equity shares have revolutionize the efficient transactions and transparency of stock exchanges, investors and brokerage companies.

Now in 2000 decades since many apps are on smart mobile telephones. These apps further encourage e-commerce through mobile telephones.

There are lots of reasons why e-commerce will not catchup with all. All are not tech savvy for on-line business; all may not have Internet connections or computer or mobile phones. For many it is cumbersome to sift through the online product information. But there is the human psychology factors also, when you want to buy, you may like to touch, feel, see the display of certain products against other and on yourself to goad you to buy.

In larger urban center you may have physical access to malls and stores but two tiers and three tiers cities as well remote villages, on-line product purchases will attract many. Recently, in India, Amazon has set up a new model for online orders from such areas where people may not be tech-savvy as well have technology devices with them to order. It is 'Store King Model', where people can go to their assigned business rep who will take their purchase orders on his laptop and they will get the delivery and pay on delivery. Thus, there are bigger business orders from such areas.

Even security of transaction fear is also there when you do not trust the delivery as money is prepaid. But recently in many countries for instance in India; where they pay on delivery.

Many e-commerce companies are planning delivery by drones for speed and remote areas accessibility. That will surely widen the scope and sales of e-commerce.

Earlier, RFID tags on the products are being used to monitor the products movements through supply chains as well tracking their deliveries. Overtime these tags have become more powerful and higher technology oriented. Now IoT emerges as a tool for supply chain visibility to monitor the flow of components and finished goods as they move through supply chains. For manufacturers, digital connectivity between the Internet and sensors attached to goods and equipment can provide data inventory and where the components are in the delivery process. Inventory management could become machine-to-machine transaction, based on shop-floor data. For logistic firms, real-time data streams from in-transit items, vehicles and drivers. This would boost efficiency and faster, more accurate decisions along the supply chain.

There are ads reminding businesses about IoT on the anvil; by 2020, 250 million vehicles will be connected and fully packed with IoT sensored technologies. Does your organisation have IoT sensored devices? Businesses are investing in IoT and 94 per cent of them have seen an incremental return. Have you invested in IoT yet?

IoT—India Focus

The addressed market is expected to reach $7.3 billion in 2021. The Indian domestic market contributes $1.6 billion to the overall IoT market, the report said, and is expected to grow to $3.8 billion in the next five years. Indian corporates are leading in spending on IoT, accounting for 80 per cent of their spend. The government contributes just 20 per cent to the domestic IoT market.... Even as Indian IT firms corner a large chunk of the market that arises from services related to the Internet of things, the country will lose about 69,000 jobs until 2021 due to the adoption of the technology, a report by consulting firm Zinnov said. This number is over and above the hundreds of thousands of jobs that experts say will be lost due to automation in IT and will predominantly impact unskilled and blue-collar workers. Internet-of-things technology will impact 120,000 jobs.

Newer technologies are expected to constrict job supply in some areas. In July, research firm HfS predicted that India's IT services industry would lose 6.4 lakh "low skilled" jobs to automation in the next five years. The HfS report stated that though "low-skilled" jobs will fall by 30%, "medium-skilled" jobs will increase by 8% and high-skilled jobs will rise by 56%. But despite the overall job losses, Indian firms are expected to benefit from adoption of IoT.

IoT Applications in India

Beside the globally accessible IoT technologies available in India, there are efforts to develop some to meets its eco and societal needs. A few salient one are mentioned.

To develop connected and smart IoT-based system for our country's economy, society, environment and global needs. "The Indian Government's plan of developing 100 smart cities in the country". It has earmarked ₹ 7,060 crores in the current budget where IoT would play a key role in developing such cities. This could lead to a quick expansion of IoT in the country. Also, the launch of the Digital India Program by the government, aims at transforming India into a digital empowered society and knowledge economy which will provide the required impetus for development of the IoT industry in the country. The various initiatives proposed to be taken under the Smart City concept and the Digital India Program to setup Digital Infrastructure in the country would provide a boost to the IoT ecosystem (Ashish Gulati tellit India Dec. 2016).

The optimistic outlook is that IoT will be an enabling technology that will help make the people and physical systems of the world—health care, food production, transportation, energy consumption—smarter and more efficient.

In India also there are new ventures going on in IoT for health, education, and manufacturing, services and devices. IOE for unbanked is being experimented. While it may not be feasible for banks to build physical branches in remote areas, they can still be accessible and provide requisite services to the people through mobile banking, interactive electronic kiosks and smart payment devices.

The other most promising challenging and exciting is working on 'Driverless car technology' Teams at the Indian Institute of Technology (IIT) in Kharagpur, Kanpur and Bombay—now household names in Silicon Valley companies—are working on 'autonomous vehicle solutions' or driverless solutions, a project evoking interest from Indian automotive companies. "We are developing technology for driverless cars keeping the Indian market in mind, in contrast to the global tech majors who are building and testing technologies in the Western market." All major auto companies were working with the three institutes.

Economic Times reported in Feb. 2017 that the government was planning amendments to motor vehicle laws to allow testing of driverless vehicles, paving the road for local companies to join the global race.

India is a complex market and creating solutions in absence of adequate infrastructure and civic sense needed for driverless vehicles becomes even more challenging, said IIT Bombay's Ankit Sharma, who is leading a team of students on the driverless technology. "If we can have a solution that can work in India, it will undoubtedly work anywhere in the world," said Sharma. IIT Bombay students, too, are running the pilot testing of the autonomous vehicle within the campus.

Each of the IITs is also individually designing a prototype vehicle using 3D laser sensor LIDAR to aid advanced road detection, which is critical to autonomous vehicle. "This car is built from scratch at the institute with only sensors being outsourced. The algorithm or the brain of the car is being developed by us," said Sharma. IIT Bombay and Kharagpur are also individually testing this technology on Mahindra's E2O (electric car) to turn it into a driverless car as part of 'Mahindra, E2O driverless car challenge and Intelligent Ground Vehicle Challenge (IGVC), through sponsorships'. India is also involving with global players in futuristic technologies of bullet trains and Hyperloop train technologies. Letting them setup and experiment in Indian situations. This is an ambitious step for Indian technologists as well governance to be involved.

Another useful recruitment technology: Talocity, as a recruitment technology startup that uses video analytics and artificial intelligence. In the HR services space, there are various companies offering sourcing of CVs, job description-to-CV match technology, assessments, video CVs, video/audio interviewing solutions, among others. However, there is no single player that offers all the services to its clients integrated through a technology platform. Talocity works at another level. Scheduling interviews with candidates mostly require making 8-10 calls per candidate before an interview can be planned. Talocity now uses scheduling algorithms and chatbots to support candidates and recruiters to schedule appointments and conduct live discussions via chatbots to enable smooth communication between the two stakeholders. So, what does such technology mean for job seekers and recruiter? "You as a job-seeker have the power to choose where you want to work and Talocity as your manager will take care of the rest. Merely upload a one way video interview and get interview invites from serious employers in your inbox. Choose where you want to be interviewed and the employer pays to meet you. Besides getting a job interview, a job-seeker or for that matter anyone can get a detailed personality report across 48 attributes about themselves based on a video pitch in real time. The personality report can be used to identify the key limitations of a personality and enable due reflection by the seeker to learn how to manage the limitations."

Recently, many startups are developing IoT products in India. There are startups like CARIQ making your car more smart efficient in driving. It is a device which records both traditional data from your car, such as mileage and speed, as well as driving patterns.

SenseGiz is to find things for you when with its small sensors you can apply to any object.

Entrib ShopWorx shows how it helps the manufacturing industry to make the shop floor smarter.

TEEWE which connects all your content to your TV; gets all your content, from pictures to movies, on your TV through a single device which connects in Wi-Fi to your laptop, phone, remote storage, whatever the platform.

LifePlot mobile electrocardiography diagnostic tool. The device is connected all time, *"taking Internet of Things where it should matter"*. It's currently the lightest electrocardiography (ECG) machine in the world, made handheld for travel. Other features include touch screen, maintenance free, remote diagnosis, paperless, all done in seconds and it required only 5 to 10 minutes of training.

'Networked readiness index' and Internet of things (IoT) promise digital dominance. As a nation we should look at more focused Internet usage to leverage IoT to impact the various programs of the Government of India.

Mobile Internet access via smartphones can lead to a 50 per cent increase in a small farmer's revenue in India, especially if the correct inputs (read: agricultural information) are used, said Vodafone in a new report, "Towards a more equal world: the mobile internet revolution."

Prime Minister's Digital India campaign is to bridge the digital divide and use the Internet as a growth enabler.

July 2016 ad campaign to opt for 'in.domain; the aim of the campaign was to popularize use of the '.in' domain name, which "creates and builds a distinct Indian identity for brands, companies and individuals in the cyberspace". As a promotional scheme, NIXI (National Internet exchange of India) will be offering the '.bharat' domain name in Hindi complementary to select businesses or categories from July 2016.

Networked Readiness Index: India

According to the WEF's Global information technology report 2016; lack of infrastructure and low levels of skills among the India population remain the key bottlenecks to widespread ICT adoption, especially in terms of individual usage. The report further said that a third of the Indian population is still illiterate and about the same number is not enrolled in secondary education. Only 15 out of 100 households have access to the Internet and mobile broadband remains a privilege of the few, with only 5.5 subscriptions for every 100 people.

'*Networked readiness index*' is a parameter that measures how economies use opportunities offered by information technology and communications for increased competitiveness and well-being. India is 91 among 139 countries for it. It has slipped down two positions.

According to the report, affordability has long been one of the strengths of the Indian ICT ecosystem, with the country ranking 8th this year. "A deep divide persists between well-connected metropolitan hubs and remote rural areas, where even the most basic infrastructure is insufficient."

The report mentioned India's ambitious Digital India program which aims to provide citizen services online, it highlighted, "India's performance in terms of providing online services and allowing e-participation has so far been in line with that of peer countries, but far from the global best (57th and 40th, respectively)". The need for new types of leadership, governance and behaviors necessitated by a growing and changing digital economy is also highlighted. A critical ingredient for the success and sustainability of the emerging system will be governance frameworks, which allow societies to anticipate and shape the impact of emerging technologies and react quickly to changing circumstances.

Terming technology as a tool to progress, the Minister (IT) said from 20 to 30 years from now things would completely change lives with digital disruption impacting lives in a big way. For instance, Video conferencing is more efficient and cost effective to cut travel bills by 50 per cent.

As mentioned in the earlier paras the Vodafone report 2016 by Independent experts has emphasized that IOT is going to help farmers and it also advocated development of locally-produced information and apps for increasing the usefulness of mobile Internet access. Although it feels this can prove a challenge due to the "high cost of creating hyperlocal apps, including those offering detailed agricultural information."

LoweBot benefits such as: (i) Enabling more time for employees to focus on delivering project expertise and personalized service. (ii) The ability to scan inventory and capture real-time data with LoweBot will also help detect patterns or gaps that will ultimately influence business decisions. (iii) Simpler and more seamless interactions with its customers.

However, if this LoweBot experiment, is successful, will have a far greater impact on the the future of IoT and retail. IoT is hot at the moment and to envisage using Blockchain maybe the booster shot it needs to take it to the next level.

Summary

Internet has become a way of life and ubiquitous around the world. All poor and the rich, educated and uneducated are fascinated by it, overwhelmed by it and at the same time find it useful source of connectivity, information and knowledge. Newer technologies such as balloon, small satellites, etc. are being used to bring Internet connectivity to the villages and remote, hilly areas to benefit one and all and for multi-functions such as from agriculture to political uprisings and counter terrorism. The new incidence of Internet of Things (IoT) connecting through the products and devices through Sensors such as driverless cars to medical assistive devices and home safety devices to robots are creating different life experiences.

At time people are getting so overwhelmed by these technologies and what next to come, that they want to detoxify themselves from Internet for a while!!

CHAPTER 5 India: Technology Focus

Affordability is a key to success of the digital revolution. Stay healthy, stay in the moment, focused on your actions, even as you work hard to let your achievements outshine your aspirations.

Science and Technology in India

Creating public awareness of the contemporary issues in research and developments in Science and Technologies are going to change the way we think and act. Modern conditions push us for innovative technologies to meet these demands.

Creating scientific ambiance and innovation essence; and creating the talent pool thus become important. Impact of Science and Technology on lifestyles in India in globalization contexts and as a prerequisite for socio-economic, cultural and political and development become important.

The Information Communication Technology (ICT) scenario has changed since decades through development and innovations in the IT. The face and shape of information societies too have undergone tremendous change world-wide; and that is true of India also. Computer and video technologies ushered in India from 90s to date. In India, the adoption of computer was resisted in 90s. It had gone through the stages of anxiety, fear and apprehensions of losing jobs. In 2000 decades, it is now well accepted and ubiquitous. In 90s the video was accepted as an inexpensive means of entertainment through video parlors. Indian Government has to censor the video entertainment for its misuse. In India, since 90s there has been revolutionary progress in telecommunications both landlines and mobile telephony and various applications.

India focus is highlighting its stake throughout all 7th revolutions and all the three waves of technology and its acceptance in national contexts and in its societal segments according to economic parameters of affordability and market availability; and compatible technology infrastructure in India; though political will and ideology to push the technology products for masses has been also one of the deciding factor. 'Political will' and ideology factors have been stronger and significant in 90s decades. Currently, the political will and ideology is impacting the digital technology scenario by pushing harder the 'digital' applications of technology in social segments and issues benefiting the lower, uneducated and specially rural strata of society and through 'Make in India' programs and in governance. Interestingly, 'People's Will' of the rural and lower segments of society is also a strong factor to make 'digital' revolutionary since they want to be part of the digital wave and not in for digital divide any more that contributes to the success of mobile telephony and its smart applications in India.

The demonetisation policy and consequent scenario in India in 2016 pushed the payment technology and its applications fast through banks as well as through people.

India focus will highlight the impact and efforts to implement some of the frontier and cutting edge technologies in current 2000 decades. Businesses and enterprises are equipped, using and innovating digital technologies for outsourcing, and for domestic applications to some extent. India through its technology companies hold a very high and significant position in outsourcing technologies, creating technologies in global contexts though it has been creating benefits for India also through national constraints and barriers. Global innovative technologies are being implemented and used for businesses outsourcing; but also many of these applications are implemented in certain areas according to the need of the hour such as more focus on *Payment technologies and Biometrics and Smartphones apps* post demonetisation; and more focus on medical devices and its applications.

Technology has been one of the components in societal change in Indian society overtime; compelling the need for changing certain social practices and related infrastructure.

In India, the implementations are need-based, urgent and selective of the populations' needs and availability of government resources as well reach and affordability to those segments of the populations.

Leaders and innovators can create vision of better future through evolving digital technologies. In India, leaders, governance and people can achieve it by their committed efforts.

Comprehensive and wide ranging perspective of technologies will drive our future; though affordability for larger number of people will be our policy parameter.

First Wave Technology

Focused on urban print media, though there was low rate of literacy both in urban and rural areas. Later, other mass media such as film, radio, TV were reachable and successful.

In 1936, British had set up Indian broadcasting company in Bombay, Calcutta, Madras and Delhi. After freedom of India, in 1959 radio was set up in other towns and covering news and information from Indian point of view. Over the years radio service become credible source of information particularly among the 90% of illiterates.

Television was set up in Delhi on experimental basis in 1959 just with one channel of news. Early television services reached a small percentage of population until 1982 when INSAT-IA first satellite of India was made operational. Within two years by 1984, additional transmitters were introduced and television programs could be beamed to rural and remote areas in India; and a national network for simultaneous relays including microwave links were established throughout the country. Color television became viable in urban areas. In 1984, a second channel of television was added specifically aimed to beam regional and local interest programs. These channels were initially operated for few hours in the evenings. But time period was also extended overtime. These changes occurred as part of the government plan to increase telecommunication facilities throughout the country.

In 1950, urban landline telephone system was started in some areas on small scale basis. Even at that time though the system was small, it was inefficient and unable to support growth. Further, telephone concentration was gradually extended to urban areas; but extending to rural areas where 90% of population was residing was not planned.

At that time, India had ambivalent attitudes and policies towards importing appropriate technologies as well issues of transfer of technologies and that restricted the acceleration of new communication technologies and participation in information societies. An integrated economic, technological and social change plan for majority of the population was considered viable by the India Government at that point. Since India focused on technology from a social development perspective to improve the life of people by social, economic and technological means. The political will of the ruling party at that point predominated which means were to be adopted and to what extent.

Second Technology Wave

1980 was the start of technology decade in India, even though many forms of distribution had been available since 1970s. Changes to policies in 80s began to focus on the following: (i) Revitalizing current technologies for more advance technologies. (ii) Emphasis on grassroots diffusion of technologies. (iii) Role of technology to improve quality of life for people through *'technology missions'* (high priority areas such as water, sanitation, immunization, health, literacy).

The social considerations determined the technology issues, priorities, policies and perspectives of the government and the masses for new communication technologies. The net achievement would have been how Will of the government and Will of the masses were/are coordinated. Thus, 'India Technology Model' was unique as compared to many other developing countries' models.

India has participated and gone through communication technology revolutions and waves with its own time lags and pace. In India, its 1st and the 2nd wave of technologies did not coincide with global technologies wave's periods of 1st and the 2nd waves.

In the first wave period, India had developed and was using Analogue technology for media channels products such as Printing, Radio, and Motion Pictures for its limited urban population because of low resources. But in later half of 80s and 90s; it was catching up with global 2nd wave new technologies channels and products and transition to digital to some extent; as well developing and manufacturing digital technology products.

It also focused on various media channels, linked ethnotronic devices such as radio and transistors, television to video and audio players; videotapes and audio tapes; motion pictures to digitalized microphones and later developing into wireless microphones. It has already successfully launched a communication satellite during this period. It was also for the first time that India focused on indigenous manufacture of fiber optics and some of the equipment needed for satellite-based communications. The manufacturing initiative had dual purpose; initially for domestic use and later to export to the neighboring developing countries.

In 2nd wave not only India pushed ahead with newer technologies for telecommunication, computerization with digital push and not with obsolete technologies of the world; and by using India's indigenous developed Satellite technology. It was also focusing on ethnotronic technologies of audio and video cassettes, and transistor radio for wider use in hard to reach areas. It has already successfully launched a communication satellite during this period.

Sam Pitroda (1987) the technology consultant for India put forth three social principles for the national focus:

1. *Connectivity:* Everybody needs to be connected to the whole nation. For communication radio, TV, telephones or interactive computer terminals need development. Rural connectivity is most important.

2. *Access to information*: Information must be shared without any distinction of social-economic status or caste through technology access. Government goal is to provide access to optimum number of people but if the technology is unaffordable it becomes constraint.
3. *Acceptability:* Information technology has to be applied and linked to people's lifestyles.

Therefore, the national focus should be to develop an integrated telecommunication national network; which should be accessible, reliable and providing connectivity to everybody.

India Government's goal throughout the 80s was to foster India's people's participation in the communication revolutions by concentrating on five major New Communication Technologies (NCTs) of television, satellites, video, computer and the enhancement of telecommunication systems. The major factor in enhancing these technologies was optimum communication and information; both physically and financially accessible to the majority of the people.

The following issues were focused by government to achieve these goals: (i) manufacturing indigenous hardware so that it is cost effective as well is able to meet the indigenous needs of the people. (ii) Encouraging advance technologies and not on basic and not on scratch technologies. (iii) Boosting the development of first-level technologies in certain areas and 'sky-level' technology in the long-range planning stages to develop technological capabilities. (iv) Most important was the development of social technologies and soft infrastructure to accept the technology hardware.

At this point, country faced a crucial reality for NCTs. The government technology policy-makers and decision-makers were thinking in terms of 21st century technologies; but when it comes to providing technology for the masses; only 15th century technology was being used and technology imperatives have been slow to develop.

The government technology policy-makers understood that efficient telecommunication was critical for moving the economy and those NCTs can be integrated through strategies for social and economic development. As part of the integrated approach the country needs to be technologically self-reliant and not become 'dumping ground' for other nations' obsolete technologies. They were realizing the capacities of NCTs indicating fast change.

In the past, there has been top-bottom; elite to people information infiltration by traditional communication channels of interpersonal or radio being the only disseminating channel. This has been very slow and inefficient. Moreover only 10 percent of the urban population benefitted. 90 percent of the rural population had low rate of literacy, mass poverty and large-scale unemployment and passive acceptance of 'exploitative linkages' of the local elites. The well-tiered interpersonal-communication model of village Panchyats set up by the government also exploited the poor and the uninformed.

Rural people including the urbanites expected government plan for new technologies of radio, TV, telephones to be easily available, accessible and cost effective with efficient and meaningful performance. Some industrial groups were ready to provide these technologies with profit motives. But majority of the population wanted government to provide NCTs to them keeping in mind their priorities.

Telephony and telecommunication: India is proud to be one of the first countries to introduce telephone shortly after its invention. It was in need of upgrading, modernization and accessibility and affordability for people. Saunders (1986) commented that under-investment is one of the factors responsible for poor telephone system in India and that hampered the India's development process. Telecommunication in India is a commercial enterprise so it is not the paucity of resources but lack of clear goals and the Governance Will have been the basic issues.

In earlier days, the Indian telephone system was run by government for a small clientele. Since 60s, there had been structural changes in the economy and that had called for new telephone management systems. A commercial service cannot operate efficiently as government department; this is a lesson public has learned worldwide. Privatization was not favored. So it was setup as autonomous department to ensure flexibility of commercial organization and responsiveness to public demands and democratic control of the government.

In the mid-80s, a very low telephone density prevailed in the country; 4 telephones per 1000. What has led to the telecommunication mess was use of borrowed technologies, technological transplant, centralized organization and failure to develop befitting human resources.

However in the latter half of the 80s, Sam Pitroda had changed technology priorities. The revitalization was made possible by updating technology expansion, using computerization and initiating new features in the telephone systems. It further enhanced rural communication by public telephone kiosks by the road system as rural telephony was still to come.

But what was still needed was an integrated telecommunication network to make use of powerline transmission, radio systems and fiber optics. These communication systems were required to support speech, telemetry, telesignalling, teleprinting, telecontrol, teleportation and facsimile transmission. Powerline carrier communication system (PLCC) has been one of the most common and popular facilities being used for this purpose. But it alone was not adequate for the potential volume of traffic; so coaxial cable and radio systems were being used.

At that point, the trend was to use digital systems instead of analogue to handle heavy telephone traffic. Digital improved telephone systems' efficiency and quality. Government was looking for both imported and indigenous technologies in this context. Both public and private sectors were assigned this task.

Digital systems were imported from France, digital electronic process control instruments were being manufactured in India with Japanese collaboration. The efforts were to import and transfer the updated technology so that telecommunication system functions efficiently. Focus on use of fiber optics for telephone cables, telephone instruments; and computerization of telephone operations and telephone instruments.

Telecommunication Intercity connections were done by fiber optics. Fiber optics was manufactured by Hindustan Cables Company in India.

The new features used in telecommunication system relied on microprocessor-based system to speed up communication and on a whole range of equipment being developed and manufactured in India for satellite-based transmission telecom system.

Later half of 80s to 90s was transition period to digital technology. 1986-92 periods were crucial for revitalization and development of modern technology features in Indian telecommunication systems to make it efficient.

Telecommunication shifted to digital within 1986-91 periods. This made the transmission system more reliable and versatile and enabled to voice data, facsimile and picture transmission services through telephone lines; even computers could be interconnected through telephone lines.

In 1985, World Bank announced $45 million loan to India to revitalize its telephone system in four metro cities of New Delhi, Calcutta (Kolkata), Bombay (Mumbai), and Madras (Chennai). World Bank felt that telephone system was seriously deficient in India and improved telecommunication is vital to market-oriented liberalization policies. UNDP and Overseas Credit funds of Japan also funded the project. These funds were to (i) help finance the digital transmission and switching facilities; and to increase telephone capacity in the abovementioned four cities. (ii) Modernize and expand satellite communication and satellite ground station networks. (iii) Setup a long distance management system to eliminate bottlenecks in the telephone network.

It was only for urban telephony in four metro cities. Costs were too expensive and unaffordable, and so it was expanded gradually to other urban cities.

Further, computerization of telephone exchanges in 1987-89 enhanced efficiency; the trunk calls booked were automated from manual handling. Telecom target set for 1992 was to reach 24 million lines. The public sector India telephone industries set the indigenous production target of seven electronic switching systems (ESS), 20 lakhs electronic push buttons using state-of-the-art technology, and to increase production of rotary dial phones, and to increase digital trunk automatic exchange (DTAX) capacity to 24 lakhs by 1992.

The other telecommunication projects focused and developed during these years (1987-92) were cellular mobile system, TV microwave links, satellite communication system equipment using digital optical fiber system, small capacity multiplexing systems, wavelength multiplexed (in electronics, a multiplexer (or mux) is a device that selects one of several analog or digital input signals and forwards the selected input into a single line. In telecommunications and computer networks, multiplexing (sometimes contracted to muxing) is a method by which multiple analog or digital signals are combined into a single line); and high speed fiber optic system.

New features in the telephone system was being upgraded gradually and making it efficient through direct dialing on national and international levels. Cellular mobile telephones, radio telephones were available in Bombay and Delhi metros. To facilitate their interface; a cordless telephone instrument was developed, and a radio base station was set up at every 10 km to ensure satisfactory performance. A pager system was also developed for paging people and displaying the caller number. Pager was used widely since it was inexpensive as compared to mobile telephone which was very expensive and not so efficient.

At that point to lower the load on the telephone system, calls were time restricted (three minutes for local, nine minutes for trunk calls).

Business System Network was designed to divert high traffic for the business subscriber from the normal network and to provide facilities of voice, data, telex, facsimile, videotext and electronic manual services to such subscribers.

PSDN (packet switch data network) an 'overlay' telecommunication network was set up for business, industry and other priority areas. In this network, a subscriber is connected to a nodal exchange/switching center either by fiber optics or radio telephone. This would communicate nationwide through roof-top microwave satellite terminals. Industrial users in backward or remote areas could hook into this network by using earth stations. An international gateway for international communication would be provided. PSDN could cover only four metropolitan towns of Calcutta, Chennai, Bombay and Delhi and eight second level industrial towns. PSDN could interface with PSTN (public-switched telephone network), public-switch data network, public telex network, and computer database.

Business Network could provide telex, message and interactive data communications at speed of 300-1200 bits per second using satellite technology; and high speed data transmission between computers; as well as interactive access from telex, PSTN and data terminals to such computers. Other features were electronic mail, access to low speed business data network and accommodating voice and data.

Such business network provided internationally compatible telecommunication services to boost trade and industry. Moreover, non-subscribers gained reliable and efficient telephone service since the load on the exchanges were reduced by diverting traffic. In the long run, it did provide impetus to set up modern national integrated communication systems.

Rural telephones: During that period, several research studies by UN telecommunication Unions and OECD indicated rural telephony as vital necessity for India. India indigenously produced rural automatic exchanges (RAX) in 1987. An experiment showed that RAX technology was effective but costs of the services and receivers was expensive and would be unaffordable for villagers to have telephones. So only one telephone per village or at roadside kiosk closer to cluster of villages was planned and setup.

An autonomous telecommunication department C.DOT was set up by government for operating, and managing government telecommunication policies.

Focus on ethnotronic technologies of audio and video cassettes, and transistor radio was mainly to provide leisure time entertainment to people at home and in informal video parlors especially to rural areas and other people since there was low penetration of TV. Government delivered video messages to facilitate local communication to rural people in their own languages and dialects in meaningful contexts and by narrow-casting special interest programs.

In late 80s government had three concerns as video use was booming: (i) social impact of uncensored programs of violence and sex, (ii) facilitating availability of low cost VCRs and encouraging indigenous production of VCR and video cassettes; and video piracy of pirating taping of original programs.

Audio cassettes were encouraging music industry boom. Government industrial policy encouraged production of audio recorder and audio cassettes. And music industry did boom.

Indigenous production of both video and audio technology meant inexpensive entertainment for people and trade gains for entertainment industry.

Transistor radio was great hit with rural people and wherever there was no electricity available. Even street vendors would use this. This was used to listen to all kind of news and entertainment and to keep connected with India at large. Moreover, indigenous production had made it very low priced.

Cellular mobile technology was being initiated but not widely used because of the cost factor.

Computers

Interestingly, in 1960s India wanted to computerize functions of banking, insurance, airlines, telephones, hotel reservations, libraries and voting in national elections; but at that time there was no indigenous hardware or software to back it up. India planned to import both but attempt was not successful since many feared loss of jobs by computerization. At that time, no amount of persuasion could convince people that computerization would create more jobs in the particular field and less time spent on traditional performances and there will be more efficiency.

Government could not implement computerization against majority of the people's will; but it did create computer awareness among people.

A few large industrial houses imported computers for computerization of their business functions especially data analysis on small scale. Government also continued computerization of national planning forecasts and planning procedures for its National Developments Plans. Some of the physical science and social science institutes used computers for data analysis. Computer awareness led to computer literacy needs and the start of teaching few basic computer courses in various institutes of technology in the country initially, then later to more advance level computer science and engineering courses. Private organization also offered short-term computer courses for software and data processing.

Government efforts to boost computerization in the country focused on computer literacy, liberalization of computer import policy, transfer of computer hardware and software technology production; and encouraged the indigenous production of computers and its ancillaries on a large scale.

The end result was between 1983-87 computerization was implemented by major network functions of banking, insurance, airlines, telecommunications, hotel reservations, transportation, travel, hospitals, police, mass media channels, and many big businesses.

Millions of dollars were being invested in creating computer culture in India through indigenous resources, assistance from developed countries and UN agencies for providing technical and hardware expertise and computer planners. UNDP project specifically aimed at creating cultural revolution in Indian industries on the use of microprocessor technology.

Projects in microprocessor use started in environment control, transport, and aeronautics and computer-aided learning systems; agriculture equipment, and a computer-controlled system was developed for satellite-based communication. UN-assisted development of basic healthcare and electro-medical equipment for more than 30,000 primary healthcare centers throughout the country.

Software packages were being developed and NASCOM—a national software center was set up for development of computer software industry.

Another major UN-assisted project was setting knowledge-based and fifth generation computer systems involving artificial intelligence. India was negotiating with USA and Soviet Union for a supercomputer to be used for defense purposes. Sites planned for installation of two supercomputers were Hyderabad, Pune with a central computer site in New Delhi.

Supercomputer provided by USA was being used for complicated aeronautical designs, defense purposes and metrological forecasts. Supercomputer from Japan was installed to build National Informatics System to process data from various government departments from district, state and national levels. Soviet Union provided ELBROS supercomputer.

Computer applications were being developed and focused on micro-level planning for food and agriculture, education, health, communication, industries, banking and environment. Initially, four major computerization projects started. These four computer projects were undertaken with aid from World Bank and UNDP.

Rail cargo movement project was aided by World Bank and under contract to Canadian railways. Computerization improved dramatically railroad freight movement, productivity, and increase in revenue.

Computer literacy in schools (CLASS) focused on preparing younger generation for computers.

Computerization of libraries and information services as well training of professionals were necessary for library documentation but interest in this was low and so was progress.

Computerization for Satellite Communications

A new computer policy was developed in November 1986 after reviewing the existing computer situation and discussions with computer manufacturers, computer experts and economists. (i) The government policy liberalized manufacture of micro and mini computers based on the latest technology both in the private and government public sector; but mainframe and supercomputer can only be manufactured by public sector. (ii) Reducing costs of inputs on computer peripherals.

(iii) Reducing duties on software codes for software makers. (iv) Simplified procedures to enable users to obtain computers from indigenous or overseas sources. (v) Promote computer applications for resource saving uses.

Satellite Communications: During this period satellites were already supplying limited telephone, television and radio services and metrological data throughout India on 12 C-band frequencies. Two extra powerful S-band channels were giving direct telecast services from satellites to small home antennae in rural areas.

INSAT IB was a joint venture of Department of Space (DOS), Post and Telegraphs (Ministry of Communications), Metrological Department, Doordarshan (television services) and All India Radio for radio services. DOS was responsible for hardware launch and other services prepared the software for ground segments.

INSAT IB has the capabilities for nationwide coverage for direct telecast of television and radio program distribution and networking. In addition, it became possible to provide national networking of all existing transmitters in order to facilitate exchange among different Doordarshan stations. Thus, it could direct telecast and nation-wide networking using existing terrestrial transmitters.

Major advantage of this system was to provide television services to rural and remote areas of the country and important events could be beamed live to all parts of the country simultaneously.

Under INSAT specific cluster areas were identified in six states of Andhra Pradesh, Gujarat, Bihar, Maharashtra, Orissa and Uttar Pradesh. Identification criteria were underdevelopment, availability of suitable physical and developmental infrastructure, and utilization of existing television production facilities. Selection of clusters focused on widest possible range of experience from projects in different cultural and linguistic settings for future expansion in other parts of the country.

2000 VHF Community television sets were installed in rural areas in these states for community viewing. Instructional and progressive programs focusing on agriculture productivity, public health and hygiene, family welfare, formal and non-formal education and national integration and news and current affairs were beamed initially, later to expand programs.

At that point the major concerns were, (i) Optimum utilization of satellite capacity, (ii) how much of the broadcast mode specifically the localized broadcast need be utilized; since this is significant because of regional subcultural and language diversity; and this posed a technological challenge.

Since this was intended to be significant mass media support for development efforts, especially for rural people; by the government. The proposed model focused on broadcast and telematics.

In urban areas, there was low density of telephones because of low availability due to technology and affordability constraints. But important point was that people were realizing the inevitable necessity to ease pressure on physical movements and transportation; and look for connectivity on many fronts through telephones.

Indians have shown that they easily adapt to new technologies. In the 3rd and 4th decades of communication revolutions computer has witnessed a plethora of new technologies, platforms, and languages. Obsolesce has become much faster whether planned obsolescence or built-in obsolescence.

In India, the major focus has been on development of computer software, hardware, training in computer use and computer applications.

The core competencies of Indians that were being utilized by global players through outsourcing of software were: high quality, low cost, state-of-the-art technologies, high math and logical expertise due to the heavy importance of those in schools and universities, and the second largest English-speaking scientific manpower pool in the world. Since outsourcing focused on software; Indian companies, universities and other academic institutions focused on software training of personnel as well development of software to the highest level and with innovative trends. Outsourcing of software in the country and in the client's locations outside India became revenue generator source.

India did not focus on total computer hardware manufacture; focused only on manufacturing of computer ancillaries' components and assembling them.

Computer literacy was swelling in the country. IT training industry was growing steadily to create a large skilled pool of manpower. IT revolution was catching up with kids, youngsters and businesses.

Software: India and U.S. have strong relationships in the field of computer software. American companies have found India a great emerging market to sell their software, especially packages. For customized software, the American companies have competitive advantage by getting their software developed through Indian companies. They choose India as No. 1 for outsourcing.

Software market was being promoted both by private and government efforts to broaden the markets. NASSCOM (National Association of Software and Service Companies) a private enterprise, and government organizations such as DOE (Department of Electronics) and commerce department promoted software strategic alliances, joint ventures, and business contracts. They organized major seminars in various countries to initiate exports to these countries. 60% of India software exports were going to the USA, 21% to Europe, and 19% to rest of the world. In 1996, with NASSCOM efforts, India and South Korea started cooperation in computer software expecting software export to South Korea worth $75 million. Pace had been slow to enter Japanese market.

Indian companies had failed to bring packaged software in the world market. They had sufficient expertise to develop packages but lacked two essentials. First, they did not have adequate funds for marketing. Two, Indian domestic market was small and therefore companies were not getting adequate opportunities to test their products locally and later export them.

In 1989, almost 95 percent of the software came from on-site. But government took steps to develop off shore software (i.e. software developed in India) by developing software technology parks, providing high speed data communication skills and adequate infrastructure. Liberalized policy regime helped to shift most of the on-site work to offshore. In 1997, 40 percent development was off-shore and 60 percent on-site. NASSCOM forecast and vision was to surpass any other country by revenue from Indian software development by 2015.

They planned strategies to do it. Indian software started receiving global acceptability. Global majors like Coca Cola, Pepsi, and Reebok and many more started relying on India Software.

India had only tapped the periphery of the global software market. It had to develop new software markets; and to explore the huge market potential for outsourcing, products and packages. Today, nearly two-third of the companies are engaged in developing end-user application products and services ranging from accounting systems to specialised products or customized services. In fact, marketing software changed with Internet connectivity in the country and globally.

Indian Government identified Software as thrust area both for export and domestic sector. But it was imperative for government to modernize the other basic infrastructures necessary for its development.

Hardware: Hardware exports were not strong, though they had been showing signs of growth. The domestic market has not been doing well because of unorganized assemblers, and the onslaught of multinational companies.

India did not have the capability of producing semiconductors and chips. In the chip area the product cycle is short. No Indian company could think of investing billions of rupees for setting up chip making facility.

India rather widened its capability to produce computer components such as mother boards, resistors, condensers for printer circuit boards, keyboards, floppy drives, and connectors for switched mode power supplies (SMPS), uninterrupted power supply (UPS) and radio frequency (RF). India was focusing on to improve the quality and productivity of these IT products in order to compete globally.

India had the world's third largest pool of skilled manpower and technical expertise, but it failed to be world leader in the design, development and production of electronics. India did not develop electronic hardware infrastructure for three reasons; (i) initially in 60s this sector was reserved for the small sector or public sector industries to provide employment. (ii) India was not allowing multinationals to set up their businesses in India and it thus lost the chance to obtain their technology, managerial techniques, quality and cost consciousness. In fact, at that point, Singapore, Thailand, Malaysia, and Taiwan invited the multinationals to shift their labor-intensive operations there. (iii) India also lacked in hardware research and development since the emphasis was on screwdriver technology in which components were imported and assembled locally.

By the late 70s the electronic industry has become highly automated and capital intensive and India was totally isolated from technological and market advances.

Even in areas where India was successful in manufacturing world class equipment. It failed to market them internationally. India's first super computer *Param 9000* unveiled at supercomputing 1994 exhibition in Washington DC could deliver high performance super-computing in the gigaflop range comparable to Cray series of supercomputers. India installed over 20 installations of *Param system* in leading academic and research institutions in India; but no sustained efforts had been made to market it abroad and it was an international disaster.

In late 90s, government (DOE) incentives offered incentives to foreign companies to set up production bases in its Electronic Hardware Technology Park. It was not successful since India did not have the manufacturing advantage due to logistic problems, inadequate power supply, inadequate telecom and transport infrastructure, delays in customs clearance and high cost of finance. Whereas other countries like Japan, Taiwan, Singapore, Malaysia could offer it. Moreover, the biggest handicap was that most of the electronic engineering graduates were either going abroad or into non-engineering jobs like management, market, finance, etc.

Global Contexts

Outsourcing abroad and national BPO (business processing outsourcing) services were booming in India for foreign investors due to increase in computer education and training. This was creating job opportunities for Indians. Later government encouraged schemes to set these BPO in two tier cities to generate jobs; but it met tepid response from the industry top and mid-tier IT companies. Most of them have already their BPOs in two-three tier and they want to operate more where customer service response is.

Information Communication Model Second Wave

Whither India: Where We Started: Then and Now

It highlights the Information Technology scenario in India in these decades and through second wave both in global contexts and domestic contexts.

Information Technology Model: There has been growing reach of Information Technology in India. There is worldwide awareness among IT majors of using India's expertise in systems design, integration, engineering, and software development.

India has emerged as a vital link on the IT chain because of growing internationalization of industries. With the opening of economy, there is interest among IT majors to invest in India. Apart from Japan, India has been largest IT base in Asia. The trend had been to choose India for product announcement, reflecting the significance of Indian market.

India was holding IT expositions periodically in India and abroad to disseminate information on new government policies, special schemes, facilities, and incentives available to IT companies in the country. The expositions also aimed to promote strategic alliances, flow of capital, and infrastructure investment in the country to promote India as a sourcing center that will bring better technology flow in the country.

Information technology helped Indian industry increase its productivity, profitability, and also integrate the urban and rural markets. It will have a multiplier effect and improve the quality of life.

MAIT (Manufacturers Association for Information Technology) had announced agenda to establish National Information Infrastructure (NII) to power India's economic growth for developing sectors such as agriculture, electronics, commerce, national data networks, defense, security, education, energy, revenue, and transportation. It aimed at an integrated complex of networks—international, national and regional. This would integrate communication infrastructure-computers to process information, software to enable utilization of information. This would enable India to be globally competitive and get tremendous economic and social benefits.

Third Wave Digital Technology: Digital India

Digital changeover: the overlapping of global digital waves in India are Communication revolutions.

World had gone through 5th communication revolution in 80s-90s consequent to the convergence of communication satellites, computers and digitalization. Digitalization converts all information—text, sound and pictures into binary codes that can promptly travel through global networks of computers linked by telephones, fiber optics and satellites. This has shifted the global power and monopolies on information in many different ways.

As mentioned in the earlier paragraphs, second wave of technology in India; in 80s and 90s India was connected to many of these global devices and benefited thereof. It was only in 2000 decades that India could develop more of its digital modes gradually depending on the Internet and telecommunication, computerization capabilities available overtime in India and that still remains more urban based even in 2016 decades.

Recently, IBM, Cisco, VM ware and Accenture, Dell, Microsoft have all called out India as their best performing or one of their best performing markets. Indian clients are investing to self-disrupt their businesses with new digital technologies.

New technologies including mobile, cloud, analytics and machine learning are disrupting traditional businesses worldwide. In India, mobile has become the primary route to the Internet, and the enormous efficiencies that the cloud brings is driving many enterprises into the cloud. "It has been a year of tremendous cloud adoption in the country," says Microsoft, which launched data centers in India in late 2015. Microsoft India Chairman Bhaskar Pramanik said 52 of the Microsoft cloud adopters include HDFC, Bank of Baroda, Axis Bank, Kotak Mahindra Bank, Fortis Healthcare, Apollo Hospitals and Narayana Health. Pramanik said e-commerce pioneers Paytm, JustDial and Snapdeal using its machine learning technologies and digital assistant Cortana (Oct. 2016).

Computers Third Wave

Quantum Computers. Kumar M.J. 2014 highlights about Quantum Computing in India. The laws of quantum physics permit us to process information using what is known as quantum computing. A quantum computer is different from a digital computer that we are so familiar with. While quantum computing sounds like a new technology, the fact is that it is a mathematical approach to finding efficient solutions to computational problems.

The challenges for the research community, therefore, include creating new models and quantum algorithms, sorting out architectural issues, and developing technological solutions if quantum computers are to become a certainty.

Broadly, the major research groups in various parts of the world are working on: (1) superconducting qubits, (2) flux-based qubits, (3) charge-based qubits, and (4) phase-based qubits.

There are very few groups working in India in the area of quantum computing. During the last decade, there were less than 100 international journal publications from India on quantum computing. This is less than 2 percent of research contribution from India to the world's research output. Within India, we need to identify groups working in the area of computer algorithms, physics, electronics, and materials engineering with interests in quantum computing. It is a highly interdisciplinary area. Computer scientists and mathematicians need to work on algorithms, architectural issues for scalable systems, data storage, and data transmission while others will focus on the physical realization of the basic elements of the quantum computers.

Quantum computers can be realized using both top-down approach (based on existing silicon CMOS technology) or bottom-up approach (self-assembly).

In India, the most cost effective method is to encourage the research groups to focus on bottom-up approaches. Existing expensive nano-research facilities in some of the IITs and IISc should be encouraged to follow the top-down approach to realize practical qubits and their chip-level integration.

The use of quantum computing can lead to many fundamental scientific breakthroughs and new technologies with wide ranging societal and commercial applications such as data encryption, new drug discovery, and weather prediction.

Developing quantum computational capacity should be India's "top national priority" simply because acquiring such technologies from outside the country will be too difficult and expensive.

The Quantum Information and Computation (QIC) Group at the Harish-Chandra Research Institute (HRI), Allahabad, India are involved in research on a wide spectrum of topics in quantum information and computation. This includes quantum algorithms, quantum communication, quantum cryptography, and theory of entanglement.

Quantum revolution will give us new material, new energy sources, and ability to create new forms of matter.

Laser Development in India

Laser (Light Amplification by Stimulated Emission of Radiation) ranks among the major fundamental inventions of this century. Invented in 1960 its unique properties make it a tool of exceptional precision and power.

India has been familiar with laser applications developed through other countries through use of CD, DVD, supermarket scanners, laser printing, and telecommunications in its second wave of technologies in 90s. Laser has ability to send billions of telephone calls using beams of light using fiber optics thus it revolutionized telecommunications. Micro-lasers are the key link in optical computers. A great deal of information can be packed on X-ray lasers.

The importance of laser was recognized by the scientific community in India fairly early and several institutions initiated research and development (R&D) projects, although modest ones, in this area in the mid-sixties. Since then, laser-related R&D programs in India have expanded considerably and now encompass most of the important areas of laser applications.

All the scientific departments of the Government of India have identified laser and its applications as a thrust area and have funded projects at academic institutions and national laboratories.

However, the support given by the Department of Atomic Energy to develop lasers and explore their applications has been quite massive. Dr. Homi Bhabha, the founder of Indian atomic energy program, always encouraged research in frontier areas of science, whether or not directly related to the atomic energy program. Thus, a modest attempt to develop semiconductor lasers at the Bhabha Atomic Research Centre (BARC) was initiated in 1964, though at that time laser was in its infancy and its applications were limited. The first semiconductor laser in India was developed at BARC in 1965. This was a major achievement for India. In another significant breakthrough an optical communication link using Indian-made semiconductor laser was established in 1966 between BARC and the Tata Institute of Fundamental Research (TIFR), a distance of 20 kms.

The laser-related activity in the Department of Atomic Energy got a fillip in 1987 when a new research institute called Centre for Advanced Technology (CAT) was established at Indore to carry out major R&D programs in the areas of lasers and accelerators. Since its inception, CAT has made commendable progress in both the areas and is widely recognized as an important R&D center of India.

CAT has given priority to developing technologies of important lasers and exploring their applications in industry, medicine and R&D. The center developed Copper vapour laser, carbon dioxide (CO_2) laser (its applications in medicine and industry).

Medical Applications

CAT has also been developing lasers for surgery. It has promoted research in this area in various hospitals through a National Laser Program.

CAT developed a surgical laser based on a 60 W CO_2 to facilitate laser surgery in India. This surgical laser has an articulated arm with seven elbows to allow the surgeon to guide the laser beam. The laser is designed for Indian conditions and can withstand the extreme ambient. Twelve such lasers have already been supplied to hospitals in India. Laser surgery has many advantages over conventional surgery. In laser surgery there is virtually no bleeding, far less trauma to the patients and healing is faster. Although use of lasers in surgery is widespread in the Western countries, its application in India was limited mainly due to the high cost of imported surgical lasers. Thus, surgical laser has proved very useful and being actively and widely used. Apart from the surgical CO_2 laser, CAT has developed nitrogen laser for medical use. Nitrogen laser has been found useful for treatment of tuberculosis. Many patients of TB develop cavities in their lungs which become breeding ground of the TB bacillus.

The treatment consists of inserting a needle from the back of the patient into the cavity and then irradiating the cavity with the nitrogen laser beam which is transmitted through an optical fiber inserted through the needle into the cavity. CAT has funded a project under the National Laser Program at a hospital in Indore and has supplied a nitrogen laser coupled with optical fiber giving 3 megawatt of average power.

The hospital has treated more than 200 patients of TB who had developed cavities in their lungs and who were on drugs for several years but had become resistant to drugs. With the nitrogen laser treatment, a large percentage of patients showed complete recovery within 2-3 months.

The hospital extended this procedure to other areas where drug resistance was encountered, for example, burn wounds infected with drug resistant Pseudomonas. Exposure of the burn wounds to nitrogen laser for about 10 minutes every day for five days resulted in complete healing of the wounds.

CAT also has a program on use of lasers in medical diagnosis. It has taken up development of analytical instruments based on lasers. One such system is a laser fluorimeter for detection of low concentration of uranium in water samples. This instrument uses a nitrogen laser to excite fluorescence in uranium source. The intensity of this fluorescence is a direct indication of the concentration of uranium in water. To suppress fluorescence from other substances generally present in water, optical and electronic filtering is used. This instrument can measure uranium concentration as low as 0.2 ppb (parts per billion).

Several such instruments are in regular use in various units of the Department of Atomic Energy which handles uranium, to check the concentration of uranium in water. The Atomic Minerals Division which explores uranium ores also uses this instrument for preliminary exploration. Scientists of Atomic Minerals Division collect water samples from deep wells and look for uranium. Recently, the Department of Atomic Energy donated two such instruments to the Seibersdorf Laboratory of International Atomic Energy Agency (IAEA), Vienna (PIB).

Industrial Applications

CO_2 lasers are being developed and used for applications in industries. However, for cutting, welding and surface treatment of metals, lasers of much higher power are required. CAT has also developed a fast glow high power CO_2 laser capable of giving up to 5 kW power continuously. This laser can cut steel sheets more than one cm. thick with ease. Workstations to handle jobs have also been developed at CAT.

The high power CO_2 laser has been used for several material processing applications such as cutting, welding and surface treatment. Laser welding is particularly suitable for welding dissimilar metals. Lasers are used for diamond cutting. CAT is collaborating with many academic institutions to study laser material processing.

Bharat Heavy Electricals Ltd. (BHEL), which makes large steam turbines for power stations, explored the possibility of repairing eroded turbine blades by laser alloying. By using the 4 kW high power CO_2 laser, CAT scientists have successfully cladded an even harder material on the blades. (Cladding is to cover a metal with another metal by bonding.) Similarly, a technique was developed to improve ceramic coating to turbine blades by laser glazing. BHEL had been importing these turbine blades made of very hard nickel super alloy at huge cost and repair of eroded blades would result in considerable savings to it in foreign exchange optic use and lasers.

New emerging technology is development and growth of power beams; the laser plasma and electron beams in material processing.

To promote and diffuse knowledge of optics, pure and applied; the areas being pursued are high power lasers, viz. combustion driven high power gas; dynamic lasers (GDL), chemical OXY-iodine (COIL); low energy solid state lasers; Nd-YAG laser designator cum range finder; beam control technologies; Electro-Optic countermeasures; laser materials; laser-related optics; thin film coatings, laser crystal/glass and NLO materials. (Laser technology uses in India currently updated April 2015. Source laser association of India, power beam society of India.)

Internet in India in 3rd Wave is discussed in Chapter 4.

Telecommunications

Telecommunication—Digital Scenario

In current 2000 decades, telecommunication revolution in India was marked by higher landline density in urban metros and two, three tier cities. Telecom connectivity, towers and telecom products have gone digital. Rural landline connectivity could not be worked out but mobile phones became ubiquitous both in urban and rural areas. Ruralites had easy access to mobile phones and were using more of these and felt connected. Currently, there is more focus to develop varied mobile applications from messaging, to healthcare, payment, commerce and entertainment, etc.

Telecommunications is arguably the hub of the Internet of things. Technology around us is communicating and helping us gather and share information and these technologies are evolving and making other technologies outdated.

Although India aspires to become a digital economy ensuring connectivity across the length and breadth of the country, the constraints of the telecom industry are hindering its true potential.

Increasing demand for telecom equipment as the telecommunication is extending in the country; both hardware and software and update technologies. The products include 2G, 3G and 4G network equipment, switches and broadband systems.

Similarly, the huge investment by the government in Digital India, smart cities, National e-Governance Project (NeGP) and National Knowledge Network would attract major equipment manufacturers. The National Optical Fiber Network project (NOFN), which will connect 250,000 gram panchayats across India, needs massive investment in telecom equipment. According to estimates of Telecom Equipment Manufacturers Association (TEMA), the demand for telecom equipment in India was about ₹ 76,940 crores in the fiscal year 2013 and companies are expected to invest about ₹ 5.2 lakh crore by 2020.

The 'Make in India' initiative will be helpful and encouraging for the home grown Telecom OEM manufacturers to build quality products. The Indian telecom equipment sector constitutes 6.6% of the global demand, but over 90% of telecom gear is being imported. As per Telecom Systems Design and Manufacturing Association (TSDMA), Indian companies, that design and manufacture and also have intellectual property, had only a 3% share of the nearly ₹ 50000 crore telecom equipment market in 2012-13. But as per industry reports, nearly 80% of the value of imported network gear comprises software which is IP-protected and cannot be manufactured locally.

Indian manufacturers have already made significant strides in exports of IT and telecom products to several countries and established that Indian IT and telecom products are of world-class quality and globally competitive on technology and price. India has all the ingredients of a globally competitive telecom industry like large domestic market, world class talent, and focus on R&D and IPR creation beside a robust framework for electronic manufacturing.

India is the fastest growing telecom network especially with advent of increased broadband penetration. This large telecom network requires top grade equipment and technology which India uses either indigenously produced or imported. Many of the world's top telecom equipment manufacturers have made India their manufacturing or assembling and trading hub.

Indian Telecom Sector has been growing at a phenomenal pace and is considered as the fastest growing telecom market in the world with the second largest subscriber base with more than 1060 million connectivity, 160 million broadband connections and 350 million plus Internet users. The rapid growth of the sector has fueled the demand for telecom equipment including mobile phones which is about 20 billion US dollars in 2015-16 and is estimated to exceed 30 billion US dollars by 2020 (Mr. Sinha Minister of Telecommunication, addressing foreign delegates Dec. 2016).

Sharma head TRAI India told members of the FICCI and ICT and Digital Economy Committee that, with the advent of technology such as cloud computing and Internet of things, ICT is transforming every sector; and telecom should also leverage it. Earlier, technology was on the periphery but in the last decade with disruptive technologies coming in, it has become a central tool. He added that ICT also brings with it efficiency and cost effectiveness.

Referring to the Prime Minister Narendra Modi's vision of Digital India to bridge the digital divide, with massive thrust on Make in India and Digital India initiatives, a large opportunity for innovative products and services has been created and India is poised for another digital and data revolution.

Telecom Secretary Deepak commented that Indian companies have exported more than 110 billion US dollars of ICT products mostly to advanced countries, which is likely to witness a big spurt in near future. He said through Digital India we are empowering the common man by giving them Choice to choose best products and services and by giving Voice that is the opportunity to give feedback on government schemes.

Foxconn makes phones and televisions in India for other brands at four plants in Sri City, Andhra Pradesh, and one near Chennai. Nokia has been making telecom equipment at its own plant at Oragadam near Chennai since 2008. Foxconn Technology Group has reached an understanding with Nokia to revive its manufacturing of mobile phones as a global manufacturing hub for mobile phones and telecom network equipment hub and bring more business to India.

Telecom's (DoT) unit is to pay a front-loaded subsidy to telecom companies for expanding telephone connectivity in rural areas. The subsidy amount is payable at the end of the quarter in which the connection is installed and made functional; and subsidies are for RDELs (Rural Household Direct Exchange Lines-landlines).

Mobile (Cellular) technology: It's not just about mobility but bringing it together with digital, media, cloud services among many other things.

We are in the midst of mobile revolution that extends far beyond our mobile phones. It is creating new global connections, empowering individuals, and driving societal change. Mobile devices are increasing both connectivity and productivity. Telecom companies have been asked to categorically support an inexpensive technology that allows mobile banking with ordinary feature phones having no Internet connection both to encourage Digital India and to reduce the chaos of demonetisation.

Mobile platforms for financial inclusion: More than 800 million people have access to mobile phones but less than half of the country's population does not hold a bank account, a UBI executive said, leaving a lot of room for growth of such initiatives. Targeting financial inclusion, more than two lakh

Nokia retail outlets would become business correspondents, or BC, enabling consumers to open no-frill accounts, deposit and withdraw cash up to 50,000 and conduct transactions of the same value every day. The bank plans to add disbursement of micro-loans, ticketing facilities and other government services in the near future; and all this being operated and enabled through mobile phone transactions.

Mobile telephones both feature and smart are increasing the consumer base. About ₹ 9,27,000 crores have been invested so far by telecom service providers (TSPs) in building world class telecom infrastructure," industry body COAI's Director General Rajan S. Mathews said (2016). Mobile phones in India have given connectivity to low income and rural areas who could not afford landline connectivity. Further smartphones with its advance features of 2G, 3G and 4G and schemes of free data are exposing these strata of society to Internet and IoT and data analytics and other features such as facetime and WhatsApp.

Airtel and other mobile telephone companies' telephone campaigns (2016) have to find an overarching theme to anchor all different pieces of communications has not been easy. At another level, the new campaign is meant to tackle an old brand problem: lack of a single-minded identity. It's a unique situation that we are in, with one brand having to address everyone from a peon to a corporate executive. Then there is also the pressure of communicating disparate messages: from network quality to tariffs and value-added services.

We told the agency that it had to convey the idea that communication dissolves boundaries and barriers break when people talk. When Airtel began searching for a possible peg to hang all its communication, it discovered one thing: for the average consumer in the mobile telephony space, the real moment of truth was invariably when the service did not perform, when there were call drop problem. No one noticed the network quality when it was up and about.

A functional differentiator simply didn't cut ice with the consumer. So the consumer connect had to be at an emotional level. And like almost all iconic brands, it also had to have a point of view that made people believe in the brand and what it stands for; a point of view that enables the consumer to have a conversation with the brand (2016).

Mobile Apps

Mobile (cell) phone has become everyday consumer appliance and a functional necessity; and even a status symbol in Asian countries and India too. Since 2000, with advance in cellular technologies globally, cell phones by many big players are available in India and that connect India heavily and specifically rural and unconnected India. It has added many indigenous applications and features in the cell phone services. This has made cell phones affordable and useful in India. Since mobile phones are virtually available to a greater number of people in rural and low income strata in the country, it is essential that we move to a mobile platform, which is easily accessible anytime, anywhere.

Even a roaming real estate agent or a car mechanic or a plumber would own cell phone since it would give them better connectivity with their customers. They find it cost effective and useful; even rural areas closer to the cellular range use cell phones. In many of these areas even landlines are not connected. Cell phones have become so ubiquitous that landline is pushed into the background for household or for businesses.

Initially, the mobile phones were feature phones. Motorola and Nokia were providing the handsets in India. The service providers were Airtel, MTNL/BSNL, Tata teleservices, Birla Idea and Vodafone. Both prepaid and postpaid services are offered with affordable price tariff; simple phone calling without Internet. This has added to rapid usage. Gradually, more value added features such as SMS messaging, etc. were added.

Overtime smartphones with its advance cellular technology and features have added applications and value to mobile phones. Smartphones feature enables, email, Internet, camera photo, and other apps. There are many mobile phone companies targeting Indian consumers in different segments with variant price tags and features.

Threefold strategy is developing for smartphones. Companies are focusing on manufacturing smartphones handsets with latest features by advance technologies; from high-end to low-end and price accordingly for different segments. (ii) Service providers focused on providing feature phones, and for 2G, 3G, 4G features in smartphones. For that telephone tower and other advance technologies are being focused. (iii) Various applications development for smartphones to increase its value for the user.

In Nov. 2016, India's first home-grown messaging app Hike Messenger has rolled out three new features—stories, a built-in camera and live filters. Stories is a new way for people on hike to share their lives and real moments with their friends through photos and videos, these stories vanish after 48 hours after being posted. In the "story" feature, a user can see how many people and who all have viewed that particular story. Hike also launched its own built-in camera into the app. It also announced the "live filters" feature that uses hike's camera to automatically detect and recognize a user's face using machine learning. Hike has 12 live filters, including one that changes a user's face to Narendra Modi. It is being rolled out across Android and iOS platforms. Messaging app Hike Messenger launched video calling feature for its users. The video calling feature has been built for a high quality video experience that works even under challenging network conditions, including good quality 2G, the release added. "We see India as primarily a sight and sound market—and we believe video calling will have a large impact on how people communicate inside of Hike," Kavin Bharti Mittal, Founder and CEO of Hike Messenger said.

There are many other mobile apps coming up as the need grow in healthcare, governance, payment, etc. A few are mentioned *Glint*, an organizational development platform to gauge how happy and engaged its employees are and the concerns they have. The platform gives visibility into employee engagement in real time. It highlights strengths, weaknesses, trends and concern areas at a glance and helps keep a finger on the pulse of the organisation.

'Swachh Paryatan' app for commenting on monuments cleanliness status.

Smartphones and many apps are being used for medical workplace and for medical devices.

Apps for Healthcare

Disruptive and innovative technologies are transforming the world today and hence we are experiencing change in almost every aspect of our lives including healthcare. In the past decade or so, the way healthcare is perceived and delivered has changed dramatically. Technology and clinical advancements have simplified diagnosis and treatment of illness while telemedicine has improved access of care in remote areas. Further, healthcare apps have created awareness regarding wellness and prevention amongst people and personalized care has become common due to innovation of wearable gadgets. India, however, stands at a cross road despite these advancements in the healthcare industry. India needs to think about healthcare beyond hospital beds and to innovate healthcare services. Therefore providing access to quality healthcare for billion plus population is a huge challenge for India to deal with.

Vishal Bali, Co-Chair, FICCI Health Services Committee & Chairman, Medwell Ventures elaborates, "unprecedented demand due to demographic changes and shifting disease patterns, coupled with rising costs and the proliferation of technology, has led to demand for efficiency, transparency in care delivery. This has paved the way for innovation of processes and products and new business models in the healthcare sector to cater to the rising demand of the consumers. In view of the new era, it is time that we look at the Indian healthcare with a different lens keeping patient needs at the core and re-engineer the entire value chain of healthcare delivery. India needs to transform its healthcare sector. Ashok Kakkar, Co-Chair, FICCI Health Services Committee and Senior MD, Varian Medical Systems International India, added, "Solving India's healthcare affordability and accessibility problems is possible only if we bring in a complete paradigm shift and strategize a journey of transformation" (2016).

Mobile apps are facilitating insurance, telemedicine, leveraging technology, training and equipping doctors for better healthcare.

Insurance Apps

Majesco announced a partnership with Life.io, a digital consumer engagement platform, transforming how insurers relate to their customers through monitoring and analyzing their behavior, preferences and more through real-time data integration. The announcement was made on October 2016.

Life.io helps insurers evolve to meet the needs of a new demographic of consumers, transforming how insurers relate to them by gaining insight that enables insurers to offer the right product at the right time based on their life-stage. The Life.io platform integrates with new technologies such as wearables and health applications to provide new sources of data to understand, assess, underwrite and service customers, encouraging healthy lifestyles while improving insurers' operational and risk management results.

As a part of this partnership, the two companies are integrating Life.io's consumer engagement platform into Majesco DigitalConnect and Majesco's core systems software to enhance the user-experience, improve risk management and support smarter selling and marketing of life insurance to consumers and customers throughout their life-stages. The Majesco DigitalConnect platform enables insurers to integrate new and innovative content, data, and collaboration capabilities together to provide a cohesive digital experience for an insurer's customers.

Telemedicine Apps

Along with training doctors on rural health and equipping the public health centers better; India must leverage technology in a big way to provide the last-mile connectivity. According to a 2012 report by PricewaterhouseCoopers, most Indians travel about 20 kilometers to reach a hospital but 90% patients don't need surgery and telemedicine can help them easily.

Early detection cannot only cure the patient but also brings down out-of-pocket expenses. In India, there are enough examples of this technology working well. For example, Devi Shetty's Narayana Health, which pioneered the concept of telemedicine, has one of the largest telemedicine networks in the world.

With nearly 900 million mobile phone connections and over 200 million Internet users, experts say wireless technology can be harnessed to decentralize India's healthcare industry, which is expected to touch $250 billion by 2020.

There are 105 state-funded telemedicine centers in the country. Some states have also individually tied up with private players under the public-private-partnership model. States like Rajasthan are experimenting with the PPP model in healthcare where private parties will run the state's PHCs.

In India, a mixed health system has evolved by default and it is loosely governed and inadequately regulated. Moreover, it is ill-equipped to tackle traditional diseases and the new ones effectively.

Along with leveraging technology, training and equipping our doctors and frontline health staff such as ASHA workers, India needs to fight old and new challenges. More importantly, it needs to engage stakeholders—public, private and voluntary sectors—to provide universally accessible, affordable and appropriate health services to all citizens through a well-coordinated universal health coverage policy.

Medical Devices

NeuroEquilibrium: The super-specialty healthcare startup chain of vertigo and balance disorders clinics advise exercises, via virtual reality (VR). VR in healthcare, even globally, is still evolving. Startups are finding its use primarily for surgery and training simulation for doctors, physiotherapy rehabilitation, fitness devices which combine VR technology with standard exercises for fitness, and platforms that help patients in dealing with stress, anxiety or other mental issues. Jaipur-based NeuroEquilibrium, founded by Anita and Rajneesh Bhandari, along with Kolkata-based Vertigo specialist Anirban Biswas, has started its experiment with VR technology in April 2016.

The Out-Patient Department (OPD) is important and one of the busiest wings of every hospital. The care and attention provided to patients here, goes a long way in building the reputation and confidence of people in the hospital. However, a common sight outside the OPD is of patients and their family members running around for information, long queues and hours of waiting for the patients to consult with the doctors.

The hospital wanted a solution to provide its patients, doctors and clinical administration and other supporting staff that would cater to effective time management and improved quality patient care. "A solution that would help patients to go online, access a doctor's details, their availability, schedule, book or modify an appointment, etc. was needed. We also wanted to provide doctors a platform to reach out to their patients for any communication or treatment," says Niranjan K. Ramakrishnan, CIO, Sir Ganga Ram Hospital, New Delhi.

The hospital rolled out an integrated mobile health platform called Smart OPD to streamline the end-to-end patient lifecycle.

"The entire ecosystem i.e. doctors, lab, pharmacy, front office, etc. are brought together and connected it with the patient. A patient can now book a doctor's appointment at the hospital through a mobile app and in return gets a queue token number. Once an appointment is booked, it also reflects in the mobile app of the concerned doctor. The app also has a provision for cancelling/re-scheduling an appointment that can be done by both the patient and the doctor.

Once a patient arrives at the hospital, a near-field communication or a NFC card is issued, which is a unique feature of this solution. Mobile tabs are made available at every counter and each consulting rooms. It is here that the patient's queue management happens.

There are dedicated staff members inside the consulting rooms who capture all information about the patient, consultation, diagnosis, prescription, subsequent orders and billing details, etc. from the NFC into a mobile tab.

This ensures that the doctors are allowed to continue treating the patient without technology acting as barrier between patients and doctors. The diagnosis entry is made into the tablet along with prescribed tests and medicine, if any. In case of tests involved, the diagnostic lab gets information in advance, and is ready when the patient arrives. The lab tests, including diagnostic images, are available on the mobile app and can be viewed by both the doctor and the patient.

A printout of the prescription can be taken directly (through Wi-Fi) from the tablet at the end of the session. Integration with the pharmacy department ensures auto delivery of order to the pharmacy once the doctor submits the prescription.

The system helps to maintain the patient records digitally, including past history, vital signs, clinical parameters, previous medical advice and diagnosis entry, lab reports and diagnostic images, etc. This allows the doctor to easily refer a patient's information in the future.

We have been able to bring a better experience to the patient, without added costs and made our doctors more productive in term of the number of patients that they can treat now. The solution has saved around 30 to 40 percent of time for both the doctors and the patients. It has also helped in avoiding long queues and waiting hours (Source doctors and administrative staff).

Healthfyme app focus is on digitally delivered fitness and weight-loss programs. App helps the customers track their lifestyle and by health coaches (nutritionists and trainers) who work with them remotely.

Practo app to set up medical appointments and reminders and consult and know about specific doctors in specific specialties.

There are many other medical apps to facilitate better healthcare.

Smartphones in India are being offered from to low to high end price by foreign companies. Blackberry was the first one on the scene globally and so in India. It faded in business.

Smartphone Micromax launched a range of 4G Volte smartphones at less than ₹ 5,000, bundled with pre-activated Reliance Jio SIM and it is Happy New Year 2017 offer of free voice and data. The new range starts with two models—Vdeo 1 and Vdeo 2 at affordable prices. Targeting first time smartphone users, the company is pitching video calling through Google Duo, which has also been embedded in the new devices. Other foreign made smart phone such as apple iPhone, Samsung and LG are widely available in India.

Asus, the Taiwanese tech giant that until past few months was limiting its smartphones to lower and mid-range segments, launched handsets priced at ₹ 50,000 and above. The company introduced its costliest smartphone in India, namely the Zenfone 3 Deluxe (Qualcomm Snapdragon 821 processor variant) priced at ₹ 62,999, which is ₹ 3,000 more than the recently-launched high-end phablet Samsung Galaxy Note 7. It also launched the Zenfone 3 Ultra and the Z It also launched the Zenfone 3 Ultra and the Zenfone 3 Deluxe (Qualcomm Snapdragon 820 processor variant) at ₹ 49,999 each.

Asus India Chief Peter Chang said that Asus wants to cater to a range of audience and not just stay limited to a particular segment. He adds that the smartphone market is fragmented in different price segments and different kind of users. So the company is trying to prove that not only can it make a mark in the mid- and low-end smartphone segment but can also offer handsets for a different range of users, specifically for those who understand the value of the product in that price tag. Asus plans to widen its product portfolio and offer more smartphones in different price brackets. There is Apple, Samsung.

Amongst Indian companies in Reliance Communication (Reliance Jio) are being made available to customers in 2016; both as service provider and product. Reliance Communications said that customers will experience significantly better app-to-app voice calls with high-definition (HD) quality and instant connections under the new plan. Further, RCom's 4G LTE network in the 850-MHz spectrum band will provide an unparalleled user experience, the company said. Under the new plan, R.Com is offering HD app-to-app calling at an introductory price of ₹ 39 for 300 minutes of calling in India and anywhere in the world.

The new plan will enable R. Com's customers to make calls worldwide through various popular data-based apps, such as JioChat, WhatsApp, FB Messenger, Skype, Google Hangouts, imo and Viber, across a range of smart devices, including mobile phones and the highly-successful Wi-Pod data access device.

With respect to sales and distribution, Jio will have half-a-million activation outlets and close to a million recharge outlets at launch. This will be in addition to the digital channels that Jio is promoting for seamless activation and recharge facilities for customers. All outlets will have real-time access to the 1,072 Jio offices set up across the country.

The Reliance Global Call service is available to all mobile phone and land-line users of the country—including prepaid and post-paid subscribers across all telecom networks. Customers can register for the RGC service via the website, or download the smartphone app from Android Play Store and iOS App Store. 'RGC India' app enables direct-dialing of international contacts, without the need to enter, toll-free number or PIN numbers."

Reliance Jio has developed its network at an extremely efficient cost base coupled with significant operating efficiencies. These efficiencies will enable it to offer services at a substantially lower cost than others. Their customer offerings are built on four key strategic dimensions, viz. widest coverage, substantially superior network quality, and transformational data capacity; and affordable services. The Reliance Jio telco has also begun the roll out of its data preview offer for Samsung 4G smartphone users in India. A similar pact with Apple and other handset vendors is also said to be in the work.

Reliance Jio launched full-fledged 4G services in September 2016. It has promised free voice calls for life along with rock-bottom data prices, once its ongoing free services come to an end on March 31, 2017. Jio had set a target of 100 million customers in the "shortest time possible" for Reliance Jio, but the new venture notched 52 million customers in just 83 days.

Multi SIM Card

Indian mobile market is seeing a growth for multi SIM phones especially dual SIM mobile handsets that offer capability to use two SIM cads on the same handset.

LePhone Mobiles which has announced the launch of its latest Triple SIM handset in the country. Its latest handset is the A10 which boasts of three SIM cards slots (2GSM + 1CDMA).

While most dual and triple SIM phones were feature phones, the LePhone A10 is claimed to run Symbian OS and is supposed to be a good smartphone.

It has a 2.2-inch display and features like an FM Radio, Bluetooth, GPRS support and USB support. There is a 3MP camera with flash light at the rear. The battery of the phone is rated at 850 mAh and is capable of providing 300 minutes of talk time and 150 hours of standby time.

Nokia offer its own dual SIM phone series in the country. Its dual SIM phone starts with the launch of Nokia C1-00 and Nokia C2-00 with the price tag of ₹ 1999 and 2,500 respectively.

Nokia C1-00 allows its users to easily switch between the two SIM cards just by holding down a key. Nokia C1-00 features a 1.8 inch TFT display with a resolution of 128 × 160 pixels and support up to 65 k colors. The handset has a 3.5 mm headset jack flashlight and FM radio. The battery offers a standby time of up to six weeks. You can get a quick access to practical features with its built-in torch. With Nokia C1-00 is simple and durable of its design.

Nokia C2-00 dual SIM phone is a stylish phone where you can swap SIM cards on the go. The handset allows you to keep one SIM inside your phone and use hot swap enabled slot to insert another SIM at any time. The phone comes with Opera Mini 4.0 and a VGA camera.

The other features and specifications of Nokia C2-00 include its music features. The phone has 3.5 mm stereo headphone plug, Nokia Music Store Support and Nokia music player. The handset has a stereo FM radio with recording feature. The phone also features S40U, GPRS, MicroSD card support and Nokia Life Tools. The connectivity options offered by Nokia C2-00 are Bluetooth v 2.0 with Enhanced Data Rate, High speed USB 2.0 and 3.5 mm AV connector.

Both the phones come with great multimedia and messaging features to stay in touch with email and access information and services. Both phones are attractive with a range of colors.

WiMAX 16E: Choices between 16M and TD-LTE. 4G, wireless networks are quickly becoming a reality. Mobile WiMAX 802.16e-2005 (16e) high speed mobile broadband networks have been commercially operational since 2007, offering an alternative to proprietary or cellular 3G technology.

Now, WiMAX 802.16 m networks (sometimes called WiMAX Release 2) are on the horizon and cellular 4G LTE (Long Term Evolution technologies) are in trials. 16 m technology is expected to be fully backward compatible with 16e and anticipated for rollout especially in emerging markets. Mobile WiMAX operators have decisions to make about what migration route to evolve for their networks.

Deloitte Haskins and Sells LLP Partner Hemant Joshi said (Dec. 2016) however that the prohibition on discriminatory tariffs has played a significant role to make data services affordable and accessible by everyone and is one of the important factors for the rising adoption of data services in India. The telecom regulator's latest recommendation to allow third party platforms to provide free data without bias towards a particular telecom operator or Internet content is likely to rekindle the debate on net neutrality in 2017. The market pulsated with action for the telecom sector in 2016 due to improved tariff affordability, falling handset prices and operator investments in improving network coverage (helped by policies like Right of Way and spectrum sale). India becomes the world's second-largest smartphone market with an installed base of 275 million devices. It is also predicted that 4G connections will grow to 280 million by 2020. According to global mobile industry body GSMA, India will add 330 million unique subscribers by 2020 (from 616 million unique users as of June 2016). In addition, the industry is set to invest heavily, with operator capex growing to USD 34 billion between 2016 and 2020, says GSMA. Demonetisation and digital push since Nov. 8, 2016 has increased need for mobile wallets on mobile phones. It will turbo charge the mobile phone market. Already, the average Indian is consuming more data, movie, gaming, connecting on social media.

Security: India should not compromise on its security and all telecommunication data-related companies will have to comply with its demands provide security agencies access to their encrypted data. Moreover, security of cellular products, equipment is important.

Cellular Operators Association of India (COAI) represents India's biggest phone companies such as Bharti Airtel, Vodafone India, Idea Cellular and Reliance Jio Infocomm.

Rajan Mathew director general of the COAI commented, it may be impractical to locally screen the same network products that have already been certified and deemed safe by globally accredited laboratories. Ideally, the government "should accept security certifications from globally reputed test labs to avoid supply chain disruptions" and not press for mandatory local screening. He further commented that there is "a grave danger of India being isolated from the rest of the world in terms of testing requirements" if the government does not align its network security testing drill with global standards. Such a scenario further delays in obtaining world-class telecom network equipment across 2G, 3G and 4G platforms and would create supply chain bottlenecks in 2017. The Department of Telecom's expert group on security is working on a framework for screening network gear while Meity (Ministry of electronics & IT) will drive the security testing drill for handsets. A senior DoT official said that Meity will be closely involved in preparing the security standards for imported end-user devices like smartphones and tablets in the run-up to their local testing. A section of bureaucrats in the government believe smartphones, by virtue of their open architecture, are particularly vulnerable for security, attracting malware if used for a mix of enterprise and personal work, and accordingly must be certified by an accredited clearing house in India. Security-linked vulnerabilities are "particularly acute in a smartphone's firmware and apps; which is why the imported telecom products (smartphones) are proposed to be screened locally, especially at a time when the government is targeting a rapid transition to a cashless digital economy where the mobile phone will play a pivotal role. Indian Cellular Association (ICA) is the apex industry association of handset makers such as Apple, Samsung, Foxconn, Xiaomi, Sony, Microsoft, Sony, BlackBerry, Lava, Micromax and Karbonn. Pankaj Mohindroo, national president of the (ICA) commented "there is a need for a robust dispensation for securing smartphones so long as it does not (negatively) impact the handset ecosystem or disrupts the supply chain, including app developers" (2016).

Moreover, the telecommunication industry can reduce the harm by providing safe online experiences which minimize the impact of online fraud. Telecom companies have a tremendous opportunity to help consumers manage their risks and strengthen their resilience by ensuring malware and cyberattacks are reduced, while improving their customer's online experience.

Early in 2000 decades the focus was on digital transformation of the telecommunication infrastructure as well as equipment. The telecommunication technology was improved and updated part by indigenous production, part by production in India by global telecommunication companies as foreign investment was being allowed; and some state of the art equipment was being imported. There were multi telecommunication service provider both for landline and mobile.

But 2010 onwards, the efforts focused on development of apps and in contexts of digitalization in India in various contexts and developing a digital economy on the periphery.

App development happened in two distinct areas: (i) the government focusing on e-governance to various products offered and (ii) private enterprises offering medical applications, payment technologies and biometrics through various startups.

Digital Economy in India

Earlier in 2nd technology wave in India; the digitalization was happening through devices in various domains from entertainment to home safety. But in third current technology wave the focus of digitalization is on facilitating people's everyday life through smaller innovative technologies and apps and those have more significance in day-to-day life.

In these contexts the digital concepts that are important for digitalization in India are digital infrastructure, digital literacy, and digital divide and individual digital empowerment.

Digital India: While the country lagged behind considerably on broadband access and policy, it made a solid mark in fields such as "protecting data and devices" and "communication and collaborating", according to the Barclays Digital Development Index. "India is placed 7th overall; bottom of the league on broadband access and policy but top on digital creation and coding," it added. The country-based survey measured the level of "Individual Digital Empowerment" among workers by assessing their digital skills in six categories ranging from basic to more advanced: researching and evaluating information; communicating and collaborating; protecting data and devices; content creation and coding; solving problems; and knowledge and attitude. The scores for Individual Digital Empowerment were then combined with analysis of policy frameworks and support for the development of digital skills in each country to create the overall ranking (July 2016).

Digital Economy in India 2014 Onwards: Modi Government Initiatives

Accessibility, affordability, quality content and online content protection will be the key drivers to sustain growth in India's digital economy. As with every paradigm shift, audience shifts will be followed by a shift in advertiser preferences and finally consumer monetization. So the digital content economy will see the exponential growth in the next 3-5 years that has been witnessed in the 2000-10 decade in TV.

Government has launched 'Atal Innovation Mission' to create an ecosystem for innovation in technology. "Let us aim to innovate. The NITI Ayog is promoting Atal Innovation Mission which will create an ecosystem for innovation, experiment and entrepreneurship. This will also create employment opportunities". Banks, consumer and consumer finance companies, which are taking the digital route, will see exponential growth. India has become one of the fastest growing markets for technology companies. The development is seen as a reflection of both, the country's good GDP growth (relative to that of other countries) and the increasing desire among Indian businesses and the government to adopt new technologies.

The need for new types of leadership, governance and behaviors are necessitated by a growing and changing digital economy. A critical ingredient for the success and sustainability of the emerging system will be governance frameworks, which allow societies to anticipate and shape the impact of emerging technologies and react quickly to changing circumstances.

Terming technology as a tool to progress, from 20 to 30 years from now, it will change how we live, work, and behave.

Digital Concepts

Digital operating concepts necessary in contexts of these objectives are digital infrastructure, digital literacy, individual digital empowerment and digital divide.

Digital Infrastructure, Digital Literacy and Individual Digital Empowerment

Digital literacy is low in India especially in ruralites and low income strata. On one hand, more individuals' standpoint; this is more because of low literacy and also due to unaffordability of tools of learning. On the other hand from government standpoint; it is lack of Internet connectivity and affordability; and also low digital tools literacy. During demonetisation phase in November 2016-17; one of government focus has been to promote cashless society and use of digital tools for monetary transacts whether to banks, businesses, vendors and even to individuals. It soon realized the shortcomings due to the two above mentioned factors and prevalence of vendor (cash based) economy in Indian society both rural and urban. Digitalization also highlighted glaring lack of digital tools including point of sale machines and security of transactions. Government is working towards both to procure effective and secure digital money tools; plus teach people how to use them simply and efficiently.

Demonetisation was announced on Nov. 8, 2016 and overnight 86 percent of India's cash was out of circulation. However, indications are that there may be many collateral risks—political and economic—associated with demonetisation that may reveal over the next year. There are concerns and challenges for digital payment modes and economy as demanded by demonetisation. That was challenging for the public and the government itself since both were caught unaware about the lack of digital literacy and tools; and other associated concerns.

Experts say the government should simultaneously give a thrust to expanding digital support infrastructure and vigilance to ensure safer online monetary transactions. When it comes to cybercrime, India is sixth in the world. The incidence of cybercrime in the country has doubled in just a year. FICCI (2017) organized an ICT policy dialogue with the agenda to discuss the challenges and opportunities that lie before the ICT sector, government and the regulators following the demonetization move.

During his address TRAI Chairman R.S. Sharma highlighted the pillars of Digital India and mentioned the need of an effective Digital Infrastructure, and how availability and affordability of digital solutions formulates the base of Digital Remonetization. He highlighted how JAM Trinity creates a robust system within India, which further creates a digital inclusion with 1.1 billion Aadhar users across India. "Cost, Convenience, and Confidence are crucial factors for a successful Digital Payment System implementation in India."

He recommended that, in order to create a well operational and sustainable digital and cashless economy, it is vital to eliminate convenience charge by the banks. He firmly suggested that interoperable or interlinked digital wallets which can additionally support the digital payment systems of India. He further suggested that the implementation of 'BharatNet' will be faster and effective with PPP model and further combined with Digital Cable Television System; India will reach a new level of digital connectivity.

A few companies made efforts to accelerate digital literacy at the grassroots level. It's not only Google that has spotted gold in regional languages. Amazon exhibited its intent in December 2016 when it launched digital books in five Indian languages in Kindle. In September 2015, Apple added support for Hindi and English to its mobile platform iOS, as well as for several dialects, including Awadhi, Maithili and Santhali.

Digital Divide in India

Digitalization will empower the governance since it will bring transparency, accountability and efficiency. Digital literacy is likely to empower individuals to enjoy the benefits accrued from such governance.

Though digital divides are narrowing between urban-based smaller towns, urban periphery rural areas but more and more efforts are being focused by India and others like Google, Facebook, and Micro Software and Oneweb to provide Internet fast in rural and hilly areas. Another notable is that gap is also reducing between generations and social classes within India. Focusing on different aspects of media use, including cultural attitudes, censorship and social media, Internet penetration has arisen; though more depends on accessibility and not the willingness of the people. Users of all media have become more open to other cultures through the availability of a broader range of international films and television programs. That gives them wider visibility of technologies abroad and their lifestyles. They include a foreign language channel, or regional language channel in their list of channels they regularly watch. But increased access to other cultures—either through international terrestrial or digital platforms has not led audiences to reject their own national or regional media. On the contrary, we see some evidence of increased use of media specific to one's own identity alongside the expanding availability of international content.

There are social, economic and political ramifications in India happening currently; when digitalization modes are being practiced or moved by different reasons or by government pressures. As discussed in demonetization and digital modes occurrence in India Nov. 2016 onwards in later part of the chapter.

Digital Initiatives

Digital e-governance

Number of products initiated to facilitate e-governance. UIDAI has issued this advisory in view of various applications of public use such as Digi-locker, eSign, eNPS, e-Hospital, e-verification of Income Tax Return (ITR), etc. being rolled out by the government departments using Aadhaar as identifier. Services like Aadhaar-based eSign facility allow residents to use digital signature to avail a number of services online in a cashless, presence-less and paperless manner.

E-governance: Modi operates Digital cabinet to implement government projects. He operates two such groups, (i) This is Modi's Digital Cabinet, not visible to the public on the My Network section of the Na-Mo app. Started almost two months ago, it allows ministers to chat freely with the PM on ideas and programs. (ii) Modi has a second private group on the app that comprises Bharatiya Janata Party's members of Parliament. (iii) Modi is planning to set up more dedicated private groups on the Na-Mo app with sportspersons, technocrats and agriculture experts. He urged them to join a private group on the Na-Mo app so all of them can converse on a common platform, the official said. The PM uses the two groups aggressively. "Unlike WhatsApp, it is a secure group as it is on our own servers," an official said. The PM wanted the pro-poor initiatives to be collated and conveyed to the people in a simple format in the manner of a brief on how they could participate and to set up a helpline if needed to spread awareness about the schemes.

The government feels many aren't aware of such initiatives, a senior official said.

Social Media and Governance in India: projecting the image: Channels being used by majority of governance are twitter and Facebook and LinkedIn. MyGov app in Facebook is a digital effort and is the government's citizen engagement platform. Government has advocated for giving freehand to ministers and bureaucrats to express themselves on social media to make government functioning transparent. But it bars officers from making "criticism of government" on television, social media or any other communication channels by any means, including a "caricature". This implies that any criticism of the government or its policies on social networking sites like Twitter and Facebook or on social networking groups like WhatsApp or through the officer drawing out a caricature will also attract disciplinary action under the Conduct Rules.

Social media provides alternate viewpoints, criticisms, comments and suggestions. Therefore in a transparent government system, there are advantages of social media. Earlier, only big metropolitan cities were looked at for opinion or suggestions but today with the advent of social media, opinions are freely available from schools, colleges, tier II, III and even downwards. The youth are more informed. Public pressures and pressure of public opinion build through social media and news media, both print and electronic play important role in forming opinion. There was a time when we did public rallies, then radio, television media have been used and then came social media whose cost is low and impact is more and it empowers all and increases accountability. The External Affairs Ministry is effectively using the social media to connect with people and help the ones in distress when abroad.

There has been a feeling in the government that its point of view had not been effectively projected on various measures it has been taking and adverse media faced by the government. Therefore, an action was initiated. The Group of Ministers will meet every day at a fixed hour, analyze the events of the day and issue suitable directions to the nodal officer to prepare appropriate material for briefing the media an order issued by the Cabinet Secretariat said. One of the ministers of the group or in certain cases, the minister concerned with the matter, if he is not a member of the group, will brief the media every day, it said. Along with the oral briefing, a written brief will also be released, the order said. The GoM will be serviced by the Ministry of Information and Broadcasting which will ensure that agenda papers or minutes of the meeting are expeditiously forwarded to the Prime Minister's Office and the Cabinet Secretariat, it said.

EO App has been developed keeping in mind the spirit of maximum governance, minimum government. The application would enable its users, which may include officers, media persons and all stakeholders to stay updated on real time basis with appointments and postings approved by the Appointments Committee of the Cabinet (ACC) and vacancies at senior level in the Government of India. By eliminating the information asymmetry in this regard, the EO App will reduce speculations regarding transfers and postings in the Government of India and will make the system completely transparent as all the relevant orders and notifications will now be instantly available in the public domain. This is an effective management tool which also empowers the IAS officers on Pan India basis and officers serving under Central Staffing Scheme by providing their personal records like Annual Performance Appraisal Report (APAR), Immovable Property Return (IPR), Executive Record (ER) sheet through secured NIC login Id and Password.

Skill base for digitalization is important for its implementation as we adopt the digital technologies. At the same time; there is apprehension that in 2017 and 2018, digital and automation will cut off a third of the contract, and nearly half the mandatory IT providers will lose part of the work, highlighting the challenge faced by Indian IT firms as they pursue growth. Nasscom has also cut its growth target for the year to 8-10 per cent from 10-12 per cent earlier.

Skill Development: The Ministry of Labor & Employment in association with Confederation of Indian Industry (CII) & Wheebox (an online skill assessment company) have launched a model career center (MCC) in Mumbai. MCC is a project of DGET, Ministry of Labor & Employment (MoLE) through National Career Service (NCS). The candidates will be provided with counseling, assessment, soft skill training, technical upskilling and placement at this MCC. The training will help the candidates in securing right career choice as per their aptitude, according to a release. It will also provide an opportunity in bridging the skills requirement by industry with the workforce available. CII Naoroji Godrej Model Career Centre in Mumbai is the first model career center in Maharashtra. Sessions are provided which are Face-to-face/ skype interaction and one week online support. Model Career Centers would go a long way in bridging the skill requirement by industry with the workforce available.

To accelerate digital literacy at the grassroots level Intel India also announced the "*Digital Unnati*" website that is being set up in collaboration with the CSC e-Governance Services India Ltd. It will enable Village Level Entrepreneurs (VLEs) to learn how to assemble a PC online and upskill their technology know-how.

Skilled Jobs Created in India by Newer Technologies

Intel India in August 2016 designed three projects designed to accelerate digital literacy at the grassroots level by reaching out to the population in non-urban India, upskill citizens in tier two cities and beyond and encouraging innovations from local level.

"We are thrilled to see the progress made through our collaboration with the government of India on various initiatives like 'Digital India' that are bringing technology and innovation mainstream in India," Robby Swinnen, general manager, Intel Corporation (Asia-Pacific & Japan).

Building on the momentum of its "Ek Kadam Unnati Ki Aur" initiative to accelerate access to technology in non-urban India, Intel India e-launched its latest "Unnati Kendra at Common Service center (UK at CSC) Intel India is working with the government to open a network of up to 100 'UK at CSC' facilities across ten states this year, with ten such facilities already set up in the state of Telangana.

In addition, inspired by the overwhelming response and the success of the first chapter of the Intel and DST-Innovate for Digital India Challenge, Intel India is laying the groundwork for launching the challenge. This challenge supports local innovation and entrepreneurship and is a nationwide competition inviting technology solutions to solve real problems faced by citizens. Intel India is fully committed to achieving the realization of a truly Digital India and has been supporting this vision by fostering innovation and upskilling of the non-urban population.

Stephen Pratt said that the large talent pool in India was what made Noodle.ai set up its development center in startup hub of the country. “Data science is different from software development life cycle and requires highly skilled professionals to build an artificially intelligent engine. We are hiring PhD and master’s degree holders from India to work for Noodle. The company is looking to hire 500 people in the next five years, out of which two-third professionals will be hired from India and will work from Noodle.ai’s new office in Delhi (2016).

Robotics for surgeries: The All India Institute of Medical Sciences (AIIMS) Delhi has introduced a robotic arm that helps in conducting complicated neurosurgeries by enabling doctors to analyze brain dysfunctions accurately and identifying the part to be treated. According to doctors, to use this robotic arm, neurosurgeons make a small hole inside the patient’s brain. Once inside the brain, the robot identifies the spot which requires treatment. “Earlier experts at AIIMS performed surgeries manually using stereotactic frame. But the robotic arm, a European technology originally, has helped identify exact spot of brain for providing better treatment. The surgeries are being conducted free of cost,” a doctor attached to neurosurgery division at AIIMS said. 60 surgeries are performed so far (Dec. 2016).

Eye-Netra, Eye-testing medical device: ***Near-Eye Tool for Refractive Assessment, or NETRA in India***

In India, Eye-Netra has launched Nayantara, a similar program to provide low-cost eye tests to the poor and uninsured in remote villages, far from eye doctors. Both efforts used

Eye-Netra's suite of tools, now available for eye-care providers worldwide.

Nayantara skills local rural youth by training them in basics of eye-care and screening methodology. They are called Visioneers. Using cloud based technology platform and associated technologies; these local rural youths organized in small teams are able to deliver expert supervised eye-screening and refraction testing. It is both scalable and sustainable. India alone has around 300 million people in need of eyeglasses.

A grant from the MIT Deshpande Center for Technological Innovation officially launched the entrepreneurial effort in 2010. "But we realized we had to start all over again," Raskar says.

This meant a complete redesign of the product and business plan to focus less on the technology and more on market need. "As much as we wanted to be disruptive in long run, the reality of the world was that we had to work with really good partners," he says.

In India, Eye-Netra teamed up with the LV Prasad Eye Institute and Lotus Eye Institute and Hospital, among other clinical partners, to help conduct tens of thousands of tests.

About 340 product iterations led to an improved device and better user interface. For instance, around three years ago, the team realized that people didn't perform well interacting with the phone. So, for the current design, they moved all buttons and knobs to the actual device. That change, and other small tweaks, made the device easier and more widely used, Raskar says.

"We were naive in thinking that if you solve the optics problem, it will be good. But in reality there are three parameters: the machine and its optical design, the eye and its involuntary activities, and the human perception," he says. "Getting all those right in the same design is nontrivial."

When asked about using augmented-reality applications developed by banks and financial services companies, 89 per cent respondents were interested in one or more of the seven augmented-reality concepts that Cisco had tested. Augmented reality (AR) is a live direct or indirect view of a physical, real-world environment whose elements are augmented (or supplemented) by computer-generated sensory input such as sound, video, graphics or GPS data. Augmented Reality (AR) is a technology enriching the real world with digital information and media, such as 3D models and videos, overlaying in real-time the camera view of your smartphone, tablet, PC or connected glasses.

Technology Product Applications

Insurance

Technology will power the new wave of change for the Indian Insurance Industry reveals the CII-EY report titled Insurer of the Future 2016. The report recommends pursuing technology to improve the traditional insurance process and to re-configure the insurance business model. The customer is at the center of digital transformations across the value chain and Insurance in India has moved from being a sellers market to that of a digitally driven buyers' market, says the report.

Technology has played an important role impacting customers, intermediaries and insurers in a holistic approach to connect with customers digitally in each stage of the value chain including product design, marketing or sales, underwriting or pricing, customer servicing and claims management. However, insurance has been slow as compared to the rest of the financial services in adopting the new technology value propositions available in the market as an enabler of business strategy: Internet of things (IoT) can play a crucial role in assessing and pricing the risk of loss. Robotic Process Automation (RPA) that replicates human behavior and executes non-judgmental sequence of activities can help insurers to automate client servicing activities:

- Insurers through collaboration with third party data service providers can make informed strategy and policy related decisions for insurance risk-management and fraud monitoring.
- Insurance bundling on e-commerce platforms has enabled greater customization in product and pricing thereby targeted marketing to customers.

- Blockchain technology has the potential to eliminate error and detect fraud by providing a decentralized digital repository to verify the veracity of customers.

Commenting on the report, Chandrajit Banerjee, Director General, CII said "The drivers of Insurance Business in India are rapidly changing. Over the last decade and a half several innovations have smoothly blended into the ecosystem of Insurance, be it in terms of products, distribution, technology or the basic way in which business is done. 'Business as Usual' of today is very different from what it was in the last decade and the Insurer of the Future will conduct business very differently in the decades to come. Technology and Digitization disruptions have brought the sector to a point of transformation and as the sector maneuvers itself to the changing paradigms there is a clear multiple level growths envisaged throughout the ecosystem of Insurance in India."

Sanjiv Bajaj, Chairman, CII National Committee on Insurance & Pensions, CII said, "The insurance industry is at the threshold of a long period of growth. With the rapid change in technology and digitization, the drivers of insurance business are changing. Those insurers who disrupt themselves continuously would be the ones who will succeed in the long run. All stakeholders—the industry, intermediaries, Government and regulator-need to work together in transforming customer experience."

Rohan Sachdev, Global Insurance Emerging Markets Leader and Partner, EY India said, "The Indian insurance sector has evolved and in order to realize the full potential, the industry must focus on aspects of technology that will fundamentally change the way customers know and interact with each other and the insurers. With increasing capital infusion and the arrival of new technologies, insurers have been readily adopting digital solutions to improve customer experience. With the rising population and changing demographics, insurers and intermediaries will have to constantly innovate to remain relevant."

Cyber and data risks are a key concern area for businesses today. The risk is expected to increase in the future, with growth in big data and data analytics requiring even more data to be accessed. While cyber liability insurance products are available in India, providing comfort to global clients on cyber risks is one of the key challenges for technology businesses. This challenge presents a great opportunity to the reinsurance through cyber-risk insurance products that can assure stakeholders of market leading preventive measures around cyber risks.

L&T Technology Services announced a digital engineering transformation partnership with Microsoft Corporation to deliver Microsoft Azure Engineering Solutions for global enterprises across industries. This strategic partnership between the two companies enables enterprises around the world to leverage L&T Technology's cutting-edge IP-led digital engineering solutions hosted on Microsoft's Azure enterprise cloud-first, mobile-first infrastructure (6 Oct. 2016).

Social Cops Data Intelligence Company

"In spite of increasing digitization of data and its availability; businesses and organizations have found it difficult to create value out of it. In the developing world, the biggest bottleneck with data is data itself. This is when we realized that the power of data combined with technology can solve some real problems," explains Prukalpa Sankar, co-founder of New Delhi-based data intelligence company Social Cops.

Take the case of a large philanthropic organization that wanted to make investments to improve the quality of life of small and marginal farmers in Bihar and Uttar Pradesh. They needed to decide which districts they could intervene to make the maximum impact.

"They used Access and Visualize on our platform to access our data about agriculture, nutrition, and female empowerment, explore the secondary data visually, and make a decision that would have otherwise taken them over six months," says Varun Banka, co-founder, Social Cops. The company found that a lot of decisions that were being made in the world were not being done on the basis of real-time updated data. That's when it decided to build a data exchange that has myriad uses—from governments deciding healthcare allocations or a marketer pondering in which villages a brand of toothpaste should be introduced.

A base layer of data was created by tapping internal organizational systems that existed in silos. Data from these systems were pulled out and now forms the base layer of their intelligent platform. An additional layer of context was added to the base layer through external information.

"In places where data didn't exist, we started to deploy an app that works without an Internet, in local languages that can be used by locals to collect two data points a day," says Sankar. For example, about 50,000 people in Jarmundi, Jharkhand use Social Cop's Android app to regularly and dynamically collect and create data that has never been created before.

The core platform leverages machine learning tools that filters and cleans the data to process and analyze it at scale and get valuable insights. "This data is visualized through interactive and easy to use dashboards that a decision maker can quickly understand and identify the problem and take corrective measures," says Sankar.

"In spite of increasing digitization of data and its availability; businesses and organizations have found it difficult to create value out of it. In the developing world, the biggest bottleneck with data is data itself. This is when we realized that the power of data combined with technology can solve some real problems," explains Prukalpa Sankar.

Social Cops is currently being used by more than 150 organizations around the world to run baseline surveys, create real-time monitoring systems, make strategic investment decisions, and generate insights to make better data-driven decisions. It has built around 600 public data sources in India and around 32 other countries across the globe. Human sensors feed the company data on a real-time basis through its app, Collect. "While growing up, we always saw some problems that were not solved for ages. The beauty of our platform is that if we solve a problem once, we solve it for life," says Banka.

Railways: The railways launched a website in December 2016 seeking inputs from all stakeholders to prepare the

National Rail Plan (NRP) which will be ready by the middle of 2017. "Railways has prepared vision documents but never National Rail Plan. Seeking suggestions from all stakeholders, he asked all concerned including Chief Ministers, different ministries, business chambers to provide inputs for finalizing the plan. NRP envisages identifying and developing new corridors."

Biotech railway technologies Tri-Netra: To reduce train accidents, the railways will soon introduce an advanced system called the Terrain Imaging for Diesel Drivers—Infrared Enhanced Optical and Radar Assisted (Tri-Netra) system in all trains. Tri-Netra will keep a record of the track maintenance and help maintain high speed during difficult weather such as fog and heavy rains to avoid delays in arrivals. It is based on a technology that fighter jets use to see through clouds and operate in pitch dark.

In 2016, Railways have taken an enormous task of providing human waste discharge free bio-toilets in all its coaches and the same would be completed by September 2019. With provision of bio-toilets in all its coaches' discharge of human waste from trains on to the track would be completely stopped which in turn would help in improving cleanliness and hygiene besides preventing corrosion of the tracks.

Drones

Production of a drone designed by Harshwardhan Zala, 14 yrs, signed a deal with the Department of Science and Technology, Government of Gujarat, to facilitate production of the drones that help detect and defuse land mines on war fields. Work has started developing the prototype of the landmine-detecting drone in 2016 and a business plan is created. The drone has been equipped with infrared, RGB sensor and thermal meter along with a 21-megapixel camera with a mechanical shutter that can take high resolution pictures as well. The drone is designed to send out waves that cover eight sq. meter area while flying two feet above the surface; the waves detect land mines and communicate their location with a base station. The drone also carries a bomb weighing 50 gram that can be used to destroy the landmine. The teenager added, I started making drones on my own and set up an interface with a base station but realized I need to do more. So I fixed payloads that detect landmines.

Developing drones for the Indian defence establishments and other government organisations is what idea Forge has been doing since 2008—the year when India's Defence Research and Development Organisation (DRDO) spotted the talented team of the three founders rubbing shoulders with the students of MIT USA. In 2009, the startup came out with the world's smallest and lightest autopilot UAV (only 10 gm) and then soon after that developed the country's first fully autonomous vertical take-off and landing UAV. The drones are used by the organisations for intelligence, surveillance and reconnaissance of moving and fixed targets. There are many missions wherein ideaForge's drones have played a primary role including Pathankot attack (2016), the 2014 Beas River tragedy.

Infosys has invested funds in Indian drone startup ideaForge, as the IT Company looks to tap its solutions for industrial uses, idea Forge's drones have been used by the Indian Armed Forces for surveillance, crowd monitoring and rescue operations, and have commercial applications in verticals such as energy, utilities, telecom and agriculture, Infosys said in a statement ideaForge's high performance UAVs, which have been designed and built in India, have significant potential in industrial use cases. We are looking forward to working with ideaForge and bringing their technology, expertise, and solutions to our clients to unlock new business insights from operational data that has previously been difficult to obtain, Ritika Suri, Global Head of Corporate Development & Ventures at Infosys, said in a statement Airport reforms—Electronic boarding passes will come in place of the paper versions under the plan finalized by the Bureau of Civil Aviation Security. Once it is notified, all that a passenger needs to do is to flash the image of the boarding pass on his mobile phone at security clearing and the gate, where it can be scanned. However, there will still be a provision for paper boarding passes for those who can't produce the electronic pass. Boarding passes will be digital and cabin tag redundant. To make the AEP airport executive and vendors' passes more secure, biometric features will be incorporated in it.

D-Health Card—a multi-purpose smart card, designed to provide patients with easy portability of their health care information and give the consultants faster access to their clinical data. The card is in the shape of a credit card. It contains a micro-chip with Smart-Chip Technology which stores all information related to patient's health. "So the patient will not have to carry his films, medical reports and details when he visits the hospital. Instead, this card will be given to the treating consultant, who by inserting it in card reader will get to know about his past medical history. This will not only save time but also will help in becoming paperless.

Secondly, this card will also be a e-Wallet cash card in which the patient can store cash and use it to pay money at any department without the need to carry physical cash. For outstation patients, it will have an added advantage of banks transferring money directly to this card. Government has started issuing smart health cards that integrate the patient's identity data with essential health information that can be quickly accessed; at government hospitals reception counters.

Digital locker: On July 1, 2015 launched digital locker facility that will help citizens to digitally store their important documents like PAN card, passport, mark sheets and degree certificates. "Digital Locker will provide secure access to government issued documents. It uses authenticity services provided by Aadhaar," an official release said.

Electricity projects: In July 2016 Government aimed at information technology-driven power distribution in the next three years that will allow users to get a supply status at 4,041 urban towns on a real-time basis. Once this project is up and running, the consumers can get the information through the URJA mobile application.

"Under the old Accelerated Power Development and Reforms Program, as many as 1,405 urban towns were to be covered for making those IT enabled. The work has already been completed in 1,222 urban towns. Under this project engineers are engaged to assist the power discoms, facilitating better consumer connect and monitoring of Integrated Power Development Scheme (IPDS) 50 discoms will be covered".

The government has appointed 50 young professionals called '*Urban Vidyut Abhiyantas*' to monitor the implementation of technology to bring down technical and commercial losses. These engineers will monitor the implementation of the Centre's ₹ 65,424 crore Integrated Power Development Scheme; and assist and support state power distribution companies—discoms in strengthening urban distribution system and in IT-enablement initiatives.

State discoms will have to mandatorily draw at least 2.75% of their total power consumption from solar plants in the current fiscal year, according to the renewable purchase obligation (RPO) norms laid down by the power ministry.

The current model follows the success of engineers engaged specifically in expediting rural electrification across the country.

e-passport, July 2016: Government is in the process of procuring devices for e-passport. The e-passport is likely to secure the data and curb the menace of fake passports. An e-passport contains an electronic chip. The chip holds the same information that is printed on the passport's data page. The government has given its approval for procurement of electronic contactless inlays for manufacturing of e-passports to India Security Press (ISP) Nasik. It intends offering e-passports to Indian citizens.

e-NAM (electronic-national agriculture market) and e-trading portal: The centre has asked state governments to speed up implementation of e-NAM to achieve the target of integrating 200 mandis (agriculture wholesale market) by September 2016. A total of 585 mandis have to be integrated with e-platform for trading commodities. Under the scheme, a pan India e-trading portal is being deployed in select regulated wholesale markets in states.

The scheme is expected to benefit farmers through enhanced market access by way of allowing remote online bidding for their produce, removal of information asymmetry between buyers and sellers, real-time price discovery based on actual demand-supply gap through transparent online auction and online payment directly to farmers' accounts.

'Digital Green' focuses on educating farmers about farming techniques through locally produced videos, in which local farmers are featured. Gandhi Rikin, MIT technology winner is the founder of this nonprofit. He demonstrated that for every dollar spent, the system persuaded seven times as many farmers to adopt new ideas as an existing program of training and visits. He helped launch the program as a 2006 project at Microsoft Research, India and spent six months testing various video schemes in villages in Karnataka before concluding that featuring local farmers is the key.

Villagers produce the videos using handheld camcorders. Workers from partner non-governmental organizations check the quality of the videos and the accuracy of the advice given; before screening them in the villages with handheld projectors.

So far 500 videos have been made. The current plan is to reach more villages—at least four times of that have been reached (MIT Technology review 2015).

Jagruti: NSE (National Stock Exchange) and India Postal start Unique Financial Inclusion Initiative India Algorithm for finance. A proposed crackdown on algorithmic trading in India could hurt the earnings of the country's two main stock exchanges just as both bourses prepare to make their much-awaited stock market debuts. The Securities and Exchange Board of India (SEBI) in August 2016 outlined new proposals aimed at curbing high frequency trading (HFT) in the country, amid fears that retail investors would be disadvantaged against such advanced and expensive systems (24th Oct. 2016 News item).

Robotics robo-advisors help investors make financial investment plans; based on structured and unstructured information about the investor. This is still at nascent stage, we need more methodologies and capabilities to understand the investor situation. Technology and Stocks, sharing high frequency trading (HFT) and algos are helping automate trading. It deepens the liquidity in the market and achieve tighter spreads.

10-20 years ago, if you were to send an order to the exchange or if you wanted to get a trade done, it took you the whole day and you would know that at the end of the day whether you failed or not or what price did you get. Today, when a retail investor goes to the market, buys share, gets done within a second. It is not by magic. It is by technology behind the depth that is provided by algo and HFT players and they are there for a reason to help match the prices across different investors and help provide the tighter spreads.

Blockchain technologies are being used for stocks and shares transactions. Since Blockchain's disintermediation powers would mean many of the middle-man in various transactions will be redundant. In August 2016, Sebi came out with its discussion paper on algo-trading. The paper had several suggestions, including a minimum resting time and batch processing of orders, speed bumps or random delays of a few milliseconds in order processing, or capping the order to trade ratio, etc. India may use it one day to power our subsidy schemes or cash transfers by government.

Technology in Banking, Robotics: HDFC Bank engages physical robots at its branches. The country's leading private sector ICICI Bank has forayed into 'software robotics'—a first by any Indian bank. Over 200 software robots are now performing over 10 lakh transactions per day for the bank which comprises 10% of its total transactions. The bank will engage 500 software robots by the end of the year which will help it to automate 20% transactions. For ICICI Bank, these 'software robots' have been deployed across functions in retail banking, agri-business, treasury, trade and forex. The bank is expecting a significant improvement in its cost to-income ratio once the initiative is rolled out in full.

Kochhar chairman ICICI Bank also dismissed apprehensions about employee retrenchment due to use of robots in their banking functions. "I don't think there will be any lay-offs," she said. "Every year we hire a few thousand people, so there is no question of any layoff because of software robotics." The use of software robots will help the bank cut down its response time by 60% and reduce the time to avail a personal loan on credit card to a mere four hours from the earlier eight hours. The bank's retail portfolio, which recently crossed ₹ 2 lakh crore, might be the biggest beneficiary of this latest move. "With our retail banking growing at 25% every year, software robotics will enable us to handle larger volumes with the same resources."

AI robot Lakshmi in banking is innovated on 11 November 2016. It handles 125 subjects for the customers; some it voice in English and in relaxed tone other it displays discreetly on its screen. Sensitive financial information like account details are displayed discreetly on the robot's screen and not voiced. It currently speaks in English, gestures, turns around and engages in very life-like conversations. The first one is put up in Union Bank, Chennai.

MFTaaS platform: Wipro successfully launched its Managed File Transfer as a Service (MFTaaS) platform on Microsoft Azure on 16 August 2016. The Software as a Service (SaaS) platform will help enterprises in seamless digital integration and cost-effective collaboration with their clients, partners and employees. The Wipro MFTaaS platform has been published on Azure Marketplace. The platform enables customers widen their reach to new markets by seamlessly integrating with their partner ecosystem. It makes use of Microsoft's cognitive capabilities and collaboration workflows to increase productivity and eliminate wastages in business processes.

Digital Payment Technologies: Pushing the Cause of Financial Inclusion

Payment technologies are being innovated to push the unbanked for financial inclusion and due to demonetisation in November 2016.

Airtel Payments Bank: The company has chosen Rajasthan as the launch pad for its banking services in November 2016. The pilot is aimed at testing systems and processes ahead of a full-scale pan-India launch. Customers across Rajasthan will now be able to open bank accounts at 10,000 Airtel retail outlets, which will double up as Airtel banking points and offer a range of basic, convenient banking services.

Airtel Payments Bank will play an important role in taking banking services to the last mile in a quick and efficient manner and benefit millions of unbanked citizens of this country. Airtel Payments Bank plans to leverage Bharti Airtel's extensive network of over 1.5 million retail outlets, with deep penetration in rural areas.

Aadhaar-based ATM is one such initiative which all of us have worked together to deliver.

This bodes well for a country like India whose smartphone market is expected to witness manifold growth in the coming years. According to Cisco's Visual Networking Index mobile forecast for 2014-19, India will have 651 million smartphones, 18.7 million tablets by 2019. Mobile data traffic is expected to grow 13-fold between 2014 and 2019.

It is these devices that will empower India's unbanked population and introduce them to the benefits of the financial ecosystem. It is these devices that will generate intelligent data and communicate with one another and iron out the creases in India's financial services landscape.

Internet Banking, Bank ATM are Another Digital Modes

Mobile payments will become ubiquitous. These apps will be an integral part of the mobile revolution powering financial inclusion. IoE will help banks keep pace with growing customer demands and help them deliver unique and real-time solutions.

In the wake of demonetisation in November 2016 and promoting cashless transactions at an exponential rate; many mobile apps have come up: Paytm, Freecharge, Bhim, Mobiqik.

With a view to introducing the benefits of banking to India's unbanked population, Cisco has launched its 'Connected ATM solution'. This technology will help banks deploy automated teller machines in remote corners of India in a faster and economical manner. The solution will offer banks connectivity options through 3G and CDMA networks. Connected ATM solution brings down the cost of deployment to nearly half making it a viable option. Cisco also offers a Remote Expert Smart Solution for retail banking that enables virtual face-to-face meetings with high-definition video. This way, banks can be more accessible to their customers and they can interact with each other in real time.

Debit card and credit cards earlier and prepayment cards after demonetization are being promoted more to encourage cashless society. But it needs increased infrastructure at point of sale.

In a country the size of India, such solutions will go a long way in helping the cause of financial inclusion and bringing more and more people under the banking system.

Government is now pushing for the rollout of unstructured supplementary service data (USSD) which can be used to carry out simple banking transactions like account balance enquiry and small fund transfers. National Payments Corporation of India (NPCI), the umbrella organisation for all retail payments systems in India, is working on the USSD platform to make it more user-friendly—so that commands are simpler, names of banks and beneficiaries can be saved on the handset and payments to utilities are feasible. Visa, one of the world's largest payment companies, is keen to be included in the menu that a customer making a USSD mobile banking transaction is asked to select from.

Although there are five lakh USSD transactions per day, the number of successful financial transactions is only 10,000-15,000. "The service is slow. Telecom companies have never been keen to co-operate. The government has lowered the charge from 1.50 to 50 paisa per transaction, but it has to push teleco; which are a formidable lobby. So far they have resisted. Some of the teleco choose to prioritize more lucrative services than USSD, which slows down the service.

Other digital supplementary fund transfer services by banks to banks such as RTGS, NTGS and within bank are useful and time saving.

Biometrics

Currently, bio-metric base Aadhaar card is being used by banks and for financial transactions for Know Your Customer (KYC) mode. Interestingly earlier and even now many of the illiterates in India have been using their thumb impression when they cannot sign their names. Now Iris is an added feature.

From Jan. 1, 2017, all ATM ad points of sale are being authenticated by biometrics—Iris or finger. There are around 1.7 billion Aadhaar cards issued in India. The payments landscape in India is also witnessing a shift to cashless transactions at an exponential rate. With around 697 million debit cards and 25 million credit cards as on July 2016, card transactions over the past two years have been growing steadily at 16% CAGR for debit cards and CAGR of 25% for credit card payments, according to a report released last quarter by Axis Capital. There is similar growth in card acceptance infrastructure as well.

India has become a hunting ground for global hackers and criminals. Of course, in order to benefit from this double safety mechanism. The Aadhaar card should be linked to user bank account. This proliferation of Aadhaar cardholders, number and worth of card present transactions along with the increase in the card acceptance infrastructure highlight the need for a safe and secure payment system. The proactive two-factor authentication mechanism, using Aadhaar-based biometric validation, is being suggested by RBI also to prevent money frauds. This will facilitate government's efforts for cashless society and sourcing of black money. Biometrics are also being used for work attendance and other digital offering modes such as e-passport, digital signature, digital locker, digital health card. More and more of it will be used for more digital offerings.

Iris technology for biometrics: The growth of recognition technology is further fueled by applications in the government, military and defense, banking and finance, consumer electronics, travel and immigration, transportation and healthcare, propelled by advanced security requirements in these domains. Iris recognition technology is also penetrating segments such as smartphones, cars and ATM machines, e-passport programs, national ID proofs, etc. Furthermore, the widespread use of cloud computing technology in order to ensure top notch security is also contributing to the growth of iris recognition biometrics market.

Compared to other forms of authentication technologies such as fingerprint scan, signatures and the like, iris recognition is considered to be more fool proof and reliable, due to the unique characteristics of each and every iris.

Today, iris recognition biometric systems are widely used in physical access control in private enterprises and government establishments. Though security concerns rule the use of this biometric system, it is also used for enhancing productivity, by tracking time, absence and attendance.

In the near future, as more and more physical and information security environments unite, iris recognition technology market will further grow, as new security challenges comes to the fore-inventory management, supply chain management and aspects like competition carves the need for better security requirements. Enterprise and the government—both foresee this amalgamation happening. Iris ID technology will revolutionize security management.

If we talk about smartphones and mobile applications, iris recognition technology is all set to appear as a trending technology fast replacing or complementing fingerprint recognition technology. ABI Research's latest report stated that the global shipments of iris scanner equipped smartphones will reach nearly 300 million by 2021. Iris scanning does not need passwords or PIN number at any stage. The mobile devices will have an iris camera, an IR LED to illuminate iris's features even in the absence of proper light source, and iris image processing software to identify and authenticate the user. Companies like Fujitsu, Microsoft, HP, Samsung, have already introduced phones and tablets enabled with iris scanning into the market.

In the mobile payments industry as well, iris recognition technology will rule the roost. In the recent wake of demonetization and the bid to go cashless, the online and mobile payment industry is all set to grow and with it—there will be growth in the iris tech market space. The technology secure user identities better than any other mediums available today. Despite growth in m-commerce, ecommerce and mobile wallet space, many people still are not comfortable adopting payment gateways because of credibility and security issues. Iris authentication technology will remove security concerns as iris recognition is not affected by external factors, age or health and therefore are more credible. Iris tech's stability and resistance to external damage will drive its future adoption, both to unlock devices as well as to certify mobile payments.

Iris is widely accepted as a more secure and reliable modality to identify and authenticate people. The iris works across a broader population, across all age groups and occupations. Iris scanning also found widespread adoption in government's initiatives pertaining to Aadhaar. Aadhaar is being made mandatory by many organizations. The need for a biometric modality that works reliably is critical for the use of Aadhaar. The use of Aadhaar for resident authentication and eKYC is expected to rapidly spread across services for government and private enterprises. It is a key component of the government's Janadhan, Aadhaar, Mobile (JAM) led initiatives. This authentication service enables an Aadhaar holder to identify himself/herself using the image of iris.

e-commerce: It is delivery of goods through telephone or online orders from regular stores. The convenience of paying online is driving many first-time users to the online grocery platform while meal orders from the working population have also moved to this space. "Before the surge, we were typically servicing 10,000, 11,000 orders daily. Right now, we expect to do about 14,000 orders a day," Online food ordering; Experts are of the view that the rise in online orders for grocery and food is driven by two factors—more metro dwellers using digital payments for everyday meals and also choosing to go online for daily essentials which they would earlier buy from the neighborhood *kirana* stores.

"Food and grocery are probably the only verticals in e-commerce that have benefited from demonetisation, all other online discretionary spends with CoD have taken a hit." This transition to digital payments in a country, which has, historically, been cash heavy expected to help ecommerce companies save on the cost of processing cash-based orders and also minimize product returns, which is pegged at 20-30% of all online retail in the country. The cost of cash-on-delivery orders is 2-2.5% of the order value or ₹ 30, ₹ 50, whichever is higher. Even some food-delivery companies are offering a credit option to customers. "One significant aspect is we have a pay later option, extended to 70,000 of our loyal customers—they can take credit from us for 15 days," said CEO, Faasos Pune-based company, which registered an increase of 20% in orders.

Mumbai-headquartered iPredictt Data Labs, an advanced data analytics company, said it has created a tool that can generate a risk score for customers on e-commerce platforms. It is similar to Cibil score for creditworthiness.

Travel sites such as MakeMyTrip, Cleartrip and Yatra have been the envy of the rest of the e-commerce and Internet industry because of their ability to push all users to make online payments.

M-commerce is through apps on your smartphones. To ease payments on mobiles that face the issue of unstable 3G connections, a startup company has developed an algorithm to determine if the connection will fail while the transaction is going through and will allow long-standing customers to defer the payment.

Smart Cities—The Digital Concept

Developing smart cities is critical to achieving the Sustainable Development Goals and creating safe, inclusive, resilient and sustainable spaces for urban communities.

Envisaged in 2013 Smart City vision is part of a larger agenda of creating Industrial Corridors between India's big metropolitan cities in India. India's Smart City plan is part of a larger agenda of creating Industrial Corridors between India's metropolitan cities. These include the Delhi-Mumbai Industrial Corridor, the Chennai-Bangalore Industrial Corridor and the Bangalore-Mumbai Economic Corridor. It is hoped that many industrial and commercial centers will be recreated as "Smart Cities" along these corridors. The Delhi-Mumbai Industrial Corridor (DMIC), which is spread across six states, seeks to create seven new smart cities as the nodes of the corridor in its first phase.

As per estimates, about 25-30 people will migrate every minute to major Indian cities from rural areas in search of better livelihood and better lifestyles. With this momentum, about 843 million people are expected to live in urban areas by 2050. To accommodate this massive urbanization, India needs to find smarter ways to manage complexities, reduce expenses, increase efficiency and improve the quality of life.

Prime Minister Narendra Modi's vision 'Digital India,' has set an ambitious plan to build 100 smart cities across the country. Modi in his speech quoted, "Cities in the past were built on riverbanks. They are now built along highways. But in the future, they will be built based on availability of optical fiber networks and next-generation infrastructure."

In India, developers both government and public are focusing on projects of developing selected smart cities facilitating urbanization with digital technology infrastructure; and smart village projects to create better living conditions of clean and safe drinking water, toilets and clean environments. Efficient healthcare and the telemedicine are among the few focuses. Innovative technologies are being leveraged to address this infrastructure fatigue, i.e. crumbing bridges, roads with potholes, road traffic jams, railways bottleneck and old tracks, old tunnels. Inadequate infrastructure investment particularly transport continues to be major drag on economy.

A 'smart city' is an urban region that is highly advanced in terms of overall infrastructure, sustainable real estate, communications and market viability. It is a city where information technology is the principal infrastructure and the basis for providing essential services to residents. There are many technological platforms involved, including but not limited to automated sensor networks and data centers.

Thus, the focus is on sustainable and inclusive development to drive economic growth and improve the quality of life of people by enabling local area development through harnessing technology; especially technology that leads to smart outcomes. Area-based development will transform existing areas (retrofit and redevelop) including slums into better planned ones thereby improving livability of the whole city. New areas (Greenfield) will be developed around cities in order to accommodate the expanding population in urban areas. Application of smart solutions will enable cities to use technology, information and data to improve infrastructure and services. Comprehensive development in this way will improve quality of life, create employment and enhance incomes for all especially for the poor and the disadvantaged. Thus, leading to inclusive cities.

Eight critical pillars of India's Smart City Program are: (i) Smart Governance, (ii) Smart energy, (iii) Smart transport, (iv) Smart environment focusing on renewable energy, Water and Waste Water Management, sanitation and safe water supply in rural and urban areas. (v) Smart buildings, (vi) Smart IT & Communications: Information and Communications Technology, (vii) Smart Health Hospitals, and (viii) Smart Education (refer appendix 11 for details).

The government machinery is working on putting together the standards for executing this mega plan, and identifying the cities to be developed in consultation with states. A few smart cities are already coming up across the country, including Kochi Smart City, Gujarat International Finance Tec-City (GIFT) in Ahmedabad, Naya Raipur in Chhattisgarh, Lavasa in Maharashtra and Wave Infratech's 4,500-acre smart city near New Delhi.

These 20 cities will be the first to receive funds in 2016, thus kick starting the process of developing them into 'smart cities'. The next two years will see the inclusion of 40 and 38 cities, respectively.

Of the 98 cities and towns that five years down will graduate into smart cities, 24 are capital cities, another 24 are business and industrial centers, 18 are culture and tourism influenced areas, five are port cities and three are education and health care hubs.

The cities were chosen through intra-city competition evaluated on parameters such as service levels, financial and institutional capacity, past track record and reforms. The cities will be developed to provide world class digital and physical connectivity as well as quality healthcare and education.

Extra weight within the National Value Capture Policy Framework will be given to Value Capture Financing (VCF) model; which may soon decide which project is implemented where in India. India's first VCF policy would help the government recover some value that public infrastructure investments generate for private landowners. VCF is based on the principle that the government makes large investments in developing public infrastructure leading to rapid economic development in those areas, including higher land prices. These add value to the people assets living in those areas.

Rurban Mission is 'Smart City Plus'. 300 villages have been identified, which will be developed as growth center for the area. All infrastructures identical to cities like digital and physical connectivity as well as quality healthcare and education will be provided. "The idea is that the soul of a village is retained while amenities of cities are provided." These selected villages are the ones where rural people from surrounding villages may visit for healthcare, education or getting mobile phones repaired or recharged.

Resource for Smart-Cities Development

The Government of India allocated INR70.6 billion (US$1.2 billion) for Smart Cities in Budget 2014-15. Given the sheer scale of the development plan, the public resources would largely be insufficient and the government is working on envisaging new financing routes to boost the program.

As per the five-year plan to develop such cities, the government will allocate ₹ 200 crore first year and follow up with ₹ 100 crore every year for remaining four years.

States/UTs and Urban Local Bodies have to make an equal matching contribution. This in effect means that central and state governments and ULBs will invest ₹ 96,000 crore over the next five years for making 100 chosen cities Smart.

However, additional resources have to be mobilized from other sources including collection of user fees, beneficiary charges, land monetization, debts and loans to execute the project. "Borrowings from financial institutions, accessing National Investment and Infrastructure Fund and from private sector through PPPs are also options available for the project. World's leading technology solution providers have been keenly waiting the unveiling of the contours of the Mission. Our own private sector is looking forward to take advantage of the investment opportunities," the minister added. It is hoped that it will attract investment to boost the economy. More than a dozen leading countries have expressed keen interest to associate themselves with this Mission which includes US (3 cities), UK, France, Spain (1 city each), Germany (3 cities), the Netherlands, Sweden, China, Singapore (1 city each) Israel, and Australia.

Japan is helping India develop its smart cities by investing US$ 4.5 billion in the first phase of the DMIC project through lending from the Japan International Cooperation Agency (JICA). JICA has also taken up master planning for three "Smart Cities"—Ponneri in Tamil Nadu, Krishnapatnam in Andhra Pradesh and Tumkur in Karnataka—in the Chennai-Bangalore Industrial Corridor. The UK is collaborating with India for developing the Bangalore-Mumbai Economic Corridor project with the help of private companies from Britain.

Implementation: Smart City Plans will be implemented by a Special Purpose Vehicle (SPV) to be set up for each identified city to enable a focused effort for effective implementation. States/UTs 50% and Urban Local Bodies will have 50% equity in SPV. Private sector can also be roped in with equity. But the management control remains with States/UTs.

Citizen engagement is crucial and important for the success of smart cities and to improve the governance to the smart level.

Facilities being Provided in Smart Cities

Cyber–control–Hub. The ₹ 400-crore state-of-the-art center, Indian Cyber Crime Coordination Centre (IC4), is being set up to tackle all cybercrime including child pornography and online abuse. Key objectives of IC4 are: to act as a nodal point in the fight against cybercrime and as an early warning system for law enforcement agencies with active cybercrime monitoring. It will also set up an open platform for victims to lodge cybercrime complaints, besides support and coordinate electronic investigation of cybercrime and assist the law enforcement agencies in criminal investigation.

Smart Cities, Art Cities—Creative Clusters in Smart Cities

The Smart Cities mission provides a significant opportunity to promote creative industries in India, notes an FICCI-EY report titled "Creative arts in India". Launched at the 'Smart Cities, Art Cities', the report covers the opportunities provided by the Indian performing arts industry.

Creative clusters in Smart Cities, which are unique to the character, resources and the local community can serve as a focal point to brand a city's unique cultural identity and embrace its historic significance.

The report also includes a survey with eminent personalities in the industry to understand the challenges faced by the sector. Inadequate infrastructure has emerged as the top most challenge, with obtaining sponsorships and onerous regulations governing the sector completing the top three.

It also highlights the regulatory support the industry expects from the government, with easing out of permissions, rationalization of entertainment tax and availability of credit emerging as the top three.

The report also highlights three key recommendations for the sustained success of the Indian theatre, dance and crafts industry: (i) Form an association/body of India theatre/dance and craft practitioners that exclusively worked for the upliftment and promotion of the sector. (ii) Involve the private sector to invest in the creative arts of the country by adequately incentivising them through tax incentives. (iii) Develop creative clusters showcasing the region's local culture within Smart Cities to attract tourists and residents.

This first ever report on the performing arts and handicrafts industry in India focuses on the current size of the industry, funding mechanisms, key opportunities and challenges faced by the industry, along with best practices followed in other countries and how they drive and fund creative arts.

Global Innovation Index

A meeting between Commerce and Industry Minister Nirmala Sitharaman and World Intellectual Property Organisation (WIPO) Director General Francis Gurry. "Discussed that the methodology of calculating GII also needs to be studied and changed, as appropriate. The parameters should be reflective of the needs and conditions existing in developing nations," the ministry said in a statement. WIPO is requested to set up a external office in India.

According to the GII 2016 report India's rank improved to 66 from 81 last year, a jump of 15 places on Global Innovation Index. To spur an innovative ecosystem across the country, it was proposed that states be ranked on a similar basis. India has requested WIPO to undertake this study, the statement said, adding that WIPO DG has agreed to examine this request. WIPO and the Indian Patent Office are co-operating in training of various IP examiners and other stakeholders, it added. An international training course was organized in RGNIIPM jointly with WIPO Academy in September 2016.

The Commerce Minister also announced setting up of a taskforce on innovation, which would suggest new ideas on best way forward in inculcating an innovative temperament in the country. Many startups in different domains are being encouraged.

Startups: Technology is an important differentiator and allows us to make a difference in many ways than one. It is aptly commented: When an innovative idea comes together with simple, beautiful design and powerful, flexible technology, it can change the way people see their world. Digital transformation brings design and technology together.

NIDHI (National Initiative for Development and Harnessing Innovations), an umbrella program is pioneered by the Department of Science and Technology (DST), Government of India, for nurturing ideas and innovations (knowledge-based and technology-driven) into successful startups. In order to realize the Prime Minister's ambitious Initiative on Startup India, DST aims to bring both speed and scale to transform the Startup Ecosystem in the country and has committed 500 crores to implement these new programs in next few years. This was announced by then Union Minister for Science and Technology and Earth Sciences, Dr. Harsh Vardhan, while addressing the media in New Delhi.

NIDHI focuses on building a seamless and innovation driven entrepreneurial ecosystem especially by channelizing youth towards it and thereby bringing in the positive impact on the socio-economic development of the country. The program aims to provide technological solutions not only to the pressing needs of the society but also targets to create new avenues for wealth and job creation.

NIDHI, by design connects and strengthens all the links of the innovation chain from scouting to sustaining, securing, scaling and showcasing. The key stakeholders of NIDHI includes various departments and ministries of the Central Government, state governments, academic and R&D institutions, mentors, financial institutions, angel investors, venture capitalists, industry champions and private sectors. NIDHI strongly addresses the new national aspirations by massively scaling up DST's experience of three decades in promoting innovative startups.

There are eight components of NIDHI that support each stage of a budding startup from idea to market. The first component PRAYAS (Promoting and Accelerating Young and Aspiring Innovators and Startups), launched on 2 September 2016, aims to support innovators to build prototypes of their ideas by providing a grant up to ₹ 10 lakhs and an access to Fabrication Laboratory (Fab Lab). The final component is the Seed Support System which provides up to one crore rupees per startup and is implemented through Technology Business Incubators.

So far, DST has established more than 100 Technology Business Incubators in academic and R&D institutions of repute. These institutions include IITs, IIMs, NITs and other institutions. Each of these incubators is focused on a Technology Domain and all of these combined together house more than 2000 startups currently and offer a total incubation space of approximately seven lakh square feet.

Various successful and high growth stories in affordable health care, diagnostics, and applications of unmanned aerial vehicles, renewable energy, and service oriented online platforms, payment gateways, etc. have emerged out of these incubators.

In the recently concluded National Expert Advisory Committee Meeting on 3 September 2016, proposal to establish six Centers of Excellence were decided, at SINE-IIT Bombay, Venture Center-NCL Pune, CIIE-IIM Ahmedabad and fourteen Technology Business Incubators which include IIT Patna and Mizoram University. Ten more Incubators to be supplemented with Seed Support Systems for startups include Startup Oasis-Jaipur, Amrita TBI-Kollam, Venture Center, and NCL-Pune etc. and establishing a Research Park at IIT Gandhinagar. In addition, a variety of other new programs including a fellowship program for entrepreneurs in residence, scaling up of startups through accelerator program and women empowerment through entrepreneurship are being setup.

Apart from setting the ground ready for the prospective startups in an enabling environment of Incubators, DST has also partnered with large corporates like Intel, Lockheed Martin, Texas Instruments and Boeing to initiate variety of technology driven and innovation based programs to promote startups. Further, DST has also partnered with Department of Higher Education, MHRD to establish Research Parks and Startup Centers in various academic institutions of national importance.

IIT Delhi, a three-month course started in October 2016; there will be regular such three months courses; for women with startup ideas and those already running startups from thousands of applicants. The course is free of cost and helps the women build their business ideas, connect with customers, network and attract funding. The women will stage a roadshow at IIT-Delhi to showcase their products. Information technologies big and small available today challenges the traditional notions and practices. One important concept is information technology relies on a global grid for international use. Any one nation's desire, decision or trial with IT inevitably links that nation to a larger, global system. It could have ramifications for that global system—depending whether that nation is adopting their older technologies or newer technologies for their use. Or a section of that nation—such as Indian technology outsourcing companies is using as well developing innovative technologies.

Startups in the making: They are coming up in various diverse domains. A few startups are mentioned.

Working on a startup idea of 3D bioprinting in the final stage of conception: It plans to cater to making biocompatible patient and tissue-specific implants for clinical applications. "After several years of lab research in 3D bioprinting technology, we proposed to formulate 3D bio-printed implants that will be patient specific, site-specific and tissue specific."

BeePositive++ startup is a socially sustainable one, is working on creating a cooperative of bee-keepers. In the first phase, BeePositive++ will train existing bee keepers to harvest simpler products like honey and bees wax while simultaneously training more farmers in bee keeping. "In the second phase we will train them to extract more complex products like propolis, royal jelly and bee venom," says Saigal. "These products have a huge market in India and abroad and are used in various industries like the pharmaceuticals and cosmetics.

Startups in Financial Inclusion: Ratan Tata, Vijay Kelkar and Nandan Nilekani have started a technology enabled financial inclusion vehicle, Avanti Finance, which will be focused on delivering affordable and timely credit to under-served and un-served segments in India. The aim is to leverage on the social sector presence of Tata Trusts and other like-minded partners and the rapidly evolving India Stack (Jan Dhan-Aadhaar-Mobile), UPI and payments bank ecosystem. Avanti would use this ecosystem and will innovate on product design in consonance with the indigenous needs, to deliver seamlessly for the end consumer. According to the press release, "the promoters strongly believe that the institutional inequalities and information asymmetries are depriving the target customer segment of access to affordable credit". The target customer segment over the last few years has displayed very low delinquency rates compared to any other customer segment, but still is charged the highest rate of interest. Avanti's primary objective is to make a difference in this sphere thereby enhancing the prosperity in these communities.

The endeavors in the last few years have been focused on creating a sustainable model for interventions which have lasting impact on communities, especially the underprivileged and the deprived.

Avanti will be a platform to impact the poor through credit at individual and community levels to create a lasting improvement in their livelihoods and standard of living, ushering prosperity.

Avanti is more driven by social motivation rather than anything else—with a view to serve the underserved and unserved and make the Tata Trusts and other likeminded partners philanthropy more effective. It will start in March 2017.

Music Saregama, a company from the RP-Sanjiv Goenka group, is turning a new leaf, betting on new technology and its legacy—a huge portfolio of Indian music, with 1.17 lakh tracks. ₹ 2 a song on the pen drive from 78 rpm records. No longer you need buy music CDs.

Technology Startups

Intel India, department of Science and Technology (DST) Department of Science and Technology (DST) and IIT Bombay's SINE, is launching a new a hardware startup incubator called Plugin to support hardware and systems-based startups through mentoring, training, lab facilities, hardware kits, prototyping, business services and funding.

"Whereas lot of innovations are happening in the IoT arena, hardware startups in India lack manufacturing, design and mentoring support," said Nivruti Rai, general manager, Intel India, will lend technical support to budding startups. Intel advocated that India needs customized solutions.

Government has set up an incubation cell at the Indian Institute of Foreign Trade (IIFT) to provide support to export startups. The cell would enable young entrepreneurs to get all the expert advice and technical guidance at one point, the initiative is named as—KITTES (Knowledge for Innovation in Trade and Technology for Entrepreneurial Start-ups). It is dedicated to startups in the domain of international business. Run by MSME center at IIFT it will support startups right from ideation stage to their internationalisation towards taking a final leap into foreign markets. Incubation cell will be supported by an advisory body consisting of industrialists, venture capitalists, technical specialists and managers established to help entrepreneurs realize their dreams through a range of infrastructure, business advisory, mentoring and financial services.

Infosys has begun training its employees and board in "**design thinking**"—a buzzword for prototype-driven innovation—hoping this will help prepare them for a future in which they have to serve as all-around advisers for clients seeking to make their businesses fully digital.

Niti Aayog, Department of Science and Technology (DST) and IIT Bombay tie-up will lead to the creation of laboratories in schools; which aims at teaching skills such as computational thinking, adaptive learning, physical computing and developing a design mindset among students.

Railway Minister Suresh Prabhu announced a 50 crore innovation fund for startups set up by its employees to solve problems unique to the organization. Startups are applying technology to help passengers find confirmed tickets by predicting availability, track PNR numbers, and even have a hot meal by delivering it to their seat. There is needed for innovative solutions to make the 163-year-old Indian Railways more agile:

Railyatri to monitor train ticket confirmation, for daily commuters, the Trainman app provides live station feed, displaying departures from a station for the next four hours. For long journey, ConfirmTKT provides users an end-to-end itinerary to help them complete the journey. It also gives information on when a traveler can break journey and shift to a bus or another train to save time and money.

Startups such as TravelKhana, KhanaGaDi, Yatrachef, RailRider and RailRestro offer food ordering and delivery to passengers on the train at their seat. RailRider aggregates restaurants, making their menus available online for the traveler covering 160 stations. It is working on a logistics model.

App Omitra addresses a basic issue most travelers face during long journeys—boredom—by connecting fellow passengers. "We realized that social networking is not enough. Soon, we will offer entertainment in the form of music or movies, and multiplayer games that work on low internet speed."

The Indian railways website and publicly available data have helped these startups. Startups are able to track trains and trends, and provide information to aid travelers.

Consumer model in the changing technology scenario: This is applicable to upcoming products now. Today, all mobile platforms or any industry is shifting to a more personalized model. The next level of business model innovation is ecosystem innovation. One consumer co-creates experience at a time. "Ecosystem innovation is the natural progression of co-creation". Innovation is moving away from one single company to all the partners. The iPhone is a great example of this kind of an innovation where each consumer gets a personalized experience even as Apple taps into resources it doesn't own, but partners with. The focus is on how to engineer. Of course, doing this isn't necessarily easy. The traditional model of companies doing innovation in research labs is changing to innovating outside one single corporate entity and the biggest challenge will be knowing how to manage this loosely bound set of partners.

Companies should look at various aspects of how they currently do business along with key stakeholders. Doing something like this needs a different kind of flexibility. It needs to think about the rate at which the market and trends are changing and how prepared consumers are. Accordingly, companies need to create current ecosystem, the changes happening and how quickly they can change their business model. Moreover, check how rigid is their supplier connections and who the other partners they need to bring in.

Technology is an important differentiator and allows us to make a difference in many ways than one. The private ecosystem in India is well capable of fostering innovation. What would be helpful from the government is to remove any regulatory uncertainty and friction from the path of innovation. There will be old economies that will be disrupted as a result; but that is how the innovation takes its course. Government can really invest in moonshot innovation—enormous problems like solving for pollution, clean water and electric vehicles—just the way ISRO is doing a fantastic job of enhancing the small satellite low cost launch service in India.

Consumer Behavior: The changes to Indian consumer behavior are being driven by increasing incomes, the younger profile of consumers and growing access to the Internet. According to the FICCI-PwC report, Shaping Consumer Trends, the greatly increased use of smartphones, conscious concerns about health and the environment, technological innovations and the rising complexity of decision-making due to the proliferation of products and points of sale are key areas of change that is impacting consumer and retail businesses.

According to the report, these drivers are reshaping where, what and how consumers' make purchases and how they want to be served. The key business trends that are visibly unfolding and creating a large number of opportunities for consumer-driven companies are:

(i) *Changing purchase patterns*: The shift in purchase behavior towards online buying, dominated by mobile phones, has been very evident over the last few years. Preferences are now clearly extending beyond the original product categories of electronics and fashion to include food and grocery as well as local origin products.

(ii) *Evolving desire for service*: Consumers are now seeking a clutter and trouble-free experience, enabled by technology and better quality sales people.

(iii) *Switch to health and wellness-driven choices*: There is a marked consumer shift towards products and services that are perceived to be relatively healthy and less harmful or enhance people's sense of physical and mental wellness and the environment.

(iv) *Rise of convenience*: Cash-rich and time-starved consumers are seeking a new dimension in 'convenience by knowledge' to help them navigate to the right products and services that are relevant for them.

(v) *Growing social networks*: The concept of (crowd clout) is gaining significance as consumers realize that their collective networks are enabling them to demand improved products and services from companies.

Discussing about the report, Mr. Krish Iyer, Chairman-FICCI Retail & Internal Trade Committee and President & CEO, Walmart India, "The continued focus on ease of doing business by the government augurs very well for India's industries across sectors. We're seeing lot of reforms by the government, not only related to FDI, but also for removing several structural and systemic bottlenecks. So while India remains one of the most attractive markets for businesses worldwide due to its favorable demographics, size of the population, growing purchasing power and the growing consuming class, effective implementation of the progressive policy reforms will further boost the economy and create an ease of doing business environment in its true spirit", added Mr. Iyer.

Mr. Anurag Mathur, Partner and Leader Consumer & Retail, PwC India, said, "India is in a strong position in the world where a growing consumption capacity, demographic shape and lifestyle changes will propel double digit growth for consumer business over the next decade. However, the Indian consumers' selective participation in global consumption trends and concerns coupled with local infrastructure challenges will require a unique response from companies to win and leapfrog on the growth cycle".

India has come a long way in regulating its policies and promoting ease of doing business, and has huge potential for growth in the sector. As per the report, the government is doing policy reforms by liberalizing foreign investment norms and creating a single window clearance policy to facilitate business in the country. But there is a need for further investment under the 'Make in India' campaign for India to compete with the developed nations of the world and make a mark in the sector.

Commenting on the steps the government has taken so far, Mr. Akash Gupta, Partner & Leader, Regulatory Services, PwC India, said, "Globally, investors are looking at India not only for its market size but as a destination with significant long-term potential. The evolving regulatory framework and the dynamism of the government have opened new avenues and have twofold benefits on fulfilling objectives of make in India, and of increasing consumption demand in the country. This is the time when most regulations are and should be created around consumers. In particular, the food and beverages segment has opened up the extensive scope of manufacturing and trading in the country. And with the implementation of 100% FDI in retail trade of food products, we can expect to see an enhanced consumer basket and a utility-driven consumption trend".

Key regulatory recommendations made in the FICCI-PwC Report: (i) Give the FMCG and Retail sector industry status so that companies are eligible for priority sector lending. (ii) Continue to focus on improving ease of doing business in the country to improve the regulatory environment in India. (iii) Rank on the global index. (iv) Implement GST early to achieve cost efficiency in the procurement and supply chain. (v) Provide fiscal incentives to the industry, including on backend infrastructure and supply chain. (vi) Introduce a unified agriculture marketing ePlatform to actualize.

Digital India Challenges

Demonetisation in India Technology Challenges: On 8 November 2016, Prime Minister of India announced to the country banning high denomination 500 and 1000 currency to block black money and counterfeit currency circulation. Later the Prime Minister unfolded their hidden agenda to turn India into cashless and paperless society by everyone changing to digital transactions. Now, all the ministries, policy-makers and government advertisements are focused on digital transactions. This change of narrative is clearly an afterthought.

Ind-Ra believes de-legalization, coupled with the government's resolve to promote the digital platform for transactions will gradually increase the share of the formal sector and expand the tax base of the economy in the medium- to long-term. Also, as transactions through the digital platform increase, it will create financial and transactional history of the informal/cash dependent segment, making them 'bankable' over the medium- to long-term.

Demonetizing Strategies

Digital Technologies Cashless Transactions will Control Black Money is the Government Strategy Put Forward: Recently, the Indian policy-maker and IT billionaire Nandan Nilekani listed some of these changes. Most important, perhaps, is the "unified payment interface" that Nilekani and RBI Governor Raghuram Rajan rolled out, which made it easier for Indian consumers to use their mobile phones to transfer money to each other. Nilekani argues that "this will also shift the business models in banking from low-volume, high-value, high-cost and high fees, to high-volume, low-value, low-cost and no fees—a banking revolution" will add to what India already has—"the most sophisticated public payments infrastructure in the world." Building on this infrastructure, a host of financial technology startups are trying to reduce transaction costs for Indians. As one such entrepreneur recently pointed out, merely transporting cash to and from villages in India cost about $335 million last year: "We are replacing that truck of cash".

But there's good reason to suppose that cashless payments could be adopted much faster in India than elsewhere. It's the classical example of leap-frogging. India's many poor people and migrants still struggle to access its chronically inefficient banking system, despite the government's efforts at reform. If presented with an easy and frictionless way of transferring cash, there's no reason to think consumers wouldn't embrace it quickly—just as most Indians skipped fixed-line telephony to go to mobile and Smartphones.

The 'Digital Payments 2020' report, jointly published by Google and Boston Consulting Group, projects that non-cash contribution in the consumer payments segment will double to 40 per cent. "The smartphone explosion will usher in a new era in Digital payments in India over the next few years that will see digital payments exceed USD 500 billion by 2020 and non-cash transactions exceed cash transactions by 2023".

It also suggested ways for leveraging Aadhaar, or any other proof of identity for authentication of card/digital transactions and setting up of a centralized KYC Registry. The committee also delved into the scope of integration of all government systems like Public Finance Management System, PayGov, Bharatkosh and eKuber.

Digital Payments: Micro ATMs, Aadhaar-enabled, interoperable micro-ATMs, PoS machines, cards. Banks are trying to make the transition and push toward cashless and mobile banking as smooth as possible for customers and themselves, despite the obvious hurdles of lack of banking infrastructure, awfully low smartphone penetration and Indians' love of cash. It is necessary to spread awareness of digital banking channels.

Banks are considering using iris-recognition technology for biometric authentication of transactions. In a step towards financial inclusion, banks that have been beta-testing or using fingerprint-recognizing ATMs on the ground say that while fingerprint scanners are effective, but there are drawbacks. Quite a sizeable number of blue-collar workers and farm laborers who use ATMs have bruises, abrasions or cuts on their fingers. It's quite possible for our fingers to be coated with a film of grease or dust. Even senior citizen finger prints may get faded. So iris-recognition is something they are considering as it is safe, non-invasive and foolproof.

Incubator Khosla Labs which has funded electronic payments startup Novo pay. The startup has 40,000 micro ATMs—no more than a smartphone with a fingerprint scanner attached and sometimes a printer—at small street-corner retail outlets. Novopay already has a presence in 130,000 village retail outlets.

The real challenge is the 350 million people without phones, many of whom are economically-challenged. The plan is to draw those enrolled in Aadhaar, and quickly enlist the remaining, toward micro ATMs promoted by large Indian lenders such as IDFC Bank and startups like Novopay.

Taisys Technologies in association with Yes Bank launch digital banking services in various states, including Goa, Bihar and Arunachal Pradesh. The service, SIMsePAY, allows any account holder to do money transfers, pay utility bills and other mobile banking services, without the need for smartphones or the Internet. The offering is based on a frugal 'sim-sleeve' technology. Sim sleeve disrupts this status quo by providing a transaction application on feature phones. Now feature phones too can initiate transactions as well as can be the merchant POS. Taisys is also planning to launch SIM se Pay in Hindi and other vernacular languages which would help widen the potential user base multi-fold.

Demonetization through digital payments: Government of India has constituted a committee of officers to enable 100 per cent conversion of Government-Citizen Transactions to the digital platform. The Committee, under the leadership of Niti Aayog CEO Mr. Amitabh Kant, will identify and operationalize in the earliest possible time frame user-friendly digital payment options in all sectors of the economy. This is integral part of the government's strategy to transform India into a cashless economy.

The committee led by NITI Aayog will also implement an action plan on advocacy, awareness and handholding efforts among public, micro enterprises and other stakeholders. That apart, it will organize training and capacity building of various States/UTs, Ministries, Departments of the Government of India, representatives of States/UTs, Trade and Industry bodies as well as other stakeholders.

As part of larger efforts to transform the country into a cashless economy, the government has also set up a panel to look into digital payments for all government-citizen transactions.

India Stack is conceived as a pyramidal structure based on the Aadhaar database as the base and unified payments interface (UPI) that is being developed by NPCI (National Payments Corporation of India) as the top; the two middle stacks comprise digital signatures and eKYC. Nilekani has explained that with the help of digital signatures customers will not need to actually sign a paper document, instead it can digitally sign it by using a smartphone. eKYC will also enable the identity of the customer to be identified digitally as well.

Creating digital payment awareness: Among officials, it has been decided that several interfaces should be made tech savvy. These include the common service centers (CSCs), Digital Seva Kendra, schools, petroleum outlets, rural development ministry's outlets and cooperative society outlets along with post offices which can play a role in not just disbursal of digital payments but also in training.

In a 'Mann Ki Baat' program by Prime Minister Narendra Modi, he urged citizens to go cashless on a mission mode and to help educate at least ten in digital payment systems; arming the recent government decision on demonetisation that has taken India "on the cusp of a major financial revolution".

Digital India Challenges erratic Internet connectivity, poor smartphone penetration. The restrictive policy and regulations etc. are major roadblocks in realizing the vision of Digital India. Some of the common policy hurdles include the following lack of clarity in foreign direct investment policies; for instance, have impacted the growth of e-commerce. Most challenging is low digital literacy and the supporting digital infrastructure. Inadequacy of appropriate skills, experience and technical capabilities is a challenge.

With the proliferation of cloud-based services like DigiLocker, data security has emerged as a major challenge.

The recent data breach in August 2016, in which debit card data for more than 3.2 million subscribers was stolen, highlights the importance of implementing foolproof security systems.

PPP models need to be explored for sustainable development of digital infrastructure, as has been the case for civic infrastructure projects like roads and metro project. In addition, the government should make efforts to make additional spectrum available to telecom service providers for deployment of high speed data networks.

Effective collaboration with the private sector is critical to the development of the digital infrastructure. Innovative engagement models that ensure commercial viability needs to developed jointly through consultation with industry bodies. This will encourage private sector participation and ensure a better response to infrastructure RFPs. In addition, startups need to be incentivized for the development of the last mile infrastructure and localized services and applications.

In rural and remote areas, private sector players should be incentivized to provide last mile connectivity. USOF (universal telecom funds) can be effectively used to incentivize and create a viable business model. The deployment of funds so far has been erratic and not been used to effectively to fund the cost of infrastructure creation in rural areas.

Satellite communication solutions could be used to speed up broadband access in rural and remote areas. For instance, banks can use VSAT technology to connect remote ATMs, remote branches that need instant access to customer data. It could be used as a last mile connectivity solution in rural areas which lack telecom networks.

Capacity building is crucial in addition to digital infrastructure development, digital literacy, skill building and higher adoption of digital solutions are all necessary for success of Digital India program.

Despite rising smartphone penetration and Internet user base, digital literacy in India has been low. Improving digital literacy is imperative for the benefits of the Digital India program to reach all sections of the population. A strong skill base is required to support the initiatives and services that are envisaged under the Digital India program.

Demonetisation will help boost digital transactions. The adoption of digital payments which could have otherwise taken three to six years would now take 3-6 months due to the government's currency overhaul process.

Shopping online: Why people in rural India are not shopping online; StoreKing, an assisted ecommerce platform; lists out a bunch of irritants: every village does not have a pin code, which makes deliveries difficult, low literacy levels, English language barrier and lack of trust in the Internet. "Over 85% of the population has no access to debit and credit cards and half of the population is not reachable by traditional courier services." So, despite having the money and the intent, people in small towns and villages are unable to shop on line. Retail analysts maintain that the task to digitize rural India might be challenging, but not impossible. India is trying to end its reliance on cash, especially in rural areas where almost every transaction is done in hard currency. Nilekani and his 13-person committee are meeting to work out how to get more Indians to adopt digital payments, via everything from their own smartphones to point-of-sale machines in local villages. While the nation has already rolled out its United Payments Interface, with hundreds of millions lacking phones or web access, a multipronged approach is needed to wean the nation of its dependence on cash. India has the underlying digital financial architecture in place to get this going.

Indian Government has invested in payment banks and payment infrastructure. Now, it is the case of building application on top of those. Bill Gates of Microsoft had expressed keen interest in digital payments, digital health and e-agriculture in India. Bill Gates (2016) "digital transactions will be a game changer, reducing inflation, interest rates and transaction fees. "Digital world lets you track things," said Gates, pointing out that some countries use very little cash and are now moving to debit cards to cell phones. The world as a whole will go cashless, but predicting for any country when that will happen is very hard to say".

Cyber security for digital modes is crucial: To prevent the government's digital payments push getting hit by e-fraud, the Reserve Bank of India has issued notification on 9 December 2016 further says: "As the rapid escalation in e-payments may put significant pressure on the existing digital infrastructure, it is imperative that the integrity of our digital ecosystem is maintained by ensuring that they remain robust and fully secure." Banks have a very high level of responsibility when adopting digital channels—to not only ensure security of the channel at infrastructure level, protect data security and personal privacy at system level, but also address the need to build customer awareness on security matters.

Information Communication Model in Third Wave

Any one nation's desire, decision or trial with IT inevitably links that nation to a larger, global system. It could have ramifications for that global system—depending whether that nation is adopting their older technologies or newer technologies for their use. Or a section of that nation—such as Indian technology outsourcing companies is using as well developing innovative technologies. In 2nd wave, there has been focus on developing technologies such as Quantum computers, laser and their applications. In India during 3rd wave, there has been digital changeover, overlapping of global digital waves in India re Communication revolutions, applications in Quantum computers, Laser development in India re Atomic energy, Medical and Industrial applications and Laser for Optic use.

Digital scenario in Mobile (Cellular) technology focused on Mobile feature and Smartphones and many digital platforms including e-governance and for financial inclusion. Primary focus has been on developing digital economy in India which spurted 2014 onwards due to Modi Government initiatives.

In 3rd wave ICT Model, there is more focus on developing apps on the technology devices unique for India/Indian population in addition to global apps. Focus has been on developing innovative devices and applications and digital modes. Hence, a wave of Startups initiated by individuals, supported by venture capitalists, technology institutes and even well-known corporates and their experts creating Startups hubs. Government is also creating facilities both technical and financial to support and encourage them. To implement Prime Minister 'Initiative on Startup India', Department of Science and Technology (DST) aims to bring both speed and scale to transform the Startup Ecosystem in the country.

The consequent information society model has been more tech savvy population, both receptivity and inclination for digital modes by the governance as well as people. Thus, 'Political Will' has created digital ambiance and a move towards a cashless society.

Information management is an art. It requires knowledge, resources, and pragmatics. Indian media is going through a metamorphosis in their management process, attitudes, and strategies to meet the changes in communication technologies. It is important to set up technology hardware as well as software. It is equally important to navigate through information highways and sort out information vs misinformation.

Efforts to provide innovative communication solutions to businesses within the communication industries—involving network management, network capacity; understanding of the problematic issues of these industries, and the experience and expertise is needed to solve these and focus on other associated needs. A confidence to integrate ideas with information and knowledge to change business approaches is challenging.

Summary

Technology is becoming more pervasive so its use and utility will also grow. However, there is a pause at this moment because the nature of the change is significant. On one hand, with automation, the need of manual intervention or need of human intervention is coming down and on other hand the use of technology is becoming hugely pervasive. India is trying to coexist with the most innovative and latest of global third wave as well as the old technologies of 1st wave (with its trickle down effects) since the digital divide among its diverse level population is wide and so is the innovative spirit of its certain segment of population and the aspirations of its governance that it goads one and all in the country towards digital modes and updated technologies.

CHAPTER 6

Futuristic Trends in Technologies

Our earlier chapters have highlighted the communication technology trend globally and also in India. But there is more to come in these directions and everyday, the media tell us, people tell us the latest and the innovative breakthroughs and also the emerging needs of people; industry and enterprises in these directions. We are highlighting these futuristic trends in many domains. These are likely to be digital and contribute towards digital revolution in many ways.

Investment in science and technology builds capability and capacity, and develops the sort of people who benefit the economy and society more widely.

Futuristic Technologies are Innovative and Revolutionary

Efficient transportation is a great connector. Third wave technology is focusing on innovative and revolutionary technologies in this context. These are focusing on surface, trains—bullet, Hyperloop and even driverless; aviation and space technologies.

Developing high speed international flights with low noise: Boom & Co., Spaceship Co. Boom has already struck a deal with the Spaceship Co., the manufacturing division of Richard Branson's Virgin Galactic, to use that company's engineering, design, and flight-test support services. The Spaceship Co. also has options for Boom's first ten aircraft as part of the arrangement. Because of the plane's sonic, the company is focused on over-water routes and doesn't plan to market its aircraft for quick zips across America or places like the Middle East to Western Europe. Working for release in early 2020.

In the strategic rivalry between Japan and China, high-speed rail contracts are one of the best ways to project power. And no Asian country offers more opportunities than India. Indian leader picked Japan as a partner for the nation's first line—a 980-billion-rupee ($15 billion) rail linking Mumbai and Ahmedabad, roughly the distance from Paris to London. Abe hopes that will make Japan the front-runner if India implements five other planned lines.

Japanese and Chinese technologies are for fast and bullet trains. Chinese technologies boast of manufacturing the trains in difficult geo areas of high terrains. India is negotiating with Japan to make its first bullet train between 2016-17.

Hyperloop technologies are being used in the next mode of transportation. A Hyperloop is a high speed, intercity transportation system which uses passenger and cargo capsules inside a reduced-pressure tube system that would reach a top speed of 800 miles per hour (1,300 km/h) with a yearly capacity of 15 million passengers. Elon Musk envisioned it as an alternative to the California High-Speed Rail project.

Hyperloop Transportation Technologies (HTT), a US startup which is hoping to revolutionize travel. The Hyperloop—high-speed travel in pods inside a partial-vacuum tube—is the brainchild of Tesla founder Elon Musk. Hyperloop technology has been explicitly open-sourced by Elon Musk and SpaceX, and others have been encouraged to take the ideas and further develop them. To that end, several companies have been formed, and dozens of interdisciplinary student-led teams are working to advance the technology.

Elon Musk, who open-sourced the basic design in 2013 in the form of a white paper. Since then, two companies—HTT and Hyperloop One, backed among others by GE Ventures and Khosla Ventures—have taken the lead in building what they hope will be commercially successful companies based on this technology. It estimates that a single tube could carry 1.44 lakh passengers daily at 40-second intervals. Over a distance of 500 km, it is aiming for ticket price under $30, or ₹ 2000. Earlier this year, it reached an agreement with Slovakia to serve as a hub in developing a Hyperloop line connecting Vienna, Bratislava, and Budapest.

The Hyperloop will run on renewable energy. There will be solar panels on the top of the tube, wind turbines in the pylons. We will generate more energy than we need. HTT says it will rely heavily on renewable and kinetic energy and keep costs low by using medians for the pylons.

"India is the perfect example of a vibrant country that could benefit immensely from more immediate, reliable and meaningful connections between markets of all sizes. We are very happy to address a country like India that has the right amount of density, lack of infrastructure and the willingness for innovation," Bibop Gresta, Chairman of HTT.

The Indian Government has been focusing on improving the infrastructure in the country. PM Narendra Modi, in particular, has talked about bringing bullet trains to India.

The first bullet train is expected to run between Mumbai and Ahmedabad and is expected to be built by 2023 at a cost of about $12 billion. But Gresta thinks bullet trains pale in comparison to the Hyperloop system. "I think it (bullet trains) would be a big mistake for India. India has the potential to really embrace new technologies. Put $1 billion in Hyperloop. And you have a faster, more efficient way to transport people," Gresta said.

HTT has been experimenting in Pune since September 2016. Once the LoI (Letter of Intent) is signed it is technically feasible to have the Hyperloop up and running in as little as 38 months, assuming all clearances and land use are processed.

HTT uses a crowd-collaboration approach by roping in about 800 engineers and companies who are working for stock options. There are about 25 people from India working on the technology, Gresta said. The company has raised $30 million in cash and an additional $70 million of land rights and services. About 15 large companies including vacuum-tube pioneers Leybold and engineering company AECOM are working with HTT. Two Indian engineering companies are also working with HTT.

The proposed routes HTT is interested and their feasibility, Hyperloop is potentially looking at five Indian sectors where the system can be built: Delhi-Mumbai, Bangalore-Thiruvananthapuram, Chennai-Bangalore, Mumbai-Chennai and a port connector project. Imagine Chennai to Bangalore in 30 minutes at fare much less than the airfare is the conceived project in India.

The way forward for the vacuum-tube transportation in India could potentially see large hurdles, as with most major infrastructure projects. Land acquisition for building the Hyperloop system and the funding itself will be one of the largest challenges in India. Even though it might sound like a cool concept, the reality of this coming to India might be a little slim at the moment. Though Modi Government is very interested in this.

Why the need for Hyperloop: Conventional means of transportation (road, water, air, and rail) tend to be expensive, slow, and environmentally harmful. Road travel is particularly problematic, given carbon emissions and the fluctuating price of oil. As the environmental dangers of energy consumption continue to worsen, mass transit will be crucial in the years to come. Rail travel is relatively energy efficient and offers the most environmentally friendly option, but is too slow and expensive to be massively adopted. For distances less than 1500 km, supersonic travel is unfeasible, as most of the journey would be spent ascending and descending (the slowest parts of a flight). Given these issues, the Hyperloop aims to make a cost-effective, high speed transportation system for use at moderate distances. The Hyperloop tubes would have solar panels installed on the roof, allowing for a clean and self-powering system.

'Hyperloop One Global Challenge', announced by the company in May 2016, was able to attract 2,600 teams of engineers and planners from across the globe, according to a report from Inverse. The 35 finalist teams were announced and will present at three showcases that will be held by the company in New Delhi on February 28, Washington DC on April 6 and London on 27 April 2017.

The company will be inviting government leaders to these showcases, to display the potential of the high-speed system in their individual regions. Nick Earle, who oversees global field operations of 'Hyperloop One' said, the feedback from governments will determine if Hyperloop One is considered for the region.

The company has shared a big list of potential routes across the globe. Earle has said that there could be multiple winners going forward, and the company is keeping all options open.

Regions that win will then be checked for feasibility before the company moves forward with any projects. "We want to have three routes in production in the next five years," said Lloyd to Inverse. This means that Hyperloop will be choosing only three systems to build out of the 35 it has projected.

"Hyperloop is a new technology and a new regulatory body will have to be formed to ensure safety and accountability. It is unlikely that the governments will allow the company to go unmonitored," said an official.

Flying Cars

Airbus, as the world's largest maker of commercial helicopters, wanted to invest to make the most of new technologies such as autonomous driving and artificial intelligence, to usher in an era of flying cars.

Airbus Group plans to test a prototype for a self-piloted flying car as a way of avoiding gridlock on city roads by the end of the year 2017, the aerospace group's chief executive said.

Airbus in 2016 formed a division called Urban Air Mobility that is exploring concepts such as a vehicle to transport individuals or a helicopter-style vehicle that can carry multiple riders. The aim would be for people to book the vehicle using an app, similar to car-sharing schemes.

"One hundred years ago, urban transport went underground, now we have the technological wherewithal to go above ground," Airbus CEO Tom Enders told the DLD digital tech conference in Munich, adding he hoped the Airbus could fly a demonstration vehicle for single-person transport by the end of the year. He said using the skies could also reduce costs for city infrastructure planners. "With flying, you don't need to pour billions into concrete bridges and roads," he said.

Driverless Cars

An autonomous car (also known as a driverless car, auto, self-driving car, robotic car) is a vehicle that is capable of sensing its environment and navigating without human input. Many such vehicles are being developed, but as of February 2017 automated cars permitted on public roads are not yet fully autonomous.

Driverless car technology is here but and it becomes abundantly clear that we have a lot more planning to do before we can unleash this new form of robot agency on the world. It's messy, difficult work, and it most likely requires we rethink core assumptions about how roads are built, whether we need precise guard rails to protect us, and whether (or what kind of) cars should even be allowed near pedestrians and inside congested city centers. In short, we most likely need an entirely new plan for transit, one that deeply rethinks the role automobiles play in our lives. Initially, highway driving is aimed at. Roads and pedestrian concerns are necessary and important to be structured and worked out.

When we imagine a world of self-driving cars, we imagine that only one thing changes: the driver shifts from a human to a generally competent AI robot. Everything else stays the same. The cars drive on the same roads, follow the same rules, and act just like when human were driving.

Currently, two options for driverless cars: (i) either human being on the steering and sensor guiding him; (ii) a robot sits and drives the car through sensor guiding him.

Many auto companies—Tesla, Mercedes, Autoliv and others are working on autonomous cars:

NVIDIA: At the Bosch Connected World 2017 in Berlin NVIDIA's CEO Jen-Hsun Huang announced that NVIDIA will provide technology enabling Level-4 autonomous driving capabilities by the end of 2018 (Source: *NVIDIA*, 2017-03-16).

Audi: Audi to introduce a self-driving car by 2020; Scott Keogh, Head of Audi America announced at the CES 2017 that an Audio that really would drive itself would be available by 2020 (Source: *IEEE Spectrum*, 2017-01-05).

Volkswagen: The company expects first self-driving cars on the market by 2019; Johann Jungwirth, Volkswagen's appointed head of Digitalization Strategy, expects the first self-driving cars to appear on the market by 2019. He did not claim that these would be Volkswagen models (Source: *Focus*, 2016-04-23).

GM: Autonomous cars could be deployed by 2020 or sooner; General Motor's head of foresight and trends Richard Holman said at a conference in Detroit that most industry participants now think that self-driving cars will be on the road by 2020 or sooner (Source: *Wall Street Journal*, 2016-05-10).

BMW CEO Harald Krueger said that BMW will launch a self-driving electric vehicle, the BMW iNext, in 2021(Source: *Elektrek*, 2016-05-12).

Ford's: Raj Nair, Ford's head of product development, expects that autonomous vehicles of *SAE level 4* (which means that the car needs no driver but may not be capable of driving everywhere) will hit the market by 2020 (Source: *autonews*, 2016-02-27).

Toyota: It plans to bring the first models capable of autonomous highway driving to the market by 2020 (Source: *Wired.com*, 2015-10-08).

Elon Musk expects first fully autonomous Tesla by 2018, approved 2021. In an interview by Danish newspaper *Borsen* (2015-09-23). Elon Musk, CEO of Tesla estimates that "five or six years from now we will be able to achieve true autonomous driving where you could literally get in the car, go to sleep and wake up at your destination.

Jaguar and Land-Rover to provide fully autonomous cars by 2024 says Director of Research and Technology at the

2014 Paris Motor Show Dr. Wolfgang Epple (Source: *Drive.com.au*, 2014-10-03).

Nissan to provide fully autonomous vehicles by 2020. Andy Palmer, the Executive Vice President of California-based Nissan Motors Ltd., has announced that Nissan will make fully autonomous vehicles available to the consumer by 2020. These cars will be able to drive in urban traffic. In contrast to Google's cars, Palmer claimed that they will not need detailed 3D maps for local navigation (Source: *Nissan Motors*, 2013-08-27).

Intel CTO predicts that autonomous car will arrive by 2022. Intel is hoping to equip autonomous smart cars with its Atom and Core processors.

***Google*:** Google's founder Sergey Brin plans to have Google driverless car in the market by 2018.

NuTonomy to provide self-driving taxi services in Singapore by 2018, expand to 10 cities around the world by 2020. The company has just started trials of its self-driving taxis in Singapore's 1 North District. It plans to deploy self-driving taxis commercially in Singapore by 2018 and aims to be operational with fleets of self-driving taxis in ten cities of the world by 2020 (Source: *Yahoo News*, 2016-08-29, Digital Trends, 2016-05-24).

Delphi and MobilEye to provide off-the-shelf self-driving system by 2019; both companies have announced that they will bring a fully self-driving (SAE level 4) system on the market for use in a variety of cars in 2019 (Source: *The Verge*, 2016-08-23).

Ford CEO announces fully autonomous vehicles for mobility services by 2021. Mark Fields, Ford's CEO announced that the company plans to offer fully self-driving vehicles by 2021. The vehicles, which will come without steering wheel and pedals, will be targeted to fleets which provide autonomous mobility services. Fields expects that it will take several years longer until Ford will sell autonomous vehicles to the public (Source: *Reuters*, 2016-08-16).

Uber fleet to be driverless by 2030; Uber CEO, Travis Kalanick, has indicated in a tweet that he expects Uber's fleet to be driverless by 2030. The service will then be so inexpensive and ubiquitous that car ownership will be obsolete (Source: *Mobility Lab*, 2015-08-18).

Baidu's Chief Scientist expects large number of self-driving cars on the road by 2019. In an interview session, Andrew Ng, the chief scientist expects that a large number self-driving cars will be on the road within three years and that mass-production will be in full swing by 2021 (Source: *Quora*, 2016-01-29).

Fully autonomous vehicles could be ready by 2025, predicts Daimler chairman, **Dieter Zetsche** fully autonomous vehicles which can drive without human intervention and might not even have a steering wheel could be available on the market by 2025. Driverless cars will be in use all over the world by 2025; US Secretary of Transportation stated at the 2015 Frankfurt Auto show. Truly autonomous cars to populate roads by 2028-32 estimates insurance think tank.

Expert members of the Institute of Electrical and Electronics Engineers (IEEE) have determined that driverless vehicles will be the most viable form of intelligent transportation. They estimate that up to 75% of all vehicles will be autonomous by 2040.

Will there be less gridlock?

With a heterogeneous mix of vehicle configurations and on-demand service delivery, autonomous vehicles will enable a higher density of passengers per road mile. Also, because AVs can travel safely closer together, and with less braking and accelerating than human drivers, traffic will flow more smoothly and congestion will decrease. On motorways more vehicles will be able to fit safely into the same length of road, effectively increasing capacity.

Will automated vehicles be vulnerable to hackers?

A driverless car has more control units, computing power, lines of code, and wireless connections with the outside world than a regular car today, which is why it's more vulnerable to hackers, explains Andy Birnie, systems engineering manager at NXP Semiconductors. "A hacker can potentially take control of the car, through exploitation of a weakness, and could cause the vehicle to refuse to start, or to crash, or it could exploit the privacy of the driver, and [their] data, including financial information."

However, a shift in the approach to security is under way, he says. "There is now more focus on the basics—applying good fundamental security to the critical areas including the interfaces that connect the vehicle to the external world; gateways, which separate safety critical systems from other car and infotainment systems; and networks that provide secure communication between control units—there can be over 150 in an autonomous vehicle." In addition, major advances to security include "over-the-air" software updates that can patch vulnerabilities seamlessly in real time, Birnie says.

Do AVs reduce the risks for pedestrians and cyclists?

We're only at the start of understanding how pedestrians and cyclists will interact with a vehicle that doesn't have a human driver at the controls. Whether a pedestrian will be able to detect whether a car is automated or not, and adapt their behavior accordingly, we still don't know. There's a risk, initially at least, that pedestrians and cyclists may try to "test" AVs to see how they react.

"In Singapore, they are currently testing autonomous vehicles in public parks and they tell us that the large majority of incidents [near misses] are not due to malfunctioning of the vehicles, but to people jumping in front of the cars to test whether they stop in time."

Mixed traffic carries risk, just as there may be risks associated with behavioral patterns we cannot foresee. "As with any new technology, there will be failures and even fatalities, but the overall benefits—in terms of [estimated] 90% fewer accidents, 40% less congestion, up to 80% less emissions, and 50% of parking space saved—are so substantial that the technological development will prevail."

What other autonomous vehicles might we see on our roads?

Our roads and pavements may have from vertical take-off and landing "flying car" prototypes to "sidewalk robots" and delivery drones, by 2030.

Scientists have developed a self-driving scooter, using the same technology that powers autonomous cars, which could help mobility-impaired people move around even in indoor spaces. The researchers had previously used the same sensor configuration and software in trials of autonomous cars and golf carts, so the new trial completes the demonstration of a comprehensive autonomous mobility system. A mobility-impaired user could use a scooter to get down the hall and through the lobby of an apartment building, take a golf cart across the building's parking lot, and pick up an autonomous car on the public roads.

Driverless trucks are already being tested around the world, with Daimler testing on public roads in the US and Germany in 2016. Bosch meanwhile, envisages that a truck will become "a 40-tonne smart device on wheels" by 2025. "[The trucks] will receive all the data they need in real time from the Bosch IoT cloud, including information on the route, congestion, detours, and unloading facilities at the destination. This will allow the driver to get on with other things [such as processing shipping documents], while the truck drives itself.

Technology about driving cars: Over the next decade, accelerating autonomous driving technology, including advances in artificial intelligence, sensors, cameras, radar and data analytics, are set to transform how we drive (or, indeed, are driven), but the notion of car ownership itself. It is also transforming the global car industry and autonomous driving has become the next major battlefield for the car industry. The new trial establishes that the researchers' control algorithms work indoors as well as out. "We were testing them in tighter spaces," said Scott Pendleton, a graduate student at the National University of Singapore (NUS). The system, designed by researchers from Massachusetts Institute of Technology (MIT) and Singapore-MIT Alliance for Research and Technology (SMART), includes several layers of software.

Algorithms use: Low-level control algorithms enable the vehicle to respond immediately to changes in its environment, such as a pedestrian darting across its path. Localization algorithms can be used to determine the vehicle's location on a map. Map-building algorithms is used to construct the map, a scheduling algorithm allocates fleet resources and an online booking a scheduling algorithm allocates fleet resources and an online booking system that allows users to schedule rides.

Using the same control algorithms for all types of vehicles—scooters, golf carts, and city cars—has several advantages. One is that it becomes much more practical to perform reliable analyses of the system's overall performance. "If you have a uniform system where all the algorithms are the same, the complexity is much lower than if you have a heterogeneous system where each vehicle does something different," said Daniela Rus, professor at MIT.

Electric Cars

Will all cars be electric: "I don't think all of them will be electric by 2030", says Danny Shapiro, senior director at NVIDIA, whose AI computer platform powers the supercomputer in Tesla vehicles. "Virtually every startup is looking at electric, and you have ever greater electric and hybrid focus from German, Japanese and US (manufacturers). But at the same time there's still a huge oil infrastructure. And, at least for the next four years, there's a very pro-oil administration in the US."

Bosch is developing a lithium-ion solid state battery that they hope will double the range of electric vehicles at half the cost of today's batteries, which Steffen Hoffmann, the corporation's UK president, believes will increase take-up among those who live in the suburbs and beyond. "We have a projection that by 2025, globally 15% of vehicles are going to have an electric component, whether that's a pure electric vehicle, a plug-in hybrid or full hybrid," he says. "For western Europe, that percentage would obviously be higher."

Electric vehicle market is not without challenges. Unlike traditional vehicles, EVs require a different value chain and processes to support them. Moreover, consumer perceptions of the practicality, functionality, and the potential advantages of EVs remain largely mixed in such areas as cost, savings, convenience, travel range, and charging infrastructure. To succeed in the current business environment, OEMs will need to adopt new strategies to realize the full potential of the evolving e-Mobility market. One important factor will be integrating and collaborating with a group of diverse players, such as utilities, charging infrastructure owners, and mobility providers in a new mobility ecosphere. OEMs have to face these challenges as to succeed in today's EV market. Therefore, Accenture has identified seven success factors for the e-Mobility market that will ensure its long-term viability.

***India*:** A joint effort by the Indian Government and automobile lobby group Society of Indian Automobile Manufacturers (Siam), was formed to develop a network of suppliers to support the efforts of consortium members to build six electric and hybrid vehicles. The consortium of companies is setup.

The consortium members are, Maruti Suzuki India Ltd., Mahindra and Mahindra Ltd., Mahindra Reva India Pvt. Ltd. and Tata Motors Ltd. Ford has moved out in March 2017.

The move is part of the Indian Government's efforts to have six million electric and hybrid vehicles on the roads by 2020 under the National Electric Mobility Mission Plan 2020 and FAME (Faster Adoption and Manufacturing of Hybrid and Electric Vehicles) programs. Under these programs, the government and industry plan to invest ₹ 12,000 crore each. In the Union Budget for 2016-17 year, the government allocated ₹ 200 crore for these programs.

For the project, code-named *xEV One*, the department of heavy industry has sanctioned an initial grant of ₹ 22 crore while each firm will invest an initial ₹ 4.4 crore for every model it wants to make.

The members of the consortium are to focus on the design, development and manufacturing of certain key components such as the motor, motor controller, charger, DC-DC converter and battery; help nurture one developer for each component; build roadworthy prototype vehicles using these components; and evaluate prototype vehicles for functional performance and safety.

The consortium planned to finalize common standards for these components within five months of the launch, by December 2016. By April 2017, it will seek an expression of interest for sourcing components. The first prototypes are expected to be rolled out by January 2018 and the deadline for the evaluation of the vehicles is set for June 2018.

Sales of electric vehicles in India rose 37.5% to 22,000 units in the year ending 31 March from 16,000 in 2014-15, according to Siam. However, only 2,000 units were four-wheelers (*Live Mint* e-paper 22 March 2017).

Bajaj Auto seems to be extremely keen on launching an electric-powered motorcycle before the turn of the decade. With the government pushing electric and hybrid automotive technology through FAME (Faster Adoption and Manufacturing of Hybrid & Electric Vehicles in India), e-vehicles/hybrids are the buzzword today with the segment receiving attractive subsidies which make the vehicles attractively priced apart from the fuel efficiency the technology offers. Maruti Suzuki India has announced Ciaz & Ertiga; Bajaj is keen to do tesla in India, and Mahindra e-20 plus car.

Space Research

Indian space research organization (ISRO) launched 83 satellites in one go using its workhorse PSLV-C37 toward the end of January 2017. Of the 83 satellites, 80 belong to Israel, Kazakhstan, Netherlands, Switzerland and the US. They weigh about 500 kg. The three Indian satellites are Cartosat-2 series, weighing 730 kg as primary payload, and INS-IA and INS-1B, weighing 30 kg. Setting a record in its space program, ISRO in June had successfully launched 20 satellites, including its earth observation Cartosat-2 series, in a single mission on board PSLV-C34 from the spaceport in Sriharikota in Andhra Pradesh.

The space agency had earlier sent ten satellites into orbit in a single mission in 2008.

Kiran Kumar Director ISRO said, the main emphasis now was on building capacity. "We need more and more capacity, launch capacity. We are working toward that; our effort is to continuously increase it (2017)".

On transponder augmentation that ISRO is looking for, he said, "GSAT-17 is having another 48 transponders, then there is a SAARC satellite which will have about 12 transponders, then we are getting into the next generation GSAT-11 and GSAT-19. We are trying to do something like 14 gigabyte and 90 gigabyte type of thing—multi beam satellites." "Noting that ISRO is conducting tests for hazard avoidance for Chandrayaan 2 as it lands then it has to avoid boulders and things; so there are some craters created and as it come down how it negotiates; verifying the performance of the system as designed. We are evaluating the performance of the system," Kiran Kumar added. ISRO has been conducting these tests at its facility in Challakere in Chitradurga district of Karnataka, India.

Space Technologies are Progressing Fast in India

Mangalyaan's contribution: The Mars Orbiter Mission (MOM) called Mangalyaan is a space probe orbiting Mars since 24 September 2014. It was launched on 5 November 2013 by ISRO. India's second interplanetary mission is planned for launch to Mars by ISRO in 2020. It will consist of an orbiter, and may include a lander and a rover. Home-grown components and technologies have also been prioritized over expensive foreign imports. Mangalyaan has gone equipped with an instrument that will try to measure methane in the atmosphere.

The enormous distances involved in interplanetary missions present a demanding challenge; developing and mastering the technologies essential for these missions that will open endless possibilities for space exploration. After leaving Earth, the Orbiter will have to endure the interplanetary space for 300 days before Mars capture. Apart from deep space communications and navigation-guidance-control capabilities, the mission will require autonomy at the spacecraft end to handle contingencies.

Even though Mangalyaan has a small payload, it will actually address some of the biggest questions at the Red Planet.

Marking India's first venture into the interplanetary space, MOM will explore and observe Mars surface features, morphology, mineralogy and the Martian atmosphere. Further, a specific search for methane in the Martian atmosphere will provide information about the possibility or the past existence of life on the planet.

ISRO's first MOM (MOM-1), which got into orbit around Mars in September 2014, has been looking for signs of atmospheric methane while studying surface features—just like the NASA MAVEN mission that started operating around the same time. Methane is considered a biomarker: a substance whose presence indicates the current or historical presence of life. The American space agency's *Curiosity* rover on the Martian surface has also been analyzing minerals and dust, looking for signs of water as well as other biomarkers.

These explorers will soon be joined by the Euro-Russian ExoMars Trace Gas Orbiter, a satellite en route to Mars and which will closely study Mars's atmospheric composition once it gets there.

Methane gas is one of the hottest topics in Mars research right now, following previous tantalising observations of the gas. Earth's atmosphere contains billions of tones of methane, the vast majority of it coming from microbes, such as the organisms found in the digestive tracts of animals. The speculation has been that some methane-producing bugs, or methanogens, could perhaps exist on Mars if they lived underground, away from the planet's harsh surface conditions.

The Indian Space Research Organisation (ISRO) wants to return to Mars with a second Mars Orbiter Mission Mangalyaan 2.0. It has published an 'announcement of opportunity' on its website soliciting proposals from institutions around India of the scientific studies that the orbiter could undertake. The mission will likely be launched in March 2018, when Earth and Mars become optimally aligned again in their orbits around the Sun for a craft to journey between them using a fuel-saving maneuver. However, no date has been officially announced.

ISRO is aiming for high-end microprocessors for use in the supercomputers onboard satellites as well as cutting-edge microwave technology for satellites and rockets An ISRO official said, "Now we are buying technologies from Europe.... But the US offers better technologies at competitive prices." ISRO will consider importing testing technology for satellites, which will allow scientists to test whether satellites can "withstand rigors of space".

Missiles Technology

DRDO (Defence Research & Development Organization) has set its sights on perfecting seeker technology for its missiles. Seekers help missiles pick and destroy targets. A DRDO source said, "Seeker and sensor technologies have not been our forte. The lifting of restrictions comes as a booster shot for the defence sector."

A DRDO source said, "So far we were collaborating with the US only in areas such as life sciences, agriculture and medicine.... Now we can look forward to the flow of well-guarded technologies in areas such as missile development, aerospace, nuclear, biological and chemical warfare and nanotechnology for military applications."

In a dramatic breakthrough in its nuclear offensive capability, India has successfully tested a Submarine-Launched Ballistic Missile (SLBM) with an eventual range of 3,500 km. March 2, 2016—K-4 Missile was tested secretly off Visakhapatnam. A longer-legged variant of the K-4 with a 5,000 km range is being worked on. The 12 m long missile is meant to arm future nuclear submarines. Source: DRDO News, *India Today*, google Latest Nov. 2010 edition.

Renewables

The water has been produced by a vending machine of Water-Gen, an Israeli startup that has developed a revolutionary technology to make water from air, capturing humidity. Water-Gen now sells its products to militaries in seven countries including Israel, US, Korea and France. It can produce clean drinking water cheaply at a cost of ₹ 1.6 per liter. And it is betting big on India. "A lot of people here do not have access to clean drinking water. I would like to help India. We have a special relationship," says Mirilashvili, president of Water-Gen, who came on board the seven-year-old company in 2014 as an investor and early this year became its leading one shareholder.

He is looking for a joint venture partner for the India business, which will target both military and civilian use. "I have met some very senior business leaders here. We have plenty of choice. But our partner must share our philosophy. We want to improve the quality of people's lives. Our partner here should share our vision and must have capabilities to fulfill that vision," he says. As part of the government's Make in India campaign, Water-Gen hopes to set up a manufacturing and R&D facility and envisages the India business to touch $1 billion in five to six years. "We want to move as fast as possible. Within a year we should be ready for mass production."

In India water sources are contaminated by bio and chemical pollutants, 21% of India's diseases are water borne. Children in 100 million homes in India lack access to clean water. Only 33% of the country has access to sanitation. "In such situation, I see tremendous potential for Water-Gen in India. If it can keep delivering quality potable water at the price it quotes across our diverse nation, it will have a lifesaving effect," says R.S. Ramasubramanian, co-chairman, Feedback Infra, an infrastructure services firm.

Another Israeli startup called Vertical Field—focusing on vertical landscaping and agriculture—in which he holds a controlling stake.

Since 2011, the two countries have been working on a range of areas, prominent being technology in areas like defense, water, energy, R&D, agriculture and education. In fact, since 2006 the two countries have worked closely in the agri-tech sector and Israel has set up high-tech agricultural centers of excellence, six of which are in Haryana.

Israel is India's third largest defense supplier, after Russia and the US supplying defense hardware worth $12 billion over the last decade.

Solarcity Gigafactory is a solar panel manufacturing plant which will produce 10,000 solar panels per day and has an estimated cost of $750 million. The dream project of Elon Musk will ensure highly efficient solar cells made at a lower price. The factory stretches for about six million square feet, or the equivalent of 126 acres. The giant factory will help it dramatically cut the cost of its batteries by "using economies of scale, innovative manufacturing, reduction of waste, and the simple optimization of locating most manufacturing process under one roof." Once the factory is fully operational by 2020, Tesla estimates the factory will enable it to reduce its battery prices by about 30%. The lowered cost of the batteries will enable the company to price its Model 3.

Futuristic Devices and Technologies

Apple Air pods, these are earbuds sans the cords, and these come armed with a five-hour battery life and can be charged through a case. Flanked by microphones, these do not get messy as there is no untangling of the wires, and, also have Siri on call with a simple double tap. ***Pokémon Go*** the free augmented reality mobile game ***Snapchat Spectacles.*** Snapchat made its hardware debut this year with a set of spectacles that had a built-in video camera, armed with a 115 degree, wide angle lens. The first wearable designed especially for the Snapchat generation, this one looks hipster enough and it enables recording content from a human eye perspective. A button on the left records a 10-second clip—and the LED bar on the frame lights up to indicate that a video recording is on (avoids covert recording). Connected with the smartphone via Bluetooth or Wi-Fi, content gets automatically added to Snapchat's Memories section. What's more—it also can record a full day's worth of video clips on a single charge!

Amazon Echo: Amazon gave us its Bluetooth speaker, which is more than a virtual assistant like Apple's Siri or Microsoft's Cortana. The smart home appliance has Alexa embedded in it and the speaker can talk back to you. With Echo, Amazon made it easier to book a cab via Uber, order pizza and even turn off the lights of your house. The tech team at Amazon is still working on making it more intuitive, and expects an improved version soon.

A 2G Nano SIM card: Light Phone company has developed a credit card-sized device that helped to disconnect one from one's smartphone. A 2G Nano SIM card, a battery life of three weeks on a single charge and a dot matrix LED display that doubles up as a torch, this one is dubbed as 'phone away from phone'. It also boasts of a touch module, microphone and a Micro-USB port. It doesn't support Internet and has no camera.

Wynd: This intelligent portable air purifier surfaced in 2016 to remove all the contaminants from your immediate surroundings. The tiny purifier can detect and automatically filter out dust, allergens, smoke, and pollution wherever you take it. The device track and display air quality trends over time and it gives a real-time air quality map using sensors from other Wynd devices.

DJI Mavic Drone: DJI's Mavic Pro is a pocket-sized drone that fits in the palm of your hand. It features a 4K camera, obstacle-avoidance technology and the ability to track objects when it is flying. Unlike the bulky drones, the Mavic drone can fold down till its size is similar to that of a loaf of bread. Its ability to fold down makes it less susceptible to accidents.

PlayStation VR: Sony's Playstation VR offer gamers a whole new way to experience their favorite games.

Using Google Glass: Siberian scientists are developing a prototype of a model to study an individual's proneness to certain brain diseases at an early stage, media reported.

Gene therapy for cancer: IBM Watson is collaborating with Broad Institute MIT for a joint research project (Nov. 2016) to identify the genes for drug delivery in cancer treatment.

Drugs become ineffective for some patient where others may be treated well. Assumption is difference in individual genes.

Kodak Ektra: Kodak has recruited Bullitt, a phone manufacturer to make the device. The camera app on the smartphone has a digital "Scene Selection Dial" that lets you access different shooting modes. Bullitt has also made Snapseed the default photo-editing app. The phone is powered by a deca-core MediaTek Helio X20 processor and 3 GB of RAM. It comes with 32 GB of internal storage, which you can supplement with a MicroSD card up to 128 GB and a 3000 mAh battery that supports "Pump Express" quick charging. The 5-inch, 1080p display has a stock version of Android 6.0 Marshmallow.

Robots: Robots create own language to work together. Software bots learn to collaborate and communicate through trial and error.

Drones: Intel Corporation put on the light show produced by hundreds of individual drones each fitted with an LED light in a football field in Germany. The company first achieved this Guinness World Records title in 2015 with 100 drones. The UAVs flew in a formation and drew the number '500' and then the company logo.

"These drones are able to fly as a fleet, this is the first time ever we can show it works so well with so many drones!" said Daniel Gurdan, Intel Engineer Lead. Corporation put on the light show produced by hundreds of individual drones each fitted with an LED light in a football field in Germany. "We're showing regulators around the world that UAV technologies used in the right ways can help shape new rules for manned and unmanned aerial vehicles," said Natalie Cheung, Intel Light Show Business Lead (Nov. 2016).

Living 'BioWall for homes of the future to have cleaner air and lower energy bills; researchers at Purdue University have developed a new technology. The new technology use a living wall of air—purifying plants built into the wall and attached to homes HVAC (heating, ventilation, air-condition) system.

- ***Internet gets*** 100 times faster with new Wi-Fi.
- ***NASA*** to use laser technology for high-speed Internet.
- ***Lip-reading AI*** to aid those with hearing loss.
- ***Skin blemishes*** use to control smartphones.
- ***Rebuild Jaw using 3D printer*** in UK by an Indian-origin doctor.
- ***NASA*** to send futuristic atomic clock to space.
- ***Bio Spray*** to heal cardiac tissues without sutures.
- ***Solar-powered skin technology*** being used for Prosthetic limbs to get better sense of feeling.

Business Printers: In 2016, HP is marketing a new business printer with new features. According to an HP document on secure printing, 53 percent of IT managers realize printers are vulnerable to cybercrime. Now, disabling printing through mobile devices would be an easy way out, but that would defeat the very purpose of BYOD (bring your own device), which lies in increased mobility, agility and efficiency of the organizations, and is no longer a workable option. In fact, today's business requirements are such that mobile and remote access to printers is a real need. For example, if a document needs to be printed while a person authorized to access that document is traveling, and then a remote printing option in a mobile device could very well address the issue. However, while bringing printers into the fold of enterprise mobility is valuable, it is equally important to ensure that all access to printers is accountable and conforms to the IT security and compliance requirements of an organization. What if the mobile device has been hacked into and an unauthorized print operation is getting triggered? Could the printer act as the first point of defense? With a new set of security features, imaging HP aims to do exactly that. It has launched a new range of business printers that employ the technology to deliver a far more secure printing environment that is constructed grounds-up—in coexistence with phenomena like BYOD and enterprise mobility. That is not easy, given the myriad of notebooks, tablets and smartphones with diverse system configurations and settings floating around. So how does HP plan to tackle the problem?

HP's approach is to monitor the devices at their very roots—the BIOS. This is because in the event of the device being compromised, its BIOS settings are most likely to get affected and hence any change in the BIOS should be a cause for red flag. With new features, printers are able to validate the integrity of BIOS before the printing gets done. The technology also ensures a continuous monitoring for any intrusion detection during run time and force-reboots to prevent any misuse or attack.

A highly effective three way step: *Protect*: The integrity of the BIOS is validated at every boot cycle by doing a white-listing lookup. Only authentic, known-good HP code that has not been tampered with is loaded into memory. *Detect*: A run-time intrusion detection helps protect devices while they are operational and connected to the network—right when most attacks occurs. *Recover:* If a compromised version or a runtime anomaly is detected, the device restarts using a safe, "golden copy" of the BIOS or is rebooted to a secure, offline state. An automatic notice goes out to IT to reload the firmware.

Facebook June 2017 has rolled out 'Find Wi-Fi' everywhere in the world on iPhone and Android. It has launched it in a handful of countries last year and found it's not only helpful for people who are travelling or on-the-go, but especially useful in areas where cellular data is scarce. "'Find Wi-Fi' helps users locate available Wi-Fi hot spots nearby that businesses have shared with Facebook from their Page. So wherever you are, you can easily map the closest connections when your data connection is weak," Alex Himel, Engineering Director at Facebook, post added.

Facebook June 2017, solar-powered drone Aquila that will beam Internet down to the estimated four billion people worldwide, has successfully completed the second full-scale test flight. Aquila's second flight, which occurred on May 22, took off just after dawn and lasted for an hour and 46 minutes. Aquila then landed perfectly on the prepared landing site.

"During the second flight, the launch speed of the drone was calculated to be at 27 mph. It rose to 3,000 feet, at a rate of 180 ft/min. We designed Aquila this way because it is meant to stay in the same area for long periods of time to supply Internet access. Aquila is solar-powered and extremely power-efficient—running on the power equivalent of three blow dryers," the post read.

In advance of the second flight, Facebook also incorporated a number of modifications to Aquila. It included adding "spoilers" to the wings, which help to increase drag and reduce lift during the landing approach; incorporating hundreds of sensors to gather new data; modifying the autopilot software; integrating new radios for the communication subsystem, applying a smoother finish on the plane and installing a horizontal propeller stopping mechanism to support a successful landing.

"Over the next year we're going to keep testing Aquila—flying higher and longer, and adding more planes and payloads. It's all part of our mission to connect the world and help more of the four billion people who are not online access all the opportunities of the Internet," Facebook CEO Mark Zuckerberg had earlier written in a post.

Microsoft in July 2017 has made its "Modern Keyboard" available that features a hidden fingerprint sensor located between the Alt and Ctrl keys to make typing hassle-free. The keyboard is rechargeable and can last up to four months on a single charge. In the upcoming Windows Fall Creators Update, the company will power Windows Defender Advanced Threat Protection (Windows Defender ATP) with its cloud-based security intelligence.

Our initial focus is to reduce the time it takes companies to detect, investigate, and respond to advanced attacks. We offer a set of new prevention capabilities designed to stop attacks as they happen and before they have impact. We will also provide a single pane of glass experience for security professionals. This means that security management teams can easily configure a broad set of Windows security stack technologies through an integrated configuration management experience. This will not only give companies a full picture of what's happening on their endpoints, but will also put them in the driver's seat to quickly react to threats as they happen. Leveraging our cloud-based security intelligence gives the optics, context, and tools that companies need to quickly investigate and remediate incidents. The update will have "Windows Defender Exploit Guard" which gives companies more control on restricting how code runs on computer networks". Avi Sagiv Principal Programme Manager, Windows Defender ATP at Microsoft, said in a blog post.

July 2017 Researchers have developed a computer code that could help robots understand body poses and movements, allowing them to perceive what people around them are doing, what moods they are in and whether they can be interrupted. "We communicate almost as much with the movement of our bodies as we do with our voice," said Yaser Sheikh, Associate Professor of Robotics at Carnegie Mellon University. "But computers are more or less blind to it," Sheikh said, adding that the new methods for tracking 2D human form and motion open up new ways for people and machines to interact with each other, and for people to use machines to better understand the world around them. A smartphone app that can detect counterfeit goods—from medicines to car parts—with 100 per cent accuracy may be available to the consumers by next year, Lancaster University researchers say due to a new quantum technology they have developed. The technology will make counterfeiting impossible, they said.

Swiss researchers said Thursday they have developed a computer algorithm that can generate brand new tunes in different musical genres. The deep artificial composer, or DAC, "can produce complete melodies, with a beginning and an end, that are completely original," said co-developer Florian Colombo of the EPFL research university in Lausanne, Switzerland. And the melodies are "quite agreeable to listen to," he told AFP. The DAC program uses a form of artificial intelligence known as "deep learning that works in a similar way to the human brain in memorising experiences and learning from them.

Erasing the line between Humans and Machine. The age of Cyborgs is upon us. Scientists and engineers are designing Brain-computer interfaces to treat diseases and even perhaps grant human beings the power of telepathy. The future of the mind from health to cognition is a fusion of mind and machine.

BRICI countries to drive digital revolution: Fast-growing economies Brazil, Russia, India, China and Indonesia will drive a "massive digital revolution" in coming years as disposable incomes increase, a study released by Boston Consulting Group (2010) suggested.

The Boston Consulting Group said more than 610 million people in the "BRICI" markets currently use the Internet regularly but that will grow to 1.2 billion by 2015—over three times more than the United States and Japan combined.

Annual growth will be between nine to 20 percent, driven predominantly by young users who "will form the digital-market eco-systems that will be in place for generations to come", the US-based management consulting firm said.

"Right now, 60 percent of BRICI Internet users are under the age of 35," said the report, The Internet's New Billion. "As they earn even higher incomes and develop more complex online needs, there will be a colossal opportunity for digital companies to monetize services and products. Those companies that manage to do so will reap the tremendous benefits of this massive digital revolution."

The study highlighted wide-ranging differences in the ownership of personal computers in the five countries, from five percent in India and Indonesia to 20 percent in China and about 32 percent in Brazil and Russia.

But while it suggested that Brazil and Russia would see a far greater take-up of PCs in the next five years, Internet users in other countries could skip the PC ownership stage and move straight into the mobile Internet market. Mobile phone ownership is already high in BRICI countries, making web-enabled smartphones a potential growth area as networks expand.

The Cost of Innovation—When Technologies Bite-back

Mokyr Joel (technology historian and economist at North-Western University (2016)) highlights that advances in technology 'Bite-Back'. Advances in technology, transport, energy and medicine do not translate into rising standards of life in the long run. Though a particular technology innovation is source of human betterment, yet it brings grim and unintended consequences. It is inconceivable to think about any innovation that does not Bite-Back.

Cellphones and other handheld devices while driving distract the driver and accidents happen. Driverless cars are being innovated with its positive and negative impact.

Cultivation of sugarcane and beetroot led to more consumption of sugar-resulting in tooth decay and diabetes. To set it right more medical technologies and drugs are innovated.

Explosion of social media and connectivity through Internet and Smartphones has brought viruses, hacking and identity thefts, cyberbullying terrorism and political uprisings. To counteract these other technologies for cybersecurity are innovated.

Railway, automobile airplanes engines were great technology innovations but the carbon emissions and noise pollutions affect the climate change and to counteract that electric and driverless car are being innovated and so are supersonic airplanes with low noise levels or airports absorbing the noise levels. Automotive engineers found alternatives to leaded gasoline.

Mokyr argues that innovations gravitate to society's greatest needs. In earlier eras, it was cheap and rapid transport, reliable energy, and basic healthcare. Today, seven of the top ten problems are in need of innovative solutions and instances of Bite-Back; such as global-warming, antibiotic resistance, obesity and information-load. Fixing these problems weigh heavily on growth. Nonetheless for every unintended consequences of one innovation brings another innovation.

The dark side of progress is that innovations bring costs as well benefits, constant connectivity boosts productivity but information load may affect the neurological health. Opiate drugs relieve extreme pain and many surgeries are recouped well; but overdose and addiction are bane for the society.

Technology innovation and acceptance in national contexts and in its societal segments is important. To push the technology products for masses through Political Will and Ideology have been deciding factors.

References

Ashton Kevin. *"IoT Will Take a Century.* Random House Penguin, New York, 2016.

——. *How to Fly a Horse* Random House. Penguin, New York, 2015.

——. That 'Internet of Things' Thing in the real world, things matter more than ideas *RFID Journal*, June 2009.

Analytics forum Boston 24-25 Oct 2016 *Big Data & Healthcare*

BASF.com 2016 Nanotechnology at BASF.

Boston Globe Oct. 18, 1999 Lasers—the thin blue line of laser research.

Bell, Daniel. 1973. *The Coming of the Post-industrial Society.* Basic Books, New York.

Beniger, J.R. 1997. *The Control Revolution: Technological and Economic Origins of the Information Society.* Harvard University Press, Cambridge, 1997.

Cook, Joel. September 18, 2016. *Managing Healthcare Data,* MedCity News.

Cairncross, Francis. 2001. *The Death of Distance: How the Communication Revolution is Changing Our Lives.* Harvard Business School Press, 2001.

Christensen, Clayton M. 1997. *Innovator's Dilemma.* Harvard Business School Press.

Daly, John A. and Patricia Daly. *Series of Essays on Information Communication Technology Applied to Millennium Goals.* World Bank, 2003.

Derek, H. Chen and Carl J. Dahlman. *Knowledge and Development: A Cross Section Approach.* World Bank Paper, 2003.

Dunning, John H. (Ed.). *Regions, Globalization and the Knowledge Based Economy.* Oxford University Press, 2002.

Dutton, William H. (Ed.). *Information and Communication Technologies: Visions and Realities.* Oxford University Press, New York, 1996.

Easterly Williams and Edge David. *The Elusive Quest for Growth: Economists' Adventures and Misadventures in the Tropics*, MIT Press, 2001.

European Journalism Observatory November, 2016.

Arab Journalism Observatory November, 2016.

Green Emily Nagle *Anywhere* McGraw-Hill New York. 1st published January 1st, 2010, 2nd publication Aug. 26, 2016.

Gartner Consultants Inc. Chris Howard Vice-President, Saul Judah, research director. Participating in *Gartner Symposium/ITxpo* (2016).

GEORGETA GRAMA-MOLDOVAN Internet, artificial intelligence, robotics: 2040, from human enhancement to human...obsolescence *Geab-Global Europe Anticipation* bulletin 103 March 2016.

Gordon Eric and Mihailidis Paul (Eds). *Era of Civic Media,* 2016.

Greg, IP. 2016 Oct. 20. *When Tech Bites Back: The Cost of Innovation, The Wall Street Journal* quotes Mokyr Joel.

Heap Nick, Ray Thomas. et al. (eds.). chapters The Social Shaping of Technology; Access and inequality; The Smart House in *Information Technology and Society.* Sage Publications, London, 1995.

Hafkin, Nancy and Taggart. *Gender, Information, Technology, and Developing Countries: An Analytic Study*, June 2001, www.usaid.gov/wid

Hyojoon, Bae and Michael Walker. et al. *Realization for high-precision mobile augmented reality systems.*

IDG *Global Mobile Survey* Oct. 2014.

IBM.com *Blockchain Technologies for healthcare* 2016.

Infosys Insight Vol. 2, 2016 *Sikka.*

International symposium on *Online journalism* Knight center for Journalism, University of Texas Austin, April 16-18, 2016.

Peter, Jonsson is project manager for Ericsson Mobility Report an industry Dec. 2016.

Lent, J.A. *India in P.T. Rosen (Ed.) International handbook of broadcasting systems* (pp. 133-45). New York: Greenwood Press, 1988.

Kumar, M.J. "Quantum Computing in India: An Opportunity that Should Not Be Missed". *IETE TECHNICAL REVIEW*, Vol. 31, No. 3, May-June 2014, pp. 187-89.

Lent, J.A. *New Information Technology: Myths, Questions and Alternatives.* Communicator 21, p. 392, 1986.

Laser association of India, Power Beam Society of India 2015.

Mani Golparvar-Fard and Hyojoon. *Fast and scalable structure-from-motion based localization for high-precision mobile augmented reality systems*, 17 July 2016. https://link.springer.com

MIT News Vol. Oct. 19, 2015, Eye Netra.

MIT technology review.com April 22, 2015. EyeNetra—Blink a-smartphone-eye-exam-service-launches in New York.

MIT Media Lab Consortium and Beth Israel Deaconess Medical Center Information Systems group, August 2, 2016.

Laser association of India, Power Beam Society of India, 2015.

Nano technology application references:

1. Microbivores: Artificial Mechanical Phagocytes using Digest and Discharge Protocol, www.jetpress.org/volume14/freitas.pdf, first described by *Journal of Evolution and Technology* 14(1) April 2005, *Journal of Materials Science and Engineering* A6 (5-6) (2016), 167-80.
2. Read about design analysis for one such cell repair nanorobot in this article: *The Ideal Gene Delivery Vector: Chromallocytes, Cell Repair Nanorobots for Chromosome Repair Therapy,* Jetpress.org/v16/freitas.pdf, *International Journal of Scientific Research Engineering and Technology.org*

Narula, Uma. "The Cultural Challenge of Communication Technology," *American Behavioural Scientist*, Vol. 32, No. 2, Nov.-Dec. 1988, pp. 194-207, Sage Publications, CA. 1988.

——. "Grassroots movements in India" in I. Singh and J. Hanson (eds.) *Advances in Telematics* (Vol. 1 pp. 127-34) Norwood NJ Ablex, 1990.

Narula, Uma and Pearce. *Development as Communication: A perspective on India.* Southern Illinois University Press, Carbondale, 1986.

——. *Culture, Politics and Research Programs.* Lawrence Erlbaum, New Jersey, 1990.

Hanson, J. and Narula, Uma. *New Communication Technologies in Developing Countries*, Lawrence Erlbaum Associates, New Jersey, 1990, 2nd edition by Francis and Taylor UK, 2010. (Cited *Social Technology Model* by Uma Narula in the text published in the above book)

Narula, Uma. Technology revisited: India case study 2003, mimeographed.

——. *Communication Perspectives: Cultural Diffusion, Dynamics and Challenges.* Haranand Publishers, New Delhi, 2000.

——. *Mass Communication Technology New Perspectives.* Haranand Publishers, New Delhi, 2001.

——. *Handbook of Communication Models, Perspectives, Strategies.* Atlantic Publishers and Distributors Pvt. Ltd., New Delhi, 2006 (Reference Information Communication technology models 4.1, 4.2, 4.3 in Chapter 4 of Handbook of Communication Models).

——. *Indian Economy: Visions, Reality, Challenges.* Atlantic Publishers and Distributors Pvt. Ltd., New Delhi, 2007.

——. *Globalization: People Empowerment Practices.* Atlantic Publishers and Distributors Pvt. Ltd., New Delhi, 2008.

——. *Global Empowerment: Emerging Practices.* Atlantic Publishers and Distributors Pvt. Ltd., New Delhi, 2008.

——. *Rising Expectations: India's Transformation.* Atlantic Publishers and Distributors Pvt. Ltd., New Delhi, 2009.

——. *Dynamics of Indian Rural Economy: Growth Perspective.* Atlantic Publishers and Distributors Pvt. Ltd., New Delhi, 2010.

——. *Development Shock*: *Dynamics of current Developments in India.* Atlantic Publishers and Distributors Pvt. Ltd., New Delhi, 2015.

——. *Skeptical Voices: Political, Economic Optimism.* Atlantic Publishers and Distributors Pvt. Ltd., New Delhi, 2015.

News items relied on, Capital Market—Live News, *Economic Times*, MEDCITY News, Healthcare IT News healthcare.com, rexeconsult.com, moneycontrol news, 2016, 2017.

Salil Prabhakar CEO and Founder, Delta: ID The growth of Iris scan technology in 2017—Projection and technology growth, Dec. 2016.

Ramaswamy, Satya. Head of Digital Enterprise Unit, TCS *Winning in the Digital Consumer Economy Requires Digital Reimagination* Tata consultancy Newsletter 2016.

Report *The Global Information Technology Report 2015—ICTs for Inclusive Growth* Insead Business School Cornell University.

Reports World Economic Forum launched the Global Information Technology Report Series.

Report Mobility Report an industry Peter Jonsson project manager for Ericsson Dec. 2016.

Report Vodafone report 2016 by Independent experts.

Report Meckinsey.com/media 2016.

Report, *A Case Study for Blockchain in Healthcare: "MedRec" prototype for electronic health records and medical research data White Paper* by Ariel Ekblaw, Asaph Azaria, John D. Halamka, MD, Andrew Lippman. https://www.media.mit.edu/publications/medrec-whitepaper/ Aug. 31, 2016.

Report, *Proceedings of the IEEE*, Vol. 102, No. 2, February 2014. *Applications of Augmented Reality—Scanning the Issue.* (White Jules, Schmidt Douglas C., Mani, Golparvar-Fard).

Report *Digital Payments 2020*, Google and Boston Consulting Group, 2016.

Report *Social Media for Business a Global Trend Report—'Mastering Digital Feedback: How the best consumer companies use social media'*. Tata Consultancy Services, 2016.

Report a research study jointly conducted by the Internet and Mobile Association of India (IAMAI) and the Indian Market Research Bureau (IMRB), 2016.

Report *The Future of Internet in India.* Nasscom and Akamai Technologies India 2016.

Report *GII 2016: Winning with Global Innovation* a collaboration between Cornell University, INSEAD and the WIPO as co-publishers, and their knowledge partners.

Report CII-EY 2016 *Insurer of the Future* India.

Report FICCI-EY 2016 *Smart cities, Art Cities* in Creative arts in India.

Report FICCI-PwC 2016 *Shaping Consumer Trends.*

Report 2014 Cisco cyber security report cisco.com

Report *Future of Digital Media Consumption.* Ernest and Young January 2016.

Report *The Future of Internet in India.* Nasscom NOIDA India, 2016.

Report *Cyber diplomacy.* Burson-Marsteller, 2016.

Report 2016 *Digital Media—Rise of On-demand Content in India.* Deloitte India.

Report Human Development. 2001. *Making New Technologies Work for Human Development.*

Report 2016. *The Internet's New Billion.* Boston Consulting Group USA.

Report 2010. *BRICI countries to drive digital revolution.* Boston Consulting Group USA.

Report "Use of Blockchain in Health IT and Health-related Research", *Ideation Challenge*, IBM Global Business Services Public Sector Team, August 2016, Office of the National Coordinator for Health Information Technology 2016.

Research team University of Texas at San Antonio (UTSA), 2016. Team Leader Kim-Kwang Raymond Choo, associate professor at UTSA, *Astroturfin.*

Saunders, Robert J. *Telecommunication and Economic Development.* World Bank Publications, 1986.

Scherer, F.M. *New Perspectives on Economic Growth and Technological Innovations,* 1999.

Schneider, S.C. *Information Overload: Causes and Consequences,* Human Systems Management 7: 143-53.

Shams, Hossein and Kamran Zamanifar. *Design guidelines for rapid and simple context-aware mobile application development—an android case study.* University of Isfahan. November 2015.

Simonite, Tom. *How Google Plans to Solve Artificial Intelligence Mastering Go is just the beginning for Google Deep Mind, which hopes to create human-like AI.* Technology Review, March 31, 2016.

Reality is the concept that governs the new nano-business world published in Small Times, micro and nanotechnology publication, New York 2016 and Smalltimes.com website.

Soni, Ameeta. *How to Succeed with Mobile Marketing.* Linked In February 25, 2015.

Soni, Tara. *Computer and Kids.* Unpublished Research Study, 2004.

Tami Blumenfield's Culture heritage politics in China case studies Springer Publishers, 2014 Springer.com

UNESCO. *Information, Communication and Knowledge: Building Contemporary Societies,* 2003.

Understandingnano.com

Vernor, Vinge. *The Coming Technological Singularity* presented at the VISION-21 Symposium sponsored by NASA Lewis Research Center and the Ohio Aerospace Institute, March 30-31, 1993. Reprint of the 1993 essay by Vernor Vinge, January 2003.

Appendices

Appendix 1. Internet

Internet Milestones in USA:

- In late 60s, USA defence department ARPA (Advance research project agency) funded an experiment to connect remote computers at various research universities doing government contract work. The experiment was inspired by MIT scientist JSR Licklider.
- In 1969, ARPANET was built by Bolt Beranek and Newman (BBN)—a Cambridge acoustic firm. Arpa awards it the contract. BBN delivers the first network switch to UCLA. Soon three more switches were installed at Stanford research institute, California University at Santa Barbara and University of Utah.
- Early 70s the network spreads east as computers are connected to nearly two dozen sites including Harvard and MIT.
- In 1972, the first e-mail message is sent via ARPANET by Ray Tomilson of BBN creator of the now ubiquitous sign @.
- In 1975 more than sixty sites are linked to the network.
- 1970s and 80s various technical standards are defined ARPANET evolves into a series of regional networks linking university campuses, research organizations, and government agencies. These subnets are connected to a nationwide backbone network run by the National Science Foundation.
- ARPANET is shut down eclipsed by the non-government Internet it has spawned.

- The commercial use of the Internet started in 1993 by inventing world wide web (WWW) by a British born engineer Tim-Berners-Lee in Switzerland. The first tool for exploring the web called Mosaic is developed at the University of Illinois.
- 1994, the Netscape communications Corp adapts Mosaic in its Netscape Navigator browsing software which it distributes free thus allowing millions to surf the web.
- 1995, major commercial internet providers including BBN, MCI, and others include control of portions of backbone network of National Science Foundation. America online, CompuServe, and Prodigy begin to provide dial up internet access. More the 20 million are on line.
- Berners-Lee establishes WWW Consortium at MIT in Cambridge to develop technical standards that will preserve the openness of web.
- 1996-97 Internet use explodes as 50 million people are surfing the web by the end of 1997.
- 1998, electronic commerce becomes a reality as more companies race to do more business on the web.

(*Source*: Katie Hafner & Mathew Lyon Where Wizard stay up late: the origin of the Internet, 1998)

Appendix 1a. Internet

UPS Makes Internet Delivery a Reality with Document Exchange; Secure, Fast, Reliable Digital Delivery

In 1998, a revolutionary way to send documents and files over Internet through UPS document exchange has become efficient way rather than to send as email attachments. Businesses around the world are now a mouse click away from using a delivery vehicle that is highly secure, easy to use, immediate and certain to greatly impact the way they do business. UPS today announced the global availability of UPS Document Exchange, the highly praised and much anticipated Internet delivery service.

Available at www.exchange.ups.com, UPS Document Exchange is a suite of delivery and information management services that industry watchers believe will transform the way companies send and receive their most critical business information.

In addition, UPS announced that it has made agreements with six leading technology providers—Adobe, Compaq Computer Corporation, iName Inc., MindSpring, QUALCOMM and VeriSign—to expand both the channels of access for customers to UPS Document Exchange and the technologies that enable the use of the Internet delivery option. The partners will facilitate the Internet business connection so that using the service is simple and seamless.

With UPS Document Exchange, customers will have a choice of two Internet delivery services, UPS OnLine Dossier and UPS OnLine Courier, each with distinct features and levels of security.

UPS OnLine Dossier, for very critical and confidential documents, offers industry leading security that utilizes a double encryption method and identity validation via digital certificates. It also features document delivery confirmation, tracking, user insurance and a third party validation by Deloitte & Touche LLP, a professional services firm.

UPS OnLine Courier is designed for customers who require universal solutions for exchanging documents over the Internet. Courier is built on an open environment that allows customers to send documents to anyone, regardless of the e-mail software, operating system or hardware being used by either sender or receiver. Customers will have several security options, including password protection and encryption, as well as tracking and receipt confirmation.

The technology supporting UPS Document Exchange was developed through strategic alliances with NetDox, Inc. (OnLine Dossier) and Tumbleweed Software (OnLine Courier). Both NetDox and Tumbleweed are recognized as early pioneers in the development of secure online delivery services.

Expanding the company's service portfolio to include electronic document delivery is the latest electronic commerce initiative undertaken by the company.

UPS has formed alliances with leading electronic commerce providers such as IBM, Open Market, Lotus, Pandesic and Harbinger, as well as several search engine companies to embed UPS tracking and other functionality into the products they are developing that meet a variety of logistics management needs.

Source: UPS services.

Appendix 2

Many disruptive technologies did not connect. A few of the disruptive technologies that did not connect.

Some of the electronic consumer products misfire badly for number of reasons. In 1964, AT&T showed Picture Phone. It was supposed to change the way we talk. It failed because it needed high speed phone lines that did not exist in many places at that time. Since 1960 other versions of video phone failed because they made the mistake of offering consumers a modest benefit at bloated price.

Another failure is betting on the wrong technology. That happened when in 1980 RCA brought select vision videodisk player. The electronic company guessed correctly that consumers would like to watch prerecorded video movies at home but they picked phono-graph like system that did not work because by this time CD players were giving better sound reception.

Videotext in 1970s fizzled out. It was supposed to give wealth of useful information to subscriber's TV like pages of news stories, sports scores, and weather information. But it had two drawbacks—slow delivery speed and warmed over material from that day's newspaper. It failed because it was not user-friendly.

Personal digital assistants of 1990s including Apple Incs Newton failed. Newton lacked the ability to communicate easily to the outside world. The information locked in the gadget could not be transferred to another computer.

Sometimes a product does not take off because there is disagreement and disputes about the technology. That happened about interactive television. It was poised to be launched in early 1990s. It was backed by NBC in USA. But it did not make ripples because first the charges for the service were high—$200 for hardware and $15 monthly for service. Ultimately, service went nowhere because consumer had no interest in it at any price. Though Interactive Network company alleged that the product did not take off as it was sabotaged by Telecommunications Inc—a cable giant that was also an investor.

Appendix 3

Broadcasting: This poses two main issues and multiple sub-issues; one, to examine various strategies in managing business, competition, finance, programming, and technology in a diverse environment. Two, to define changing roles of public service broadcasting amid increasing competition (from private services), and changing preferences of the audience.

Public service broadcasting is vital to promoting democratic rights and responsibilities of its citizens; and the social, cultural, and economic aspirations of their society. The major concerns are for fair competition for growth and expansion. Should public service broadcasters be more profit-driven than policy-driven? Should private broadcasters share more in addressing public service objectives? Is autonomy the key for survival of public service broadcasting? What are the challenges and opportunities related to autonomy. Will public service broadcasters compete effectively given more independence? Is there a more effective system to ensure its growth?

Regulating the quality of commercial private services raises concerns about key elements of quality programming. Are they better achieved in a regulated environment? What financing strategies can be adopted to ensure program and business viability?

Governments' role is also important for regulating broadcasting programming, ownership, financing, and technology. The concern is whether less government control in broadcasting will enhance the quality of public life, empower individuals, and social groups to participate fully and equitably.

Broadcasters need strategies to address audience needs and their changing preferences. They have to decide whether priority should be given to local or imported programs in order to capture bigger audience share.

Cable technology may make Internet as accessible as T.V.

The Internet will never become a mass medium unless every user has access to high-speed, no-hassle connections that are always available without placing a call. One such technology-Cable Model stands a chance of coming over to households in the next few years. Cable modem permits the users to receive the internet over the same common T.V. cable already in homes and businesses without interrupting the normal T.V. reception.

Cable modems can be fast. It can deliver up to 10 million bits of data per second, nearly 350 times the speed of the fastest standard modem. Telephone modems on standard telephone lines can deliver 28,800 bits of data per second to the PC. With a special kind of modem-ISDN (hard to install high speed phone connection) you can get up to 128,000 bit per second.

Moreover, cable modems are always 'on' and waiting for you like a T.V. channel and does not require dialing or placing a call.

Some cable companies are experimenting with cable modems, and upgrading the cable system to handle digital two-way data. One drawback of cable modem could be that cable modem speeds can slow sharply when numerous users choose to log in at the same time.

There will be digital sets which are not HDTV capable, sets that are fully HDTV-capable (but require converter boxes), and HDTV sets which have built-in decoders and everything with them. The first two kinds will be available at relatively low price. In these you are getting a far superior picture to any analogs, and you can use it with computer and other things because it is digital.

Interaction with your television is going to be a way of life. How that interaction happens, whether it is web TV, or it is the Internet on TV. But it has got to be easier to use than what it is today.

Web TV (Microsoft's set-top device for accessing the Internet and downloading video on demand. It is fairly awkward way to access TV, but is not awkward when you take PC out of the equation for people. Web TV is a nice alternative when you are not computer-literate. The first generation of web TV is better than the second generation. It has evolved dramatically in the usefulness and functionality of that product. It has now a storage drive which can basically store video. With disk space being cheaper every year and compression technology being better every year, web TV will be finding more and more uses and potentialities. Such as video on your TV every morning when you turn it on; which gives the opportunity overtime for television on demand. Web TV which starts as an Internet device is becoming more and more of Microsoft's vision of digital television—which is not necessarily HDTV but digital services that go to TV.

Fifteen years from now probably, there will be several means to get high speed transmissions to your house, and home server could be one component. When electronic good become commodities and price competition intensifies, people tend to buy more and more of these gadgets.

We had VCR in 70s, CD in early 80s. Digitization began with CD. The other products are going to be DVD (digital video disk), webTV digital television, and Dolby digital sound system. DVIX (digital video express) is a DVD player with additional encryption technology in a 'modem' that allows you to buy disk whenever you want and when you want to watch it you stick it in your machine and the machine tells you the cost for the number of hours you have been watching off and off and your store charges you accordingly. It will be added convenience and likely to be successful (Information counting on digital interview Bob Guntz 15 June 2006).

The CDs were in and LPs were vanishing. The CDs impact went beyond sound. It created expectations of standardizations that did not exist for LPs. Every disk sounded the same. You cannot wear a CD down. DVD is still better. It will expand the capacity of the disk—they can be lot longer or sound a lot better.

Peripheral devices like camcorders and tape players are also going digital. DVD players were launched in 1996. The digital camcorder permit more sophisticated editing of images, a simpler co connection to PC and other digital devices; and effects such as filming in black and white and sepia. Engineers however face a challenge designing a VCR that can hold the dense amount of information in a high-definition digital signal. No solution is expected for several years.

Video Technology

People from a variety of disciplines have produced a substantial body of research addressing these issues from a wide range of analytical perspectives. Decades after their introduction, video systems are beginning to realize their potential in supporting working from home, teaching and learning at a distance, conferencing, and interpersonal communication. In the face of upsurge of interests in this developing video technology—the questions are being asked: what functions does video really serve. What advantage does it provide over the telephone? How and why the video-mediated interaction is different from face to face interaction. How can we best configure video technology to support different kind of work at a distance? What is the future role of video technology?

Digital Media: Entertainment Plus Technology

Digital is setting aside the old analog ways. It may be more efficient. It may allow all sorts of gadgets to do all sorts of tricks. For starters, the wonders of digital have come at the expense of clarity and depth. Digital describe things that rely on computing technology to operate. It is efficient, but not enough to satisfy those who work with the technology and many of those who use it. Digital technology has come to stay but the systems will get better by innovative technologies.

Digitalization in broadcasting and the growing use of satellite communication technology has provided the opportunities to reach wider audience, and people in remote areas, in different regions, and internationally. It creates new markets, programs, and products in the regions.

Take the problems of integrating digital technology into communication networks. Such networks with computerized switches, laser-driven fiber optics and signaling systems, have replaced the old electro-mechanical gear, that once required larger number of maintenance and technicians to run the system. The newer digital gear is more efficient, able to handle more calls and data traffic. Digital communication is tough to tap with cell phones and other security features. Much of the world paging industry relies on one or two satellites to beam pages worldwide. But if the satellites fail as it did in May 1998 —when the PanAM Sat Galaxy spun out of orbit it knocked out of commission more than 95% of the 45 million pagers across the countries. Granted the digital era open up a new world. But part of the old ones will be missed. Just get the right information to the right people at the right time for key players, and reduced the cost to the consumers.

Two driving forces for digital came about in 60s and 70s as methods were developed in turning every information—a sound, a moving image, an odor into binary or digital language of computers. Now much of the discussion about digital technology advance is about how to make connections happen. Most of the today's advances in digital in consumer's electronics are done with an eye towards more connections in the future. Digital technology will change the face of consumer electronics in near future—and the obstacles each of the product have to overcome.

In just the 90s the Internet has changed the ways how companies behave internally and with customers and suppliers, It has changed from relatively obscure network being used by government agencies and colleges to a global library and business tool used by millions.

Chip innovations—Smaller the better are enabling designers to put formerly separate functions on a single chip. Such feats of integration are allowing digital cameras, advanced video games. Chip makers use fine lenses and etching materials to miniaturize them. Designers can use smaller chips; expand capability and cramming more circuitry on each chip. Wavelet-based compression chips would work five or ten times more efficiently MPEG-2 compression, allowing for faster processing. The next generation video-encoding method—compression algorithms that take snapshot of an entire image, then look at eliminating the redundancies across a much larger amount of data. With chip innovations, credit cards will be getting smarter with features such as touch-sensitive fingerprint identification.

Digital media are still in their infancy. But the early efforts are beginning to provide hints about what will and what won't work. Soon the digital media from the World Wide Web to 3-D video games to technologies, still to come will exercise a force as pervasive and powerful in our lives as films and television today. These new media will bring us drama and diversions unlike anything we have known. They will change the way we think about entertainment and leisure. But what will this entertainment look like? In short, what will make digital media work?

There is disagreement among broadcasters, cable companies, and computer industries as how to use the extra transmission or the bandwidth that is being allotted for digital signals. Digital channels can be used in multitude ways. The broadcasters can use that space for one channel to give an ultra-clear picture and CD quality sound. Cable companies are worried they have to sacrifice the variety of channels they offer in order to squeeze in the fatter digital channels. Cable companies' capacity difficulty may provide an opening for satellite program firms to win more customers.

Another popular digital technology is responsible for popular innovation in audio, i.e. separation of sound among five or more speakers, which helped drive consumers to turn TV watching rooms into home theaters.

The personal computer is the product most associated with digital wave. It first brought new productivity and educational tools in the home. Recently, it has become new portal to connect people to Internet.

Tim Fohl's Model of Technology Development. Sometimes, technology seems to follow a pattern: many small incremental advances followed by an explosion of change. Fads and fashions break out like that. Such as you can heat water from 33 to 211 degrees without seeing much change, but raise the temperature just one more degree and you will see the difference—a totally new thing appears. A deeper understanding of dynamics of Innovations becomes imperative. Traditional models of innovation show a steep increase followed by diminishing returns—the familiar 'learning curve'.

Suggests that at a constant level of efforts, technologies first advanced slowly—then erupted—like water at the boiling point. After the explosive period they return to slow advance. In other words, their progress follows a clear S curve. The model proved so reliable that it could forecast product development cycles.

The results became more interesting and potentially more useful when he plotted additional variable of—though a new technology advanced in small steps in the beginning; it did so with big swings in performance between individual successes and failures. The greater the variations, the steeper the slope of the progress that followed; in other tolerating, encouraging a wider range of possibilities early seemed to nudge a project towards a steeper takeoff.

This model can forecast the course of technology development efforts and find out about dynamics of progress. This modeling technique can be applied to complex social systems like fads and fashions, traffic jams, etc.

These agents can be reinforced into motion by simulating word of mouth patterns that varied according to such factors as airplay, video promotion, chart position, and further word of mouth. The simulation program is touting to cinema, apparel, toys, entertainment in general. The path is powerfully influenced in the early stages, as consumers explore a wide range of possibilities in search of something viable and better.

In a simpler time, one could predict the course of technology (a man on the moon by the end of decade). But today science bolts from the blue; fashion is born in the street (compare with traditional diffusion model of innovation, Narula technology and social technology models).

Digital Television: What is different about digital television? Broadcasters will be able to tell.

Telecommunication

The wireless and cell telecommunication technology has been revolutionary and the development of its infrastructure as well as the hardware and software components of telephones have been revolutionary. An expanded scenario of innovations from 1960 to 1990s created more and more.

Early mobile FM (frequency modulation radio was invented by Edwin H. Armstrong in 1935) radio telephones had been in use in the USA since 1946, but since the number of radio frequencies are very limited in any area, the number of phone calls was also very limited. Only a dozen or two calls could be made at the same time in an area. To solve this problem, there could be many small areas (called cells) which share the same frequencies. But when users moved from one area to another while calling, the call would have to be switched over automatically without losing the call. In this system, a small number of radio frequencies could accommodate a huge number of calls. A team of researchers at Bell Labs devised this cellular phone concept in 1947, but there were no computers available to do the switching. As small inexpensive computers were developed, cell phones could be produced. Motorola holds the US patents for the cell phone. Henry Taylor Sampson and George H. Miley hold a 1968 patent on a 'gamma electric cell' which is not a component of cellular phones.

Details of Cell Phones Development from 1994 Onwards Adding New Features

Alcatel, the French company is already marketing the 'one touch Com' which has taken all the functions of a palm-size organizer installed in a mobile handset and small enough to slip in a shirt pocket. The landline phones that plug into your walls are also getting snazzy Internet features. The iPhone from Cidco features a 6" × 4-1/2" screen which users can use to check e-mail, and surf the web without ever booting the personal computers. Despite offering cool features, the makers of smart phones have yet to figure out the exact combination of features, size, and price that will make millions of users see the new devices as must-haves. Nokia and other companies are trying to create devices that synchronize easily with PCs. With Nokia's 9110 communicator in Europe and in USA, users will be able to move information between phone and PC by simply dropping the phone in a cradle on the PC and pressing a button. Qualcomm Inc with 3Com Corp the maker of palm-pilot has developed a phone that combines the functions of PDA and a mobile phone in a single gadget; Nokia communicator 9500 Wi-Fi (wireless local area) network compatible available in 2004. The perception that devices need to be cheaper has driven several phone makers for less expensive models.

The phones use a special browser developed by Unwired Planet Inc Calif. It works on 40 or so sites which pair down their data to run with the browser. At the moment standard websites are virtually unreadable at that size. A new version of the browser expected soon would have technology that will make these pages easier to read.

First generation cell phones: Geowork Corp which develops software for Nokia 9000i says studies indicate that 85% of the consumers use mobile phones for making calls, eschewing address books, and other useful features. All the other functionality is too difficult to use. Our aim is to develop easier-to-use phone; it is not changing the functionality but giving people a graphical. In the beginning cellular engineers aimed for too much channel capacity at the expense of voice quality. They were compressing speech too soon, looking to grow capacity over conventional networks by a factor of 10 instead of 5.

The first generation cellular phones miscoded background noise in a car or in a street corner. The phone would actually turn the noises into voices that led to 'warbling'. First generation digital cellular used eight-bit technology, while newer systems today used 16 bits or higher. The more bit of computer code used, the more information calls can transmit for full faith reproduction. The most critical mission is to synchronize various components of sound reproduction so that high quality multimedia transmission will be possible by phone or computer network.

The joint venture called Symbian (joint venture of Nokia, Motorola, Ericsson) intends license Psion's software for new generation of smart devices ranging from mobile phones that receive e-mail, surf the Internet, and even pay for transactions; to laptop computers that can go online automatically without anyone having to open the carrying case. The battle between Symbian and Microsoft is not who will make next era's cool gadgets but who will control the next era of personal computers.

European companies have triumphed over American for mobile phones; whereas the European computer maker such as Britain's Amigo, France Bull, Italy's Olivetti are crushed by American competition. Also European use more of mobile phones and Americans are hooked more on computers at home and in offices. One reason is Europe's more cooperative approach to technical issues: In 1991 manufacturers, network operators, and regulators all agreed on a single digital standard called GSM (global system for mobile communications). It spread quickly to Hong Kong, Australia, etc. This gave Europe a competitive edge in the global marketplace.

Business model for payment: The US companies chose a variety of incompatible standards that made it hard to use a single phone while traveling from New York to Los Angeles or from Boston to Bombay. The fact that European companies have the volume benefit of a standard applied in more than 100 countries gave a kick to the whole industry and lowered risks. Two other marketing innovations have helped boost demand in Europe. Phone companies there quickly realized that people would leave their cell phone switched on longer if the cost of the call was paid by the caller and not by the receiver of the mobile call. The opposite of the system is common in

USA and India. The US economists realize that the US business model—subsidizing the cost of the phone handset in order to lure customers to sign up for the service is less appealing to consumers than an approach by which customers pay full price for the phone set but get cheaper talk time.

Alcatel claims to have 10% of the world phone market with cheap handset available in rainbow colors. Nokia reports half of its (Finland's) population about 5.1 million uses mobile phone to manage their daily lives in 1998. It is assumed that 100% market penetration will be achieved in the next five years.

Sven Christer Nilsson President of Ericsson observed (1998) that it has taken 120 years from Alexander Graham Bell's invention of the conventional telephone to wire up one billion customers worldwide. Current estimates of mobile operators suggest same number to be achieved by 2005 for mobile phones. Symbian a joint venture of Nokia, Ericsson, and Motorola are planning to use Psion operating system EPOC as the basis for the smart phones. So far only Philips has licensed Psion software for smart phone. Ericsson Vice President Jan Ahrenbring (1998) adds that Microsoft operating system was not actually applicable for mobile. But Microsoft maintains that its software is modular and can be customized to suit customers' needs. In addition to Symbian, telecommunication industry has formed two other alliances to improve the usability of wireless devices. One of them WAP forum (wireless applications protocol) is designing special browsers to being Internet data to mobile phones. The second group Bluetooth is trying to set a universal standard for radio communication between smart devices like palm computers and mobile phones.

The third generation of mobile phones will switch on around 2003 resulting in real sprint for technological superiority. For this, European and Japanese have agreed on a technical standard called Wideband Code—Division Multiple Access (CDMA) as the successor to GSM. Probably, Qualcomm USA will adopt different standard from Europe and Asia. The vision of the future may be: Hand-held computer makers could offer machines made with Symbian's software in the hope of making them more appealing to consumers with mobile phones. Or the mobile phone industry could adopt Window CE to ensure that their devices link easily with existing desktop PCs. That depends how the battle between Microsoft and Symbian is resolved. But likelihood is Europe will be communicating with a single standard. "Watch out Bill Gates: Europeans are getting a jump on the next information revolution. A British company Psion is giving brains to new mobile phones that receive e-mail, surf the Internet, and can even pay for transactions". The satellite phones—The super cell phones. The Iridium Consortium and rival joint ventures are closing on their goal of making sat-phones into multibillion-dollar mainstays of the Info-superhighway (Material is based on—High Flying phones by Charles P. Wallace, *Times*, Sept. 28, 1998).

In consequence to Nokia's 9110 communicator, Nokia is bringing into the market Communicator 9500—Wi-Fi (wireless local area) compatible handsets. The Wi-Fi chips are built-in the handsets. It will be able to bypass conventional cell phone networks, but still access the web and even make phone calls using the Wi-Fi (wireless local area) network. Key to its operation are 'hot spots' within 300 ft of a Wi-Fi base station connected to the Internet by a fixed line. Its limitation is that people will be able to use the Wi-Fi function within a hot spot. At present consumer needs a specially equipped laptop or a personal organizer to use these hot spots. Communicator 9500 set will be a threat to other cell operators who were trying to sell data wireless services such as web browsing and e-mail (March 2004). Wi-Fi uses unlicensed spectrum meaning any property owner can offer wireless Internet access in the proximity of their premises. Today cell phone operators can largely access the content delivered over their networks. But media companies using Wi-Fi networks can sell video clips and music to mobile phone users without any intervention by an operator. Nokia and other cell phone manufacturers.

Airplane phone: The airplane phone is an incredible concept. They have the constraints of poor connections, poor sound quality, lack of privacy, and exorbitant rates. There are potentialities and promises for air phones in the next generation. There may be service where through calling a central number in the plane will locate you and the phone at your seat will ring.

Rural Cellular Networks: The concept of global cellular communication using intermediate-circular-orbit, and low-earth-orbit offer a hope for rural communication for rural areas in developing countries. Four mobile satellite operators—Globalstar, Odyssey, Iridium, and Immarsat ICO are developing such systems to offer a global system by 2000 (*The APT Yearbook* 1997). The current cost of such global cellular is beyond the reach of rural folks.

Personal Communication Services (PCS): This is another kind of micro-cellular digital network, which use low power and high frequency radio waves. Current cellular transmissions move from cell to cell geo unit. Each of which is equipped with high-powered transmitter. Micro cells will be much smaller, allowing phones to use less power and smaller batteries thus reducing the size and cost. Low power also means the ability to use the entire frequency all over again in each micro cell transmission area. PCS networks will be twenty times as efficient as existing cellular analog systems and provide much better services and quality.

Appendix 4: ICT Initiative

In the context of a particular communication medium, there is an incubation period, i.e. the early stage of initiating the medium. During this period, the medium faces hardware and software problematic issues and social issues of acceptance or rejection of the medium. At this stage, there is experimentation and adaptation with various modes of the medium.

The innovators, adapters and administrators and early adopters are at the helm of medium during this period. This period may spread over to about 10-15 years according to the resources and political will of the country.

The next is the rapid growth period that is revolutionary period for the medium and may catch up within five years. Quite likely more developed and technologically advanced countries may have already passed over that particular revolution which is making headway and ripples now in the developing and less technology advanced countries. Analysis and observation show that passing of the specific communication revolution will impact and revolutionized the other less resourceful countries. The information revolution will open tremendous new opportunities for developing countries.

A significant point in setting up ICT initiatives is setting up Info-dev incubator initiative (2000). It established the first common repository of knowledge, best practices, experience and services—specifically targeted to address the challenges and opportunities facing technology and business incubators in developing countries. The ICT incubator support center would provide information, organization and technical support to incubators from developing countries during the implementation of the incubator initiative. People are exploring creative business approaches, public private partnership, and other sustainable ways to bridge the global digital divide and create lasting economic, social and environmental benefits. ICTs for development are seeking convergence between ICT have and have-nots.

By weakening the influence of geography on development and opening opportunities for countries to leapfrog stages of development, ICTs are challenging some aspects of conventional wisdom in economic development theory.

It is advocated that development and deployment of open source software should be encouraged, as appropriate open standard for ICT.

What are the main issues in international assistance related to the use of these technologies in developing countries?

Katherine Sierra (2000) advocates that the information revolution are opening tremendous new opportunities for developing countries by promoting foreign direct investment in emerging markets, contributing to better governance, improvement of public services, amplifying the voices of the poor.

But the digital-divide necessitates a response that encompasses fibers, computers, and the switches but also the development of the soft infrastructure required for building knowledge economies including education, cyber law, and modern regulatory institutions. Developing countries have to face the new challenges and opportunities offered by information revolution particularly Internet. The regulators, entrepreneurs, donor agencies have to go through the 'cultural-revolution' to fully tap the potential of new economy. Some emphasized the dangers of technological determinism and the need to maintain a human development focus in ICT efforts and supporting information development proposed initiative for promoting incubators designed to foster Internet-centered start-up companies and social applications in emerging markets. Other necessary and significant social applications of ICTs are 'Rural Information Network'. These need to be created using Internet technology for employment, education and empowerment of the villages in India particularly and other developing countries in general. It is fundamental to service industries as well as to rural development.

Appendix 5: India: Technology Applications

Talks are also on with Reliance Infocomm for developing a program to make ticketing via SMS possible. "In India, the penetration of internet is still not as wide as is the penetration of cellular phones. There are over 10 crore mobile phone users and this creates a huge opportunity for offering customer conveniences. Ticketing via SMS will save time and effort and can also turn out to be a money churner," a Rail Bhawan official told *ET*.

Here's what is being planned. A 24/7 call center will be set up for booking tickets and answering customer queries. Thereafter, once ticketing via SMS is introduced, all it will take to book a ticket is a call to the call center and a customer identification number. The customer ID will be stored on the computer and the berth and seat number will be SMS ed to the buyer. The payment will automatically be credited to the phone bill in case of a post-paid connection or will be deducted from the pre-paid card.

"Apart from introducing ticketing via SMS, we also want to make home delivery of tickets a reality. Though nothing concrete has been planned, discussions are on to work out a way to introduce home delivery service," the official said. Our main objective is to reduce the queues at ticket counters in railway stations, he added.

Falcon Cable System, connecting India to rest of the world, was inaugurated, on September 5, 2006. The inaugural call of the 2.56 terabit Falcon Cable System will be spreading over four continents and 11 countries. The Flag Global Network bridges the distance between 35 diverse developed and developing economies, connecting the global economic hubs in USA, UK, Germany, France, Middle East, India, Hong Kong, Singapore, China and Japan to name a few. The company's FLAG is the first and only global network of this scale to provide integrated connectivity on one seamless network to the three highest growing regions, namely India, Middle East and China, in terms of international bandwidth demand.

Intel Curie 2015

Features Low-power 32-bit Intel Quark microcontroller 384 kB flash memory 80 kB SRAM Low-power integrated DSP sensor hub and pattern matching technology	Bluetooth Low Energy (BLE) 6-axis combo sensor with accelerometer and gyroscope Battery charging circuitry (PMIC)

eSys is the largest hard disk drive distribution company with a global market share of 23 per cent. The new facility will augment the installed capacity of the company in India from 3,00,000 units to three million units per annum.

India-using Augmented Reality

Augmented reality market will radically increase the consumer engagement time with various brands, depending on the quality of the content, Shopsense: This Mumbai-based startup offers the ease of online shopping in stores. It installs large touchscreens connected with the store's inventory, which allow customers to zero in on clothes easily. Customers can create various looks—which kurti goes with a given pair of slacks before trying them on and even seek friends' opinions over e-mail and whatsapp using screen.

Houssup: It is a technology-backed platform that bridges the gap between design inspiration and its implementation for home owners. With an aim to provide interior designing solutions using advanced technology such as artificial intelligence, augmented reality and virtual reality, this company aims to provide an unsurpassed home decoration experience to its customers.

LensKart: This company has introduced a virtual trial room feature, where its potential buyers can try on the spectacles. Buyers can click a selfie through their webcam and pick out glasses that best suit their face through a 3D feature.

CommonFloor: This one has forayed into virtual reality-based property listings with CommonFloor Retina, based on Google's Cardboard project. Users can then launch the app, insert the phone inside the headgear and start viewing a virtual tour of the property. The headgear also comes with a magnet that acts as navigational tool allowing users to switch between different parts of property—bedrooms, dining/drawing, kitchen, etc.

Imaginate: It is a renowned AR and VR-based technology enterprise, which offers innovative visualization products and services. Through its strong and proven technology expertise, it offers experiential solutions in the fields of retail, defense, enterprise, finance, entertainment and healthcare sectors.

Google Foray in AI

Hassabis cofounded DeepMind in 2010 to transfer some of what he learned about biological intelligence to machines. The company revealed software that learned to master Atari games in December 2013, and early in 2014 it was purchased by Google for an amount reported to be 400 million pounds, more than $600 million at the time (see "Google's Intelligence Designer"). DeepMind quickly expanded, hiring dozens more researchers and publishing scores of papers in leading machine-learning and artificial-intelligence conferences. It revealed the existence of AlphaGo, and that it had defeated Europe's best Go player in October 2015. AlphaGo beat an 18-time world champion, Lee Sedol, earlier this month (see "Five Lessons from AlphaGo's Historic Victory").

Atari games and Go are very different, but DeepMind tackled them both using the same approach, loosely inspired by the way animals can be taught new tricks using rewards and punishments from a trainer. In reinforcement learning, as it is called, software is programmed to explore a new environment and adjust its behavior to increase some kind of virtual reward.

AlphaGo combines reinforcement learning with other components, Hassabis believes the reinforcement learning approach is the key to getting machine-learning software to do much more complex things than the tricks it performs for us today, such as transcribing our words, or understanding the content of photos. "We don't think just observing is enough for intelligence, you also have to act," he says. "Ultimately that's the only way you can really understand the world." Future challenges might require more complex planning—for example, learning that keys can be used to open doors. The company will also test software in other ways, and is considering taking on the video game StarCraft and even poker. But posing harder and harder challenges inside Labyrinth will be a major thread of research for some time, says Hassabis. "It should be good for the next couple of years," he says.

Other companies and researchers working on artificial intelligence will be watching closely. The success of DeepMind's reinforcement learning has surprised many machine-learning researchers. The technique was established in the 1980s, and has not proved to be as widely useful or very powerful as other ways of training software, says Pedro Domingos, a professor who works on machine learning at the University of Washington. DeepMind strengthened the venerable technique by combining it with a method called deep learning, which has recently produced big advances in how well computers can decode information such as images and triggered a recent boom in machine-learning technology (see "10 Breakthrough Technologies 2013: Deep Learning").

Looking farther ahead, DeepMind will need many breakthroughs to keep moving toward Hassabis's goal of solving intelligence, even in the next couple of years of experimenting inside Labyrinth. One of the most critical missing pieces is a trick called chunking that human and animal brains use to handle the world's complexities. Hassabis explains it using the example of needing to go to the airport. You can conceive of how you'll get there and carry out that plan without having to consider exactly where to place your feet as you walk to the door, how to turn its handle or control every twitch of your muscle fibers. We can plan and take actions by working with high-level concepts that hide many details, and adapt to new situations by recombining the "chunks," or concepts, we already know. "It's probably one of the most core problems left in AI," says Hassabis.

It's a problem being worked on by many research groups, including others inside Google. But one unusual way DeepMind hopes to solve it is by studying real brains. The company has a team of neuroscientists led by a prominent researcher, Matthew Botvinick, who until late last year was a Princeton professor. Unlike most neuroscience research, its experiments are aimed as much at informing how DeepMind designs software as revealing how the brain works.

One recent experiment tested a theory of Hassabis's about the way human brains organize concepts, using a standard procedure that creates false memories. It involves presenting test subjects with a list of related words, for example "cold," "snow," and "ice." People often falsely remember hearing other related words, too, such as "winter."

"With my machine-learning hat on I thought that has to be a huge clue as to how that kind of conceptual information is organized in the brain," says Hassabis. The DeepMind team worked out a theory of how the brain's anterior temporal lobe works with concepts, and confirmed its predictions by watching the brains of people doing the memory task inside a scanner. The results might help change how DeepMind designs its artificial neural networks to represent information.

Other things on DeepMind's "to discover" list include a way to combine research it has done on software to grasp the meaning of text with its work on agents that roam inside Labyrinth—one possibility is to start putting up signs inside the virtual space. Hassabis says he's also planning an "ambitious" way to test agents when they are ready for a more realistic world than Labyrinth. At some point he wants to see DeepMind software take control of robots, which he says are held back by the inability of software to understand the world. "There are amazing robots around that cannot be used to their full capabilities because the algorithms aren't there," he says.

Appendix 6: Blockchain Technologies

6.1. We explore a blockchain structure applied to EHRs. We build on this distributed ledger protocol originally associated with Bitcoin. The blockchain uses public key cryptography to create an append-only, immutable, timestamped chain of content. Copies of the blockchain are distributed on each participating node in the network. The Proof of Work algorithm used to secure the content from tampering depends on a "trustless" model, where individual nodes must compete to solve computationally-intensive "puzzles" (hashing exercises) before the next block of content can be appended to the chain. These worker nodes are known as "miners," and the work required of miners to append blocks ensures that it is difficult to rewrite history on the blockchain. Our MedRec blockchain implementation addresses the four major issues highlighted above: fragmented, slow access to medical data; system interoperability; patient agency; improved data quality and quantity for medical research.

We build on the work of Zyskind et al. to assemble references to data and encode these as hashed pointers onto a blockchain ledger. We then organize these references to explicitly create an accessible bread crumb trail for medical history, without storing raw medical data on the blockchain. Our system supplements these pointers with on-chain permission and data integrity logic, empowering individuals with record authenticity, auditability and data sharing. We build robust, modular APIs to integrate with existing provider databases for interoperability. A novel data-mining scheme is proposed to sustain the MedRec network and bring open, big data to medical researchers. We present MedRec not as the panacea for medical record management, but as a foray into this space to demonstrate innovative EHR solutions with blockchain technology. A novel data-mining scheme is proposed to sustain the MedRec network and bring open, big data to medical researchers. We present MedRec not as the panacea for medical record management, but as a foray into this space to demonstrate innovative EHR solutions with blockchain technology.

6.2. Overview For MedRec, the block content represents data ownership and viewership permissions shared by members of a private, peer-to-peer network. Blockchain technology supports the use of "smart contracts," which allow us to automate and track certain state transitions (such as a change in viewership rights, or the birth of a new record in the system). Via smart contracts on an Ethereum blockchain, we log patient-provider relationships that associate a medical record with viewing permissions and data retrieval instructions (essentially data pointers) for execution on external databases. We include on the blockchain a cryptographic hash of the record to ensure against tampering, thus guaranteeing data integrity. Providers can add a new record associated with a particular patient, and patients can authorize sharing of records between providers. In both cases, the party receiving new information receives an automated notification and can verify the proposed record before accepting or rejecting the data. This keeps participants informed and engaged in the evolution of their records. MedRec prioritizes usability by also offering a designated contract which aggregates references to all of a user's patient-provider relationships, thus providing a single point of reference to check for any updates to medical history. We handle identity confirmation via public key cryptography and employ a DNS-like implementation that maps an already existing and widely accepted form of ID (e.g. name, or social security number) to the person's Ethereum address. A syncing algorithm handles data exchange "off-chain" between a patient database and a provider database, after referencing the blockchain to confirm permissions via our database authentication server.

Blockchain for Healthcare Use Cases: The potential uses of blockchain technology in healthcare are multiple and varied. Here we present a wide-ranging list of prospective healthcare-related use cases that the industry has been debating.

- Notarization/Identity Verification: Registration of EMR, insurance, and other records.
- Collaborative Crowdsourcing: Open bazaar for services, transparency in pricing, and health property exchange.
- Medical Banking: Disintermediating counterparties.
- Counterfeit Drug Prevention and Detection: Introduce blockchain-enabled solutions to protect and enhance the pharmaceutical supply chain.
- Genomics Research: Accessibility to genetic data secured on blockchain.
- Population Health Management: A blockchain-based personal health record (PHR) system measuring consumer outcomes and influencing medical actions (for example, cases of influenza and preventative vaccines).
- Internet of Things and Blockchain: Consumer-generated health data meets IoT wearables through data accessibility and interconnection with health records.
- Validation and Payment of Claims: Reduce process time and friction, including compliance with contract terms.
- Outcome-based Payments: Assigns each consumer a unique digital identity with data from blockchain (payers measure metrics for positive outcomes).
- Clinical Trial Results: Improve accountability and transparency in the clinical trial reporting process.
- Smart Property: Track provenance and introduce anti-counterfeit measures for healthcare assets.

- Real-Time/Contextual Forms of Insurance: Using smart controls, introduce new tools and services for growth, improving fraud detection and pricing, and reducing administrative costs.
- EMR: Personal health record storage and access administered using blockchain, with user-key permission for doctors and other authorized parties.
- Health Research Commons: Aggregated personal medical records, quantified self-data commons (DNA bits), genome and connectome files.
- Health Document Notary Services: Proof-of-insurance, test results, prescriptions, status, condition, treatment, physician referrals.
- Doctor-Vendor RFP Services: Similar to Uber car services, doctors and health provider.

Appendix 7: Eye-Netra, Eye-testing medical device: *Near-Eye Tool for Refractive Assessment, or NETRA*

Eye Netra the Eye-testing technology experimented in India in 2003 by MIT researchers and now in 2016 further expanded and used in varied improved applications both in India and USA. MIT researchers have invented eye tests through cell phones. It is being widely used in Indian villages partnering with LV eye institute in India; and in USA as health solution technologies to homes and schools and also with virtual reality development companies.

Around the world, half a billion people live with uncorrected vision problems, according to World Health Organization estimates, in part because eye specialists are rare in the developing world. But a team at the MIT Media Lab believes it can help restore sharp eyesight to many of these people, with a vision test that uses cellphones, an inexpensive clip-on eyepiece, and free software.

"As much as we want to solve the prescription glasses market, we could also [help] bring virtual reality to the masses," says Eye-Netra co-founder Ramesh Raskar, an associate professor of media arts and sciences at the MIT Media Lab who co-invented the device.

The device, called Netra, is a plastic, binocular-like headset. Users attach a smartphone, with the startup's app, to the front and peer through the headset at the phone's display. Patterns, such as separate red and green lines or circles, appear on the screen. The user turns a dial to align the patterns and pushes a button to lock them in place. After eight interactions, the app calculates the difference between what the user sees as "aligned" and the actual alignment of the patterns. This signals any refractive errors, such as nearsightedness, farsightedness, and astigmatism. The app then displays the refractive powers, axis of astigmatism, and pupillary distance required for eyeglasses prescriptions.

Ramesh Raskar says his team has developed a prototype eye test that rivals what vastly more expensive machines do in eye doctors' offices. The implications could be significant for the developing world, where cellphones are far more common than opportunities for eye care. The device, called the Near-Eye Tool for Refractive Assessment, or NETRA, won't eliminate the need for eye doctors, Raskar said, but it could signal a problem and make it easy for people to get the right glasses from agencies that collect donated ones. The eyepiece costs about a dollar or two to make, Raskar said.

"Just like we have thermometers at home, we need a thermometer for the eye," he said. "It's not a replacement for the optometrist or ophthalmologist in any way. Like a thermometer, it makes you aware. It measures but it does not prescribe."

Here's how it works: Instead of staring at an eye chart while different lenses are flipped into place before their eyes, people look through an eyepiece at two lines on the cellphone screen. If the red and green lines are aligned, then their vision is fine. If they are not, they click on the phone's arrow buttons until the two lines come together. Users repeat the steps with the lines at different angles, and the number of times they need to click reveals how their eyes focus best. Software then translates the results into what corrective lenses they might need.

Team at MIT has created a simple, inexpensive eye test using a cell phone. Software in the cell phone works in conjunction with an eye piece attachment.

If you've ever squinted through a phoropter; it is an instrument for evaluation of vision, with lenses placed on dials in a unit that is positioned in front of the patient while the optometrist switches lenses and demands that you decide which one makes the letters clearer. But in the new method; it does not rely on your ability to discern between blurry letters and sharp characters.

Using this new Netra system, all you need to do is look into the eye piece clipped to your cell phone and make two green lines overlap. You accomplish this by using the arrow keys on the cell phone. When the images line up, your visual ability is determined, and a prescription can be written from the results during the exam. *The combined cell phone and software shows promise for testing eyesight in rural areas in developing countries where a phoropter is impractical, and optometrists are hard to come by. It makes testing accessible and easy.*

The Netra eye test method resulted from a system to develop small bar codes, called bokode, which are imperceptible visual tags for camera-based interaction from a distance. They were created to replace optical tags that must be read at short range, such as the scanning we are familiar with at the checkout counters. The current sized codes take up valuable space on produce packaging that could be used for advertising, product recognition, and instructions on use.

The system is safer than other methods in that it does not use lasers, and doesn't need cycloplegic drugs (cycloplegic eye drop is also sometimes used after surgery to place the iris at rest during the healing process), which paralyze the muscles of the eye.

The bokodes can be used to determine if a person has a refractive error. As Ankit Mohan, one of the MIT researchers says: "People have tried all kinds of things, some very clever. What's really great about our technique is that it contains no moving parts, all the intelligence is in the software and we can make it very cheap and simple."

You might not see the Netra at your local optometrist's office soon, but inhabitants in remote areas of developing countries may see an improvement in eye care in the near future.

A unique social initiative associated with basic primary eye care in rural areas.

In India, Eye-Netra has launched Nayantara, a similar program to provide low-cost eye tests to the poor and uninsured in remote villages, far from eye doctors. Both efforts used Eye-Netra's suite of tools, now available for eye-care providers worldwide.

Nayantara skills local rural youth by training them in basics of eye-care and screening methodology; they are called Visioneers. Using cloud-based technology platform and associated technologies; these local rural youths organized in small teams are able to deliver expert supervised eye-screening and refraction testing. It is both scalable and sustainable.

In 2015, after five years of development and about 40,000 tests worldwide, project started in 2000; the smartphone-powered eye-test devices developed by MIT spinout Eye-Netra is coming to hospitals, optometric clinics, optical stores, and even homes nationwide.

But on the heels of its commercial release, Eye-Netra says it's been pursuing opportunities to collaborate with virtual-reality companies seeking to use the technology to develop "vision-corrected" virtual-reality displays.

According to the World Health Organization, uncorrected refractive errors are the world's second-highest cause of blindness. Eye-Netra originally invented the device for the developing world—specifically, for poor and remote regions of Africa and Asia, where many people can't find health care easily. India alone has around 300 million people in need of eyeglasses.

But the United States has offered the best market, in terms of adoption, Raskar says. "The consumerization of health is happening much faster here in the U.S. than in the developing world," he says. "If you're to play that role of smartphone-based personalized health solutions, then we have an amazing lead over anyone else 'Personalized correction'".

Over the past six months, Eye-Netra has been in discussion with virtual-reality companies in USA to integrate the technology into virtual-reality displays, Raskar says. The idea, he says, is to use the startup's technology to develop custom screens to fit a user's eyeglass prescription.

Prescription screens could make virtual-reality devices more form-fitting for a more immersive and comfortable experience, Raskar says: Right now, devices are built with extra space on the viewing end for people wearing glasses.

Such an approach could be game-changing, Raskar says, as billions of dollars have recently been invested into virtual-reality technology:

In 2014, Facebook acquired Oculus Rift for $2 billion; Google and other big companies recently backed Magic Leap with more than $540 million; and Microsoft has starting pooling resources into virtual-reality research.

"In addition to the major business [Eye-Netra] is doing for prescriptions, it can also disrupt virtual reality, which is potentially an even bigger market," Raskar says.

User-friendly Optics

Around 2009, Raskar and some of his Media Lab students developed a prototype of Netra: A small, plastic device was clipped to a smartphone, and viewers used the phone's keyboard to align the patterns.

The device was designed as an inverse of a traditional Shack-Hartmann wave-front sensor machine, which shines a laser into the patient's eye and measures the refracted light with a photon sensor to find optical aberrations that affect eyesight. Essentially, Netra replaces the expensive sensor with a smartphone display. Because the red and green light goes through different parts of the eye, aligning the two colors similarly demonstrates any optical aberrations.

Later that year, Raskar and Eye-Netra co-founder and chief technology officer Vitor Pamplona, who co-invented the technology, brought the invention to MAS.533 (Imaging and Fabrication Ventures), a class he co-teaches that presents image-based projects for students to further innovate. There, teams of students ran the device through several case studies, researched markets, and established a network of investors.

Over the next few months, Raskar, Pamplona, and other students entered the prototype in MIT's IDEAS competition, where they won a prize, and the MIT $100K Business Plan Competition, where they earned a spot as semifinalists.

Then, a grant from the MIT Deshpande Center for Technological Innovation officially launched the entrepreneurial effort in 2010. "But we realized we had to start all over again," Raskar says.

This meant a complete redesign of the product and business plan to focus less on the technology and more on market need. "As much as we wanted to be disruptive in long run, the reality of the world was that we had to work with really good partners," he says.

About 340 product iterations led to an improved device and better user interface. For instance, around three years ago, the team realized that people didn't perform well interacting with the phone. So, for the current design, they moved all buttons and knobs to the actual device.

That change, and other small tweaks, made the device easier and more widely used, Raskar says. "We were naive in thinking that if you solve the optics problem, it will be good. But in reality there are three parameters: the machine and its optical design, the eye and its involuntary activities, and the human perception," he says. "Getting all those right in the same design is nontrivial."

Moving forward, Raskar says Eye-Netra aims to capitalize on the "consumerization of health" phenomenon in the United States, where consumers are gaining access to innovative medical tools for personal use. "The biggest impact we could have is playing a key role in bringing health solution technologies to people at the their homes or schools," he says (MIT News, Oct. 2015).

Appendix 8: Laser Technology Health Products

Raman Heads for the Clinic

The Latest Laser Lipo Innovation: SmartLipo Triplex, 3 Wavelengths to Melt Fat and Tighten Skin

Laser liposuction: No-surgery weight loss

New surgical technique uses laser energy to destroy brain tumors

Laser technology may soon be used for corneal transplants

No more d-d-dentist drill with revolutionary new laser

Can lasers stimulate a hair-growth spurt?

Procedure uses laser to get rid of fat

Laser Treatment Offers Hope for Vitiligo Patients

HealthWatch: Radio Frequency Laser Resurfacing

Laser scalpel deployed in scar wars

Laser Technology Spots Cavities Before They Start

Laser Reduces Wrinkles

Laser Dentist Drill

Tongue Cancer Laser

Laser Brings Relief to Achy Backs

Femtosecond laser has dentistry applications

YAG laser dental procedure considered 'effective' in treating gum disease

Laser therapy option to avoid surgery

Laser Helps Smokers Kick the Habit

Laser best for eyelid surgery

Laser imaging beats the bends

New laser treatment helps people with gum disease

Laser teeth whitening procedure-key facts

Eye surgery leaves many with problems

New laser treatment cures neck pain without surgery

Laser hair removal system—how does it work?

Laser scan of veins detects cancer

The brain dances to a laser tune

Laser hair removal as hirsutism treatment

Lasering that enlarged prostate!

Defense Products

Russia developing laser weapons

Fighter jets laser blinds heat-seeking missiles

Planes being attacked by lasers at Birmingham Airport

In test, US airborne laser shoots down missile: Pentagon

Hefty 'battle strength' electro-laser breaks 100 kW barrier

Air Force Uses Airborne Lasers to Create High-Speed Data Links

Key Reviews for HEL-TD Laser Program Completed

Laser attacks on jets rising: Police

City airport to get laser guns to check bird hits

'Blinding' lasers to protect superyachts from pirates

Boeing Advanced Tactical Laser Strikes Moving Target in Test

Elbit Systems unit, US Army complete helicopter tests

Pain weapon in a potable version may end up in police hands

Pew! Airborne military laser takes out truck on video

Jet pilots blinded by laser pen yob

Laser energetics demonstrates dazer laser(tm) at the Emmy awards

Truck-mounted laser raises hopes of unmanned military defense

U.S.-India Strategic Partnership on Laser-Based Missile Defense

Boeing: we zapped a uav with a laser

Laser 1, drone 0 in boeing test

Boeing Laser Avenger Shoots Down Unmanned Aerial Vehicle in Tests

Thompson Files: Fuzed weapons are good

Air Force Looks to Laser-Proof its Weapons

'Laser jumbo' testing moves ahead

Boeing Designs Laser Weapon

Compact laser dazzlers for canadian forces small arms

Revellers blinded by laser show in Russia

U.S. Sonic Blaster + Laser = New Weapon

Pilots dazzled by laser pointers

Taking Terror Threat Out of Flying

Ferries targeted in laser attacks

Navy Pushing Laser 'Holy Grail' to Weapons Grade

Defense officials view laser as future of anti-missile technology

X-47B manhunter drone could fly next year, to carry laser weapons and more

French champion lyon fined after fan aimed laser at Cristiano Ronaldo

Israeli town demands anti-missile laser

Video: army lasers zap bikers in Afghanistan

U.S. Tests anti-ied laser

Testing needed on laser weapons, military observers say

Boeing Tests Avenger Solid State Laser Weapon

SKorea seen developing laser weapons

Blackwater's New Weapon: Laser Dazzlers

Aircraft laser attacks on the increase

Israel Air Force to be Equipped with Elbit Systems' Lizard Laser-Guided Bombs

Laser blinds copter pilot carrying sick patient

5-mile laser rifle in the terrifying works

Portable Solid-State Pulse Laser Latest Hope for Laser Gun

Boeing's new laser pod can take out roadside bombs, UAVs

Laser pod could destroy bombs

Laser Dazzlers for the Police and Military

Indian Army to induct portable laser weapons

US Army eyes truck-mounted laser

Boeing developing truck-mounted laser cannons for US Army

Record power for military laser

Israel Defense Ministry to re-examine anti-missile laser

Lasers Over LAX (Skyguard)

High-Energy Lasers Could Defend Commercial Aircraft From MANPADs

Mid-Infrared Lasers Confuse Heat-Seeking Missiles

High Powered Laser Pointers Save U.S. Military Lives in Iraq

Laser technology products–environment & other areas

Laser makes molecules super-cool

Laser Made Rain Clouds

Featured Application: Laser Cutting Carbon Fiber Composite

Laser Etching Safe Alternative for Labeling Grapefruit

Scientist shines laser light on methane in pursuit of clean fuel

'Mini lasers' illuminate dark molecules

Modeling a black hole with a 300 GigaWatt laser

Laser land-levelling project for farmers initiated

NPL Develops Femtosecond Laser Tech for Formation Space Flying

Using Lasers to Map Bird Habitat

Port wine stains now easy to wipe off with laser therapy

Nsu's trying to develop a laser for wee frontiers

Smoke and lasers could disrupt microphone market

Researchers use laser-induced breakdown spectroscopy to collect elemental fingerprints

Liquid mirror shows promise for adaptive optics

Laser technology application progress in other areas

BEAM COMBINING: High-power fiber-laser beams are combined incoherently

Lasers need lenses no more

Replacing wire with Laser, Sun Tries to Speed Up Data

A High Power Laser Zap to Nanotechnology

Scientist in Texas Runs NASA's Lunar Laser Program

Laser System cuts up to 1.25 in. thick steel/.750 in. SS.

Japanese Team Invents Tiny Laser Light Powered Motor

No shooting the birds bengals settle on lasers, not guns, to shoo pigeons

All that glitter is tech

New laser method helps detect hidden liquid explosives

Solar Converted to Laser Light

Japan develops new space laser

Laser-based analyzer gives ultra fast and accurate measurement of trace moisture

Dancing atoms hold prospect of superfast computing

Laser detects danger liquids

Laser system offers cheaper, faster pathogen detection

Laser-based Thermometer (Red hot gadget)

Free Electron Laser Achieves 10 kilowatts of Infrared Laser Light

What's New in Laser Optics could Lead to "Light Bullets"

SDSU professor uses laser beam to study forest conditions (LIDAR)

Brookhaven Lab Physicist Ilan Ben-Zvi Wins Free Electron Laser Prize

Diamonds, a super efficient laser material

Pore-free Ceramics Shine New Light on Lasers, Electronics and Biomedical Implants

Lasermaterials.info

Plastic Laser Materials

Characteristics of a continuous-wave Yb:GdVO4 laser end pumped by a high-power diode

Diode-pumped continuous-wave Nd:LuVO4 laser operating at 916 nm

Concentration quenching in fine-grained ceramic Nd:YAG

Source: http://www.newkerala.com/news/fullnews-95826.html

Richard Mildren, associate professor, and his colleagues at the Macquarie University Photonics Research Centre discovered in late 2008 that it was possible to generate a coherent laser beam from synthetic diamond. They have now demonstrated diamond lasers with efficiency higher than almost all other materials. "The major achievement is that we are able to use synthetic diamond to create high performing laser devices, Mildren said. We are now in a good position to explore the highly exotic laser properties of diamond, many of which are not so widely appreciated. "For example, the speed at which heat travels through diamond is the highest of all known materials and it is hoped that this property will enable us to simultaneously miniaturize the device and increase the laser beam power to unprecedented levels." April 2016 at Sydney. The diamonds used in the laser research are colorless, approximately eight mm long, and weigh a bit less than a carat. They are grown to the researcher's specifications using a process called chemical vapour deposition that essentially creates the crystal lattice carbon by carbon atom layer by layer on top of a large flat diamond crystal substrate. The synthetic diamond forms the core component of what is called a Raman laser, a type of laser that is optically stimulated rather than electrically powered. "Though there has been little take up of this type of diamond in the gem market, it is very well suited to our purposes. Diamonds larger than one centimeter are likely to be available very soon which will also be an advantage for our studies." Diamond is also the most transparent material known, in terms of the range of light wavelengths (or colors) that can pass through the material, said a Macquarie University release. Mildren said satellite borne diamond lasers for mapping greenhouse gases in the atmosphere were also a possibility. He said it is only now—in the 50th year since the invention of the first laser—that the full potential of diamond lasers is starting to be understood. Pore-free Ceramics Shine New Light on Lasers, Electronics and Biomedical Implants (*Source*: http://www.nanotech-now.com/news.cgi?story_id=32049 http://www.usnews.com/articles/science/technology/ 2009/02/02/ advanced-ceramics-shine-new-light-on-lasers-electronics-and-biomedical-implants.html).

To most people, the word "ceramics," refers to opaque clay flower pots or translucent porcelain tea cups. But not all ceramics block or scatter light. Gary L. Messing, distinguished professor of ceramic science and engineering, and his group at Pennsylvania State University, are developing a brand new class of ceramics that are so pure and perfectly transparent; they can be used as a substitute for crystals in solid-state lasers. To test their new method, Messing and his group made neodymium-doped yttrium aluminum garnet (Nd:YAG) laser ceramics, because they are important in industrial and military applications. The Nd:YAG crystal structure also works well with ceramic processing. "Most high power, solid-state lasers use single crystals made by melt-growth methods," said Stevenson. "These require high temperatures of greater than 1950 degrees Celsius, and weeks or months to grow a single crystal boule [block] of Nd:YAG." According to Stevenson, switching to ceramic processing could reduce the temperatures needed to make an Nd:YAG laser ceramic by at least 250 degrees Celsius and reduce the time it takes down to just days.

To make the ceramics, the group started with powders and mixed them with liquids and polymers to make a material similar in consistency to paint. "We used a process called tape casting to make long thin sheets of the material," Messing explained. "Next, we cut the sheets into squares and stacked them to form thicker squares about 1 cm × 5 cm × 5 cm." After applying heat to sinter the squares, the ceramics became transparent. But the material still contained enough pores to degrade a laser's performance. "We did a final step, called hot isostatic pressing (HIP), where we heated the ceramics to over 1600 degrees Celsius and applied high pressures with argon gas." "By combining heat with pressure, we eliminated the few remaining pores."

(Nd:YAG lasers are optically pumped using a flashtube or laser diodes. These are one of the most common types of laser, and are used for many different applications).

Lasermaterials.info lasermaterials.info is supposed to be an Open Source project providing data of modern solid state laser gain media. Primarily, this information board is addressed to laser physicists and laser engineers requiring property parameters and spectra of solid state laser materials. Still not complete, the data content will be extended. Due to the large number of crystal or glass parameters a certain variation of the presented data must be taken into account. Although non-commercial, this site additionally gives an overview about suppliers and institutions for crystal growth or glass fabrication (*Source:* http://www.lasermaterials.net/ytterbium.htm). Plastic Laser Materials). (http://www.patentdigi.com/tide_time_calculating/plastic_laser_materials.html). A material exhibiting narrow line fluorescence when excited by high-energy radiation, hence suitable for laser applications, is formed by dispersion of rare earth ions bonded to organic molecules in the form of an organometallic chelate, in solid solution in a plastic host. Characteristics of a continuous-wave Yb:GdVO4 laser end pumped by a high-power diode Characteristics of a continuous-wave Yb:GdVO4 laser end pumped by a high-power diode Optics Letters, Vol. 31, Issue 17, pp. 2580-82. An efficient and compact diode-pumped continuous-wave Yb:GdVO4 laser is demonstrated, generating an output power of 4.0 W with an optical conversion efficiency of 61% and a slope efficiency as high as 78%. With increasing pump power the polarization of the laser output changes from s to p, while in a certain intermediate power range the two polarization states coexist with different emission wavelengths. Diode-pumped continuous-wave Nd:LuVO4 laser operating at 916 nm Optics Letters, Vol. 31, Issue 10, pp. 1435-37. We realized an efficient diode-pumped Nd:LuVO4 continuous-wave (CW) laser operating at 916 nm. Laser experiments with 0.5at. % Nd-doped Nd: LuVO4 crystals of various lengths and cutting directions were also investigated. The maximum output power of 930 mW was obtained with a slope efficiency of 27.2% and an optical conversion efficiency of 20.8% at the absorbed pump power of 4.5 W. The laser experiment shows that Nd:LuVO4 crystal can be used for an efficient diode-pumped laser system.

Appendix 8a: Laser: Industrial and Medical Applications

The first laser built at CAT was a copper vapour laser. It is the most powerful laser emitting visible light. Copper vapour lasers capable of giving up to 40 Watt average power had been developed at CAT. These lasers are also used to pump tunable dye lasers whose wavelengths can be changed. Several such lasers have been given by CAT to universities and other research laboratories for spectroscopic studies.

Another important laser developed by CAT is the carbon dioxide (CO_2) laser. Incidentally, the CO_2 laser was invented by a well-known Indian scientist, Dr. C.K.N. Patel, who was then working at Bell Labs in USA. CAT has developed technologies of several types of CO_2 lasers namely, low power slow flow CO_2 laser, high power fast flow CO_2 laser, tunable CO_2 laser and high pressure pulsed CO_2 laser and is also pursuing applications of these CO_2 lasers in medicine and industry.

Industrial Application

Some time ago CAT scientists were approached by the Bharat Heavy Electricals Ltd. (BHEL), which makes large steam turbines for power stations, to explore the possibility of repairing eroded turbine blades by laser alloying. BHEL imports these turbine blades made of very hard nickel super alloy at huge cost and repair of eroded blades would result in considerable savings to it in foreign exchange. Using the 4 kW high power CO_2 laser, CAT scientists have successfully cladded (to cover a metal) with another metal by bonding an even harder material on the blades. Similarly, a technique was developed to improve ceramic coating to turbine blades by laser glazing.

Medical Applications

CAT has also been developing lasers for surgery. It has promoted research in this area in various hospitals through a National Laser Program. Apart from the surgical CO_2 laser, CAT has developed nitrogen laser for medical use. Nitrogen laser has been found useful for treatment of tuberculosis. Many patients of TB develop cavities in their lungs which become breeding ground of the TB bacillus.

The treatment consists of inserting a needle from the back of the patient into the cavity and then irradiating the cavity with the nitrogen laser beam which is transmitted through an optical fiber inserted through the needle into the cavity. CAT has funded a project under the National Laser Program at a hospital in Indore and has supplied a nitrogen laser coupled with optical fiber giving 3 megawatt of average power. The hospital has treated more than 200 patients of TB who had developed cavities in their lungs and who were on drugs for several years but had become resistant to drugs. With the nitrogen laser treatment, a large percentage of patients showed complete recovery within 2-3 months.

The hospital extended this procedure to other areas where drug resistance was encountered, for example, burn wounds infected with drug resistant Pseudomonas. Exposure of the burn wounds to nitrogen laser for about 10 minutes every day for five days resulted in complete healing of the wounds.

CAT also has a program on use of lasers in medical diagnosis. It has taken up development of analytical instruments based on lasers. One such system is a laser fluorimeter for detection of low concentration of uranium in water samples. This instrument uses a nitrogen laser to excite fluorescence in uranium source. The intensity of this fluorescence is a direct indication of the concentration of uranium in water. To suppress fluorescence from other substances generally present in water, optical and electronic filtering is used. This instrument can measure uranium concentration as low as 0.2 ppb (parts per billion).

Several such instruments are in regular use in various units of the Department of Atomic Energy which handles uranium, to check the concentration of uranium in water. The Atomic Minerals Division which explores uranium ores also uses this instrument for preliminary exploration. Scientists of Atomic Minerals Division collect water samples from deep wells and look for uranium. Recently, the Department of Atomic Energy donated two such instruments to the Seibersdorf Laboratory of International Atomic Energy Agency (IAEA), Vienna (PIB).

Appendix 9: Eight Critical Pillars of India's Smart City Program

1. Smart Governance: Investments of about US$1.2 trillion will be required over the next 20 years across areas such as transportation, energy and public security to build smart cities in India. Highlights:

   US$1.2 billion allocated for smart cities and FDI norms relaxed.

   US$83 million allocated for Digital India Initiative.

   PPP Model to be used to upgrade infrastructure in 500 urban areas.

   Smart City projects to create 10-15% rise in employment.

   Ministry of Urban Development has plans to develop two smart cities in each of India's 29 states.

   Delhi-Mumbai Industrial Corridor Development Corporation Ltd. (DMICDC) plans seven "smart cities" along the 1,500 km industrial corridor across six states with a total investment of US$100 billion.

2. Smart Energy: Three crucial dimensions of smart energy systems are: Smart Grid.

   Electrification of all households with power available for at least eight hours per day by 2017

   Establish smart grid test bed by 2014 and smart grid knowledge centre by 2015

   Implementation of eight smart grid pilot projects in India with an investment of US$10 million

   Energy Storage

   Addition of 88,000 MW of power generation capacity in the Twelfth Five Year Plan (2012-17)

   India needs to add at least 250-400 GW of new power generation capacity by 2030

   The Power Grid Corporation of India has planned to invest US$26 billion in the next five years

   Smart Meters

   India to install 130 million smart meters by 2021.

3. Smart Environment: Three crucial dimensions of ensuring sustainable development are

   Renewable Energy

   Ministry of New and Renewable Energy has plans to add capacity of 30,000 MW in the 12th Five Year Plan (2012-17)

   Water and Waste Water Management

   The Indian Ministry of Water Resources plans to invest US$50 billion in the water sector in the coming years

   The Yamuna Action Plan Phase III project for Delhi is approved at an estimated cost of US$276 million

   Sanitation

   About 67% of the rural population continues to defecate in the open, and India accounts for about 50% of the world's open defecation

   The Government of India and the World Bank have signed a US$500 million credit for the Rural Water Supply and Sanitation (RWSS) project in the Indian states of Assam, Bihar, Jharkhand and Uttar Pradesh.

4. Smart Transportation: The Government of India has set ambitious targets of developing public transportation system to support the ever growing urban populace. Green Transport

   The Government of India has approved a US$4.13 billion plan to spur electric and hybrid vehicle production by setting an ambitious target of six million vehicles by 2020

   Electric vehicle charging stations in all urban areas and along all state and national highways by 2027 Railways

   Metro: Ministry of Urban Development plans to invest more than US$20 billion on the metro rail projects in coming years

   High Speed Rail: The proposed 534 km Mumbai-Ahmedabad high speed rail project will have an investment of around US$10.5 billion

Monorail: India's first monorail project at Mumbai will cost around US$500 million, of which US$183 million has been spent on phase I.

5. Smart IT & Communications: Information and Communications Technology

   Cloud computing will evolve into a US$4.5 billion market in India by 2016

   Broadband connections to 175 million users by 2017

   Security and Surveillance

   Under the flagship "Safe City" project, the Union Ministry proposes US$333 million to make seven big cities (Delhi, Mumbai, Kolkata, Chennai, Ahmedabad, Bangalore and Hyderabad) to focus on technological advancement rather than manpower

   Disaster Management

   The Government of India and World Bank signed US$236 million agreement for reducing disaster risks in coastal villages of Tamil Nadu and Puducherry.

6. Smart Buildings: India is expected to emerge as the world's 3rd largest construction market by 2020, by adding 11.5 million homes every year

   The Intelligent Building Management Systems market is around US$621 million and is expected to reach US$1,891 million by 2016

   Smart Buildings will save up to 30% of water usage, 40% of energy usage and reduction of building maintenance costs by 10 to 30%.

7. Smart Health Hospitals

   Health budget up by 27% in FY 2014-15 to US$5.26 billion, with special focus on improving affordable healthcare for all

   To establish six new AIIMS like institutes and 12 government medical colleges in the country

   Accessible, affordable and effective healthcare system for 1.2+ billion citizens

Insurance

FDI limit in the insurance sector increased to 49% from 26%

Insurance industry has potential to reach US$1 trillion by 2020

Medical Devices

Indian medical devices market to reach US$11 billion by 2023

100% FDI allowed in the medical devices sector under the automatic route

Wellness

Indian wellness industry is expected to reach around US$16.65 billion by 2015.

8. Smart Education: The Government of India has allocated US$13.95 billion in the Union Budget 2014-15 for the education sector, up by 12.3% from the previous year

   Budget has allocated US$78.5 million to set-up five new IITs and five new IIMs

   The Ministry of Human Resource Development plans to have 1,000 private universities for producing trained manpower to meet services and industry requirements

   100% FDI allowed in the education sector

   India's online education market size expected to be US$40 billion by 2017.

Appendix 10: Microsoft Technology Paradigm

Cloud-first, mobile-first is not the mobility of one device; it's the mobility of the human experience that spans across all your devices. Even today, when we are looking at all the startups, you can increasingly see it.

Take the Internet of Things, the fact is data is coming from all the computing and cloud will enable that mobility. Therefore, cloud infrastructure is important for the emerging trends of distributed computing; as well the realities of running a worldwide cloud infrastructure.

We will also always have the hybrid cloud because of the Azure stack. This means that there is no lock-in. Customers care about it, governments care about it.

India Stack's vision of having a presence less-cashless-paperless vision—which is fundamentally about bringing down transaction costs in the economy so that every citizen, small business and large business can all benefit. This is a grand vision. Microsoft are very focused on making Office 365, Dynamics 365, Windows 10 or Azure help India Stack leverage all of its (Microsoft) technology. We need new technology breakthroughs in order to have the type of growth we had in the 20th century.

Automation in technology is here and will need re-skilling of human capital and a different approach to human resources. Automation is radically changing the DNA of the organization and has thrown a daunting challenge for human resources. Artificial Intelligence (AI) is definitely going to be instrumental. The question is, as surplus gets created how is it going to be equitably distributed?

When you have to train people for these new jobs; continuous learning and skilling, not just high-end, but even mid skills, vocational training with machines and AI become important. In a country like India, where there is going to be a service-led economy, there are going to be many jobs. But there are many things that AI will never be able to do. Who is AI helping in India?

We (Microsoft) have to create opportunity. There are over 10,000 partners, the health of those partners, how are they creating employment, what is their business model evolution is important. How are we helping, be it in education or in health, or in public sector, small and large business? That's at the core. The overall labor mobility in the world is going to be defined by every country's immigration policy, every country's trade deal or protectionism. Every country thinks about their own national goals.

Invisible forces "such as people's motivations and habits, as well as their environmental settings, also contribute to how they behave. By understanding this concept, organizations aiming to change people's behavior to improve their health would have better chances of achieving their goals. We need to understand the settings better because they control us," Curtis said during a TEDx Talk in November 2015. "And if we understand them, we can control them."

Curtis said disrupting settings; for example, like changing social norms in a community could lead people to change their behavior. Curtis and Aunger based on *theory of change*, developed an approach they call behavior-centered design, which they've employed in several health-related projects for the past five years.

Index